# The New Age Catalogue

# The New Age Catalogue

## Access to Information and Sources

*By the Editors of*

BODY MIND
SPIRIT
M A G A Z I N E

A Dolphin Book
Doubleday
New York
1988

*We would like to acknowledge the following people for their contributions to the creation of* The New Age Catalogue:

*Carol Iozzi,* Body, Mind & Spirit's *managing editor for her energy, expertise and vision; the rest of the* Body, Mind & Spirit *staff for their help, patience and proofing; Cheryl Maio, our typesetter extraordinaire; Hazel Underhill, for getting the graphics together; my wife Deborah, for her endless patience and support, and Jim Fitzgerald, for his unyielding faith in us and this project.*

- Paul Zuromski
*Editor & Publisher*
Body, Mind & Spirit *Magazine*

Library of Congress Cataloging-in-Publication Data

The New Age catalogue: access to information and sources / by the
 editors of Body, mind & spirit magazine.
     p.      cm.
   "A Dolphin book."
   Includes index.
   ISBN 0-385-2483-9 (pbk.): $14.95
     1. New Age movement — Catalogs. 2. New Age movement — Directories.
 I. Body, mind, spirit.
 BP605. N48N47 1988
 130′ .29′473—dc19                                          87-30698
 ISBN 0-385-24383-9                                         CIP
Copyright © 1988 by Island Publishing Company, Inc.
ALL RIGHTS RESERVED
PRINTED IN THE UNITED STATES OF AMERICA
FIRST EDITION

Illustration pg. 88 from USE BOTH SIDES
OF YOUR BRAIN by Tony Buzan.
Copyright © 1974, 1983 by Tony Buzan.
Reproduced by permission of the publisher,
E.P. Dutton, a division of NAL Penguin Inc.

Illustration pg. 77 reprinted with permission
of Macmillan Publishing Company from
BEYOND THE QUANTUM by Michael
Talbot. Copyright © 1986 by
Michael Talbot.

Illustrations pg. 218, 219 by Mayumi Oda.
Copyright © 1987 from BEING PEACE
by Thich Nhat Hanh. Reprinted with
permission of Parallax Press.

# Contents

*Those who hide behind their masks of fear and confusion hope this thing called the New Age will pass. However, that which is truly new in this age of rising consciousness will be the bridge to the future and the hope of humanity.*

*- Lazaris*
*Channeled by Jach Pursel*
(See page 3)

# Why Publish a New Age Catalogue?

*"A leaderless, but powerful network is working to bring out radical change in the United States."*

- Marilyn Ferguson
From The Aquarian Conspiracy

America is currently being flooded with New Age ideas, concepts, awareness, spirituality and organizations. You've awakened to trance mediums on "Good Morning America." Shirley MacLaine gave us a close look at her metaphysical adventures in her best selling books and TV movie, *Out on a Limb.* Subliminal and hypnosis tape programs are being sold in shopping mall bookstores. Business executives admit that their intuition was an important vehicle on their road to success and physicians are finally acknowledging that the true healer lies within each of us.

You are participating in a revolution of consciousness. The goal is an understanding of who you are, learning why you're here and exercising your unlimited potential in this lifetime. The problem is the often confusing glut of information sources, tools, experts and organizations ready to help you travel down your unique pathway to awareness.

We're here to help you make informed choices.

That's why *Body, Mind & Spirit* magazine was created. Since 1982, we've helped our readers sort out and understand New Age ideas and resources. Today over one half million readers look to us to help them explore the latest New Age trends and ideas. *The New Age Catalogue* is a natural extension of our work. This book lays out the broad spectrum of things New Age from channeling to Zen. It gives you the basic concepts behind each topic and the finest quality resources including books, tape programs, organizations, magazines and manufacturers. We selected each item listed in this book based on the following criteria:

1. We needed to have an actual sample of the product or service in our hands so we could experience what we recommended.

2. It had to *feel* good. We used our own intuitive abilities to decide its value, usefulness and ability to help people learn more about a particular subject area.

3. Due to space limitations we had to concentrate on universal or national reach. That means we had to virtually eliminate sources like regional organizations and individual practitioners unless they could contribute to a greater understanding in a subject area.

_____

Basic metaphysics says that the Earth plane is a wonderfully instructive school. What we perceive in this reality is just illusion created by each one of us for the grand and important purpose of learning.

Spirit entities, the Bible, Nostradamus, Ruth Montgomery's spirit Guides and virtually any other New Age-conscious person you talk to says this Earth plane is currently undergoing profound changes. These ideas range from a destructive shifting of the Earth's poles that will take place in the year 2000 to simply an upward shift in this plane's vibrational rate (assuming, of course, that we are basically composed of energy).

According to Jose Arguelles, the Harmonic Convergence that took place in August 1987 marked the final 25-year-cycle of this planet as indicated by the ancient Mayan calendar. What follows is what has been called throughout history as "The Golden Age," "The Millenium" or "The Promised Land."

Assuming that we do create this plane of reality, then it follows that we are also creating these changes. We need to be aware of our role in creation, since the seeds of change are our individual efforts. Consciousness is being raised. Awareness is being heightened. When you picked this book up, you acknowledged the curiosity — the fire within you — that yearns to *know* the very nature of your being.

*Body, Mind & Spirit* and now *The New Age Catalogue* exist to help fuel that fire within and help you discover the answers and pathways that are right for you. As you travel through these pages, trust your intuitiveness and allow it to be your guide.

We selected what we felt were the best quality sources of insight in the major New Age topic areas, intended to serve as a take off point for your own explorations.

The final choices are up to you, as they should be.

*Paul Zuromski*

*Paul Zuromski
Editor & Publisher
Body, Mind & Spirit
Magazine*

*For information on how to subscribe to* Body, Mind & Spirit, *see page 237.*

# How to Use This Catalogue

Use it *intuitively*.

Your intuitiveness, along with a mix of logic, practicality and common sense are the factors you should use in the process of selecting what to use, visit and get involved with in this *Catalogue*.

Intuitiveness is simply capturing the very *first* thought, feeling or emotion that enters your consciousness in relation, for example, to what you look at in this book. Once you start consciously analyzing, your intuitive ability (yes we all have it) is no longer at work. For more information on how to develop intuitiveness, check under the "Intuitive Development" part of the *Catalogue*.

The last few pages of the *Catalogue* contain a comprehensive index that will help you find a particular subject area you are interested in.

If you write to a publisher, company, organization or magazine and find that they are out of business or no longer offer, make or publish what you want, don't be discouraged. Due to the fast-changing nature of the New Age, things often come and go quite rapidly. You can check with your library for books and periodicals. Also write us at the *Body, Mind & Spirit* Book Shop. Sometimes we have an inventory of out-of-print books or we can suggest alternatives.

For information on how to order from this *Catalogue*, see page 237.

## Contribute to future *New Age Catalogues*...

*The New Age Catalogue* will be updated periodically. If you have, or know of any product, service, organization, company, idea, or concept that should be included in future editions, send complete information, along with a sample, current literature and anything else that will help in our selection decision. Send it to Selection Committee, New Age Catalogue, Body, Mind & Spirit, Box 701, Providence, R.I. 02901.

# Defining the New Age

*By David Spangler*

What is the New Age? The simplest answer for me is that it is the condition that emerges when I live life in a creative, empowering, compassionate manner. It manifests when I recognize and honor both the intrinsic wholeness of my world and the value and importance of everything within it. It arises when I honor each person, animal, plant, or object as unique yet also as a part of myself, imbued with a spirit of personhood, sharing whatever worthiness and sacredness I claim for myself.

I see the New Age as a metaphor for the expression of a transformative, creative spirit rather than as a future event. This means that I discover the shape of the New Age in the ordinary proportions of everyday life. I find it, for example, in nurturing my marriage or in gracefully meeting the demands of parenthood. I find a New Age in doing my work well and in improving my craft. I find it in my questions about myself that impel me to confront my shortcomings and my boundaries. I find it in the never-ending quest to understand the nature and purpose of a God who is not just (or even primarily) the inner divinity on which so many New Age writers focus but the evocative Other whose very differences impel me to reach beyond myself and participate in the larger communion and community of life. I find the New Age in the daily effort we all share to live with integrity, grow with courage and be a willing partner with life to allow expression of dreams and capabilities.

I see the New Age as an added dimension to our daily, ordinary living. It is a sense of empowerment and enthusiasm arising from the presence of the unexpected in our lives. It is the inner power to imagine and give birth to something new which complements the power to nurture the maturation of what already exists.

For most folk, however, the popular notion of the New Age is

not that of a reminder of their creative capability but that of an event, one that will end or transform history as we know it. It is something to be anticipated, and as such an image, it becomes a vehicle defined by people's unmet expectations. For those who see the New Age in this way, it will always be foreplay in search of climax, a tension that is never relieved except in disillusionment. Worse, it can become a cause of deeper "illusionment" that further divides them between the world as it is and the world as they would like it or need it to be. Seeing the New Age only as a special event limits their ability to experience it as a special creative attitude to bring to everyday, ordinary affairs.

I understand the New Age as a metaphor for being in the world in a manner that opens us to the presence of God — the presence of love and possibility — in the midst of our ordinariness. For this reason the New Age is found only tangentially for me in the context of prophecies. Seeing psychics and their prophecies come and go over the years with a minimal record of accuracy, I have generally learned to disregard them in favor of the potentialities of the immediate moment. This is especially so when the prophecies of a New Age pluck

our questing spirits from the present, like fish from the sea, and leave us heaving and gasping with expectations or with fears on the beaches of someone else's imagination.

The New Age idea really has little to do with prophecy. It is an invitation to encounter today in a joyous, nurturing, and creative way. Although it is presented in a context of transformation, it calls us not simply to transform but to live in a delicate and creative balance between transformation and routine, between metamorphosis and maturation, between the birth of what could be and the care of what is, between empowerment and surrender, between the sacred and the ordinary.

Often the New Age is seen as the pursuit of pagan religions, interest in Eastern philosophies or in the occult, or involvement with channeling, crystals, reincarnation, and other psychic phenomena. People who have these interests may well see themselves as forces for change and identify themselves as being part of a "New Age movement." However, to equate the New Age with psychic phenomena, the occult, or with a specific kind of spirituality is a limited and potentially distorting approach. New Age activities take many forms that are not involved with the paranormal or the religious.

For example, there are John and Nancy Todd, whose work with The New Alchemy Institute and Ocean Arks International (10 Shanks Pond Rd., Falmouth, MA 02540) addresses ecological restoration and balance and led to the development of the bioshelter; Dee Dickinson and the New Horizons for Learning Foundation (P.O. Box 51140, Seattle, WA 98115), who are pioneering new understandings of education and of the capabilities of the human intellect; William Shaw and the CrossCurrents International Institute (16 Enid, Dayton, OH 45429-2382) who is a leading organizer of citizen diplomacy missions to the Soviet Union; Mark Satin, whose newsletter *New Options* (P.O. Box 19324, Washington, DC 20036) is a forum for exploring decentralist, empowerment politics; and Robert Gilman, who publishes *In Context* (P.O. Box 2107, Sequim, WA 98382), a journal covering holistic thought and activity in numerous areas such as science, the arts, and business.

These people and hundreds like them are all examples of pragmatic efforts toward social change and betterment inspired by the spirit, if not always the nomenclature, of the New Age. Their work is based on and promotes rigorous intellectual activity, compassion, artistic sensitivity, good human relations, communication skills, business acumen, and a sense of caring for the human community. They have little, if anything, to do with psychic phenomena.

The New Age deals with issues of planetarization and the emergence of an awareness that we are all one people living on one world that shares a common destiny. The New Age represents social, political, economic, psychological, and spiritual efforts to recognize and include all that our modern society has tended to exclude: the poor, the dispossessed, the feminine, the ecological, and, inwardly, all the painful, repressed and unintegrated material that Carl Jung called the Shadow. The New Age is the integration of all these hidden and suppressed elements of our personal and collective lives so that we may individually and as a species achieve wholeness. It is a redefinition of

humanity's role within creation, emphasizing our servanthood rather than our mastery, our stewardship rather than our dominion.

The New Age is often seen as a time of individual empowerment, and New Age literature is filled with books on how to claim one's divinity, to proclaim "I am God!" and be more creative, abundant, happy, prosperous, and spiritual. Personal empowerment is important, but the essence of the New Age is the expression of a compassionate love and a social awareness and responsibility that reaches beyond the self to embrace and empower others. The New Age is the initiation of the Human Self into becoming a Planetary Self; in this context, empowerment is a means to an end, not the end itself. The individual who says "I am God!" should thus be aware that what he or she seeks to emulate and embody is not an all-powerful creator but a compassionate and giving servant, a nourisher of all life who lives and works amidst the ordinary and the seemingly trivial and is, in His/Her/Its love, the most vulnerable and accessible being of all.

Outwardly, the emergence of a New Age is primarily based on efforts to implement holistic, and planetary values. It is in the nature of these efforts often to draw little notice to themselves because they seem so ordinary. Competing for news space, the efforts of a manager to empower employees more deeply or the struggles of a father to go beyond traditional patriarchal attitudes to express his own nurturing and "maternal" instincts may not be as dramatic as the allegedly channeled spirit of a 30,000-year-old Atlantean warlord prophesying destruction, but they will have a more lasting and transformative effect. It is such individual efforts to explore and implement values of empowerment and compassion in very ordinary settings that are the core of the New Age movement.

Inwardly, the New Age continues the historical effort of humanity to delve deeply into the mysteries of the nature of God, of ourselves, and of reality. In the midst of materialism, it is a rebirth of our sense of the sacred, an inner impulse

to understand and express our own divinity in cocreation and synergy with the divinity within creation and with the Source of that divinity whose ultimate nature we are still seeking to know.

Therefore, for those of us who profess belief in a New Age, it is important to understand that the New Age is essentially a symbol representing the human heart and intellect in partnership with God building a better world that can celebrate values of community, wholeness and sacredness. It is a symbol for the emergence of social behavior based on a worldview that stimulates creativity, discipline, abundance and wholeness; it is a symbol for a more mature and unobstructed expression of the sacredness and love at the heart of life. It has very little to do with the emergence of psychic phenomena.

The media may so identify the idea of a New Age with irrationality, glamour and self-centered lifestyles that the very image will lose its transformative currency. This would be a shame, but it would not alter anything. The real transformation occurring in our society will continue. The New Age has little to do with prophecy or the imaging of a new world but everything to do with the imagination to see our world in new ways that can empower us toward compassionate, transformative actions and attitudes. If we remember this, then we can forget the New Age of channels, crystals, and charisma and get on with discovering and cocreating a harmonious world that will nourish and empower all of us on this planet and all our children who will be the inheritors of our future.

*David Spangler is a philosopher and educator who has been writing and lecturing on spirituality and the New Age for twenty-five years. He is President of the Lorian Association and was a Co-Director of the Findhorn Foundation community in Northern Scotland in the early Seventies. He is currently working on an introductory book called simply* The New Age. *His last book, published by Doubleday, is* Emergence: The Rebirth of the Sacred, *which also deals extensively with the New Age and with David's mystical experiences. For further information on David's work and writings, please contact the Lorian Association, P.O. Box 663, Issaquah, WA 98067, USA.*

## Part I: Intuitive Development/Channeling
# What Is Channeling and Why Is It So Popular?

Channeling is the communication of information to or through a physically embodied human being from a source that is said to exist on some other level or dimension of reality than the physical as we know it, and that is not from the normal mind (or self) of the channel. Although the human mind might be considered nonphysical, I want to rule out by my definition not only communication from one's own normal mind as source, but communication from fellow physically embodied minds.

Currently there is an extra-ordinary upswing in public interest in the phenomenon we now call channeling. In the last few years, tens of thousands of people have sought out channels privately or in workshop situations, while millions more have read material or have listened to or viewed tapes said to be channeled. The *Seth Material*, the *Findhorn* books, and *A Course in Miracles* are some of the recent major bodies of work that are either channeled or based on channeling. They have enjoyed a remarkable following among people of varied personalities, world views, and walks of life.

There have been times in history when channeling and related phenomena have been accepted, in keeping with the mainstream world view and notion of what a human being is and can be. At other times, phenomena such as channeling have been deemed unusual or paranormal and have been treated as fads or voguish — which may be the case today. And at other times, such phenomena have been devalued, ignored, or considered a type of confidence game or even a punishable crime.

Channeling, like mysticism, is a phenomenon that has been part of human experience as far back as human records go. It appears to be an essential element in the origins of virtually all of the great spiritual paths. It is not just a curiosity of current interest based on a resurgence of inner voices, visions, trance seances, and automatic writing. Rather, the phenomenon is an important aspect of human consciousness, a crucial experience for human beings in all cultures and times, even though we do not yet understand its origins or mechanisms."

*- Jon Klimo*
*From Channeling*

---

**Channeling**
*Investigations on Receiving Information from Paranormal Sources*
By Jon Klimo
1987/384 pages
**$17.95**
$20.35 postpaid from:
Jeremy P. Tarcher, Inc.
9110 Sunset Blvd.
Los Angeles, CA 90069

*This is the source book for understanding the phenomenon called channeling. This process is very popular today and has received extensive media coverage.*

*Channeling can mean trance mediumship, when a person goes into a trance and the spirit entity "takes over" his or her body to speak to human audiences or automatic writing — Ruth Montgomery's mode of channeling — when a person goes into an altered state and a spirit entity "takes over" the person's writing arm and hand (or in Montgomery's case her typing fingers) and communicates via the written or typewritten word.*

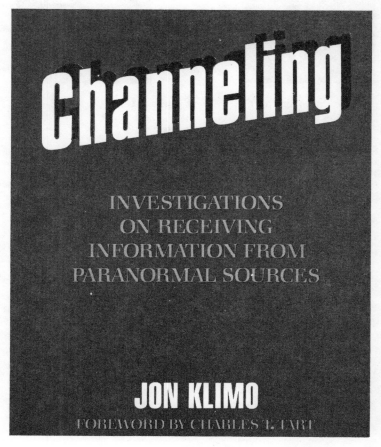

Channeling

INVESTIGATIONS ON RECEIVING INFORMATION FROM PARANORMAL SOURCES

JON KLIMO

FOREWORD BY CHARLES T. TART

# Edgar Cayce *The Sleeping Prophet*

"When we turn within, we are initially confronted by our own personal subconscious. *However, all subconscious minds are in contact with one another.* When we open ourselves without direction to these levels of consciousness, we are sensitive to or even vulnerable to the thoughts of others. As we go deeper, we find levels such as the spirit planes and other planes of consciousness to which we may attune or which may intrude into our awareness if we are not properly directed.

Through attunement of the spiritual centers to these planes, we may communicate with discarnate entities, spirit guides, and even archangels. Our goal should always be to seek attunement with God alone."

> *- Herbert B. Puryear*
> *From* The Edgar Cayce Primer

---

### The Edgar Cayce Primer
*Discovering the Path to Self-Transformation*

By Herbert B. Puryear, Ph.D.
1982/250 pages
**$3.95**
$5.95 postpaid from:
A.R.E. Press
Box 595
Virginia Beach, VA 23451

*A complete course in psychic development and understanding based on the channeled work of Edgar Cayce.*

### Edgar Cayce
*The Sleeping Prophet*

By Jess Stearn
1967/288 pages
**$3.95**
$5.95 postpaid from:
A.R.E. Press
Box 595
Virginia Beach, VA 23451

*An in-depth biography of America's best-known channeler: Edgar Cayce.*

### There Is a River

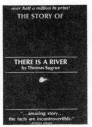

By Thomas Sugrue
1945/376 pages
**$3.95**
$5.95 postpaid from:
A.R.E. Press
Box 595
Virginia Beach, VA 23451

*A biography of Edgar Cayce first written while America's most famous channeler was still alive.*

---

Remember — let every purpose, every desire, every hope be tempered with the spirit of truth; sowing only the seed of the spirit, love, kindness, patience. Those things bring into the experience not that of longfacedness, not those forces that would hinder from finding real joy. For remember, He is God of love, for He IS love. He is God of Joy, for He IS joy; a God of Happiness, for He IS happiness! And only those forces that are in the nature of fear and doubt, hate and jealousy and such, bring those influences that are destructive or disappointing in the experience.

> *- #2403-1*
> *Edgar Cayce Reading*

# Lazaris

Lazaris is a nonphysical entity whose wisdom, techniques and concern for and understanding of psychological and spiritual growth have transformed the lives of many people all over the world through seminars, video and audio tapes, and private consultations. Lazaris, as he says, is "waiting at the edge of your reality," there to love you when you are ready to be loved, and to guide you on your spiritual journey home to God/Goddess/All That Is. Lazaris channels only through Jach Pursel. For information about Lazaris Seminars, contact Concept: Synergy, 279 S. Beverly Drive, Los Angeles, CA 90212.

# Lazaris Videotapes

## Awakening the Love

By Lazaris, Channeled by Jach Pursel
1986/VHS or Beta
**$59.95**
$63.95 postpaid from:
Concept: Synergy
279 S. Beverly Dr., Suite 604
Los Angeles, CA 90212

This is a wonderful introductory tape as Jach, who channels Lazaris, talks about his experience of discovering Lazaris. Then Lazaris proceeds to explain Lazaris in a delightful talk. Lazaris then unfolds the most beautiful discussion on: "What Is Love" and "How to Love Yourself More." So many tell us to love ourselves — Lazaris explains how to do it.

## The Secrets of Manifesting What You Want

By Lazaris, Channeled by Jach Pursel
1986/VHS or Beta
**$59.95**
$63.95 postpaid from:
Concept: Synergy
279 S. Beverly Dr., Suite 604
Los Angeles, CA 90212

This is Lazaris' classic discussion on how we manifest our reality, the blockages that stand in our way, and how to overcome them. It is also a powerhouse of metaphysical tools, from the 33-Second Technique to the use of the Causal Plane in programming.

## Developing a Relationship with Your Higher Self

By Lazaris, Channeled by Jach Pursel
1986/VHS or Beta
**$59.95**
$63.95 postpaid from:
Concept: Synergy
279 S. Beverly Dr., Suite 604
Los Angeles, CA 90212

This is an incredibly beautiful tape about your Higher Self — the magnificent part of you toward which you are growing — and talks about how we can reach for and experience our Higher Self as an empowering means for our growth.

## Other Lazaris Videos include:

**Forgiving Yourself**

**Personal Power & Beyond ...**

**Releasing Negative Ego**

**Achieving Intimacy & Loving Relationships**

**Unlocking the Power To Change Your Life**

**Spiritual Mastery: The Journey Begins**

**Unconditional Love**

$59.95 each
$63.95 each postpaid from:
Concept: Synergy
279 S. Beverly Dr., Suite 604
Los Angeles, CA 90212

## The Sacred Journey: You and Your Higher Self

By Lazaris, Channeled by Jach Pursel
1987/160 pages
**$9.95**
$12.95 postpaid from:
Concept: Synergy
279 S. Beverly Dr., Suite 604
Los Angeles, CA 90212

Once in a great while there comes a book that can change the way you view reality. Such a book is The Sacred Journey, Lazaris' tender, truthful, and thunderously empowering work on You and Your Higher Self. Lazaris begins by exploring the New Age — what it is and is not — and then takes the reader through the steps of preparation to meet his or her Higher Self. Finally, in a series of three incredibly beautiful meditations, you meet your Higher Self, and then are given guidelines for a continuing relationship with your Higher Self that can change your life.

# Lazaris Audio Tapes

By Lazaris, Channeled by Jach Pursel
VHS or Beta/60 minute cassette
**$24.95** each
$27.95 postpaid from:
Concept: Synergy
279 S. Beverly Dr., Suite 604
Los Angeles, CA 90212

## Crystals: Their Power & Use

In this landmark work on crystals Lazaris describes the piezo-electric qualities of crystals and outlines their uses in previous civilizations (Atlantis, Egypt, Mesopotamia, and Europe) and their applications in present-day metaphysics. Includes a delightful meditation.

## The Unseen Friends

The spiritual path has often been described as a lonely one — but it is really crowded with Friends there to help us in our growth.

## Consciously Creating Success

Learning to consciously create success is one of the most important things we can do, and Lazaris guides us on this journey of understanding with elegance.

# SETH

"You will reincarnate whether or not you believe that you will. It is much easier if your theories fit reality, but if they do not, you will not change the nature of reincarnation one iota."

- *Seth, channeled by Jane Roberts From Seth Speaks*

## Austin Seth Center

This organization is devoted entirely to the study of Jane Roberts' Seth channeling. They hold annual conferences, seminars and Seth material study classes. They also publish a quarterly magazine called *Reality Change*. For information contact: Austin Seth Center, Box 7786, Austin, TX

Seth is a spirit personality "no longer focused in physical reality" who channeled through Jane Roberts (1929-1984). This is the most widely published spirit entity in the twentieth century.

"My present existence is the most challenging one that I have known, and I have known many, both physical and nonphysical. There is not just one dimension in which nonphysical consciousness resides, any more than there is only one country on your planet or planet within your solar system.

My environment, now, is not the one in which you will find yourself immediately after death. I cannot help speaking humorously, but you must die many times before you enter this particular plane of existence. (Birth is much more of a shock than death. Sometimes when you die you do not realize it, but birth almost always implies a sharp and sudden recognitiion. So there is no need to fear death. And I, who have died more times than I care to tell, write this book to tell you so.)

*Seth, channeled by Jane Roberts From Seth Speaks*

## The Seth Material

By Jane Roberts
1970/334 pages
**$4.50**
$6.45 postpaid from:
Bantam Books
Direct Response Dept.
414 E. Golf Rd.
Des Plaines, IL 60016

*This is the first Seth book - a landmark work in the presentation of channeled material.*

---

## Seth Speaks

By Jane Roberts
1972/486 pages
**$4.95**
$6.45 postpaid from:
Bantam Books
Direct Response Dept.
414 E. Golf Rd.
Des Plaines, IL 60016

*A continuation of the "Seth Material" that contains mostly transcripts of Seth channeling.*

## The Nature of the Psyche
*It's Human Expression*

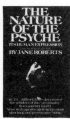

By Jane Roberts
1979/256 pages
**$4.50**
$6.00 postpaid from:
Bantam Books
Direct Response Dept.
414 E. Golf Rd.
Des Plaines, IL 60016

*Seth gets into controversial issues like sexuality, choosing our time of death and the power of dreams.*

## Another Seth Channel?

One of the best known Seth channelers is Jean Loomis, a frequent contributor to *Body, Mind & Spirit* Magazine. She does workshops channeling an entity who calls himself Seth. Is this the same as Jane Roberts' Seth? "Just another point on the same circle" says Loomis' Seth. Contact her at 116 Montowese Street, Branford, CT 06405

"Western society has attempted to force all expression of love into sexual activity, or otherwise ban it entirely. Sexual performance is considered the one safe way of using the great potential of human emotions. When it seems to you that society is becoming licentious, in many ways it is most inhibited ..."

- *Seth, channeled by Jane Roberts From The Nature of the Psyche*

# RAMTHA

The controversial spirit entity called Ramtha is channeled by J. Z. Knight, a former housewife living in Washington state.

"I am a sovereign entity who lived a long time ago upon Earth. In that life I did not die: I ascended, for I learned to harness the power of my mind and to take my body with me into an unseen dimension of life. In doing so, I realized an existence of unlimited freedom, unlimited joy, unlimited life.

I am now part of an unseen brotherhood who love mankind greatly. We are your brothers who hear your prayers and your meditations and observe your movements to and fro.

All of you are very important and precious to us, because the life that

flows through you and the thought that is coming to every one of you, however you entertain it, is the intelligence and life-force that you have termed God. It is this essence that connects all of us, not only to those upon your plane, but to those in untold universes which you have not yet the eyes to see.

Throughout history, we have tried many different avenues to remind you of your greatness, your power, and the foreverness of your life. We have been king, conqueror, crucified Christ, teacher, friend, philosopher — anything that would permit *knowledge* to occur. At times we have intervened in your affairs to keep you from annihilating yourselves, so that life here would continue to provide a playground for your experiences and your evolution into joy.

- *Ramtha*
*Channeled by*
*J. Z. Knight*

## Ramtha
*Ramtha Channeled Through*
*J. Z. Knight*

Edited by Steven Lee Weinberg, Ph.D.
1986/218 pages
**$19.95**
$21.95 postpaid from:
Sovereignty
Box 926
Eastsound, WA 98245

## Ramtha Intensive: Soulmates
*Ramtha Channeled Through*
*J.Z. Knight*

1987/128 pages
**$10.00**
$12.75 postpaid from:
Sovereignty
Box 926
Eastsound, WA 98245

*Ramtha dispels the misconceptions about love and romance and helps you confront illusions which cause frustration and obsession in mankind's search for love.*

## Ramtha Videos

VHS or Beta
**The Power of Manifestation**
(4 cassettes):
**$160.00/$162.75** postpaid
**Ramtha and His Teachings**
(1 cassette):
**$48.00/$50.75** postpaid
**Audience with Ramtha**
(2 cassettes):
**$90.00/$92.75** postpaid
From: Sovereignty
Box 909
Eastsound, WA 98245

# ELWOOD BABBITT

*Known as "the medium from Massachusetts," for many years Babbitt has been channeling entities like Mark Twain, Einstein, Wordsworth, Jesus Christ and Vishnu. Charles Hapgood, a Harvard University professor, studied Babbitt's work extensively and produced three books as a result.*

## Elwood Babbitt Audio Tapes

*These 60-minute cassette tapes feature Elwood Babbitt channeling some well-known spirit entities. The sessions were moderated by Charles Hapgood.*

**Elwood Babbitt Tape #1 features Mohandas Gandhi and Albert Einstein.**
**Elwood Babbitt Tape #2 features Winston Churchill, John F. Kennedy and Mark Twain.**
Order Babbitt tapes through the

**$10.95 each.**

## Talks with Christ and His Teachers

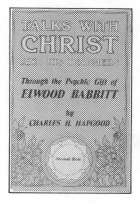

By Charles H. Hapgood
1981/234 pages
**$9.95**
$10.95 postpaid from:
Fine Line Books
Box 281
Turners Falls, MA 03176

## The Law of One (The Ra Material)
By Ra (An Humble Messenger)
1984/229 pages
*Read and return our book at no cost or make a donation of any amount if you wish to keep it.*
From: L/L Research
Box 5195
Louisville, KY 40205
*This is channeled material from an off-planet entity called Ra. Fascinating.*

## Kevin Ryerson

Ryerson is a trance channel for a host of spirit entities including Shirley MacLaine's spirit guides. He figures prominently in MacLaine's books *Out on a Limb, Dancing in the Light* and her latest, *It's All in the Playing.* For a schedule of Ryerson's events contact Lynn Tate Ryerson, 3315 Sacramento Street, San Francisco, CA 94118

## Voices of Spirit

By Charles H. Hapgood & Elwood Babbitt
1975/344 pages
**$11.95**
$12.95 postpaid from:
Fine Line Books
Box 281
Turners Falls, MA 01376

*The story of Babbitt's channeling experience, and research into the validity of his experiences.*

## You Are One

Open your spirit to your soul of being. Witness all your lifetimes. Seek all the mansions of the soul, and in that glimpse, that crevice where the glory glimmers through, you will know and understand your reason for returning to the physical world. And it is your reason alone (your free will) that returns you to a resurrection of the spirit (in the body) to express once again your idealistic tendencies toward the perfecting of all mankind.

But treat spirit not as man or woman. Separate it not in your word of sex. Only look upon it as pure energy and as you do so comes the realization, the images, the Word — and the Word is true. Realize it flowing through every part of your house of flesh, each of which in itself has a full consciousness of being. Speak to it, love each cell for its division. For you, in your own individuality, are a division of the Soul of Being, yet in all of your members you are united as one, the one and only great universe of Self.

- *Christ*
*Channeled by*
*Elwood Babbitt*
*From* Talks with Christ

# A COURSE IN MIRACLES

*Channeled through Helen Schucman*
*Transcribed by William Thetford*

"Three startling months preceded the actual writing, during which time Bill suggested that I write down the highly symbolic dreams and descriptions of the strange images that were coming to me. Although I had grown more accustomed to the unexpected by that time, I was still very surprised when I wrote, "This is a course in miracles ..." That was my introduction to the Voice. It made no sound, but seemed to be giving me a kind of rapid, inner dictation which I took down in a shorthand notebook. The writing was never automatic. It could be interrupted at any time and later picked up again. It made me very uncomfortable, but it never seriously occurred to me to stop. It seemed to be a special assignment I had somehow, somewhere agreed to complete. It represented a truly collaborative venture between Bill and myself, and much of its significance, I am sure, lies in that. I would take down what the Voice 'said' and read it to him the next day, and he typed it from my dictation. I expect he had his special assignment, too. Without his encouragement and support I would never have been able to fulfill mine. The whole process took about seven years. The Text came first, then the Workbook for Students, and finally the Manual for Teachers. Only a few minor changes have been made. Chapter titles and subheadings have been inserted in the Text, and some of the more personal references that occurred at the beginning have been omitted. Otherwise the material is substantially unchanged.

This Course is a beginning, not an end ... No more specific lessons are assigned, for there is no more need of them. Henceforth, hear but the Voice for God ... He will direct your efforts, telling you exactly what to do, how to direct your mind, and when to come to Him in silence, asking for His sure direction and His certain Word."

"Nothing real can be threatened.
Nothing unreal exists.
Herein lies the peace of God."

*From A Course in Miracles*

## A Course in Miracles

Channeled by Helen Schucman
1975/1100 pages
**$25.00**
Order from:
Foundation for Inner Peace
Box 635
Tiburon, CA 94920

## Down to Earth:
### *The Jason Journal*

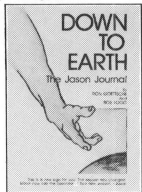

By Ron Goettsche and Bob Fogg
1984/250 pages
**$6.95**
$7.95 postpaid from:
Synergy Publishers
Box 18268
Denver, CO 80218

*Jason is a nonphysical entity channeled through Ron Goettsche who "only (wishes) to assist in a better understanding of how this physical reality functions ..."*

# The Complete Guide to Channeling

1987/60 minutes
**$49.95** Video/VHS or Beta
**$10.00** Audio cassette tape
**$51.95** Video/**$11.00** Audio postpaid from:
Starseed Seminars
Star Route Box 70
Mtn. View, MO 65548

*This video provides the do's and don't's involved with the process of spirit channeling and features some of the best known names in the field including Barbara Marx Hubbard, Ken Carey, Terry Cole Whittaker, Lazaris channeled through Jach Pursel and Marcel Vogel.*

## Agartha
### *A Journey to the Stars*

By Meredith Lady Young,
Channeling Mentor
1981/340 pages
**$9.95**
$10.95 postpaid from:
Stillpoint Publishing
Box 640
Walpole, NH 03068

*Agartha channels a spirit entity called Mentor.*

"Do not fear what you do not understand, instead seek to learn."
- Mentor
Channeled by
Meredith Lady Young
From Agartha

# Should You Follow Channeled Advice?

There is sometimes confusion about whether or not to follow the advice of a particular guide. It is up to you to use your own ability to discriminate and recognize wisdom. When you receive advice from your guide or from someone else's guide, ask yourself, "Is it appropriate for me to follow this information? Does the information limit me or expand me? Is it accurate? Does it have practical value for me, and is it immediately useful? Does it feel like my inner truth?" Remember the last time you got advice from a friend or guide that didn't turn out well. Wasn't it true that there was a part of you that didn't want to follow the advice? You generally know what is best for you. Weigh the information you receive carefully. Use your common sense to decide whether to use the information or not; don't just blindly accept information about your life. High-level guidance will assist you in having greater confidence in your own truth. Channeled advice is to be followed only if it rings true to you, not just because it is channeled. Do only those things that feel joyful or right to you.

> Only accept those messages which ring true to the deepest part of your being.
>
> - *Sanaya Roman and Duane Packer*
> *From* Opening to Channel

## Opening to Channel
*How to Connect with Your Guide*

By Sanaya Roman and Duane Packer
1987/228 pages
**$12.95**
$15.95 postpaid from:
Lumin Essence Productions
Box 19117
Oakland, CA 94619

*A book full of simple exercises a person can use to learn to channel their spirit guide or higher self. The authors are long-time teachers of this skill.*

# Magazines Devoted Entirely to Channeling

## Metapsychology
Edited by Tam Mossman
Quarterly/$20.00 for one year, $5.00 single issue
P.O. Box 3295
Charlottesville, VA 22903

*This elegantly produced magazine features a variety of spirit entities discussing topics ranging from after effects of near death experiences to soulmates to decoding your personal symbolism.*

*Mossman was the editor for the early Jane Roberts/Seth books. This is quality material.*

## Spirit Speaks

Edited by Molli Nickell
Bimonthly/ $24 one year, 6 issues
$40 two years, 12 issues
$4.95 for single issue
P.O. Box 84304
Los Angeles, CA 90073

*Each issue is a lively, easy-to-read flow of channeled material from a number of diverse spirit entities channeled through mediums located primarily in southern California. Topics like Disease, Relationships or Channeling Your Higher Self are the focus of each issue.*

## The Starseed Transmissions
By Raphael
1982/96 pages
**$5.95**
$6.95 postpaid from:
Uni-Sun
Box 25421
Kansas City, MO 64119

"I look out across the slumbering sea of humanity and I whisper these words in the night. And I know that I address a great being sleeping still in ignorance of itself. I know that if the wild winter winds of your communication systems sends tatters or fragments of this message echoing in the darkness, it will still be to the unconscious that I speak.

> - *Extraterrestrial Consciousness Channeled by Raphael*
> *From* The Starseed Transmissions

# Ruth Montgomery

For those who are unfamiliar with my ... books in the psychic field, I should explain that the ones I call "my Guides" are souls like ourselves who have had many previous lifetimes but are currently in the spirit plane, as we will be when we pass through the mysterious door called death. They introduced themselves to me a quarter century ago, after famed medium Arthur Ford said that I had the ability to do "automatic writing" and told me how to go about it. Since then the Guides are always on tap for the daily sessions, and after Ford's death in January 1971 he also joined the group.

In succeeding years, utilizing the voluminous material that the Guides write through my typing fingers, we have jointly produced eight books on subjects of their own choosing that run the gamut from life after death to reincarnation, and from a prehistoric view of the world to Walk-ins who rejuvenate dying or unwanted bodies in order to help humankind. A political rival once said of my friend Barry Goldwater that he was "dragged kicking and screaming into the eighteenth century." My Guides might say the same about my own resistance each time that they have urged me to break new ground by writing about psychic concepts that seem to be ahead of their times. After all, as a long-time syndicated Washington columnist on politics and world affairs. I had a reputation to maintain, and no desire to be regarded as a kook.

But somehow the Guides have always been vindicated in their judgment. When I reluctantly wrote *A Search for the Truth* in 1965 I feared ostracism by the religious community. Instead, I was flooded by invitations from protestant ministers to speak from their pulpits, and from Catholic academia to address their student bodies. After I published *Here and Hereafter*, a big bestseller in the field of reincarnation, bookstalls began to burgeon with volumes on that formerly controversial subject. And when *A World Beyond*, my book

describing what happens immediately after death, also became a bestseller, suddenly doctors and psychiatrists rushed into print with books about the experiences of their patients who came back from clinical death to describe what they had experienced.

The role of Pathfinder can be a lonely one, but each time my faithful Guides have pushed me only one step forward at a time. They did not inundate me with vast quantities of material on a wide range of subjects, but simply nudged me along, allowing me to complete a book on one subject before challenging me with another. Yet each broke new ground. The term "Walk-in" had never seen the light of print until my Guides and I introduced the concept in *Strangers Among Us*, and followed that with specific cases delineated in *Threshold to Tomorrow*. I feared a hooting reaction from the nonbelievers, but nowadays it is virtually impossible to pick up any publication in the parapsychology field without running across references to Walk-ins, and a number of distinguished psychiatrists and psychologists are exploring the phenomenon as an explanation for their patients' radically altered personalities and goals after a near brush with death.

- Ruth Montgomery
From Aliens Among Us

---

## A Search for Truth

By Ruth Montgomery
1967/256 pages
**$3.50**
$4.50 postpaid from:
Random House
400 Hahn Rd.
Westminister, MD 21157

*This is Ruth's first book that describes her introduction to her Guides and the spirit realms via automatic writing. She describes the basic working of the spiritual and physical planes of existence and psychic ability. An excellent introduction to New Age concepts from a former skeptic.*

## Here and Hereafter

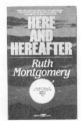

By Ruth Montgomery
1968/176 pages
**$3.50**
$4.50 postpaid from:
Random House
400 Hahn Rd.
Westminister, MD 21157

*This is Ruth's introduction to the concepts of reincarnation and karma. She draws heavily on the work of Edgar Cayce to seek out the truth about this controversial concept.*

## A World Beyond

By Ruth Montgomery
1971/176 pages
**$3.50**
$4.50 postpaid from:
Random House
400 Hahn Rd.
Westminister, MD 21157

*This is Arthur Ford's account of what happens when you die, the nature of existence in the spirit and the physical realms of existence. Ford was a famous Spiritualist medium who channeled his spirit guide Fletcher.*

## Born to Heal

By Ruth Montgomery
1973/224 pages
**$3.50**
$4.50 postpaid from:
Random House
400 Hahn Rd.
Westminister, MD 21157

*This is the story of the amazing Mr. A — later identified as William Gray of Berkeley, California. Now deceased, he was a healer who was able to cure seemingly hopeless medical cases ranging from malignant tumors to blindness. Mr. A used "laying on of hands," the most ancient of healing arts.*

## Companions Along the Way

By Ruth Montgomery
1974/256 pages
**$3.50**
$4.50 postpaid from:
Random House
400 Hahn Rd.
Westminister, MD 21157

*Arthur Ford and Ruth's other Guides from "the other side" tell an incredible tale of past life incarnations of Ruth, Arthur Ford and many famous people living today.*

## The World Before

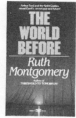

By Ruth Montgomery
1976/288 pages
**$3.50**
$4.50 postpaid from:
Random House
400 Hahn Rd.
Westminister, MD 21157

*Were there once people living on Earth who were half human and half animal? Did cataclysms occur in Earth's history? Ruth answers these and many other questions in this fascinating look at our planet's past and future as provided by her spirit Guides. There is much information on the history of Atlantis and Lemuria.*

---

# Ruth Montgomery's Guidelines for Automatic Writing

1. Practice it only at the same hour each day, in order to establish a date with a superior discarnate who is willing to become your Guide.

2. Do not pick up the pencil until you have first meditated for ten or fifteen minutes, to place yourself in the proper spiritual attunement and to induce the alpha state through which the writing flows. Then murmur a prayer for protection or mentally enclose yourself in a protective circle of light.

It is well to remember that when we open ourselves to unseen forces, a mischievous or evil entity can contact us as easily as a benevolent one, unless we have attuned ourselves to a high-minded Guide who is alerted to our signal and will guard the opened doorway. However, Arthur Ford insisted that if we remain "God centered," or "Christ oriented," no harm can befall us through psychic delving.

— *Ruth Montgomery*
From Born to Heal

# What Happens When You Die?

"We welcome a newcomer with love and open arms. He is surprised at first, unless he has prepared for this step through study and meditation. He hungers and we produce food. It is a thought pattern, but as real to him as that which he once used to sustain his physical body. He thirsts, and we give him drink. He is gradually making the transition, and has not yet accustomed himself to the idea that he will no longer need food and drink. He asks about loved ones whom he does not see around him. Some are still in physical body, some here, some already progressed to a higher state or gone back into another earthly body. We tell him to wait, that within a short time he will understand more, and that meanwhile he is to do whatever suits his fancy. Some will explore the countryside, gasping in awe at the brilliant colors and lush foliage. Others may wish themselves in a big city and immediately will be there, soaking up the sounds and dodging traffic as excitedly as if they needed to do so. For a time we let them do exactly as they choose. It's up to them. But we are ever within call, and the day comes that they tire of this way and begin to wonder more about their present circumstances. If of a studious nature they will want to join classes, for we have them here. Others may join groups who are experimenting with earthly contact.

— *Arthur Ford*
*Communicating via Automatic Writing through Ruth Montgomery from*
A World Beyond

# Psychic Functioning

## We All Have Psychic Skills

At one time or another everyone has had a hunch which has paid off. The phone rings, but *before* you answer it you already know who it is. You go to your mailbox and know *ahead of time* that a letter from a particular person will be there waiting for you. You see a stranger on a street and know that that unknown person will somehow be important in your life. These are all examples of psychic happenings. Locked within each of us lies the power to expand our consciousness beyond our present awareness. For want of a better term, this power is called "psychic ability." Everyone has it. Few know how to use it or how to command it. Like most people, you may be aware of your ability to perceive things beyond the level of the accepted five senses, sight, sound, touch, smell and taste, but unlike most people you are about to learn to awaken this ability and develop your psychic skills.

How to get at these psychic abilities has long been considered mysterious. Popular opinion holds that some people, the lucky ones, are born with "the gift." These lucky people come equipped with psychic abilities. The truth of the matter is that these people have enough awareness of their hunches to take the time to develop their intellect, their athletic competence and so on, one step at a time. Everyone has the ability to think; no one would argue with that. But it is evident that some people are able to think better than others. This is not so much a matter of native ability as it is of *training* that native ability to get the most out of it. It is from this premise that I have taken the liberty to term these so-called psychic gifts, *skills*. It is my belief that anyone, with a little practice, can develop psychic skills.

- *Enid Hoffman from*
Develop Your Psychic Skills

### Develop Your Psychic Skills

By Enid Hoffman
1981/180 pages
**$7.95**
$9.95 postpaid from:
Para Research
1469 Morstein Rd.
West Chester, PA 19380

### Expand Your Psychic Skills

By Enid Hoffman
1987/132 pages
**$9.95**
$11.95 postpaid from:
Para Research
1469 Morstein Rd.
West Chester, PA 19380

### The Psychic Energy Workbook

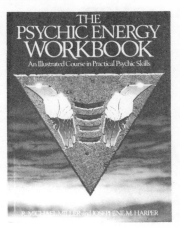

By R. M. Miller &
Josephine M. Harper
1986/112 pages
**$10.95**
$12.45 postpaid from:
Aquarian Press
Sterling Publishers
2 Park Ave.
New York, NY 10016

*Psychic events and abilities are part of our human heritage. We are all psychic. Often we do not see our hunches and perceptions for what they are, nor do we understand their relationship to the spectacular abilities demonstrated by some psychics.*

*This unique workbook guides the reader through a graduated course in psychic skills based on a fundamental awareness of the psychic energy we all possess. It shows how this energy is generated by all living things, how it forms the basis of all psychic events, and how perception and control of it can be put to practical use.*

*The Workbook — illustrated throughout with stunning photographs — provides a progressive exercise program for two or more people to develop their awareness and control of psychic energy. It also covers: psychic cleansing, communication, tuning, self-defense, telepathy and clairvoyance.*

*The exercises in this book are designed for two or more people. This allows for immediate feedback — an essential element in psychic training.*

# Unlocking Your Intuition

## The Intuitive Edge

By Philip Goldberg
1983/242 pages
**$7.95**
$9.45 postpaid from:
Jeremy P. Tarcher, Inc.
c/o St. Martins Press
175 Fifth Ave.
New York, NY 10010

*The really valuable thing is intuition.*
*Albert Einstein*

Until recently intuition has been treated like an employee who, forced to retire, keeps going to work because he is indispensable. Attitudes about him vary: some people don't know he exists, some downgrade his contributions as trivial, some revere him privately while trying to keep his presence a secret. A growing minority are exuberant supporters who feel that credit is long overdue and that such a valuable asset can function even better when recognized and encouraged. This book is in the latter category, part of the corrective effort to bring intuition out into the open, to demystify it, to see what it is, how it works, and what can be done to cultivate its full potential.

In recent years, the subject has emerged from obscurity. Intuition is increasingly recognized as a natural mental faculty, a key element in discovery, problem solving, and decision making, a generator of creative ideas, a forecaster, a revealer of truth. An important ingredient in what we call genius, it is also a subtle guide to daily living. Those people who always seem to be in the right place at the right time, and for whom good things happen with uncanny frequency, are not just lucky; they have an intuitive sense of what to choose and how to act. We are also coming to realize that intuition is not just a chance phenomenon or a mysterious gift, like jumping ability or perfect pitch. While individual capacities vary, we are all intuitive, and we can all be *more* intuitive, just as we can all learn to jump higher and sing on key.

*Philip Goldberg*
*From Unlocking Your*
*Intuition*

## Psychic Energy
## *For Achieving Wealth, Success and Happiness*

By Joseph I. Weed
1981/208 pages
**$4.95**
$6.95 postpaid from:
Simon & Schuster
200 Old Tappan Rd.
Old Tappan, NJ 07675

*This is a classic work that describes how psychic abilities are very normal powers available to everyone of us to use in our daily lives ... from precognition to telepathy and out-of-body experiences.*

## 60 Minutes To Unlocking Your Intuition

By Philip Goldberg
1987/60-minute audio cassette tape
**$9.95**
$10.95 postpaid from:
St. Martin's Press
175 Fifth Ave.
New York, NY 10010

*This is the companion audio tape to Goldberg's book* The Intuitive Edge.
*This great seminar-in-a box comes with a 32-page handbook.*

## Be Your Own Psychic
## *Based on the Edgar Cayce Readings*

By Doris Patterson & Violet Shelley
1975/82 pages
**$4.95**
$6.95 postpaid from:
A.R.E. Press
Box 595
Virginia Beach, VA 23451

When asked "Has the entity any psychic ability or powers and if so, in what way may this be developed and used, primarily for the welfare of others?" Edgar Cayce's reply was:

"These are latent in each and every individual, as has been given. The mystic as calls to the entity in and through the Neptune forces, as has been seen as regarding waters and of the universal forces — as is relating to water, as the creative force; for, as is seen, from out of these all force or form, or matter, begins *its* development, and in this relation the entity has his share — and it may *be* developed by application, not just by thinking — but by applying. To think is to act, to some; to others it is only an interesting pastime. *Application* is a different condition.
*Q-6. In what way may this be developed and used?*
*A-6. As given. Application!"*

*- Doris Patterson and*
*Violet Shelley*
*From Be Your Own Psychic*
*Researchers who based their work on the Edgar Cayce readings have created some of the most useful and sensible guides to developing your inner powers.*

## Balance

In guiding or observing others as well as undertaking any personal exploration of psychic experiences, one of the most important considerations is the matter of an even distribution of energy in physical, mental, and spiritual activities. This may be called balance. This idea may appear to be in contradiction to the experiences of many sensitive people. Psychic phenomena seem to occur more often when the body or mind is tired or exhausted, or when overstimulated. The suggestions that follow are in line, however, with the concept that psychic experiences may be the activities of the real self and are not by nature confined to the realm of abnormality. Certainly one will find it much easier to measure and understand such experiences if they can be observed through the clarity of a state of physical, mental, and spiritual balance. Diet is an extremely important factor in such balance.

- *Hugh Lynn Cayce*
*From* Venture Inward

### The Psi Center

*The PSI Center is a clearinghouse for information on research, findings, theories, organizations, publications and persons that are involved in parapsychology.*

*Its semi-annual journal,* Parapsychology Abstracts International *lists a comprehensive list of information sources in this field. They also publish a number of other bibliographic abstracts and book lists. For a list of PSI Center Publications: 2 Plane Tree Drive, Dix Hills, NY 11746.*

# How to Receive Vivid Impressions Using Self-Hypnosis and Meditation

About 85 percent of those using self-hypnosis and meditation techniques to explore the unknown will easily receive vivid impressions. The remaining 15 percent must be convinced to trust themselves. They expect subjective input to be perceived in a particular way, and when their experience doesn't live up to the expectation, they block themselves. Their attitude is, *"I won't accept it unless it happens according to my expectations!"* Their belief literally destroys their experience, for they expect to receive perfect dreamlike impressions, and that simply isn't the way it works for most people.

There is absolutely no excuse for anyone not to receive. It is a simple process of self-trust. The experience is different for everyone, though, and this seems to be what some people find frustrating. The primary misconception is that the experience isn't real unless you can see pictures in your mind.

Though many people receive visual or fantasy-like impressions, others simply perceive thoughts or feelings. Some claim to see nothing at all and yet they are able to relate numerous details. Others get the impression that during the regression they are making it all up, even though later their experiences have been historically documented. You have to be willing to trust your mind and your impressions.

Most people perceive as if they were creating a fantasy in their own mind. Think about the last time you mentally relived an argument or experienced a sexual fantasy. You imagined the situation and became emotionally involved in it, yet you also remained fully aware of your surroundings; you realized you were creating the fantasy. Now stop and reread those last few sentences. They sum up the way you will probably feel while receiving in an altered state.

There are, of course, many other ways to perceive. For example, some people receive single pictures that shift like watching slides through a slide projector. Others hear a voice or read words. And each of you may perceive through any of these forms at any time. Sometimes you may be emotionally involved, as if you were actually reliving the experience, while at other times you'll be detached, perceiving the events as an observer.

*Dick Sutphen*
*From* How to Rapidly Develop Psychic Ability

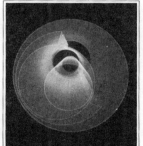

### How to Rapidly Develop Psychic Ability

*This is a complete course in psychic development that employs exercises, hypnosis and subliminal programming.*

# Open Yourself Up to the Possible

*America's Foremost Mentalist*
*Does the "Impossible." So Can You.*

You may wonder why I am writing this introduction to a section dealing with material that takes on metaphysical-like quality.

Certainly it is not because I have changed my general opinions regarding the phenomena, as I do not necessarily accept much of what is considered metaphysical, but to throw out potential truths as well as certain areas of mental development because they are shrouded in a cloak of mystery becomes a kind of intellectual and emotional bias and narrowmindedness.

Most new "truths" of science were originally condemned and subjected to ridicule and vitriolic condemnation by the contemporary scientists of that period.

I believe there are very possibly underlying truths that are common in much of the phenomena that is discussed in this chapter. When Dr. Margaret Mead admonished me for calling myself a "mentalist," she felt instead I should use the title "sensitive." She pointed out that the phenomena in which I was involved has been reported all through history but defined differently, and at times much misunderstood. Indeed, I would not have wanted to be around during the days of Salem and its witchcraft trials, let alone the period of the dark ages.

Let's take the tarot card readers and other kinds of psychic advice givers. It may very well be that the cards are in themselves only tools or vehicles by which the "sensitive" is able to reveal what he intuitively picks up from the stimuli around him. Stimuli that we are not consciously aware of. Interestingly, the old crystal ball of the gypsy fortune teller has in a more sophisticated way found its route into the psychotherapeutic clinic and office, for today some psychiatrists have certain patients gaze into crystal balls or glasses of water in order to project their inner feelings, visions, memories, etc.

We all need to find our own personal signals to bring out the best within us. If we haven't, it becomes

part of our search to find the correct tool and switch. It very well may be that this search is one of the great ventures of our lives.

In my career, from childhood on, I found myself searching and often groping with frustration. Other times I was like a child discovering a new toy. I kept going until I carved a pathway so that I was able to handle my intuitive abilities with a style that has effectively allowed me to perform time after time, day after day in public and in private demonstrations. I have never said that my work is conclusive proof of some paranormal phenomena but it certainly does become a demonstration of certain inner talents and capacities. Abilities that I think are inherent in all of us.

Whatever the reasons for man's voyage into the paranormal he will always find it intriguing and mysterious, but aren't all great truths in life somewhat mysterious and almost miraculous? Look at how little we know of electricity, let alone magnetism.

As you test some of the areas that are covered in this book, you may do so with a critical mind but that is not the same as blind skepticism. The latter attitude is so rigid and narrow that all you will succeed in

doing is shutting the door to some of the richnesses that can be found in new experiences. I held to the conviction that I could somehow find a way of exercising certain inner abilities even though others said they were not plausible or even possible. Keep in mind that it is your belief that such things are possible accompanied by a strong desire to achieve that will help you find your way in a field that has not been clearly defined or understood. What is really exciting about the material that is available in this catalog is that we, at long last, have an opportunity of testing the waters by sampling the ideas and techniques of some of the Eastern and "foreign" philosophies and by doing so, finding skills that will enable us to achieve our own goals. The first step is to study and examine the available literature, materials and teaching on each subject.

Let us remember that the word "education" comes from a Latin word "educo," which means to bring out of ourselves. For again, as has been suggested by great teachers from time in memorial ... the greatest answers and truths are within ourselves ... only waiting to be discovered.

*- Kreskin*

## The Donning International Encyclopedic Psychic Dictionary

By June G. Bletzer
1986/876 pages
**$19.95**
$21.45 postpaid from:
The Donning Company Publishers
5659 Virginia Beach Blvd.
Norfolk, VA 23502

*Consider this volume as a condensed, comprehensive, technical, parapsychology textbook, complete with "do-it-by-yourself" instructions. Because the entries are "categorized" under their particular field and in alphabetical order, one can very quickly find much information about the subject of their choice. And for a full basic, but in capsule form, education in this field, there are instructions outlining graduated steps for not only the individual just becoming interested but also the long-time instructor.*

*June Bletzer*
*Encyclopedic Psychic*
*Dictionary*

---

## Expand Your Mind Power
### Develop An Amazing Memory

By Kreskin
1986/55-minute cassette tape
**$6.95**
$7.95 postpaid from:
Listen USA
60 Arch St.
Greenwich, CT 06830

*Kreskin takes you step by step through the exercises he has developed to increase memory capacity. He developed his amazing mental abilities with simple and direct methods like the ones on this tape.*

---

O-LINE
OBJECT-KNOWING PRINCIPLE                                                  O

**O-LINE**—see CRITICAL DAYS.

**OAK PEOPLE**—the Druids who lived in England.

**OAK TREE**—(Celtic, Germany, Slavic, Rome) (esoteric) a tree species believed to be chosen by God Himself; everyone who drew energy from it would go to heaven; worshipped in ceremonies, and used as a psychic tool for energy, protection and information; has the vibrational frequency that its leaves can speak to mankind. [cf. ACORN, DRUIDS, INSTINCT PERCEPTION, SENSATIONAL CONSCIOUSNESS]

**OAN**—(Babylonia) an intelligent NATURE SPIRIT that had the face, limbs, and speech of human beings, the skin of a fish, lived in the sea; taught his people science, art, craft, written language and how to construct temples and cities; wrote a book on such.

**OBAIFO**—(Africa) a phosphorescent light seen floating in the night; an ETHERIC WORLD ENTITY seeking blood from humans. [cf. ASTRAL VAMPIRE, DOG-GHOST]

**OBE**—abbr. for OUT-OF-BODY EXPERIENCES, see ASTRAL PROJECTION.

**OBEAH**—(Jamaica, West Indies) PSYCHISM and MEDIUMSHIP including about every kind of psychic and mediumistic skill.

**OBEAH DOCTOR**—(Jamaica, West Indies) see MEDICINE MAN and SHAMAN.

**OBEAHMAN**—(Jamaica, West Indies) psychic male who is capable of many psychic skills, mediumship skills, and possesses healing abilities; female is called Obeahwoman.

**OBEer**—(laboratory) one who has the OUT-OF-BODY EXPERIENCE.

**OBI**—(West Indies) psychics.

**OBJECT PSYCHOKINESIS**—abbr. OBJECT-PK; to manipulate inert third-dimensional matter with mind activity only; (excludes living organisms); psychic builds dense concentrated energy in her or his mind giving undivided attention to the activity desired; this puts the PSYCHIC in an ALPHA STATE OF CONSCIOUSNESS, working with the SUBCONSCIOUS MIND; methods to alter the object's shape, area of location, vibrational frequency, placement of parts, or form, varies; 1. psychic concentrates on the object with his or her eyes focused on the object until it changes; 2. psychic gathers and holds

energy in his or her mind until it is dense and then stares directly at the object and shoots a mass of mind energy all at once; 3. psychic beams the concentrated energy out of the palms by placing his or her hands over the object, with palms facing the object; (controlled experiments put the object in a bottle to eliminate air movements from the hands); 4. psychic holds the object in the hand and performs feats that the hand cannot physically perform; energy is sent out of the mind, down the SYMPATHETIC NERVOUS SYSTEM and out the palm and the object is altered; e.g., matchstick is moved across a surface by staring at it (in an area without drafts); a broken watch is held in the hand and soon it is repaired by mind activity; (do not confuse with alchemical DEMATERIALIZATION or with OBJECT TELEKINESIS in which the guides perform the task). Syn. ARTICLE-PK, NONHUMAN-PK. [cf. NONHUMAN PSYCHOKINESIS, MOTOR PSYCHOKINESIS, NONHUMAN TELEKINESIS, ALCHEMY, GRAVITY CONTROL]

**OBJECT READING**—to perceive PSYCHIC INFORMATION by holding an article in the palms of the hands; psychic can determine data regarding the article itself or data regarding the owner of the article; see PSYCHOMETRY. [cf. PRACTICAL PSYCHOMETRY, PSYCHOSCOPY]

**OBJECT TELEKINESIS**—abbr. OBJECT-TK; to manipulate inert third-dimensional matter with the aid of the ETHERIC WORLD INTELLIGENCES, while in a TRANCE state of consciousness; accomplished in the SEANCE room with the assistance of the SITTERS, or in daylight by one's self; intelligence intervenes when directed to do so and alters matter in shape, vibrational frequency, placement of parts, or area where placed; e.g., (authenticated case) two wooden loops with no breaks in their construction were hooked together in a seance; a candy dish floated through the air, unattended, to serve the sitters; piano keys began to play without human hands touching the keys; (do not confuse with POLTERGEISTRY which is unexpected as this phenomenon is planned and willed). [cf. OBJECT PSYCHOKINESIS, LEVITATION TELEKINESIS, GRAVITY CONTROL, TELEPORTATION, PSYCHIC PHOTOGRAPHY]

**OBJECT-KNOWING PRINCIPLE**—(Tiber) the SOUL-MIND of a human being compacted with all the memories and concepts of past lives forever surfacing and used in present consciousness. Syn. SOUL-MIND, CONSCIOUSNESS-PRINCIPLE.

OBSIDIAN
OCTAHEDRON

POSSESSION, SIMPLE OBSESSION, FASCINATION, SUBJUGATION, PHYSICAL OBSESSION]

**OBSIDIAN**—a natural black glass of volcanic origin used for SCRYING. [cf. QUARTZ, SOLOMON'S MIRROR]

**OC**—(Latin) prefix meaning "opposed to, against, inversely, oppositely, reversely."

**OCCIPITAL HEMISPHERE BRAINWAVE MONITORING**—to place a redbead electrode about one inch to the right or left of the skull bone, when using the EEG biofeedback instrument. [cf. ELECTROENCEPHALOGRAPH, BRAIN FREQUENCY ALTERATION]

**OCCULT**—(Latin occulere, "to conceal") 1. (ancient) that which is hidden behind outer appearances and must be studied to be understood; that which is magical or mystical; only available for the initiates; a system of methods compatible with nature to develop psychic power; knowledge of the invisible world and its relationship to mankind; 2. (current Western philosophies) to use nature to develop psychic skills and to constructively probe ancient mysteries and philosophies and to relate these to science; includes knowledge of the invisible world. Sim. MYSTICISM. [cf. Appendix 4 OCCULT]

**OCCULT ATTACK**—see PSYCHIC ATTACK.

**OCCULT FIRE**—see SERPENT POWER.

**OCCULT FORCE**—see PSYCHIC ENERGY.

**OCCULT GUARDIANS OF MANKIND**—see ETHERIC WORLD INTELLIGENCES

**OCCULT HYPNOTISM**—(antiquity) to use the MAGNETIC FLUID in the subject's body and the operator's body to induce a deep hypnotic state which relates to the SUPERCONSCIOUS MIND whereby the subject can establish contact with her or his own OVERSOUL; subject travels through the higher planes with complete memory of the teachings received; used by Pythagoras, Rene Descartes, Theophrastus Paracelsus, Hermes, Plato, Robert Fludd, and the Druids; see ESOTERIC HYPNOSIS and HYPNOTHERAPY.

**OCCULT MEDICINE**—(current) alternative or unorthodox methods, therapies, and medicines that aim for HOLISTIC HEALTH. [cf. ROLFING, DANCE THERAPY, NEUROMUSCULAR MASSAGE, ALTERNATIVES]

**OCCULT PHILOSOPHY**—originated in the Eastern

teachings of antiquity; see OCCULTISM.

**OCCULT POLICE**—highly intelligent ETHERIC WORLD INTELLIGENCES who concern themselves with psychism applied toward criminal ends and offense against society; answerable to anyone who needs help and calls upon them through telepathic communication. [cf. ETHERIC WORLD, EMPATHY-PK, UP-FOR-GRABS, BODY BRUISES]

**OCCULT SCIENCES**—study of OCCULTISM; includes astrology, parapsychology, nature psi, hypnotherapy, holistic health, yoga, meditation, pyramidology, reincarnation, etc.

**OCCULTISM**—(Latin) the science and study of the nature of human beings, the function, operation, purpose, origin, and destiny of mankind; aim is to bring the HIGHER SELF through into manifestation in consciousness through this knowledge; study of the secrets of nature and the relationship between the invisible and visible forces pertaining to progress of the earth; suggests developing INDIVIDUALITY; this hidden material is now being released for anyone. Sim. MYSTICISM, PARAPSYCHOLOGY. [cf. MYSTICISM, PARAPSYCHOLOGY]

**OCEAN**—(esoteric, Tiber) symbolizes the second layer of stratum of ethers (air) resting on the warp and woof. [cf. IMMATERIAL DIMENSION, OCEAN OF LIVING ENERGY]

**OCEAN OF FIRE**—(Sufi) see SOLAR PLEXUS.

**OCEAN OF LIVING ENERGY**—the atmosphere containing the various levels of vibrational frequency and each level having life suited to that level; meaning no emptiness; ETHERIA substance in its entirety. [cf. ETHERIC WORLD, UNSEEN REALM, HIGHER SIDE OF LIFE]

**OCEAN SURF**—the sound of the ocean waves breaking as it rolls up to the shore, is used for meditation: its natural sound has a soothing and hynotic effect to aid in quieting the mind, emotions and body. Syn. WHITE NOISE, WHITE SOUND. [cf. SELF-GENERATED, REPEATED STIMULUS, TANTRIC MEDITATION]

**OCEANIDE**—(Greece) a nature spirit, known as a daughter of the ocean, capable of communicating with and helping mankind; inhabitating the oceans and presiding over its function.

**OCTAHEDRON**—two three-dimensional triangles placed bottom to bottom giving a solid figure with eight faces; has a vibrational frequency that in-

---

## American Society for Psychical Research

### Purpose and Scope of the Society

1. The investigation of telepathy, clairvoyance, precognition, veridical hallucinations and dreams, psychometry, and other forms of paranormal cognition; of phenomena bearing upon the hypothesis of survival of bodily death; of claims of paranormal physical phenomena such as psychokinesis and poltergeists; the study of automatic writing, trance speech, alterations of personality, and other subconscious processes insofar as they may be related to paranormal processes; in short, all types of phenomena called parapsychological or paranormal.

2. The collection, classification, study, and publication of reports dealing with the above phenomena. Readers are asked to report incidents and cases. Names and places must be given, but on request will be treated as confidential.

3. The maintenance of a library on psychical research and related subjects. Contributions of books and periodical files will be welcomed.

From the
*Journal of the ASPR*

*The ASPR is one of America's oldest — it was founded in the 1885 — and most respected organizations devoted to parapsychological research and the collection of related information. Their approach is scholarly. An excellent source for parapsychological research conducted since the late 1800's.*

*Members receive the quarterly* Journal of the ASPR *and the ASPR* Newsletter *plus notice of workshops and seminars sponsored by the Society. For membership information, contact ASPR, 5 West 73rd St., New York, NY 10023.*

## Pathways to Mastership

By Jonathan Parker
1986/12 cassette tapes/2 volumes
13 hours
**$98.95**
$103.45 postpaid from:
Institute for Human Development
Box 1616
Ojai, CA 93023

*This complete self-development course is one of the most ambitious and all-encompassing ever created. It includes 33 guided meditations. Jonathan Parker guides the listener from understanding your inner self to developing intuitive abilities, removing success blocks, aura reading, the nature of God, past and future lives, mental mastery and reaching levels of love and tranquillity and control in life.*

# Self Power

### Inner Guides, Visions, Dreams & Dr. Einstein
### A *Field Guide To Inner Resources*
By Hal Zina Bennett
**$6.95**
$7.95 postpaid from:
Celestial Arts
Box 7327
Berkeley, CA 94707

I have always felt that my greatest journeys were not taken in automobiles or airplanes or trains or boats, transporting me over the countryside or across the water or the sky, but in vehicles made of mind stuff, transporting me through the inner world. For me, the inner world has always seemed filled with limitless possibilities. I have to agree with the psychologist C. G. Jung that this inner world is "the greatest of all cosmic wonders." By comparison, as exciting and fulfilling as it can be, the external world seems filled with frustrating restrictions.

- Hal Zina Bennett
From Inner Guides ...

# Metaphysical Organizations

*There are hundreds of metaphysical organizations operating all over America offering services that range from classes to regional symposiums.*

*We have listed the few organizations that have a base facility and a national range of activities. Contact them for more information about their activities.*

Berkeley Psychic Institute
2436 Haste Street
Berkeley, CA 94704

International Association of Metaphysicians
9440 Lexington N.E.
Albuquerque, NM 87112

Psychic Science International
Special Interest Group
7514 Belleplaine Drive
Huber Heights, OH 45424

Psychical Research Society of Kansas City
Box 151
Belton, MO 64012

Spiritual Advisory Council
2965 West State Road, 434
Longwood, FL 32779

## Developing Intuition

By Shakti Gawain
1987/60 minute cassette tape
**$10.95**
$13.45 postpaid from:
Whatever Publishing
Box 13257
Northgate Station
San Rafael, CA 94913

*Shakti Gawain shows us how simple and natural it is to develop our intuition, and "to tap into the power of the Universe." Side One ends with an excellent basic practice to help you connect with your intuition. Side Two helps you deal with the fears that so often come up, and ends with another useful practice.*

## Natural ESP

By Ingo Swann
1987/218 pages
**$8.95**
$11.45 postpaid from:
Bantam Books
414 E. Golf Rd.
Des Plaines, IL 60016

*From Ingo Swann, a gifted artist and pioneer in the field of psychic research, comes an exciting new approach to understanding ESP. Now, you can learn how to unlock this extraordinary faculty within yourself.*

# Is Experimenting with Psychic Phenomena Dangerous?

To answer this question an individual must take a good look at himself. Superstition, gullibility, emotionalism, neurotic tendencies, a body which is physically sick — all of these are characteristics that should be warning lights. Careful, personal controls that apply in other fields of investigation must be observed: honesty with oneself and others, open-mindedness, persistence, etc. The real dangers of investigation in psychic areas exist in the very nature of the person himself: the wish to be the center of attention, desire for power over others, greed, hate, anger, self-pity, or fear. If one has stored within his own subconscious a great deal of any of these negative emotions or attitudes, such influences will pour out as he opens a door into psychic realms. More than this, the relationship with other minds, such as the possibility of the existence of a collective unconscious, or perhaps the operation of telepathy, must be considered. Psychiatrists and psychologists would be the first to point out that fears, guilt, and other conflicts are suppressed or repressed in the subconscious, and that to open doors that would release these urges without proper guidance might bring disturbing results.

- *Hugh Lynn Cayce*
*From* Ventu.e Inward

## Edgar Cayce on ESP

By Doris Agee
Edited by Hugh Lynn Cayce
**$2.95**
$4.95 postpaid from:
A.R.E. Press
Box 595
Virginia Beach, VA 23451

Edgar Cayce, in one reading, stated, "*Every* entity has clairvoyant, mystic, psychic powers." This theory was advanced in many Cayce readings.

At another time he said, "In the study of phenomena of this nature there should be, first, the analysis as to purpose ... What is the source of the information .. that goes beyond ... ordinary ... guessing? What is the basis of telepathic or clairvoyant communication? What are these in their elemental activity?

"To be sure, this experience is [in] a portion of the mind; but mind, as we have given, is both material and spiritual ...

"It is not, then, to be a calling upon, a depending upon, a seeking for, that which is without, outside of self; but rather the attuning of self to the divine within, which is a universal, or the universal, consciousness ...

"As to making practical application — it is what you do with the abilities that are developed by this attunement in coordinating, cooperating one with another in such experiment. For the universal consciousness is constructive, not destructive in any manner, but ever constructive in its activity with the elements that make up an entity's experience in the physical consciousness ...

"The more each is impelled by that which is intuitive, or the relying upon the soul force within, the greater, the farther, the deeper, the broader, the more constructive may be the result.

"More and more, then, turn to those experiments that are not only helpful but that give hope to others, that make for the activity of the fruits of the Spirit.

"Wait on the Lord; not making for a show, an activity of any kind that would be for self-glorification, self-exaltation, but rather that which is helpful, hopeful for others."

- *Doris Agee*
*From* Edgar Cayce on ESP

## The Warrior Within
### *A Guide to Inner Power*

By Shale Paul
1983/142 pages
**$9.95**
$11.95 postpaid from:
Delta Group Press
245 Ponderosa Way
Evergreen, CO 80439

This book is really three things. It's an explanation of the author's philosophy, a handbook for personal growth, and finally, it's an almost poetic illustration of what his discovered self looks like from the inside. In his two final chapters ("Discoveries" and "Return to the River"), we see an inner view that is attractive, peaceful, and if we are to believe the author, available to all of us. *The Warrior Within* is recommended reading for anyone who thinks there ought to be more to life than money, fast cars and big houses.

- *Shale Paul*
*From* The Warrior Within

## Psychic Development Course

By Jonathan Parker
1986/3 cassette tapes
**$29.95**
$32.95 postpaid from:
Institute for Human Development
Box 1616
Ojai, CA 93023

*Jonathan Parker will take you on an inner journey that explores and refines your personal intuitive abilities. He provides guided meditations to help remove blocks which may be stopping you from accessing your psychic centers and then teaches you psychic functioning in forms like psychometry, precognition and remote viewing.*

# Chakras/Auras

The different energy fields connected to the body are much like various frequencies through which human life can be expressed. These energy centers are called *chakras*, from the Hindu word for wheel. The chakras are thought to be spinning wheels, creating a vortex of energy.

The energy spins more slowly at the base of the spine, becoming faster and brighter as it reaches the top of the spine. Breath, consciousness, and awareness are the tools that are required to keep the energy spinning.

The chakras create the energy field that is known as the luminous body or aura, which surrounds all forms of life. There are some sensitive people who perceive the aura as colors or an electrical field, but a great number do not perceive it at all. The aura is constantly changing and is a manifestation of the energy of your entire being. How you physically, emotionally, mentally, and spiritually feel is reflected in the aura. It is to your direct advantage to be sensitive to this energy field in yourself and in those with whom you come in contact.

The chakras are the batteries for the body. They receive and store energy by interacting with the universal life force. They then direct the energy to supply the needs of the body. The freedom with which energy can flow back and forth between you and the universe is in direct correlation to the total health and well-being you may experience.

Any blocks or restrictions that you might have in either reception or expression of this life energy will result in a malfunction of the organism as a whole and will be experienced as disease, discomfort, lack of energy, or an ailment. By acquainting yourself with your chakras, how they work, and how they should operate when totally healthy, you can diagnose your own blocks and restrictions and have some guidelines for relieving them. (By "blocks" we mean restrictions — complete blockage would result in disconnection with the universal life force, or death.) Everyone has chakras and all of them are functioning. The degree of efficiency is the factor that varies between individuals and between different stages in your life. The chakras can more simply be viewed as seven pathways to consciousness, which work together to create a sense of joy and holistic love for life.

*- David & Lucy Pond*
The Metaphysical Handbook

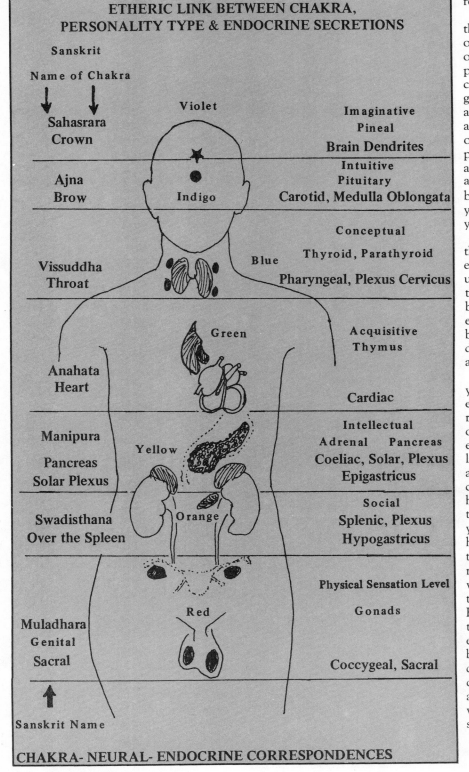

**ETHERIC LINK BETWEEN CHAKRA, PERSONALITY TYPE & ENDOCRINE SECRETIONS**

Sanskrit

Name of Chakra

**Sahasrara Crown** — Violet — **Imaginative / Pineal / Brain Dendrites**

**Ajna Brow** — Indigo — **Intuitive / Pituitary / Carotid, Medulla Oblongata**

**Vissuddha Throat** — Blue — **Conceptual / Thyroid, Parathyroid / Pharyngeal, Plexus Cervicus**

**Anahata Heart** — Green — **Acquisitive / Thymus / Cardiac**

**Manipura / Pancreas Solar Plexus** — Yellow — **Intellectual / Adrenal Pancreas / Coeliac, Solar, Plexus Epigastricus**

**Swadisthana Over the Spleen** — Orange — **Social / Splenic, Plexus Hypogastricus**

**Muladhara Genital Sacral** — Red — **Physical Sensation Level / Gonads / Coccygeal, Sacral**

Sanskrit Name

**CHAKRA- NEURAL- ENDOCRINE CORRESPONDENCES**

## Nuclear Evolution
### *Discovery of the Rainbow Body*

By Christopher Hills
1977/1010 pages
**$24.95**
$26.95 postpaid from:
University of the Trees
P.O. Box 66
Boulder Creek, CA 95006

*Christopher Hills, a true Yogi of the New Age, provides a unique synthesis of scientific evidence and spiritual guidance in this text. It explores the levels of the personality spectrum, mapping out the nature of man's being through light, aura colors, the chakras, Einstein's theory, Jungian typologies, the I Ching and the highest Yogic teachers.*

## Chakra Balance

By Dick Sutphen
1980/60-minute cassette tape
**$12.50**
$14.00 postpaid from:
Valley of the Sun Publishing
Box 3004
Agoura Hills, CA 91301

*Sutphen takes you through guided meditation exercises so you can work on your chakras areas. He helps you get in touch with each energy point and shows you how to use it effectively.*

## The Human Aura

By Kuthumi and Djwal Kul
1972, 1977, 1986/240 pages
**$4.95**
$6.95 postpaid from:
Summit University Press
Box A
Livingston, MT 59047

*This is the messages of the great saints and sages of the East and West on the mysteries of the human aura.*

As we commence these auric studies, let it be understood that the combined manifestation of body, soul, and mind creates around the spinal column and the medulla oblongata those emanations called by some the human aura and by others the magnetic forcefield of the body of man. Let it be understood by all who read that each individual in whom is the flame of life reveals himself as though he were to shout it from the housetops — all that he really is, all that he has done and even the portent of that which he shall be — right in the forcefield of his being and in the magnetic emanations surrounding his physical form.

- *Kuthumi and Djwal Kul*
*From* The Human Aura

## Discover Your Rainbow Body
### *How You Can See & Understand the Aura*

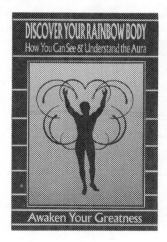

1985/60-minute cassette tape
**$9.95**
$11.95 postpaid from:
University of the Trees
P.O. Box 66
Boulder Creek, CA 95006

Why is the Aura so important? It tells who you are. It reveals what goes on in your subconscious mind, your needs, your aspirations, your hidden potentials, and how you respond to the universe around you. It is the signature of your inner and outer self. By seeing the Aura around others you can discover who they are and how best to respond to them.

- *From* Discover Your Rainbow Body

## The Chakras & Esoteric Healing

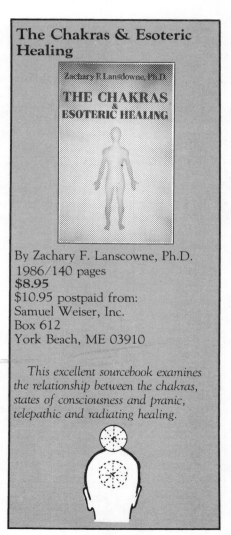

By Zachary F. Lanscowne, Ph.D.
1986/140 pages
**$8.95**
$10.95 postpaid from:
Samuel Weiser, Inc.
Box 612
York Beach, ME 03910

*This excellent sourcebook examines the relationship between the chakras, states of consciousness and pranic, telepathic and radiating healing.*

# Crystals

# Clear Quartz Crystals

When most people talk about crystals, they are usually referring to clear quartz. This type of crystal is the most common and well known and could be related to as "the grandfather" of the mineral kingdom. Generally speaking, clear quartz can be used for all purposes as it vibrates the clear white light which contains all other colors.

Quartz is the salt of the earth and is indigenous to this planet. It is comprised of silicon dioxide which is one of the earth's most common mineral compounds. It is interesting to note that human beings are also largely comprised of silicon dioxide. Would this make us cousins of different kingdoms in the family of earth?

Quartz crystals represent the sum total of material plane evolution. The six sides of the quartz crystal symbolize the six chakras with the termination being the crown; that which connects one with the infinite. Most quartz crystals have a flat base which was their roots to the earth. Oftentimes quartz are cloudy or milky at the bottom and gain more clarity as they reach the terminated peak. This also symbolizes a similar growth pattern in which the cloudiness and dullness of consciousness is cleared as we grow closer to the point of union with our infinite self. Clear Quartz Crystals prove that the material plane can and does reach a state of physical perfection capable of containing and reflecting pure white light. Clear Quartz Crystals are a symbol of coming into alignment with cosmic harmony. They demonstrate that purity and unity in every molecule and atom of their being. Clear quartz radiates with divine white light and by seeing, touching, wearing, using or meditating with these crystals one can actually work with that light in a physical form.

The Clear Quartz Crystals that one attracts into one's life are stones that in some way will facilitate that particular person's growth of awareness. To

unawakened minds, they will work subliminally through the subconscious. For the aware souls who are walking upon this planet, crystals will be like beacons that will add more light and positive energy to be used in their lives and integrated onto the earth. Quartz crystals represent perfected material form, aligned and harmonized with the cosmic force. They are much like the pyramids in that they channel high frequency energy onto the physical earth plane. Clear Quartz Crystals reflect pure white light that can be channeled into daily thoughts, feelings, words, and actions. They stimulate the finer, more subtle realms of our being which can then be integrated and manifested into our lives.

The evolution of the quartz crystal is much different than ours in many ways, and very similar in others. Quartz crystals are conceived within the womb of the earth and matured there until they are born onto the surface of the planet, much in the same way that humans incubate within the warmth of the maternal womb while grounding their spirit into a physical body before entering the material world. Each crystal is unique and unlike any others, each with its own personality, lessons

and experiences, (as with humans). The purpose and destiny of both is to unite with cosmic consciousness and manifest that on the material plane. Crystals and humans can become working partners in that process and serve each other's evolution. When the mineral kingdom and the human kingdom link their forces together, new worlds of consciousness unfold. As the healing essence of quartz crystals vibrate the soul of humanity, vast horizons of hope and joy appear.

Quartz has the remarkable ability to vibrate its energy at all of the color frequencies, from black to yellow, green to pink, and on into the blue and purple spectrum. In this way, quartz demonstrates how to manifest the clarity and purity of white light into denser and lower frequencies. This ability to be multi-colorful can teach us how to vibrate all of our seven chakra centers simultaneously while maintaining perfect alignment with the light. This is the ultimate challenge of being in a physical form; to fully utilize all creative centers while consciously expressing the multi-faceted use of light.

*- Katrina Raphaell*
*From Crystal*
*Enlightenment*

# Crystal Sources

The finest, clearest, quartz crystal in the United States comes from the Mt. Ida region of Arkansas. There are a number of quartz crystal mines in the area that allow visitors to come and, for a small fee, pick their own stones. For more information, contact the Mt. Ida Chamber of Commerce, Mt. Ida, AR 71957. They will send a map that shows the location of mines in the area and lists crystal-related events.

The Middleville area of Herkimer County, New York is the source of the famous Herkimer "Diamonds" — which are actually quartz crystals that are so perfect in clarity and symmetry that they are mistaken for diamonds.

Brazil is another important source for quartz crystal. The stones mined in this South American country almost always have a milky coloring, making them less desirable, perhaps just aesthetically, than Arkansas specimens.

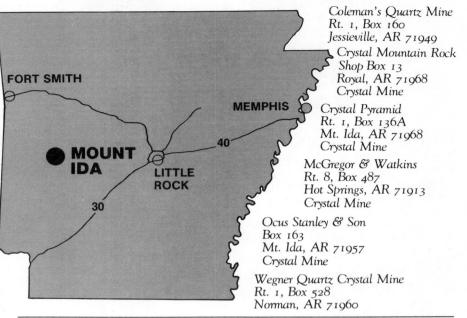

## Arkansas

FORT SMITH

MEMPHIS

**MOUNT IDA**

LITTLE ROCK

40

30

**Quartz Crystal Sources:**

Body, Mind & Spirit Book Shop
Box 701
Providence, RI 02901

Coleman's Quartz Mine
Rt. 1, Box 160
Jessieville, AR 71949

Crystal Mountain Rock
Shop Box 13
Royal, AR 71968
Crystal Mine

Crystal Pyramid
Rt. 1, Box 136A
Mt. Ida, AR 71968
Crystal Mine

McGregor & Watkins
Rt. 8, Box 487
Hot Springs, AR 71913
Crystal Mine

Ocus Stanley & Son
Box 163
Mt. Ida, AR 71957
Crystal Mine

Wegner Quartz Crystal Mine
Rt. 1, Box 528
Norman, AR 71960

## The Crystal Sourcebook

THE CRYSTAL SOURCEBOOK

### From Science to Metaphysics

By John Milewski &
Virginia Harford
1987/350 pages
**$24.95**
$26.95 postpaid from:
Mystic Crystal Publications
1439 W. Highway 39
Sedona, AZ 86336

This is an excellent crystal resource book for beginners as well as the crystal experts. It contains essays from some of the leading practitioners who work with crystals including Marcel Vogel, John Adams, M.D., Ken Silvy and Judith Larkin, Ph.D. This book explains how to use crystals for personal development, plus information on mining, medical uses, history, and extensive resources to help the reader acquire and use crystals.

## Herkimer Diamonds

Herkimer diamonds are very brilliant clear quartz crystals composed of silicon dioxide and hard enough to scratch glass. The crystals are double-terminated (points formed on both ends) of hexagonal structure and are colorless. They range in size from microscopic to several inches. Primarily, these crystals are found in Herkimer Country, thus their name.

The diamonds are found in a rock formation known as dolomite, originally limestone. This rock was buried ages ago. These crystals were formed under tremendous heat and pressure. Subsequently, weathering and erosion by glaciers of overburden rock have exposed the strata containing the diamonds. Apparently, this unique geological happening occurs only in and around the village of Middleville, New York, in Herkimer county.

*The Ace of Diamonds* is one of the oldest mines in the Village of Middleville, New York, where the diamonds are found. The crystals are found mostly in pockets in the rocks. Primarily, they are used for mineral specimens; but many of satisfactory gem quality are used in art and jewelry. Rare ones are found with liquid bubble inclusions called *Hydros*.

Smooth crystal faces of high quality quartz with smooth crystal faces are not uncommon. What makes Herkimer diamonds special is that, unlike quartz crystals, they are often found loose in the rock and are double-terminated. Perfect specimens contain eighteen sides each and are so smooth, they look hand-faceted. Their clarity and refraction may rival the brilliance of real diamonds.

Smaller specimens, generally, are more brilliant and contain fewer flaws. Larger crystals, which sometimes exceed three inches in length, may contain internal fractures or carbon called *anthroxolite*. Some imperfections, such as an enclosed drop of water of smoky color, actually add to the value.

Several miles from the New York State Throughway (Herkimer Exit 30, Route 28 North), there are a number of mines and campgrounds: *Diamond Ledge, Crystal Grove, Hickory Hill, Herkimer Diamond Development Corporation* and the *Ace of Diamonds.*

Ken Silvy
From The Crystal Sourcebook

# Crystal Healing

Crystal healing is a progressive art, one that has the potential to create complete healing, inclusive of the mental, emotional, physical, and spiritual bodies. Practicing crystal healing is an opportunity to let go and let God. It is the time when the heart listens to the messages of the soul, a time to plunge deeply into trust in the inner self. Crystal healing is dedicated to the highest energies of light and color as they act upon the subtle levels of the human being. When this energy interaction takes place, the deepest essence of a person can be accessed. It then becomes possible to see why we have created the realities that we have in our lives. When we understand why we have attracted our circumstances and what the invaluable spiritual lessons are inherent in our life's events, we can then take complete responsibility for ourselves and create our lives the way we choose. Peace and personal empowerment are the natural way of being to one who is in harmony with the self and understands the sometimes hidden purpose behind why events happen in life the way that they do. It is then no longer necessary to play the role of victim, of the controlled, the powerless, and the prisoner of life.
- *Katrina Raphaell*
*From* Crystal Healing

## Windows of Light

### *Quartz Crystals and Self-Transformation*
By Randall & Vicki Baer
1984/176 pages
**$8.95**
$10.45 postpaid from:
Harper & Row
2350 Virginia Ave.
Hagerstown, MD 21740

## Crystal Enlightenment, Vol. 1
### *The Transforming Properties of Crystals and Healing Stones*

By Katrina Raphaell
1985/172 pages
**$9.95**
$11.95 postpaid

## Crystal Healing, Vol, 2
### *The Therapeutic Application of Crystals and Stones*

By Katrina Raphaell
1987/214 pages
**$14.95**
$16.95 postpaid from:
Aurora Press
Box 573
Santa Fe, NM 87504

*Katrina Raphael offers two very esoteric volumes of crystal information.* Crystal Enlightenment *gives the basics of working with crystals and stones.* Crystal Healing *details the uses of crystal for healing, reprogramming and guidance.*

## Gems and Stones
### *Based on the Edgar Cayce Readings*
By the Association for Research and Enlightenment
1960, 1979/74 pages
**$4.95**
$6.95 postpaid from:
A.R.E.
Box 595
Virginia Beach, VA 23451

*This details the many therapeutic and spiritual uses of various stones, including crystal, based on the Edgar Cayce readings.*

## The Crystal Connection

### *A Guidebook for Personal and Planetary Ascension*
By Randall & Vicki Baer
1986/378 pages
**$16.95**
$18.45 postpaid from:
Harper & Row
2350 Virginia Ave.

*Randall & Vicki Baer are a husband and wife team who have devoted themselves to the study and application of crystal for self-transformation.* Windows of Light *and* The Crystal Connection *are written to introduce the reader to the many ways crystal can be used to aid in processes like healing, stress management and telethought communication.*

## Crystal Energy

### *Put the Power in the Palm of Your Hand*

By Gari Gold
1987/114 pages/paperback
**$7.95** (includes free one-inch crystal)
$9.95 postpaid from:
Contemporary Books
180 N. Michigan Ave.
Chicago, IL 60601 ⎯⎯⎯⎯⎯

### Gemstones, Crystals & Healing

By Thelma Isaacs
1982/146 pages/paperback
**$8.00**
$9.00 postpaid from:
Lorien House
Box 1112
Black Mountain, NC 28711

### Cosmic Crystals
*Crystal Consciousness and the New Age*

By Ra Bonewitz
1983/192 pages/paperback
**$9.95**
$11.70 postpaid from:
Newcastle Publishing
Box 7589
Van Nuys, CA 91409

*An excellent book focusing on the spiritual aspect of crystals. Includes healing and meditation with crystals and even how to grow your own.*

# Clearing and Charging Crystal

Clearing your crystal and charging it can often be accomplished simultaneously. For example, exposure to the sun will both clear a crystal of old energy and recharge it with new. Sometimes, however, old energy won't be gotten rid of simply by exposure to new, positive energy; while the crystal is charged with new energy, it also retains the old. I usually do a salt-water cleansing before charging in the sun, but it is not always necessary. Do whatever you feel your crystal needs. If you desire a quick cleanse and charge, cleansing and charging with intent is particularly effective.

*Gary Gold*
*From* Crystal Energy

# 1988 Crystal Calendar

If you love crystal, you must have this colorful calendar on your wall. It features crystals photographed in natural environments. The calendar itself details phases of the sun and moon respective to their astrological coordinates. A 1989 version will be published.

### Crystal Calendar

By Michael Tivana
**$9.95** postpaid from:
Brotherhood of Life
110 Dartmouth, S.E.
Albuquerque, NM 87106

## Crystal Awareness and Techniques

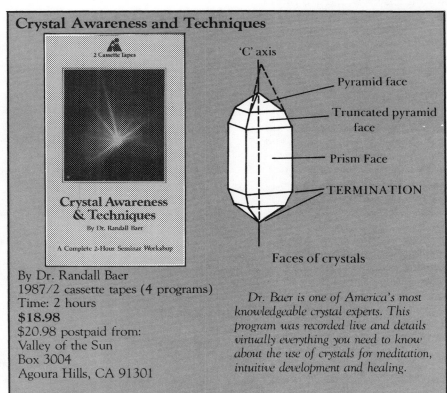

Faces of crystals

By Dr. Randall Baer
1987/2 cassette tapes (4 programs)
Time: 2 hours
**$18.98**
$20.98 postpaid from:
Valley of the Sun
Box 3004
Agoura Hills, CA 91301

*Dr. Baer is one of America's most knowledgeable crystal experts. This program was recorded live and details virtually everything you need to know about the use of crystals for meditation, intuitive development and healing.*

# Divination

## Systems of Divination

*By David Pond*

The modern renaissance of consciousness exploration has brought a renewed interest to the various systems of divination such as astrology, tarot, I Ching, numerology and palmistry. No longer are these oracles simply thought of as gypsy fortune-telling techniques. Modern methods of using these ancient tools help individuals become aware of the many influences surrounding a given situation to assist them in making choices. Yes, choice is important. Divination does not exclude free will; it helps make you more aware of the choices available. Divination is the process of acquiring knowledge directly through intuition and the systems of divination presented in the following books are methods for sharpening and developing your intuition.

We all have intuition; it is a natural process of human intelligence. However, education typically prepares a person for using only the analytical, rational part of intelligence. The old world view that we are emerging from held that the individual was separate from the rest of life. Modern science as well as consciousness explorers are realizing that all of life is interconnected. The holograph is often used as a symbol to represent this phenomenon. A holograph is a projected image that has been split by a lazer beam and then reunited with mirrors. Each piece of the holographic image contains the information of the whole picture. Applied to consciousness, this analogy implies that each individual contains the information of the collective consciousness within himself. Divination creates a vehicle for accessing this information. Each person can be both a receiver and a transmitter of universal knowledge. In the art of divination you seek to align yourself with the clearest channel of information between your essential nature and the wisdom inherent in the universe.

The systems of divination offered in the following books operate on the premise that there are many aspects of life that are beyond the physical. The study of these systems is the study and synthesis of those aspects of ourselves that go beyond what is physically apparent. There are also mental, emotional and spiritual aspects that need to be considered in order to fully understand situations. All of life is interconnected and the health and well being of the individual is a product of the natural flow of communication between all aspects of the whole. The various systems presented in the following books are methods for the individual to see how the whole relates to the parts and to help organize these perceptions into meaningful concepts.

Fortune-telling aside, using these systems can assist you in coming to a greater understanding of yourself and the underlying motivations that prompt you into action. They can help you find a greater meaning in your life by helping you establish a means of communication with your higher-self. These systems become tools for exploring consciousness by revealing the meaning behind events. You begin to see the role that your attitudes and beliefs have in creating the circumstances in your life and how you can effectively improve the quality of your life through inner work. For those interested in developing their consciousness and spirituality, divination provides a window into the self and beyond.

From The Metaphysical Handbook

## The Metaphysical Handbook

By David & Lucy Pond;
Illustrated by Jim Sorensen
1985/342 pages
**$8.95**
$10.00 postpaid from:
Reflecting Pond Publications
P.O. Box 292
Port Ludlow, WA 98365

*This is an indispensible handbook for learning the basic metaphysical techniques of astrology, tarot, I Ching, numerology, and palmistry. The essentials are given step by step so that even without prior experience you can personalize the information to benefit immediately from the expanded perspective on life that studying metaphysics offers.*

# Random Generation of Symbols:
### *Tools for Sharpening Your Intuition*

**Tarot:** Keep a deck of Tarot cards readily accessible in your home. When the telephone rings, cut the cards and ask yourself, who is it and what is the message? Another quickie is to fan the cards on the table and draw one on any given situation. Drawing one card from the deck to represent a general theme for the day is yet another method.

**Palmistry:** Notice where you are getting cuts and hurts on your hands. You can use the symbols of palmistry to connect the afflicted area in your hand to an aspect of your life that needs more attention.

**Numerology:** There are numerous occasions during the day when numbers randomly pop up before you. Each of these times is an opportunity to sharpen your intuition. Notice the number of your parking stall, keep it in mind as a clue to the theme of what you will experience after parking the car. Addresses, ticket stub numbers, telephone numbers, and license plate numbers are all opportunities to use numerology in daily life.

**Astrology:** Notice the types of people you are attracting into your life. Is there a dominant sign represented? Often this is symbolic of a part of your birth chart that you are working on.

**I Ching:** The method of opening the book at random and pointing to a line for a spontaneous reading works exceptionally well. This method also works with the *Bible* and other books of wisdom.

**Events:** Once you have sharpened your intuition to the point that you can see the meaning of seemingly unrelated events, then all of life becomes symbolic. An example is when you are working in the kitchen and accidently cut your finger. It is often revealing to analyze what you were thinking about at the moment you cut yourself. Were you thinking cutting thoughts about someone? There are myriad clues throughout the day that can show you both the power of your thoughts and how interconnected the world really is.

When you have extended your intuition to include the events of life as a source of symbols, you will never be without the tools of the trade. When you first begin on this path, the cards, coins, and planets are necessary tools. These sharpen and strengthen your primary tool: intuition. Now that you have opened this door, all of life is available for reading.

- *David & Lucy Pond*
*From* The Metaphysical Handbook

## Seven Paths to Understanding

By Zipporah Dobyns and William Wrobel
1985/340 pages
**$12.95**
$14.95 postpaid from:
ACS Publications, Inc.
P.O. Box 16430
San Diego, CA 92116-0430

*A synthesis of seven of the many different ways to approach the task of understanding human existence and experience including astrology, numerology, handwriting analysis, palmistry, personal interviews, psychological tests and self-analysis.*

# Astrology

## Compendium of Astrology

By Rose Lineman and Jan Popelka
1984/304 pages
**$14.95**
$16.95 postpaid from:
Para Research
c/o Schiffer Publishing Ltd.
1469 Morstein Rd.
West Chester, PA 19380

*One complete volume explains the basics of astrology. Learn to cast a chart, delineate planet positions and interpret entire horoscopes.*

## World Ephemeris for the 20th Century
### *Noon and Midnight Editions*

1983/624 pages/2 volumes
**$13.95 each**
$15.95 postpaid from:
Para Research
c/o Schiffer Publishing Ltd.
1469 Morstein Rd.
West Chester, PA 19380

*Computer calculated and typeset with letter-quality printing which provides complete accuracy. Sun's position is calculated to the second of arc, the Moon's mean node and nine planetary positions are given to the minute of arc.*

**JUNE 1952**

|   | Jup. | Saturn | Uranus | Nept. | Pluto | N.Node |
|---|------|--------|--------|-------|-------|--------|
| R | 7Ta40 | 8L116R | 12Cn 9 | 19L1 9R | 19Le19 | 25Aq24 |
|   | 7 53 | 8 15 | 12 12 | 19 8 | 19 20 | 25 21 |
|   | 8 6 | 8 14 | 12 16 | 19 7 | 19 21 | 25 18 |
|   | 8 19 | 8 13 | 12 19 | 19 7 | 19 22 | 25 15 |
|   | 8 32 | 8 13 | 12 22 | 19 6 | 19 22 | 25 12 |
|   | 8 45 | 8 12 | 12 25 | 19 5 | 19 23 | 25 9 |
|   | 8 58 | 8 12 | 12 29 | 19 4 | 19 24 | 25 5 |
|   | 9 11 | 8 11 | 12 32 | 19 4 | 19 25 | 25 2 |
|   | 9 24 | 8 11 | 12 35 | 19 3 | 19 26 | 24 59 |

## Complete Horoscope Interpretation
### *Putting Together Your Planetary Profile*

By Maritha Pottenger
1986/540 pages
**$19.95**
$21.95 postpaid from:
ACS Publications
P.O. Box 16430, San Diego, CA
92116-0430

*Contains everything an astrologer would need to analyze a natal chart, emphazing how to quickly and easily spot themes and essential messages of a horoscope.*

## The Only Way to ... Learn Astrology

The Lunar Cycle

By Marion D. March and
Joan McEvers
**Vol. I, Basic Principles**
320 pages
**Vol. II, Math & Interpretation Techniques**
264 pages
**Vol. III Horoscope Analysis**
272 pages
**$9.95 each**

$11.95 postpaid from:
ACS Publications
P.O. Box 16430, San Diego, CA
92116-0430

*Clear, concise and easy to read. Excellent for self-study or as a text, with a Teacher's Guide available upon request.*

## Person-Centered Astrology

By Dane Rudhyar
1980, 1987/386 pages
**$14.00**
$16.00 postpaid from:
Aurora Press
P.O. Box 573
Santa Fe, NM 87504

*Inspired guidance on the value of Astrology in the New Age focusing on a person-centered view vs. the event-oriented approach.*

## The Astrology Workbook
### *Understanding the Art of Natal Interpretation*

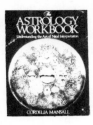

By Cordelia Mansal
1985/176 pages
**$10.95**
$12.45 postpaid from:
Thorsons Publishing Group England
c/o Sterling Publishers
2 Park Ave.
New York, NY 10016

## Astro Computing Services
P.O. Box 16430
San Diego, CA 92116

*Well-established astrological computing service which caters to both serious students and the general public by providing charts, graphs, and a catalog (ACS Publications) of books and supplies concerning all aspects of astrology.*

## Cycles Research
## Conferences & Seminars
P.O. Box 1460
Sebastopol, CA 95472

*Sponsors international conferences on modern astrology drawing speakers from throughout the U.S. as well as overseas.*

# The Triplicities (the Elements) and Their Corresponding Signs and Houses

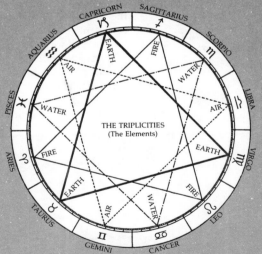

*The triplicities (the elements)*

**The Earth Triplcity**
(Taurus, Virgo, Capricorn)
Key Phrase: "I shall wait until I know what it is all about!"

**The Water Triplicity**
(Cancer, Scorpio, Pisces)
Key Phrase:"I shall wait and see if my first impression is correct!"

**The Air Triplicity**
(Gemini, Libra, Aquarius)
Key Phrase: "I have to know what is going on and why!"

**The Fire Triplicity**
(Aries, Leo, Sagittarius)
Key Phrase: "Now I am here, let's get on with it!"
*Cordelia Mansall*
*From The Astrology Workbook*

## American Federation of Astrologers, Inc. (AFA)

6535 S. Rural Rd.
Tempe, AZ 85285

*This organization is dedicated to encourage study of all scientific methods of astrology. Offers membership, classes, certification, a catalog of publications and products. They also sponsor bi-annual conventions.*

# Numerology

*Evolution is the law of Life.*
*Number is the law of the Universe.*
*Unity is the law of God.*
> *Pythagoras*

Numerologists believe that we are born at a certain date, hour and minute not merely by chance, but in order to learn important lessons and to perform specific tasks during our lifetimes and that the conditions and vibrations prevailing at the precise moment of our birth must be favourable if we are to fulfil our mission in life. Some also believe that that transmigration of souls and the possibility of reincarnation plays an important role in their philosophy of life. Numerology is also a method of character analysis which uses the numbers of names and birthdates in an attempt to solve the age-old question "Who am I?" Its study enables us to take an objective, unbiased look at ourselves and discover our innate talents and abilities.

> *Julia Line*
> *The Numerology*
> *Workbook*

## Numerology and the Divine Triangle

By Faith Javane and Dusty Bunker
1979/288 pages
**$14.95**
$16.95 postpaid from:
Para Research, Inc.
c/o Schiffer Publishing Ltd.
1469 Morstein Road
West Chester, PA 19380

*A masterful explanation of our changing life cycles of "9" with a complete introduction to esoteric numerology and its relationship to the 78-card tarot deck.*

# Finding Your Birth Number

The date of birth is one number which cannot be altered. Probably the most often used method of analysing a birth date is by reduction. Here the date is written out in full (months are always expressed numerically) and the resulting numbers are added together.

eg.

| 27th | Dec. | 1963 | |
|------|------|------|---|
| 2+7 | +1+2 | +1+9+6+3 | =31/4 |
| Date | Month | Year | |
| ___ + | _____ + | _____ = | ___ |

Some American numerologists use a slightly different method. They would reduce the date of birth as follows:

| Dec. | 27th | 1963 |
|------|------|------|
| 12 | +27 | +1963 |
| 12 | +27 | +19 (1+9+6+3) |
| 12 | +27 | +19 = 58/4 |

The double digit number is different but the total, when reduced, is still the same.

The single number arrived at (11 and 22, the master numbers, being the only double-digited exceptions) represents the lessons which have to be learned during the lifetime under analysis and indicates the path which should be taken in order to reach that particular goal.
> *Julia Line*
> *From* The Numerology Workbook

---

## Instant Numerology
### *A Manual for the Beginner*

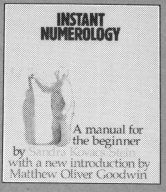

By Sandra Kovacs Stein
1979/98 pages
**$7.95**
$9.70 postpaid from:
Newcastle Publishing Co., Inc.
P.O. Box 7589
Van Nuys, CA 91409

*A series of clear, easy to follow, step-by-step exercises with plenty of graphic aids.*

# Numerical Value of Letters

| | | |
|---|---|---|
| 1 | A | J | S |
| 2 | B | K | T |
| 3 | C | L | U |
| 4 | D | M | V |
| 5 | E | N | W |
| 6 | F | O | X |
| 7 | G | P | Y |
| 8 | H | Q | Z |
| 9 | I | R | |

*-Sandra Kovacs Stein*
*From* Instant Numerology

## The Numerology Workbook
### Understanding and Using the Power of Numbers

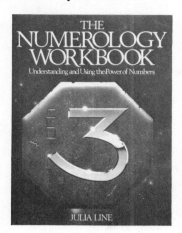

By Julia Line
1985/224 pages
**$10.95**
$12.45 postpaid from:
Thorsons Publishing Group England
c/o Sterling Publishers
2 Park Avenue
New York, NY 10016

*A comprehensive look at the many systems of numerology, with special emphasis on the Pythagorean, Golden Dawn and Cheiro methods. The author provides a step-by-step study of the basics of numerology. Especially good for the beginner.*

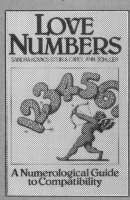
# Numbers of the Twelve Signs of the Zodiac

**Aries, the Ram
(21 March — 20 April)**
Number = 9 (positive)
Element: Fire
Key words: I am

**Taurus, the Bull
(21 April — 20 May)**
Number = 6 (positive)
Element: Earth
Key words: I have

**Gemini, the Twins
(21 May — 20 June)**
Number = 5 (positive)
Element: Air
Key words: I think

**Cancer, the Crab
(21 June — 20 July)**
Number = 2
Element: Water
Key words: I feel

**Leo, the Lion
(21 July — 20 August)**
Number = 1
Element: Fire
Key words: I will

**Virgo, the Virgin
(21 August — 20 September)**
Number = 5 (negative)
Element: Earth
Key words: I analyze

**Libra, the Scales
(21 September — 20 October)**
Number = 6 (negative)
Element: Air
Key words: I balance

**Scorpio, the Scorpion
(21 October — 20 November)**
Number = 9 (negative)
Element: Water
Key words: I desire

**Sagittarius, the Archer
(21 November — 20 December)**
Number = 3 (positive)
Element: Fire
Key words: I see

**Capricorn, the Goat
(21 December — 20 January)**
Number = 8 (positive)
Element: Earth
Key words: I use

**Aquarius, the Water-Carrier
(21 January — 20 February)**
Number = 8 (negative) and 4
Element: Air
Key words: I know

**Pisces, the Fishes
(21 February — 20 March)**
Number = 3 (negative) and 7
Element: Water
Key words: I believe

*From* The Numerology Workbook

# Tarot

Tarot cards, or symbolic representations of the truth, have always been used to help man relate not only with the mind, but internally through the feelings invoked by the colors and forms. The nature of these cards is that they can produce a strong awakening of one's unconscious forces. They are like a spiritual mirror in which we can recognize and examine ourselves.

We can then understand that the reasons for our fate lie within ourselves, which changes by the mere fact that we begin to react differently to everything that happens to us. The cards are a valuable key to understand our present state, our past and in a deeper sense, how we create our future.

- *Elizabeth Haich*
  From Wisdom of the Tarot

## The Tarot Revealed

By Eden Gray
1960/240 pages
**$3.95**
$4.95 postpaid from:
New American Library
P.O. Box 999
Bergenfield, NJ 07621

*The ancient lore of the Tarot is presented in simple language for the beginning reader.*

## Encyclopedia of Tarot, Vol. I & II

Stuart R. Kaplan
**Vol. I:**
**$25.00**
$28.00 postpaid
**Vol. II:**
**$35.00**
$38.50 postpaid from:
U.S. Games Systems, Inc.
179 Ludlow Street
Stamford, CT 06902

*A fascinating overview of the history, artwork, and uses of the tarot and related playing cards is provided in this mammoth reference work. The Encyclopedia also contains chapters on the interpretations of the Major and Minor Arcana cards, and how to spread the tarot decks. The Best of Cards Catalog ($2.00), also available from U.S. Games Systems. It contains the most complete selection of tarot decks, books, and other playing cards.*

## Tarot: A New Handbook for the Apprentice

By Eileen Connolly
1979/244 pages
**$9.95**
$11.70 postpaid from:
Newcastle Publishing Company, Inc.
P.O. Box 7589
Van Nuys, CA 91409

*A self-discovery workbook, which relates the tarot to other occult sciences such as astrology, the kabalah and numerology, for greater enlightenment and powers of divination.*

# The Knight of Cups

KNIGHT of CUPS.

**DESCRIPTION:** A knight riding quietly and wearing a winged helmet, symbol of imagination. He is contemplative, not warlike; he bears his cup firmly as the horse prepares to cross the stream and approach the distant peaks.
**DIVINATORY MEANING:** A young man with light brown hair and hazel eyes, of high intelligence and romantic dreams. Love may come from him to the subject of the reading. He may also be the bearer of messages. May indicate advances, a proposition or an invitation.
**REVERSED:** Propositions should be carefully looked into. There may be subtlety, fraud, trickery, rivalry.

- *Eden Gray*
  From The Tarot Revealed

## Choice-Centered Tarot

By Gail Fairfield
1984/152 pages
**$7.95**
$9.70 postpaid from:
Newcastle Publishing Company, Inc.
P.O. Box 7589
Van Nuys, CA 91409

*A fresh, creative exploration of the variety of ways Tarot can be used as a tool in our lives.*

## Tarot for Your Self

By Mary K. Greer
1984/254 pages
**$12.95**
$14.70 postpaid from:
Newcastle Publishing Company, Inc.
P.O. Box 7589
Van Nuys, CA 91409

*This book focuses on self-readings and the personal use of the Tarot. Excellent for both beginning students and advanced practitioners.*

## Builders of the Adytum (B.O.T.A.)
*Temple of Tarot and Holy Qabalah*

5101-05 North Figueroa Street
Los Angeles, CA 90042

*B.O.T.A., a national organization, was founded by Paul Foster Case in 1947. It is devoted to studying and disseminating information on the Tarot and the Qabalah (a.k.a. Kaballah). This "Mystery School" teaches that the Tarot is a pictorial book of spiritual instruction meant to communicate information to everyone symbolically, thereby avoiding any language barrier. Established B.O.T.A. chapters are located in cities across the country offering classes and related meditation groups.*

## The Tarot

By Paul Foster Case
1947/216 pages
**$7.95**
$9.45 postpaid from:
Macoy Publishing Co.
P.O. Box 9759
Richmond, VA 23228

*An esoteric study of the occult meaning of numbers, symbols and tones corresponding with the Tarot.*

## Wisdom of the Tarot

By Elizabeth Haich
1975/174 pages
**$12.95**
$14.95 postpaid from:
Aurora Press
P.O. Box 573
Santa Fe, NM 87504

*The path of higher consciousness is studied through the color, shape, and symbolic forms on each of the twenty-two Major Arcana cards. A meditation is offered for each card (step) encountered on the journey towards the Light.*

# Tarot Decks

Available from:
U.S. Games Systems, Inc.
179 Ludlow St.
Stamford, CT 06909

**Native American Tarot Deck**
$12.00
$2.00 postage

**Rider-Waite Tarot Deck**
$12.00
$2.00 postage

**Aquarian Tarot Deck**
$12.00
$2.00 postage

# *Palmistry*

## Cheiro's Language of the Hand
### *The Classic of Palmistry*

By Count Louis Hamon (Cheiro)
1987/254 pages
**$7.95**
$9.95 postpaid from:
Prentice Hall Press
A division of
Simon & Schuster, Inc.
200 Old Tappan Road
Old Tappan, NJ 07675
Attn: Mail Order Dept.

*A classic palmistry text, well illustrated and supplemented by Cheiro's 30 thirty years of study in this field.*

## Hands
### *A Complete Guide to Palmistry*

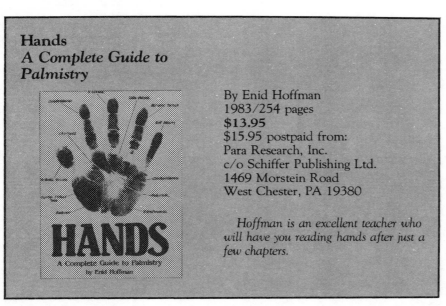

By Enid Hoffman
1983/254 pages
**$13.95**
$15.95 postpaid from:
Para Research, Inc.
c/o Schiffer Publishing Ltd.
1469 Morstein Road
West Chester, PA 19380

*Hoffman is an excellent teacher who will have you reading hands after just a few chapters.*

## Secrets of the Palm

By Darlene
Hansen
1985/192 pages
**$9.95**
$11.95 postpaid
from: ACS
Publications, Inc.
P.O. Box 16430
San Diego,
CA 92116-0430

*This book is an excellent course in palmistry. It features mini-exams in each chapter that allow you to test your knowledge as you proceed through the book.*

## Chinese Hand Analysis

By Shifu Terence Dukes
1987/348 pages
**$29.95**
$31.45 postpaid from:
Samuel Weiser, Inc.
Box 612
York Beach, ME 03910

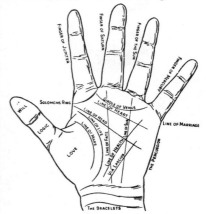

*The Chinese method of hand analysis focuses on "why" and "how" lines mean what they do. Terence Dukes gives special emphasis on the fact that our hands can help diagnose our psychological, physical and spiritual health.*

# What to Look For in Hand Lines ...

The rules in relation to the lines are, in the first place, that they should be clear and well marked, neither broad nor pale in color; that they should be free from all breaks, islands, or irregularities of any kind.

Lines very pale in color indicate, in the first place, want of robust health, and, in the second, lack of energy and decision.

Lines red in color indicate the sanguine, hopeful disposition; they show an active, robust temperament.

Yellow lines, as well as being indicative of biliousness and liver trouble, are indicators of a nature self-contained, reserved, and proud.

**The Map of the Hand from Cheiro's Language of the Hand**

Lines very dark in color, almost black, tell of a melancholy, grave temperament, and also indicate a haughty, distant nature, one usually very revengeful and unforgiving.

Lines may appear, diminish, or fade, which must always be borne in mind when reading the hand. The province of the palmist, therefore, is to warn the subject of approaching danger by pointing out the evil tendencies of his nature. It is purely a matter of the subject's will whether or not he will overcome these tendencies, and it is by seeing how the nature has modified evils in the past that the palmist can predict whether or not evils will be overcome in the future.

- Cheiro
From Language of the Hand

# How You Think Is Reflected in Your M's, N's, and R's

**Sharp Needle Points** reveal a penetrating, fast, and intuitive thinker, one who sizes up situations and grasps facts instantly. The sharper and higher the points the more vivid and rapid the comprehension

**Upside-down V, or Spade Shape** shows a critical and investigative mind which explores and digs for knowledge, always asking questions and seeking answers; an intellectually thirsty person with eagerness to learn.

**Rounded m's, n's, r's** reveal the careful and creative mind that accumulates observations and facts and finally uses each piece logically to build a mental structure. Each piece has to fit. Facts should be proven.

**Overly Rounded Tops of the Small m, n, or r** show childish tendencies on the part of the writer. There is a lack of mental acuity, immaturity, with the yielding and submissive traits of one who is obedient and follows the rules. Not easily adaptable to circumstances, and can be somewhat dull and lazy.

**Sharp Needle Points with Very Rounded Connections** indicate an inner conflict between a keen mind and a very yielding nature, between mental maturity and emotional immaturity. The emotional nature cannot carry through with what the mind perceives, and the person feels weak and frustrated.

> - *Karen Amend and Mary Ruiz From* Handwriting Analysis

## Handwriting Analysis

By Karen Amend & Mary S. Ruiz
1980/196 pages
**$9.95**
$11.95 postpaid from:
Newcastle Publishing Co.
P.O. Box 7589
Van Nuys, CA 91409

*This book includes a variety of actual handwriting samples explained in clear, precise terms. The authors teach by example.*

## Graphology Handbook

By Curtis W. Casewit
1980/154 pages
**$11.95**
$13.95 postpaid from:
Para Research
c/o Schiffer Publishing Ltd.
1469 Morstein Road
West Chester, PA 19380

*Illustrated with over a hundred handwriting samples including presidents, movie stars and everyday folks. The author gives advice on how to become a graphologist and make a living doing it.*

# What Good Is Graphology?

You will definitely benefit from learning about handwriting analysis. A Chicago school that trains analysts puts it this way: "You can quickly sift from any specimen of handwriting the signs of special talents and aptitudes as well as general character traits. Musical ability ... scientific endowments ... mathematical proficiency ... a bent for management and leadership ... skill in handling people ... research and investigative capabilities ... sound judgment ... selling talents — all of these, and more, are brought sharply into focus.

Graphology proves especially valuable in business. Analysis cuts through appearances and lets you see a person as he or she really is.

> - *Curtis W. Casewit From the* Graphology Handbook

## Dowsing

# How Can I Tell If I Am a Dowser?

Try one of the basic devices described below. Hold it in the search position and walk forward, keeping the mind focused on your potential target, i.e. underground flowing water. If you feel you have covered too much ground, or passed over a known stream without result, try one of the other devices. Remember that with a little practice and some patience nearly everyone can achieve a dowsing reaction. As with all human skills, aptitude will vary. We believe, however, that dowsing is a basic ability and that familiarization with it is a simple matter for old and young alike.

### Which Device Shall I Start With?

*Angle rods* will respond to most people on the very first attempt. You can make them from round metal stock, preferably 1/8 to 3/16 inch in diameter, and from 18 to 30 inches long. Bend two such rods at a point approximately 6 inches from the ends to form a right angle "grip." Metal or plastic tubing slipped over the "grips" will permit the rods to swivel more easily but is not necessary to get a reaction. Hold the rods at waist level, pointing forward like two pistols. As you walk forward, mentally ask for an underground stream of water, water pipe, electric or gas line — whatever it is you seek. The rods will swivel, either crossing inward or diverging outward, as you pass over its actual location. As you pass beyond it, they should resume their original fore-and-aft position, aligned with your forearms.

The *forked stick*, however, may suit you just as well. It has an age-old connection with dowsing. It is pictured, for instance, as the device used by miners on a tenth-century German coin. Simply cut a fork about 18 to 20 inches long, 1/8 to 1/4 inch in diameter, from a tree or bush. It should be limber enough to be responsive when the two ends are held firmly in a palms-up position, yet stiff enough to resist all but a definite pull from a vertical, or search, position. Proceed as with the angle rods, mentally holding the desired target until the forked stick

reacts over it by a pulling motion. This may be toward or away from the body, though many dowsers find the latter response to be the norm. You may also want to try forked "sticks" made of metal, whale bone, or plastic.

*The pendulum* is equally favored by beginners. Anything of 1/4 to 1/2 ounce weight such as a finger ring, or a 3/8-inch hexagonal nut will serve. Secure it to a 6-inch string or small chain. Hold the string or chain between thumb and forefinger of your master hand about two to four inches above the suspended weight. Position it above your right knee and set it in motion. Then, keeping the hand steady, allow the weight to find its pattern of movement. This will often be a clockwise circle, but whatever *the pattern*, let this be your "signal" or sign for "positive" and "yes." After stopping the swing, move the hand over the left knee and, after an initiatory motion, let the weight settle into a pattern. Frequently this will be counterclockwise or the opposite of "yes." Let this pattern be your signal for "negative" and "no." Finally, move the hand to a position between the knees and, as above, let the weight describe a pattern. Often, this will be a straight back-and-forth swing. Let this be your signal for "neutral" (starting movement) or "don't know." If after repeated trials the modes appear differently to you, do not attempt to change them, but use the pattern that is consistent *for you*. It is only necessary to set the weight swinging in the neutral mode and proceed over a target area until it reaches the positive mode in order for you to know that you have made a "hit" and are on target.

*The wand* or bobber is another device and can be made from a four foot branch of a tree, stripped of leaves and shoots, about 1/2 to 1/4 inch in diameter. A similar length of rigid wire or the plastic tip of a fishing rod will also serve. Grasp the wand close to the smaller end and set it in motion, either vertically or horizontally. As you walk over the target area, the opposite motion or a

circular motion will prevail and signal to you that the search has been a success.
*American Society of Dowsers*

## The American Society of Dowsers, Inc.
Danville, VT 05828

*The ASD is a nonprofit educational and scientific society open to anyone who wishes to join. There are 64 chapters throughout the United States. The American Dowser is a quarterly publication sent to all members including a national directory and schedule of events and notice of seminars and conferences. The ASD is dedicated to teaching dowsing skills and promoting this practice as a service to mankind.*

## Life Understanding Foundation
Box 30305
Santa Barbara, CA 93130
*Provides information, tools, publications, and videos on dowsing, pyramid energy, and pendulums. Write for free catalog.*

# Making an Angle-Rod From a Coat Hanger

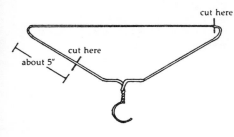

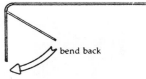

cut here

cut here

about 5"

bend back

1   *Making an angle-rod from a coat-hanger*

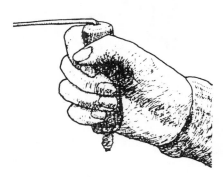

2   *Holding an angle-rod*

*- Tom Graves*
*From* The Diviner's Handbook

## The Practical Pendulum Book

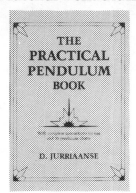

By D. Jurriaanse
1986/76 pages
**$5.95**
$7.45 postpaid from:
Samuel Weiser Inc.
P.O. Box 612
York Beach, ME 03910

*A simple, easy-to-read introduction on how to use the pendulum. It details 38 pendulum "swing" charts to help you answer many questions about your life.*

# What Should a Pendulum Look Like?

The best pendulum shape to look for is one that tapers to a point.
- *D. Jurriaanse*
*From* The Practical Pendulum Book

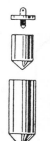

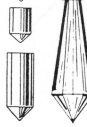

## The Diviner's Handbook

By Tom Graves
1986/180 pages
**$5.95**
$7.45 postpaid from:
Inner Traditions
P.O. Box 1534
Hagerstown, MD 21741

*This book explores the divining of all types of physical objects from both a practical and psychospiritual perspective.*

## The Divining Hand

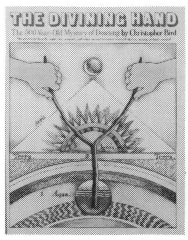

By Christopher Bird
1979/340 pages
**$15.00**
$17.00 postpaid from:
New Age Press
P.O. Box 1216
Black Mountain, NC 28711

*A well-illustrated, encyclopedic work which provides a complete history of the art of dowsing around the world.*

# Oracles

Ancient oracles were places where a god was believed to speak to human beings through the mouths of priests or priestesses.

Today what we call oracles are tools that can be used to access our subconscious and tap into the universe for helpful information we might not

consciously know. You can turn to an oracle to make decisions, get to the root of a problem, or become clear on the direction to take in relation to an opportunity. They can provide a clear voice especially when a situation is clouded by emotional issues.

---

# Runes

## The Book of Runes

By Ralph Blum
1984/128 pages
**$24.95**/128 page book &
25 ceramic rune stones in a cloth drawstring bag
$26.45 postpaid from:
St. Martin's Press
175 Fifth Ave.
New York, NY 10010

*Are you worried about the future? Are you facing a crucial decision? Are you concerned about your relationship*

*with someone? Money? Business? Love?*

*Then do what the Vikings did ... reach for your runes. A valuable guide to your future from out of the past.*

*When facing a decision, pull out the bag of runes, and proceed to get some remarkably insightful guidance from this oracle that first originated prior to 800 A.D.*

*Ralph Blum, a Fullbright scholar and Harvard graduate, has resurrected this ancient oracle and adapted it for use by modern folks. The Book of Runes package consists of 25 ceramic runes (each one inscribed with a letter from the Viking alphabet), a handsome clothbound book that simply and clearly explains how to cast and read them, and a drawstring cloth bag to hold your runes. Blum details a number of ways to cast your runes, based on the concept that, like other oracles, they provide a more direct route to help you tap into the answers contained in your higher self or subconscious. The runes are a valuable and interesting source of insight and advice. They can help recognize patterns of behavior and address questions that need answers.*

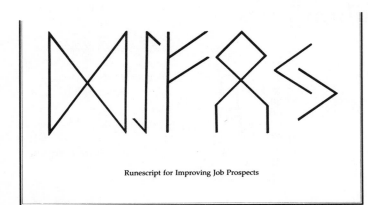

Runescript for Improving Job Prospects

## Rune Play

By Ralph Blum
1985/202 pages
**$14.95**
$16.45 postpaid from:
St. Martin's Press
175 Fifth Ave.
New York, NY 10010

*Rune Play is a workbook/logbook for serious rune users. It's arranged according to season and includes 12 rune casting techniques.*

"The Runes I draw seem to reflect what I already subconsciously know, but sometimes find hard to admit or accept without reassurance or confirmation. They make me feel more tranquil and help settle inner conflicts even though their message is not always what I want to hear. Since starting this journal, I often catch myself 'making nice,' putting everybody's wants and needs ahead of my own. Next time a similar situation confronts me, I'll go back, find today's page number, enter it on the current page. By comparing the Runes I drew on both occasions, my behavior patterns really jump out at me. I am taking responsibility for my own needs at last."

*A comment of a Rune user from Rune Play*

## The Runic Workbook
### *Understanding and Using the Power of Runes*

By Tony Willis
1986/192 pages
**$10.95**
$12.45 postpaid from:
Sterling Publishers
2 Park Ave.
New York, NY 10016

*The Runic Workbook is a course-within-a-book that offers a complete working knowledge of rune work. This work differs from* The Book of Runes *by offering information or alternative methods, rune styles, and casting concepts. The author gives the reader a chance to choose the meanings and methods that work best for them.*

| | |
|---|---|
| *Alternatives* | : ʖ Ϲ ⅃ |
| *Letter* | : P |
| *Name* | : PEORTH |
| *Meaning* | : A Dice Cup |
| *Planetary Rulership* | : Mars and the South Node |

---

## Star + Gate

By Richard Geer
1986/96 cards, 2 spread boards, and
250-page illustrated guidebook
**$29.95**
$31.95 postpaid from:
Star+Gate Enterprises
Box 1006
Orinda, CA 94563

STAR+GATE may well help you to direct the course of your life. Or it may provide a level of assistance for you in understanding a personal relationship or in moving through a professional crisis. You may ask, "How can STAR+GATE do that? It looks like a game."

And it would not be inaccurate to describe STAR+GATE as a game, for it has all the elements which comprise a rather sophisticated, delightful form of entertainment. Like many other games, it has cards (96 to be exact) and a game board. But the object of this game is dramatically different from any other you will ever possess.

Simply put, the board (the Circle Pattern) is a map of consciousness — orderly, patterned, and yet unlimited in its possibilities. And the designs on the cards represent the symbols most commonly recognized by the human subconscious. Formally, these symbols are called archetypes — or original patterns from which all things of the same nature are represented.

A player forms a question in his mind, shuffles the cards, and then lays them down according to the STAR+GATE Sky Spread. Three cards represent the energy of the past or, literally, the background of a given circumstance. Three other cards represent the energy forming around future events, and four cards are used to represent the present moment.

Once the cards have been laid in place, the player is directed through a process of interpretation — one which involves both sides of these unique cards. The picture side of the cards evokes hunches and impressions from the player, and the word side triggers rational associations and certain levels experienced in personal situations. Interpretation also entails building creative and self-revealing pictures, and this leads to a plan of action for improving or resolving the personal topic.

Completing this stage of the game, the player positions the cards by number to their corresponding points on the Circle Pattern map of consciousness. At this point, the object is to use the map as a guide which directs the player to the elements or energy a situation lacks and/or requires in order to bring it to completion.

*- From the introduction to Star+Gate*

# I-Ching

## How to Use the I-Ching

The traditional Chinese method of consulting the *I-Ching* for divination is with the use of yarrow stalks, the manipulation of which allows time for concentration and meditation on the question to be asked as the hexagram is laboriously constructed. This method is described in detail in Part I of this volume.

However, today's readers do not always have the time or inclination for such a drawn-out procedure, and there are other, quicker ways of using the *I-Ching* which are just as effective in the long run. Today, in the West as well as in China, the most popular method is the tossing of coins. All you need is three identical coins of any denomination, which are tossed six times. The first toss gives you the *bottom* or *first* line of the first trigram. The second toss will give you the second line, which is placed *above* the first. All the lines are built from the *bottom up*. Thus, when you have completed three tosses, you have constructed your first trigram. Three more tosses will give you your second trigram, on top of the first. Together, these two trigrams form a hexagram.

Some practitioners may prefer to have two tails and one head equal Yang, etc.; any arrangement may be utilized, so long as all possible combinations are assigned a value.

Complications arise with the last two categories, which produce so-called "moving lines" or "changing lines." These are lines which change from Yang to Yin or vice versa. For example, say you throw the coins six times and come up with the following hexagram: ≣ Line 6 is a moving line (Yang changed to Yin); therefore, the hexagram is changed to this new one: ≣ *Both* hexagrams must now be taken into account in determining the outcome of the situation in question. The same thing applies to any Yin lines which are changed to Yang.

When you have constructed all six lines (two trigrams), you will have the hexagram(s) which is/are pertinent to your question. Then, merely turn to that/those hexagram(s) in Part II of this book and read the interpretations of the trigrams, the hexagrams themselves, and the individual lines. It is up to you to determine how their meanings apply to your situation. More general advice on interpretation can be found in this book.

The meanings and their application to you will never be immediately clear, for each hexagram has layer upon layer of meaning, but a little conscientious study and concentration on the problem will usually result in some exceedingly beneficial insights and revelations. The more you apply your intuition to the advice of the *I-Ching*, the more it will have to say to you. Good luck!

- *From* The Authentic I-Ching

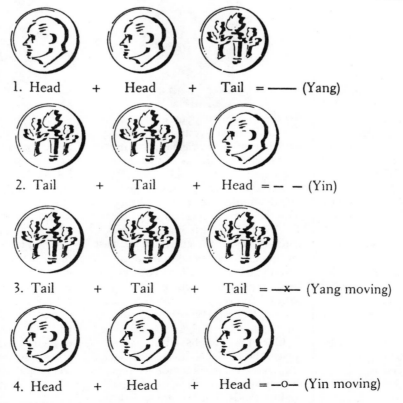

1. Head + Head + Tail = —— (Yang)

2. Tail + Tail + Head = — — (Yin)

3. Tail + Tail + Tail = —x— (Yang moving)

4. Head + Head + Head = —o— (Yin moving)

## The Authentic I-Ching

By Henry Wei, Ph.D.
1987/420 pages
**$12.95**
$14.70 postpaid from:
Newcastle Publishing
Box 7589
Van Nuys, CA 91409

A new translation of the I Ching (Book of Changes) by a scholar who understands both Chinese and Western culture. Up to now, translations of the I Ching have been done by Westerners with an incomplete understanding of the nuances of Chinese culture.

## I Ching
## A New Interpretation for Modern Times

By Sam Reifler
1974/280 pages
**$3.95**
$5.45 postpaid from:
Bantam Books
Direct Response Dept.
414 E. Golf Rd.
Des Plaines, IL 60016

A Westerner's interpretation of the I Ching with modern interpretations.

# 1

KH-YEN ☰ YANG

☰ Heaven below    Heaven ☰ above

ORACLE

Heaven in motion;
the strength of the dragon.
The man nerves himself
for ceaseless activity.

*Creative activity.*
*Influence.*
*Improvement.*
*Keep to your course.*

---

## The Way of Cartouche
### An Oracle of Ancient Egyptian Magic
By Murry Hope
1985/206- page book and deck of 25 cards
**$19.95**
$21.45 postpaid from:
St. Martin's Press
175 Fifth Ave.
New York, NY 10010

The Way of Cartouche is a set of 25 cards with symbolism taken from ancient Egyptian concepts. It is similar to the Tarot since the cards are set out in spreads designed to elicit subconscious information from the user.

As with any oracle, this is an attractive, interesting tool you can use to help access the information you already possess.

Use the Star Spread to ascertain what conditions are likely to prevail

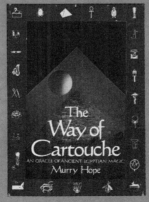

if you intend to take a journey, entertain someone important, embark on a first date, or simply plan ahead a little. Let us suppose that it looks like a fair day for a picnic but the weather forecast is a little suspect and one of the younger members of your family seems somewhat off color. Will the day

turn out well, and if anything unforeseen does occur what precautions can be taken in advance? Example:

*Point 1. Air* suggests the nature of the inquiry which concerns travel

*Point 2. Fire* indicates a nice sunny day with no rain, despite the weatherman's predictions.

*Point 3. Horus* reversed advises that the suspected upset will develop in one of the children, but ...

*Point 4. Thoth* says it is nothing that cannot be put right quickly if you take the right medication with you.

*Point 5. Anubis* will lead you to just the right spot for a successful picnic and, as long as everything is handled sensibly and diplomatically, a happy day will be had by all.

- Murry Hope
From The Way of
Cartouche

## Shirley MacLaine

*A truly inspiring story in three volumes, Shirley MacLaine's spiritual odyssey is a classic in transformational literature. Shirley's questioning mind becomes public knowledge in* Out on a Limb. *Through her intense love affair with a prominent politician and her karmic connection with her friend David, we are invited to explore the mysteries of karma, reincarnation, and "higher selves" in the new metaphysical world.*

*Continuing on with* Dancing in the Light, *Shirley is exposed to deeper truths and becomes intensely involved in life-altering experiences from the metaphysical realm. Her new vision allows her a perspective of unlimited power from which she can actively pursue her goals and purposes of this lifetime.*

It's All in the Playing *is Shirley's culmination of this trilogy set amidst the filming of her* Out on a Limb *mini-series. In it, she comes to the realization that we are the creators of the very situations in which we live, and it is our choice to make them what we want.*

"The way I look at it, this is all my dream. I'm making all of it happen — good and bad — and I have the choice of how I'll relate to it and what I'll do about it. What is the lesson in this? Perhaps we are all telling the truth — our truth as we see it. Perhaps everyone has his own truth, and truth as an objective reality doesn't exist.

"There's nothing like making a movie to bring home that point, because you can make the truth anything you want it to be. Particularly if what you're dealing with is your own life. I have been accused by some of 'remarkable' hubris in making the television movie *Out on a Limb*, but because of the experience of playing myself in a film, I was able to look closely at the illusion within the illusion. It began in Peru ten years ago and ended in Peru ten years later. But the stops along the way were the real story."

> *- Shirley MacLaine*
> From It's All in the Playing

Lately, more and more people are claiming to have seen the actual "light," the blinding, indescribably loving light that they are certain is "Heaven." "God is light," they say after having had an out-of-body experience. "I died and lived to tell of it," they say. And account follows account of such experiences. The reports are increasing, almost as though the numbers of people experiencing the light are increasing as a testament to the level of receptivity and openness to higher and higher consciousness. The chasm between Heaven and Earth is narrowing, and to no one's surprise.

The light is expected now. It had always been there, but more and more we are beginning to recognize that in fact we are the light, if only we can bring ourselves to hold that evolved and sophisticated concept. The light is not outside of us. And whenever we recognize that light inside of us, we know we have found the secret to life well kept. We have been a secret to ourselves. That is what has been missing. We have been missing the light from ourselves. *We are the light.*

> *- Shirley MacLaine*
> From It's All in the Playing

### It's All in the Playing

By Shirley MacLaine
1987/338 pages
**$18.95**
$20.45 postpaid from:
Bantam Books *Direct Response Dept.*
414 E. Golf Rd.
Des Plaines, IL 60016

*Shirley MacLaine's latest narrative of her spiritual quest.* It's All in the Playing *traces her steps from her earliest metaphysical investigations to her experiences while filming the mini-series* Out on a Limb.

"The night before I left for Peru I sat and meditated. I was beginning to see I could take control of my destiny in every way. My work would not only be person to person now, but person to humanity. It was now important for me to take complete responsibility and to be aware of what was going on around me, but not afraid. I recognized and acknowledged that I had prepared for my trip to Peru for a very long time; that the first time I went I decided to use that trip as a vision quest, and knew then that I would write the book that would become a film that would take me back again."

> *- Shirley MacLaine*
> From It's All in the Playing

## Dancing in the Light

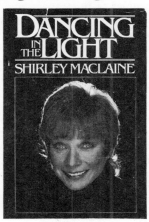

By Shirley MacLaine
1985/420 pages
$4.50
$6.00 postpaid from:
Bantam Books
Direct Response Dept.
414 E. Golf Rd.
Des Plaines, IL 60016

*Amidst personal and emotional turmoil, Shirley delves into her past lives and uncovers some startling information about her present friends, family and her lover.*

## Out on a Limb

By Shirley MacLaine
1983/366 pages
$4.50
$6.00 postpaid from:
Bantam Books
Direct Response Dept.
414 E. Golf Rd.
Des Plaines, IL 60016

---

# Connections with H.S.

The following morning, I experimented with connecting to my higher self without the use of Chris's (Griscom) needles. It was there every time. If I had misplaced something, I asked H.S. where it was. I was always guided in the right direction. It was never wrong.

I asked H.S. what to eat, who was on the other end of a ringing telephone, what direction an address might be. It was astonishing how correct the answers were. I wondered how long it would last. The answer came: "As long as you can find me, you can find anything."

And so my concern that I had never had a really "revelatory" experience evaporated. It had always bothered me that I seemed to be progressing slowly and surely, but without any major revelation. Not so anymore.

Getting in touch with my unlimited soul was an extraordinary event, a milestone in growth and understanding and an experience that flooded me with joy. I felt that this was some kind of coming of age for me. Yet if anyone else had related that discovery to me about themselves, I guess I would have thought they were "dreaming."

. . . . .

Apart from insights into my relationships with family, friends, and lovers, it would be difficult for me to define accurately the effect my time with Chris (Griscom), and achieving connection with my higher self, have had on my life. But there are perhaps three significant areas in living where my growing spiritual maturation has assumed major importance for me: first, in energy control and resource; second, in reality perception; and third, in experiential reality.

As for the first, my energy is "phenomenal." People tell me this — and I surely know it in every phase of daily living and work. Secondly, more and more I am convinced of the truth of Flaubert's statement: "There is no such thing as reality. There is only perception." And that perception of one's own reality relates directly to the third — experiential reality.

Now, when I encounter something that seems too negative or confusing to deal with, the knowledge that I have chosen it for my own learning experience makes it less difficult to cope with. The task then becomes an attempt to investigate why events occur so that the pieces can be fitted into the larger picture.

*- Shirley MacLaine*
*From* Dancing in the Light

---

That is what this book is about ... it's about the experience of getting in touch with myself when I was in my early forties; it's about what the experience did to my mind, to my forbearance, to my spirit, and for my patience and belief. It's about the connection between mind, body, and spirit. And what I learned as a result has enabled me to get on with the rest of my life as an almost transformed human being.

So this book is about a quest for my self — a quest which took me on a long journey that was gradually revealing and at all times simply amazing. I tried to keep an open mind as I went because I found myself gently but firmly exposed to dimensions of time and space that heretofore, for me, belonged in science fiction or what I would describe as the occult. But it happened to me. It happened slowly. It happened at a pace that apparently was peculiarly my own, as I believe all people experience such events. People progress according to what they're ready for. I must have been ready for what I learned because it was the right time.

*- Shirley MacLaine*
*From* Out On A Limb

## Ruth Montgomery: *Herald of the New Age*

By Ruth Montgomery with
Joanne Garland
1986/278 pages
**$3.50**
$4.50 postpaid from:
Random House
400 Hahn Rd.
Westminister, MD 21157

*Millions of lives have been touched
and transformed by Ruth Montgomery
and her "Guides". From a highly
respected syndicated political columnist
and foreign correspondent to a herald of
planetary vision and human*
responsibility, *Ruth's journey inspires
emergence in each of us.*

If it is true, as many thousands of
fan letters attest, that my books have
forever changed the lives of readers
and helped them to understand the
deeper meaning of life, then the
credit should go to those unseen
mentors whom I call "the Guides."
I have simply been the chosen
instrument for their imperative
project to enlighten humanity
about everything from spirit
communication and reincarnation to
Walk-ins, extraterrestrials, and the
New Age that is beginning to dawn.

I was ever the skeptical reporter,
requiring convincing proof before
taking my readers alone with me on
each of the quantum leaps into a
largely unexplored and mysterious
realm. But if we are to grow and
develop spiritually, it is essential that
we maintain an open mind and a
willingness to begin tapping into that
90 percent of human brain capability
that scientists tell us is currently
unutilized by most of us.

As the Guides gradually stretched
my own thinking to encompass these
new realities of time, space, and
eternity, my faith in a benevolent
Creator unfolded and expanded, as it
inevitably will do for all who
sincerely seek a richer purpose for
living. During the past quarter
century I have pursued an often
lonely search for answers to some of
life's most impelling questions: Why
were we born? Do we have a mission
in life? If so, how can we determine
that mission? Did we live before? Are
we forever? Is there a divine plan for
us earthlings? Then what is our
ultimate goal?

The Guides, in my previous
books, have provided many thought-
provoking answers to these posers
that have long perplexed humankind.
The intent of this biography is
therefore to inspire others to set
forth on their own voyage of
discovery, to awaken the slumbering
awareness within, and to realize that
we are not our physical selves, but
individual sparks of the Creator.

> *- Ruth Montgomery*
> *From* Ruth Montgomery:
> Herald of the New Age

---

## Dying to Live: *A True Story of Life After Death*

By Tolly Burkan
1984/212 pages
**$8.95**
$10.40 postpaid from:
Reunion Press, Inc.
Box 1738
Twain Harte, CA 95383

*Tolly Burkan's journey from an
entertainment magician to the founding
father of the American firewalking
movement is an inspiring story of a
strange journey that eventually leads us
to mastery over our fears and unlimited
personal growth.*

As I continued to research
firewalking, I found that over the
years numerous theories, based on
changes in blood pressure and laws
of physics, have been presented to
try to explain it. The more I read,
however, the more clearly I saw that
scientists and medical experts were
continually contradicting each other,
and most of them finally admitted
that flesh should burn instantly at
these temperatures.

I left my inquiry with the
conviction that firewalking was still a
mystery: it wasn't that Universal laws
were being violated in firewalking;
rather, firewalking was another
example of our not yet knowing all
the laws of the Universe. What I was
left with was my own experience of
it — an experience that I knew, from
the moment I had walked across the
coals, would change my entire life.

I didn't know then that future
years would find me traveling all
over the planet teaching classes in
firewalking, nor did I have any idea
that my firewalking seminars would
eventually be in such demand that I
would have to train dozens of others
to teach firewalking, too. From my
trailer in the woods I didn't have the
least glimmering of a notion that the
media would discover my firewalking
workshops, make them world-
famous, and credit me with being the
first person on earth to introduce
firewalking to the general public as a
simple class open to all. I knew only
that I had been changed by
firewalking, that I felt freer now and
more joyful and I felt deeply grateful
to Linda for being the catalyst of this
change.

> *- Tolly Burkan*
> *From* Dying to Live

## A Painter's Quest
### *Art as a Way of Revelation*

By Peter Rogers
1987/160 pages
**$14.95**
$16.95 postpaid from:
Bear & Company
P.O. Drawer 2860
Santa Fe, NM 87504-2860

*This book is illustrated with extraordinary paintings that are part of the artist's insightful journey into the archetypal dreamscape on his quest for enlightenment.*

That the imagery of *The Quest* series stems from the *collective* unconscious only gradually became apparent to me as I began to run across precedents in the cultures of past ages; there are echoes, not only of Christian myth, but also of Buddhist, ancient Egyptian, ancient Greek, Chinese, and pre-Christian Irish myth. This merely corroborates what many others have discovered: that there is and always has been only one story — one quest for one goal — and that the same story is to be found in some shape or form within the religious records of all races, regardless from where or when they derive. *The Quest* is my own attempt to find new forms to express this timeless myth, the evolution of the theme being partly the result of my own quest and, paradoxically, partly the means to it.

Nowhere in this book will the reader find the story of *The Quest* told in so many words; it would take a poet to do so successfully and I am not a poet. Instead, towards the middle of the book there is a brief pictorial Quest. I make little attempt at annotation. Paintings should speak for themselves, and it would be wrong to suppose that they are meant to say precisely the same thing to everyone — they never do. Even my own interpretation is subject to change, so I have learned better than to state categorically what my paintings mean. Not that I mean to give the impression that my imagery is obscure; it is mostly self-explanatory and, where it is not, ample clues will be found throughout the book.

*- Peter Rogers*
*From A Painter's Quest*

## Joy's Way
### *A Map for the Transformational Journey*

By W. Brugh Joy, M.D.
1979/290 pages
**$7.95**
$10.35 postpaid from:
Jeremy P. Tarcher, Inc.
9110 Sunset Blvd.
Los Angeles, CA 90069

*A rare morsel of the emerging body of knowledge on true esoteric healing, transformational psychology, and the transformation of humanity.*

It was a Saturday morning. I had finished rounds at the hospital and was working on some patients' charts in my office when I felt an incredibly strong urge to enter into meditation. It was so strong that I did not understand what was happening to me. I completed the patients' charts and gave in to the impress. A vortex of energy, of a magnitude I had never before experienced, reverberated through my body and threw my awareness into a super-heightened state. Then a loud voice — not that of the Inner Teacher — said, in essence: "Your experience and training as an orthodox physician is completed. It's over. The time has come for you to embark on a rededication of your Beingness to a deeper commitment and action ..."

The voice didn't care about my many personal concerns and commitments. It next presented to my awareness that I would soon begin a journey into the world, going first to Findhorn and to England, Egypt, India, Nepal near the Tibetan border and perhaps to Japan. This journey was to reawaken old soul memories. They in turn would bring to my awareness knowledge not then available to my outer mind. The voice explained clearly that my vision of being a physician had been distorted by boyhood ideals and by the current concepts of science and medicine, which overemphasized the body and external causes and ignored the journey of the soul. I was to begin the study of alternative healing practices and reach insights Western medicine had not yet dared to dream, insights that would unify exoteric and esoteric traditions and thus form the basis of an integrated approach to the art of healing. The last instruction the voice gave me was simply to detach from everything.

*- W. Brugh Joy, M.D.*
*From Joy's Way*

## Lupus Novice
### *Toward Self-Healing*

By Laura Chester
1987/170 pages
**$16.95**
$17.95 postpaid from:
Station Hill Press
Barrytown, NY. 12507

*Laura Chester involves the reader in her moving account of her struggle and personal breakthrough with SLE (systemic lupus erythematosus), a potentially fatal auto-immune disease shared by hundreds of thousands of Americans.*

*We share the author's discovery that physical symptoms include spiritual and psychological processes that are reflected in the process of the body attacking itself.*

*Chester shows us how to move from inner conflict to self-renewal.*

I personally don't believe that any disease is truly incurable. I think that label leads many patients to make a similar search, going from doctor to doctor, in hopes that some answer will be found, "out there." I did find this journey to be illuminating, and I did receive much reassuring care, but again and again, I found that I was being redirected back to my own self. I had to look inward, rather than solely attempting to escape the situation by searching outwardly for some cure or solution.

All along I think I realized that I had to confront more than just the physical realm, my sick body, and though this was a big struggle for me, it eventually lent me strength. My leaning toward the healing alternatives, and in particular, an anthroposophical approach to illness, stemmed from this desire to be well on a deeper level.

> *- Laura Chester*
> *From Lupus Novice*

---

## The Inner Path from Where You Are to Where You Want to Be
### *A Spiritual Odyssey*

By Terry Cole-Whittaker
1986/238 pages
**$14.95**
$16.45 postpaid from:
Rawson Associates
866 3rd Ave.
New York, NY 10022

*Terry's story of how and why the collapse of her TV evangelical ministry became the catalyst for self-transformation and the start of her Foundation for Spiritual Study.*

*This book is written to lead you to where you've always wanted to go — to the Highest Part of Yourself for The Great Adventure of the Soul.*

*In this book is an immense discovery: a method you can use in your life right now to bring yourself the experience of love, success, peace, abundance, and joy that you have always wanted.*

*This discovery is shared with you openly and candidly by spiritual leader Terry Cole-Whittaker, for whom it produced a revelation of the highest order.*

*It will help you decide what you want to feel for the rest of your life, and to choose which path you will take, the outer path of the world or an inner path into the world you would like to create, and in which you would like to dwell for the rest of your life.*

You may choose to dream the seemingly impossible dream.

What you choose will not matter to anyone, least of all to God. God allows. God does not judge, God does not get damaged, God does not go off in a corner and huff and puff and blow the house down to show you who is boss. God allows. God allows because God is That Which Includes All. God allows because God is not a being, God is That Which Includes All Beings. God is the All of it and the Everything, and God cannot be apart from any of it in any way.

What you choose will matter only to you, and only to the degree that you care who you are.

> *- Terry Cole-Whittaker*
> *From The Inner Path from Where You Are to Where You Want to Be*

## The Black Butterfly
*An Invitation to Radical Aliveness*

By Richard Moss, M.D.
1986/300 pages
**$9.95**
$10.95 postpaid from:
Celestial Arts
P.O. Box 7327
Berkeley, CA 94707

*A truly remarkable account of individual transformation and growth.*

Awakening is going on in varying degrees in every person. It is not something from which we can turn away. On the contrary, it is something that all humanity must engage more consciously. Yet its manifestations are so varied that, in the end, it is not the label we give or that others may place upon us, but the depth of integration that is of real significance. Many people are having opening experiences of various kinds. Many are terrified and attempt to deny the experience if they can. Many simply have no idea of the possibilities that are dawning in consciousness during these episodes of multidimensional transformation. New models are needed, contemporary examples of the awakening process, its trials and wonders, what it brings to life, and how it may be integrated. The greatest gift of any such model is not that he or she can tell you what to do, but rather that they expand the panorama of what is possible. Their very lives grant permission to trust more deeply, to invite a creative relationship to oneself. It does not matter how bizarre, difficult, or wondrously transcendent your experience may be. What matters is

what you do with it. It is for this reason that I wish to share my own experience.

... I was sitting quietly in the morning sunshine. I observed two butterflies dancing in the air. One was predominantly black and the other white. They alighted on a branch and, to my amazement and delight, I saw them mate. I watched their wings opening and closing in unison. After some minutes, they once again resumed their dance in the air. Suddenly, the black one flew to me and landed right between my eyebrows.

At that moment life changed forever.

> *- Richard Moss*
> *From* The Black Butterfly

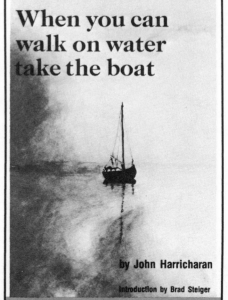

## When You Can Walk on Water Take the Boat

By John Harricharan
1986/120 pages
**$9.95**
$11.95 postpaid from:
New World Publishing
1401 Johnson Ferry Rd.
Suite 328-M7
Marietta, GA 30062

What follows will mean different things to different people. For some, it will be a lovely other-worldly adventure but for others, it will be a powerful re-awakening.

Life is lived from within and one can never be hurt by what appears to be happening outside. You can change circumstances if you so desire. Your only purpose in life is to make choices. Once the choice is made, the entire universe moves to bring into fruition that which you chose.

Read them with an open mind and let yourself ask you questions. Many of these things you already know but may have only forgotten. Let us remember together the true nature of our being.

> *- John Harricharan*
> *From* When You Can Walk on Water, Take the Boat

## Star Woman

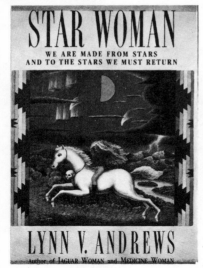

By Lynn V. Andrews
1986/246 pages
**$9.95**
$10.95 postpaid from:
Warner Books, Inc.
P.O. Box 690
New York, NY 10019

*Experience the true account of one woman's spiritual quest in the Native American tradition. Lynn Andrews faces the challenge of the dark side of her own spirit, aided by the wisdom and magic of two American Indian medicine women.*

Without hesitation, I did what this inner or outer voice commanded. I was not sure where the speech was coming from, nor did I care. I fairly flew to Arion's side and lifted easily up onto his bare back. We seemed bathed in an extraordinary shower of prismatic colors. Arion began to run like a meteor around the many acres of flat meadow. I lay down on his neck, feeling the power of the universe pounding between my legs. I did not become afraid until I had the sensation of becoming smaller. Or was it Arion becoming larger? There was a merging sensation. I looked down at my fingers entwined in Arion's rainbow-colored mane and saw pulsing rainbows emerging from my own hands. There was no delineation between me and the stallion, or anything else, for that matter. My consciousness imploded all at once. The curves of my body began to die, fading into the pulsations of the northern lights. I had the experience of being only golden light and becoming the golden shimmer of Arion's withers and neck.

Then I looked down at the ground, and we were at least one hundred stories high. I should never have done that.

"Don't look down," Twin Dreamers commanded. Her voice was within me. But it was too late, for I was terrified. I lost my concentration and my intent. I fell headlong off Arion's back. The last thing I remember was the cracking noise of breaking bones and a sound like a melon hitting bedrock.

*- Lynn V. Andrews*
*From* Star Woman

## Crystal Woman
### *The Sisters of the Dreamtime*
By Lynn V. Andrews
1987/270 pages
**$16.95**
$17.95 postpaid from:
Warner Books, Inc.
P.O. Box 690
New York, NY 10019

*This is Lynn Andrews' latest book documenting her personal transformation as a shamaness in the native tradition. Compelled by a vision, Lynn goes to Australia and participates in the sacred dreamtime of the aborigine women. Pitted against two evil sorcerers, she must reach new levels in her abilities as she is inexorably drawn into a life and death struggle.*

"Buzzie," I called to her. I wasn't able to see anything inside except for some vague shadows.

"What you want from me?" I heard Buzzie demand.

"I don't know," I said, walking a few steps inside. I looked around as my eyes adjusted to the darkness. Buzzie stood defiant in the filtered light. All manner of bones and odd-looking things hung from the curve of the ceiling. Too late I heard the warning scream from the nari. Buzzie had turned her body around to the right and out of the left side of her head came a vision or the real face of Two Hearts, the sorcerer from my dream. He was screaming, blood dripping from his hands as he reached out and grabbed me by the throat.

I tried to yell, but Two Hearts was strangling me. I could not utter a sound. He threw me around the wurley as if I were a paper bird on a string. I tore at the grasses and branches trying to stop the spinning. He smashed the wurley into a heap of rubble using my flailing body as a club. He threw me into Buzzie time and time again until we were both lying in a beaten heap under a mound of grass and the demolished wurley. I heard screams of alarm from the women in the village. The last thing I remember seeing was the nari flying after a dark whirlwind spinning out of the village. Then they disappeared over the hill. I heard Ginevee and Ruby as they pulled away the branches and debris.

*- Lynn V. Andrews*
*From* Crystal Woman

# Basics of Creative Visualization

*By Shakti Gawain*

When we create something, we always create it first in a thought form. The idea is like a blueprint; it creates an image of the form, which then magnetizes and guides the physical energy to flow into that form and eventually manifests it on the physical plane.

When we are negative and fearful, insecure or anxious, we will tend to attract the very experiences, situations, or people that we are seeking to avoid. If we are basically positive in attitude, expecting and envisioning pleasure, satisfaction, and happiness, we will attract and create people, situations, and events which conform to our positive expectations. So the more positive energy we put into imagining what we want, the more it begins to manifest in our lives.

## Using Creative Visualization

The process of change does not occur on superficial levels, through mere "positive thinking." It involves exploring, discovering and changing our deepest, most basic attitudes toward life. That is why learning to use creative visualization can become a process of deep and meaningful growth. In the process we often discover ways in which we have been holding ourselves back, through our fears and negative concepts. Once seen clearly, these limiting attitudes can be dissolved through the creative visualization process, leaving space for us to find and live our natural state of happiness, fulfillment and love ...

The ultimate point of creative visualization is to make every moment of our lives a moment of wondrous creation, in which we are just naturally choosing the best, the most beautiful, the most fulfilling lives we can imagine ...

Here is an exercise in the basic technique of creative visualization:

First, think of something you would like. For this exercise choose something simple, that you can *easily* imagine attaining. It might be an object you would like to have, an event which you would like to happen, a situation in which you'd like to find yourself, or some circumstance in your life which you'd like to improve.

Get in a comfortable position, either sitting or lying down, in a quiet place where you won't be disturbed. Relax your body completely. Breathe deeply and slowly, from your belly. Count down slowly from 10 to 1, feeling yourself getting more deeply relaxed with each count.

When you feel deeply relaxed, start to imagine the things you want exactly as you would like it. If it is an object, imagine yourself with the object, using it, admiring it, enjoying it, showing it to friends. If it is a situation or event, imagine yourself there and everything happening just as you want it to. Have fun with it. It should be a thoroughly enjoyable experience, like a child daydreaming about what he wants for his birthday.

Now keeping the idea of image still in your mind, mentally make some very positive, affirmative statements to yourself about it, such as:

"I now have a wonderful, happy relationship with ＿＿＿＿＿.

We are really learning to understand each other".

"I now have a perfect, satisfying, well-paying job."

These positive statements, called affirmations, are a very important part of creative visualization. Always end your visualization with the firm statement to yourself: "This or something better, now manifests for me in totally satisfying and harmonious ways, for the highest good of all concerned."

This leaves room for something different and even better than you had originally envisioned to happen, and serves as a reminder to you that this process only functions for the mutual benefit of all.

If doubts or contradictory thoughts arise, don't resist them or try to prevent them. This will tend to give them a power they don't otherwise have. Just let them flow through your consciousness, and return to your positive statements and images.

As you see, the basic process is relatively simple. To use it really effectively, however, usually requires some understanding and refinement. As you get more in the habit of using it, and begin to trust the results it can bring you, you will find that it becomes an integral part of your thinking process.

## Creative Visualization

By Shakti Gawain
1979/160 pages
**$7.95**
$9.45 postpaid from:
The Good Living Catalog
Box 13257
Northgate Station
San Rafael, CA 94913

*Shakti Gawain has the ability to translate spiritual matters into simple practical language and concepts. She also adds the very important ingredient of making the entire process of self-help fun!*

*Creative Visualization is simply the art of using your mental energy to transform and greatly improve your life.*

*Gawain provides lots of meditations, affirmations, exercises, and other techniques that will help you learn to understand who you are and provide the keys to creating positive change in your reality.*

## Creative Visualization Workshop Video

With Shakti Gawain
1986/100-minute videocassette,
VHS or Beta
**$39.95**
$41.45 postpaid from:
The Good Living Catalog
Box 13257
Northgate Station
San Rafael, CA 94913

---

# Four Basic Steps for Effective Creative Visualization

### 1. Set Your Goal
Decide on something you would like to have, work toward, realize, or create. It can be on any level — a job, house, a relationship, a change in yourself, increased prosperity, a happier state of mind, improved health, beauty, or better physical condition, or whatever.

At first, choose goals that are fairly easy for you to believe in, that you feel are possible to realize in the fairly near future. That way you won't have to deal with too much negative resistance in yourself, and you can maximize your feelings of success as you are learning creative visualization. Later, when you have more practice, you can take on more difficult or challenging problems.

### 2. Create a Clear Idea or Picture
Create an idea or mental picture of the object or situation exactly as you want it. You should think of it in the present tense as *already* existing the way you want it to be. Picture yourself with the situation as you desire it now. Include as many details as you can.

You may wish to make an actual physical picture of it as well, by making a treasure map (described in detail later). This is an optional step, not at all necessary, but often helpful (and fun!).

### 3. Focus on it Often
Bring your idea or mental picture to mind often, both in quiet meditation periods, and also casually throughout the day when you happen to think of it. In this way it becomes an integrated part of your life, it becomes more of a reality for you, and you project it more successfully.

Focus on it clearly, yet in a light, gentle way. It's important not to feel like you are striving too hard for it or putting an excessive amount of energy into it — that would tend to hinder rather than help.

### 4. Give it Positive Energy
As you focus on your goal, think about it in a positive, encouraging way. Make strong positive statements to yourself: that it exists, that it has come or is now coming to you. See yourself receiving or achieving it. These positive statements are called "affirmations." While you are using affirmations, try to temporarily suspend any doubts or disbelief you may have, at least for the moment, and practice getting the feeling that that which you desire is very real and possible.

Continue to work with this process until you achieve your goal, or no longer have the desire to do so. Remember that goals often

change before they are realized, which is a perfectly natural part of the human process of change and growth. So don't try to prolong it any longer than you have energy for it — if you lose interest it may mean that it's time for a new look at what you want.

If you find that a goal has changed for you, be sure to acknowledge that to yourself. Get clear in your mind about the fact that you are no longer focusing on your previous goal. End cycle on the old, and begin cycle on the new. This helps you avoid getting confused, or feeling like you've "failed" when you have simply changed.

When you achieve a goal, be sure to acknowledge consciously to yourself that it has been completed. Often we achieve things which we have been desiring and visualizing, and we forget to even notice that we have succeeded! So give yourself some appreciation and a pat on the back, and be sure to thank the universe for fulfilling your requests.
- *Shakti Gawain*
*From* Creative Visualization

## I Want to Change But I Don't Know How

By Tom Rusk & Randy Read, M.D.
1986/330 page book,
60-minute cassette tape
**$14.95**
$15.95 postpaid from:
Price/Stern/Sloan Publishing
360 North La Cienega Blvd.
Los Angeles, CA 90048

# Need a Change?

Almost everyone wants to change in some way — become a better lover, parent, golfer, or cook — become less lonely or depressed — become more assertive, make new friends — learn to love and be loved. If you find yourself curious about other people's problems, absorbed in their life stories, it may be a clue that for *you* something is missing.

... You want to change, get a new deal, a different script for your life. At off-moments you brood about your life, poke at it like an aching tooth. You may not be in agony but then again, you're not *really* getting what you want either. You settle for your life as it is, put up with it, hoping things will somehow improve. But like decaying teeth, lives that ache usually get worse unless something is done.

**"I want to change but I don't know how. I'm stuck, I know things aren't quite right, but I just don't know what to do."**

We hear variations of this lament several times a day in our practice and so does every other psychiatrist. You've heard it too. It's an honest statement describing a very human dilemma.

And it is widespread. Many people don't really live. They merely exist, passing from one uneventful day to the next, if they are fortunate, or puddle-jumping from one hectic crisis to another if their luck turns bad.

If you only want to get by like that, okay. It is certainly the simplest way. It's easiest because you don't have to do anything differently — don't have to think those complicated thoughts about how and what to change. If that's all you want, then except for its entertainment value, you may as well stop reading this book right now.

On the other hand, if you choose it, there's a whole different way to go. It's up to you. Wouldn't you like the rest of your life to be a lot more exciting and rewarding than it has been up to now? You know what we mean: satisfying, like your daydream fantasies; fulfilling, like the lives of those people you secretly envy.

That's pretty outrageous, isn't it? We're already intruding into your daydreams. But we're serious. You can probably get much more from life. We've seen people do it. Oh sure, you may think you're unusual, a special case — that your problems are unique and your life different from every other human in the history of our species. Right?

Forget it! No one is that alone, that unusual. Whatever you've got going for or against you is just a variation on the same theme to which everyone dances. Anyway, we don't have your answer. You do. We just want to provoke you into finding it for yourself.

> *- Tom Rusk &*
> *Randy Read, M.D.*
> *From* I Want to Change But I Don't Know How

## Living in the Light
### A Guide to Personal and Planetary Transformation

By Shakti Gawain
1986/192 pages
**$8.95**
$10.45 postpaid from:
Whatever Publishing
Box 13257
Northgate Station
San Rafael, CA 94913

*According to Gawain, "the key is learning to listen to your intuition and act on it at all times, even at the risk of going against old patterns, expectations and belief systems. The reward is complete, creative transformation."*

# Believe It!

Almost since the beginning of the human race, men have been molded by those who knew something of thought's great power. All the great religious leaders, kings, warriors, and statesmen understood this science and have known that people act as they think — and also react to the thought of others, especially when it is stronger and more convincing than their own. Accordingly, men of powerful dynamic thought have always swayed people by appealing to their minds — whether sometimes to lead them into freedom or into slavery. There never was a period in history when we had more reason to study our own thoughts, understand them, and learn how to use them to improve our lives by drawing upon the great source of power within each of us.

Undoubtedly, we become what we envisage. There was a time when I would have laughed at people who talked about the magnetic force of thought, how thought correlates with its object, how it can affect people and inanimate things even at great distances. But I no longer laugh, nor do others who know something of its power, for anyone who has any intelligence sooner or later comes to realize that thought can change the surface of the entire globe.

George Russell, the famous Irish editor and poet, was once quoted as saying that we become what we contemplate; and he certainly demonstrated it in his own life by becoming a great writer, lecturer, painter, and poet. However, it must be kept in mind that many of the thoughts we think are not ours at all, at least not of our own originating. We are molded by the thoughts of others; by what we hear in conversation, what we read in newspapers, magazines, and books, what we hear in the movies, on TV, and on the radio; even by chance remarks from bystanders.

But too often these thoughts are upsetting, weaken our self-confidence, and turn us away from our higher purposes. It is these outside thoughts that are the trouble makers ...

*- Claude M. Bristol*
*From* The Magic of Believing

## Spirit Guides
## *We Are Not Alone*

By Iris Belhayes
1985/180 pages
**$12.95**
$14.95 postpaid from:
ACS Publications
Box 16430
San Diego, CA 92116-0430

# Spirit Guides

Humankind has always known or at least felt there was someone out there looking over us ... Loving us ... Protecting us from the dangers of this "unfriendly" planet. This knowing or feeling has been translated in many ways ... ways in which humankind has tried to explain its own existence. Most societies or groups of people have decided that the presence or presences they feel must be connected to a kind of superparent or guardian who watches our actions and judges whether or not we deserve award or punishment.

There are, indeed, *beings* "out there" who care for us but they are not judgmental. They do not deal in punishment neither do they hold one of us above the rest, nor view anyone as being bad or wrong. They see each of us as perfect, playing out life on this plane as best we can with the circumstances we have given ourselves. They understand that each of us is experiencing those things necessary for us to experience in order to fulfill our own thrusts for learning, development, adventure and growth.

*- Iris Belhayes*
*From* Spirit Guides

## The Magic of Believing
## *Setting Your Goal ...*
## *and Reaching It!*

By Claude M. Bristol
1985/172 pages
**$7.95**
$9.95 postpaid from:
Simon & Schuster
200 Old Tappan Rd.
Old Tappan, NJ 07675

*This is an earthy, effective book that's sure to get you moving and start making changes in your life. Bristol is very goal-oriented in the style of Napoleon Hill of* Think & Grow Rich *fame.*

## Dianetics
### The Modern Science of Mental Health

By L. Ron Hubbard
1985/638 pages
**$4.95**
$5.95 postpaid from:
Bridge Publications
1414 Catalina St.
Los Angeles, CA 90027

*This is the very controversial "science" of Dianetics. The author claims the reader can gain more confidence, relieve stress, better understand and control the mind and find success and happiness. Over 8,000,000 copies are in print. There are Churches of Scientology all over the world.*

## Love Is Letting Go of Fear

By Gerald G. Jampolsky, M.D.
1979/128 pages
**$5.95**
$6.95 postpaid from:
Celestial Arts
Box 7327
Berkeley, CA 94707

*Fear is our greatest limiter. By letting go of fear and preoccupation with the past and future, we can live now, remembering that love is our essence. That's personal transformation and Jampolsky conveys these concepts beautifully.*

## Reconstructing the Cabin
### Superconscious Symbol Visualization/Meditation to Assist You to Reconstruct Your Own Life Exactly the Way You Desire It to Be

By Dick Sutphen
New Age music by Upper Astral
1984/60-minute cassette tape
**$8.98**
$10.48 postpaid from:
Valley of the Sun Publishing Co.
Box 3004
Agoura Hills, CA 91301

*This tape is based on Psychosynthesis, a technique used by many psychiatrists to generate positive change. The symbol creates a new line of force in your psyche and can change inner attitudes and outer behavior. Produced with soothing New Age music. Instructions: Lie down or sit comfortably, close your eyes and breathe deeply for 3 minutes. Turn on tape. Dick will direct you through a complete body relaxation, then ask you to vividly fantasize the situation he is describing. Make it real. Perceive everything. You'll be counted up at the end of the tape. For maximum self-change results, use of the tape several times a week. Also, during the day, quickly fantasize the symbol on your own when you have an opportunity.*

## Themes to Live By on the Road to Personal Transformation

In making practical application of the material covered in this book to everyday situations, it will be helpful to keep the following underlying themes in mind:

1. Peace of mind is our single goal.
2. Forgiveness is our single function, and the way to achieve our goal of peace of mind.
3. Through forgiveness, we can learn not to judge others and to see everyone, including ourselves, as guiltless.
4. We can let go of fear when we stop judging and stop projecting the past into the future, and live only in the now.
5. We can learn to accept direction from our inner, intuitive voice, which is our guide to knowing.
6. After our inner voice gives us direction, it will also provide the means for accomplishing whatever is necessary.
7. In following one's inner guidance, it is frequently necessary to make a commitment to a specific goal.even when the means for achieving it are not immediately apparent. This is a reversal of the customary logic of the world, and can be thought of as "putting the cart before the horse."
8. We do have a choice in determining what we perceive and the feelings we experience.
9. Through retraining of the mind we can learn to use positive active imagination. Positive active imagination enables us to develop positive, loving motion pictures in our minds.

- Gerald G. Jampolsky, M.D.
From Love is Letting
Go to Fear

# Create Your Reality

Self-Help is a major dimension of the New Age movement because most people are drawn to metaphysics and a New Age consciousness in search of something that will improve their lives. While most people are concerned with spiritual needs, self-help can include anything from subliminal aid in dieting to realizing psychic abilities like telepathy or clairvoyance or attaining mastery of life.

The key is that you create your own reality. This means that you are not a victim, you can exert control over your life, you can shape your future and you can transform yourself. The responsibility is yours and the answers, your answers, lie within you — not with some established code of behavior or belief. That is what separates the New Age from the past.

But before we can accomplish a great many positive things we have to eliminate a lot of negative programming. In conducting seminars across the United States each year for New Age enthusiasts, I teach many psychologists, psychiatrists and medical practitioners. They attend the seminars to learn about hypnotic regression techniques, reincarnation and karma, because years of research with thousands of seminar participants has proven to me that past life experiences affect our daily lives here and now.

Remember that two thirds of the world has always accepted reincarnation as a metaphysical doctrine. Meanwhile, acceptance of reincarnation is growing rapidly in the United States while the organized religions are losing ground. I believe this is because reincarnation and karma offer the only reasonable explanation of total justice. For me, reincarnation and karma is not a belief: fifteen years of research verifying past life regressions and psychic data have convinced me that past lives are influencing our present life.

In my seminars, the participants are put into a hypnotic altered state of awareness and then regressed to the cause of their problems or anxiety, and this is often a situation remembered from a previous life, stored deep in the subconscious. The situation is a source of pain and the subconscious will go to great lengths to avoid that pain again. The result is subconscious programming which is out of alignment with the present life desires. This can create a profound fear and personality conflict that is hard to explain or resolve. So what I call Past Life Therapy can relieve hidden anxiety, resolve personal fears and problems, and throw light on the cause of much of our negative programming.

The use of subliminals, which I have been exploring since the mid-Seventies, is another powerful tool for self-help programming. Most of us say we want something but fail to acknowledge that we don't really believe we should have it or deserve it. The repetition of strong, positive affirmations about our chosen goals, both consciously and subliminally, has helped many people to achieve results where they had failed before. I believe our methods, utilizing both audio tapes and new, four-way video-tapes, are the most powerful subliminal tools available today.

I often say that if fear is the problem, love is the answer, and I believe everyone is already a Master of Life but that we have an overlay of a lot of negative stuff that we've accumulated along the way. It is this fear-based, negative programming that we need to eliminate in order to realize who we truly are.

- Dick Sutphen
  Valley of the Sun
  Box 3004
  Aqoura Hills, CA 91301

## Video Hypnosis
### *Personality Transformation*

By Dick Sutphen
1987/30-minute video, VHS only
**$19.95**
$21.95 postpaid from:
Valley of the Sun
Box 3004
Agoura Hills, CA 91301

*This is Dick Sutphen's "next generation" hypnosis video. It programs both consciously and subconsciously with hypnosis and audio/video subliminal suggestions. This tape helps you let go of fears, create your own reality, avoid negativity and become balanced, harmonious, independent and self-responsible.*

*If you need some positive programming for change, this is an excellent resource.*

## Self-Hypnosis
### *Creating Your Own Destiny*

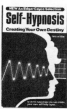

By Henry Leo Bolduc
1985/164 pages
**$7.95**
$9.95 postpaid from:
A.R.E. Press
Box 595
Virginia Beach, VA 23451

*This is an excellent source of information on self-hypnosis. Bolduc has 22 years of experience in this field. He explains the processes involved and gives detailed information on how to create your own self-help tapes to help create personal changes from losing weight to developing psychic abilities.*

# Hypnosis

The word "hypnosis" stems from *hypnos*, the Greek word for sleep. However, people experiencing hypnosis are not actually sleeping — far from it! They may *appear* to others to be asleep, but they can think, talk, open their eyes, respond to suggestion, and move in any way. People experiencing hypnosis are usually aware of their surroundings and can hear other sounds besides the voice of the hypnotist.

Hypnosis, like love, is difficult to define because every person experiences it a little differently. The hardest part most people have with it is simply getting past the word "hypnosis."

Hypnosis is a tool for modern minds; it is 100% natural. Sometimes it is called a *waking* dream, at other times a *working* dream. It means different things to different people (even the experts can't agree on how to define it!). Although many have been helped and inspired by hypnosis, some think of it as only a stage show; the reality, however, is somewhere in between. Far more profound than a mere show, there is nothing really amazing about hypnosis except the use of the unlimited potential of the human mind.

It is also a method of relaxing the physical body and utilizing another level of awareness through suggestion and visualization. This level of awareness, called "alpha," refers to a state of electrical activity in the brain. We all experience this activity as we go into regular nighttime sleep and again later as we awaken in the morning.

The levels of hypnosis are measured by brain-wave frequency. Technically, sleep researchers, biofeedback technicians, and medical practitioners look upon the human brain as consisting of four levels of activity, each having a particular cycle-per-second rate.

Although there is still ambiguity in this new field, researchers have called the normal, everyday waking state *beta*. *Alpha* is that transitional time people experience when they are half awake and half asleep. *Theta* occurs in deep hypnosis, intense meditation, and during the early stages of nighttime sleep. *Delta*, perhaps the least understood level of the human mind, is the deepest sleep or unconsciousness.

Most people experience the hypnotic state when they are in alpha, where attention is focused on their objective but where they may be aware of noises or of other people in the room. They usually have recollection of most of the session unless a specific suggestion is otherwise given and accepted. Because it is such a familiar feeling (people experience it at least twice a day and oftentimes also when watching television or even daydreaming), some people, after their first session, question whether they were truly hypnotized. This altered state of consciousness is called "trance" by some people and "controlled relaxation" by others.

Despite the misconceptions, hypnosis is not really mysterious. Once learned, it is a *tool* which allows a person to use more of his or her mind and to use it more dynamically and effectively. Hypnosis is relaxed receptivity with increased perception, a state of deep relaxation which quiets the body and opens the mind. With its defenses down, the mind is especially open to suggestion, the type of which is determined by a person's goals and ideals — the reasons for wanting to use hypnosis.

Like a gardener, you choose the specific thought-seeds you want to plant. Hypnosis helps you to care for and nourish those thought-seeds to grow and bear fruit. Your subconscious mind is your secret garden where the thoughts you plant grow to become your reality. This garden is far more fertile than you may realize, so plan carefully! As the Edgar Cayce readings often assert, "Thoughts are things."

- Henry Bolduc
From Self-Hypnosis

**Triggers
A New Approach to
Self-Motivation**

By Stanley Mann, A.C.S.W.
1987/200 pages
**$8.95**
$10.95 postpaid from:
Simon & Schuster, Inc.
200 Old Tappan Rd.
Old Tappan, NJ 07675

*Trigger a new reality for yourself. Actually this is more like tricking yourself into enjoying and succeeding at projects, careers and even maintaining your health.*

# How to Trigger Your Motivation

Here is an outline of the steps to use to increase your motivation to do some activity. Although you could use sound or sight as your trigger, this is an example of how to achieve the desired result by using your sense of touch.

1. Decide what your target and reservoir* will be.
2. Imagine your reservoir vividly (fishing, dancing, reading, or whatever you most enjoy). Create a trigger by pressing your right knee.
3. Imagine your target, and, when it is clear in your mind, create another trigger by pressing your left knee.
4. Using your intuition, be sure your reservoir is definitely stronger than your target.
5. If necessary, build your reservoir's trigger until it is stronger.
6. Fire off both triggers at the same time by pressing both knees, remembering both your reservoir and your target.
7. Allow a minute or two for this to combine.
8. Imagine yourself in the future, performing your target with your newly acquired eagerness. Adjust this image so it feels real. Imagine the *rewards* of performing your target successfully.

You can use this outline to make notes to yourself, which you might want to refer to while you are doing the procedure.

I also used this technique on what, for me, is a tougher problem than

getting myself to write — cleaning "the room." We have a large, rambling house with one large room that used to be a two-and-a-half car garage. It now serves as a storage area. I had a bad habit of putting things there "temporarily" until they were piled all over the place in utter chaos. It was frustrating when I wanted to find something in there, but when I faced the prospect of cleaning it up, I felt my stomach twist and I became unaccountably tired. After a few minutes of feeble attempts, I found something "more important" to do.

So, I went through this double-triggering routine, which helped. Now I can enjoy working on the room and straightening it up for only about an hour. The reason this outcome was not outstanding was because my abhorrence of cleaning

that room almost equalled my enjoyment of fishing. As I said before, the trick is to pair the undesirable feeling with a much stronger, enjoyable one.
- *Stanley Mann*
  *From* Triggers

* positive feelings in your memory of past experiences

## Troubleshooting Chart If Double Triggering Does Not Work

| Possible problem | Solutions |
|---|---|
| 1. Target too difficult | Choose an easy one, work up to harder ones |
| 2. Reservoir experience weak | Find a stronger one. Build two or more |
| 3. Mental rehearsal is not realistic | Adjust it until it feels believable |
| 4. Target is a phobia | Read Chapter 2 |
| 5. Imagination too weak | Read Chapter 4 |
| 6. Trying *not* to do something | Read Chapter 11 |

## Master of Life Manual
*Metaphysics, Brain/Mind Awareness and Human Potential Principles to Create Your Own Reality Now!*

By Dick Sutphen
1987/128 pages
**$3.95**
$4.95 postpaid from:
Valley of the Sun
Box 3004
Agoura Hills, CA 91301

*Sutphen promises ... and delivers! This hard-hitting manual gets to the basics of how you work, why you work the way you do, and how you can change it.*

# You Create Your Own Reality, or Karma, with Your Thoughts

Many people have no idea how frequently they think in a negative manner. If you climb out of bed cursing the alarm clock, grumble your way through breakfast, then dwell on how much you dislike the rain and the traffic during your commute to work, and brood unhappily about your job, and on throughout the day, you are literally creating a worse reality for yourself. Because you are thinking more negative thoughts than positive ones, there is simply no way you can be creating anything but a negative reality. With all that negative programming in your computer, how could it do anything but create the programmed result: more negativity?

You do not *have* a mind, you *are* mind. You are using your current body, but your body isn't you. You have a soul or a spirit or whatever you want to call it. Whatever it is, it must be mind, for any study of regressive hypnosis will show that the mind carries all the memories of the past. Every individual carries memories of previous lifetimes, and the events in these past lives often seem to be affecting the present. This in itself does not prove reincarnation, but does show that a lineage of cause and effect (karma) is evident.

If you are mind and that mind operates likes a computer, that makes you a computer ... a machine. Naturally, there is more to you than the mechanical aspect, but few people are presently working with the larger aspects of their totality.

To become a Master of Life means to transform the way you experience your life. In so doing, you learn to let fear and negativity flow through you without affecting you, and to be direct and natural, in balance and harmony.

Everyone has the potential to create their own reality, so if you are not happy with the way it is, what mind has created, mind can change.
- *Dick Sutphen*
  *From Master of Life Manual*

## Explore the Mysteries of Your Mind
*How to Unlock Your Mind's Potential*

By Charles Thomas Cayce

By Charles Thomas Cayce
1986/3 60-minute cassette tapes,
72-page book
**$24.95**
$26.95 postpaid from:
A.R.E. Press
Box 595
Virginia Beach, VA 23451

*Charles Thomas is Edgar Cayce's grandson and head of the Association for Research and Enlightenment. In this program he shares case histories, personal experiences, and information drawn from the Cayce readings. He shows you how to create your future with your thoughts, how you limit yourself with your own thoughts, and how to replace those limiting thoughts with new ones that expand your potential. He teaches how to access your psychic ability and learn to use it in your life along with the basic principles of self-hypnosis and pre-sleep suggestions. A complete home study course to help you truly shape your reality.*

For mind is the builder, and that entertained, that builded, that pattern set in same is that to which the body, the mind and the soul attains by this constancy held before same.
- *Edgar Cayce*
  *Reading #370-3*
  *From* Explore the Mysteries of Your Mind

## You Can Heal Your Life

By Louise L. Hay
1984/224 pages
**$10.00**
$13.00 postpaid from:
Hay House
3029 Wilshire Blvd. #206
Santa Monica, CA 90404

*This book is a workbook that takes you chapter by chapter through processes that help you recognize and change negative belief patterns using powerful affirmations and healing methods.*

## Discovering Your Soul's Purpose

By Mark Thurston, Ph.D.
1985/4 60-minute cassette tapes
160-page book
**$24.95**
$26.95 postpaid from:
A.R.E. Press
Box 595
Virginia Beach, VA 23451

*You were born for a very special, unique mission in life. Until you find and live that mission or purpose, your life will seem unfulfilled, no matter how many signs of success you achieve in material life. But your mission can be discovered.*

*Using techniques described in the Edgar Cayce readings, you will find a practical five-step program for discovering the mission or purpose your soul planned for this lifetime.*

*In-depth lectures and workshops will lead you through experiences to help you make the most of your creative talents and abilities and turn your weakness into strengths. You'll find how your personality can become a blueprint to your mission in life rather than a roadblock and gain a new perspective on the spiritual meaning of your vocation. You'll also discover some of the karmic patterns which have kept you from your mission.*

### As You Think
#### Become the Master of Your Own Destiny

By James Allen
1987/74 pages
**$5.95**
$6.40 postpaid from:
Whatever Publishing
Box 13257
Northgate Station
San Rafael, CA 94913

*This classic work was written almost 100 years ago and remains one of the best self-help/self development books ever published. Allen shows how truly you are what you think.*

# Think About Your Health

The body is the servant of the mind. It obeys the operations of the mind, whether they be deliberately chosen or automatically expressed. At the bidding of unhealthy thoughts the body sinks rapidly into disease and decay; at the command of glad and beautiful thoughts it becomes clothed with youthfulness and beauty.

Disease and health, like circumstances, are rooted in thought. Sickly thoughts will express themselves through a sickly body. Thoughts of fear have been known to kill a person as speedily as a bullet, and they are continually killing thousands of people just as surely, though less rapidly. The people who live in fear of disease are the people who get it. Anxiety quickly demoralizes the whole body, and lays it open to the entrance of disease; impure thoughts, even if not physically indulged, will soon shatter the nervous system.

Strong, pure, and happy thoughts build up the body in vigor and grace. The body is a delicate and plastic instrument, which responds readily to the thoughts by which it is impressed, and habits of thought will produce their own effects, good or bad, upon it.

People will continue to have impure and poisoned blood, so long as they propagate unclean thoughts. Out of a clean heart comes a clean life and a clean body. Out of a defiled mind proceeds a defiled life and an impure body. Thought is the source of action, life, and manifestation; make the source pure, and all will be pure.

A change of diet will not help those who will not change their thoughts. When our thoughts are pure, we no longer desire impure food.

Clean thoughts make clean habits. Those who have strengthened and purified their thoughts do not need to consider the malevolent microbe.

- *James Allen*
From *Become the Master of Your Own Destiny*

**EDGAR CAYCE FOUNDATION and
A.R.E. LIBRARY/VISITORS CENTER**
Virginia Beach, Va.
*OVER 50 YEARS OF SERVICE*

**Tantra for the West**
*A Guide to Personal Freedom*

By Marcus Allen
1981/236 pages
**$7.95**
$8.45 postpaid from:
Whatever Publishing
Box 13257
Northgate Station
San Rafael, CA 94913

*Tantra, the author says, is the yoga of everything. It is defined as "the union of everything" and is the awareness that creates "personal freedom within every moment of our daily lives, rejecting nothing."*

# Writing Affirmations

The measure of an affirmation's success is whether or not it soon manifests in your world. You should be able to manifest almost anything you are affirming within 21 days. There are some exceptions to this, if the project is vast or complicated, or the goal is distant. But the results should become clearly evident to you in a short time. You should be able to feel the change. If the results aren't happening, it is only because you are affirming something else on deeper, perhaps less conscious, level which is creating something contradictory to what you are affirming consciously.

If you're repeating to yourself, for example,

*"My connection with infinite intelligence is yielding me a vast personal fortune."*

every day, with emotion, and after three weeks you are still broke, then you have to find out what else you have been telling yourself that is creating a contradictory reality. Writing affirmations and their responses is the best way to do this.

Take a notebook. On one page, write "Affirmations" across the top. On the next page, write "Thank you!" across the top. Then begin writing your affirmation on the page headed "Affirmations." Put your attention into it; pour your feeling into it. You want to be self-sufficient, or beautiful, or whatever — and the truth of the matter is that *you deserve*

*it*, so you might as well create it for yourself.

Keep on writing the same affirmation, and keep putting your full attention on it. Soon you will probably notice some kind of inner resistance popping up — some words you are telling yourself (affirming to yourself) on deep levels. Whatever they are, write them down on your "Thank you!" page. On this page, you are encouraged to voice all of your reactions to your affirmation.

Say you're writing, for example, *"My connection with infinite intelligence ...,"* and you find yourself thinking, "What connection? I'm a blundering idiot!' Immediately turn to your "Thank you!" page and write those words. It is called your "Thank you" page because, as you write those words, you want to mentally thank yourself for sharing them with you (this may sound artificial or strange, perhaps, but it *works*). Then go back to writing your affirmation *"... is yielding me a vast personal fortune."* Then you may find yourself thinking, "A vast personal fortune? I could never handle it!" — so write that down too on your "Thank you" page. Then go back and write your affirmation again. And so on.

After writing your affirmation 10 or 20 times, you may have 10 or 20 or 30 comments on your "Thank you!" page. Look at them carefully

— these are the things you are affirming to yourself on deeper levels which are creating your present reality. Sometimes it is enough just to look at them and see how foolish they are, and how they are not really true for you. Sometimes these negative affirmations dissolve as soon as you look at them. At other times, you may have to create new affirmations for yourself that are especially designed to counteract what you have been telling yourself. In the example above, where you found that you were thinking you could never handle a vast personal fortune, you may want to affirm something like, *"I am capable of handling a vast personal fortune easily and skillfully"* — or, if that is too confronting, lower the gradient for yourself and affirm, *"I am capable of skillfully handling my finances."*

Do this daily, if necessary. Break down your resistances with more affirmations. That is all that is necessary to do. When you finally get to the core of your resistance — to the "biggie" which you are holding onto, the one terrible thing about yourself that you haven't dared to admit even to yourself — when you finally find yourself writing it out on your "Thank you!" sheet, you'll feel something releasing in you. Then find the affirmation which deals with it directly and releases it for all time from your consciousness. You'll find yourself feeling wonderful (literally — *wonder full*). Now you are coming into your own power. Now you're not limiting yourself any more. You're free to be who you want, and to create the life you want. It is your birthright.

• • • •

*"＿＿＿＿＿＿ comes to me easily and effortlessly."* Fill in the blank with whatever you desire.

- Marc Allen
From Tantra for
the West

**Ecstasy
Is a New Frequency**
*Teachings of the Light
Institute*

By Chris Griscom
1987/180 pages
**$9.95**
$11.95 postpaid from:
Bear & Company
P.O. Drawer 2860
Santa Fe, NM 87504-2860

*Chris Griscom's healing work was
featured in Shirley MacLaine's* Dancing
in the Light. *Griscom concentrates on
healing the emotional body, the part of
us holding feelings and experiences. She
says that once our higher self brings the
soul through the emotional body and
into the physical body, the result is
ecstasy.*

**Working Inside Out**
*Tools for Change*

By Margo Adair
1984/420 pages
**$12.00** postpaid from:
Tools for Change
Box 14141
San Francisco, CA 94114

# Think About Your Emotional Body

The mind is the most powerful instrument that we have, except that we're not in contact with our higher mind. We're not in contact with the mind in ourselves that decides if we age or become ill or die. The mind is a wonderful instrument, and it *does* control our physical body.

You are not directing your body because the imprint of all the deaths and illnesses you've had — or your friends and lovers have experienced — is impinging on you too intensely. We know scientifically that the mind does control the body. We can slow down our heartbeat. We can change almost anything. We can feel anything we want if we have enough intentionality, if we are clear enough in that message from the mind to the body that says, "Yes, I want you to be well." If we send a clear message to the body, it will do exactly what our brain tells it.

If you send a message to your emotional body and you say, "Emotional body, I don't want to be angry any more; it scares me to get angry," nothing·happens. You can

change your behavior for a while, and that's useful because we're social beings. We depend on each other, we mirror off each other all the time. We don't know who we are except when someone tells us we are so and so. So we can change our behavior, but the energy just goes someplace else. The blueprint is not altered because we simply stay within one little space that's safe. "Whoops, if I don't do anything with this then I'm OK and nobody will ever know, including myself." What's going on? The mind does not control the emotional body.

We have to change our emotional bodies in order to manifest in this lifetime, to engage in enough power, to create a world outside of ourselves that is a world we truly deserve. The only part of ourselves that can change the emotional body is our spiritual body or higher self, which does not know judgment, which does not know negativity.

*- Chris Griscom
From Ecstasy*

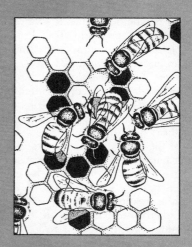

Working Inside Out *provides safe structures to explore the vast realms within you. The training gives you a language to communicate with your deeper self as well as providing methods to employ it for problem solving. This will rekindle your intelligence. The guided meditations create a clear and simple navigational course through your inner dimensions so you can use the resources available within you to improve the quality of your life; this is Applied Meditation. The purpose of this book is to help you to be more effective in making the changes you want. Whether that be in your health, your behavior, your relationships, your work. Whatever it is, your inner-consciousness can help you.*

# Subliminal Programming

## What Is Subliminal Programming?

The concept of subliminal programming is based on the idea that you only pay attention to, and are conscious of, a small amount of the information your body, mind and brain can assimilate. Many studies, including evoked response research, have shown that subliminal information is absolutely registered even though you are not conscious of it. Scientists have discovered through the use of standard measurements of brain activity — electroencephalograms (EEGs), Galvanic Skin Response (GSRs), pulse rate, respiration and biofeedback — that a rise in brain wave activity occurs when a listener is using a subliminal tape, versus a tape with the same music on it, but without subliminal messages.

The remarkable sales and interest in subliminal tapes indicate a new trend and dimension that may revolutionize the self-improvement field. Tape manufacturers claim rapidly-increasing sales while the number of new companies producing tapes continues to grow.

Advocates of the tapes say that listening to them brings changes in your life without effort, conscious thought patterning or strain. The positive subliminal affirmations beneath music or natural sounds are believed to melt away negative, limiting beliefs. Repeated listening to tapes could therefore reaffirm positive thoughts to the subconscious and conscious mind and thus help to create a desired new reality.

The use of subliminal messages was pioneered by Hal C. Becker, Ph.D., a former member of the Tulane University Medical School staff. Becker invented the sound-mixing equipment that has been dubbed the "Black Box." In the mid-1960's, Becker patented subliminal induction devices and later used them in department store chains to reduce shoplifting and in medical clinics to ease the anxiety of patients.

Subliminal messages came under fire after some well-publicized instances during the 1950's when movie patrons would feel hungry when the message "eat popcorn" flashed across the big screen.

Much controversy has arisen over the implications of the use of subliminal programming and the issue of mind control. Dick Sutphen, nationally-known hypnotherapist and founder of Valley of the Sun, a company that creates altered state of consciousness tapes responds that "directly proposed suggestions cannot make you do anything against your morals, religion or self-preservation." Dr. Paul Tuthill, president of Mind Communication, Inc., states that the individual using a subliminal tape must be predisposed to want to use the tape. "If the individual listening to the tape does not want to hear the messages on it, subconscious rejection may occur and they will stop playing the tape."

Although there is little scientific proof that subliminal messages work, many people say they do and claim to have gained self-confidence, quit smoking and improved their lives. Some scientists argue that the desired changes occur because listeners expect them to and thus fulfill their own expectations.

*- From Subliminal Persuasion, Psychic Guide Magazine, September 1986*

---

### I Can Do Anything
*Subliminal Affirmation Tape*
1984/60-minute cassette tape
**$9.95**
$11.95 postpaid from:
Mind Communication
Box 9429
Grand Rapids, MI 49509

*This is just one of hundreds of subliminal programs offered by Mind Communication. The tapes come with a complete list of affirmations your sub-conscious mind hears on the tape.*

*The following affirmations are included on the "I Can Do Anything" tape:*

I feel my own power
I am willing to take a chance
I do more each day
I relax
I am unique
I am willing to change, positively
I am happy
I breathe deeply
All things are possible for me
I listen daily to my program
I am always improving
I can do more
My mind is clear
I feel stronger and stronger
I do it now
I remember my goals
Success is with me
I can do anything I want to do

# Sources of Subliminal Programs

*The following companies offer a wide range of subliminal programs to help you with problems ranging from smoking and excess weight to self-confidence and spiritual awakening. Each offers a catalog of their subliminal products.*

## Audio Activation
Bantam Audio Publishing
666 Fifth Ave.
New York,. NY 10103
800-223-6834
in NY 212-765-6500 ext. 479

*A line of subliminals that includes special tapes for men and women.*

## Effective Learning Systems
5221 Edina Industrial Blvd.
Edina, MN 55435
612-893-1680

*The "Love Tapes" are a series of subliminal and hypnosis tapes created by Bob Griswold.*

## Futurehealth
975 Bristol Pike
Bensalem, PA 19020
800-3-FUTURE

*Thomas Budzynski, a psychologist, has developed left/right brain subliminals with special messages focused to the brain hemisphere responsible for action.*

## Institute for Human Development
Box 1616
Ojai, CA 93023
800-443-0100

*An excellent source for subliminals to tackle an amazing array of problems. You can even customize your subliminals with your favorite music.*

## Light of Mind
Box 280, Dept. PH80
Topanga, CA 90290
818-992-0880

*A complete line of self-help subliminals, with original New Age music from David and Steve Gordon.*

## Mind Communication
Box 9429
Grand Rapids, MI 49509
800-237-1974

*Dr. Paul Tuthill offers 100 subliminal ways to help yourself.*

## Subliminal Persuasion Tapes
## Money-Prosperity

By Barrie Konicov
1978/60-minute cassette tape
**$9.98**
$12.23 postpaid from:
Potentials Unlimited
Box 891
Grand Rapids, MI 49518

*Side one has subliminal suggestions only your subconscious hears and is programmed by. Side two has hypnosis to reinforce the message that prosperity can be yours.*

---

## Potentials Unlimited
Box 891
Grand Rapids, MI 49518
616-698-7830

*Created by hypnotist Barrie Konicov, offers over 150 titles with or without subliminals along with hypnosis.*

## Psychodynamics Research Institute
Box 875
Zephyr Cove, NV 89448

*A full line of subliminals, including a sports and gaming series.*

## Success Education Institute
Box 90608
San Diego, CA 92109
800-248-2737

*Here are the "Randolph Tapes" subliminals created by Betty Lee Randolph, Ph.D.*

## Valley of the Sun
Box 3004
Agoura Hills, CA 91301
800-421-6603

*This is Dick Sutphen's company devoted to self-help products, including subliminals.*

## Stop Smoking
## Video Subliminal

By Dick Sutphen
1986/30-minute Videocassette, VHS
**$19.95**
$21.95 postpaid from:
Valley of the Sun
Box 3004
Agoura Hills, CA 91301

*Dick Sutphen has created a new type of subliminal video that incorporates simultaneous programming of your conscious and subconscious mind. A special video has been created that is unlike any other on the market today.*

## Subliminal Persuasion Video
## *Weight Loss*

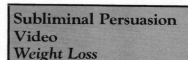

By Barrie Konicov
1983/30-minute Videocassette/VHS
**$14.98**
$18.58 postpaid from:
Potentials Unlimited
Box 891
Grand Rapids, MI 49518

*Just pop this video into your VCR and watch lush nature scenes and listen to stereo sounds as subliminal audio and video messages are sent to you to help you program thin thoughts about yourself.*

# Meditation
## What to Expect from Meditation

When you begin to meditate you may notice changes right away. You may feel anxious or more alert. You may be better able to concentrate, have more energy, be more at ease socially, or be more powerful intellectually. Or nothing much may seem to change. Don't count on anything dramatic. Most changes happen slowly.

There is a wide variety of experiences you will have during meditation itself, such as feelings of a pleasant calmness, a slight exhilaration, or, if you're fatigued, strong drowsiness. A common report is the feeling of the mind speeding up. Actually, this is not what is happening, but rather your awareness, is standing back a bit so that for the first time you notice the normal speediness of your thoughts. Other kinds of experiences can include seeing images with your eyes closed, hearing inner sounds, or having inner smells, tastes, or new sensations in the body; these are less common. Outside meditation, you may find a sense of spaciousness in your life, a new peace.

All of these experiences, because of their novelty, have a great

### Journey of Awakening
### A *Meditator's Guidebook*

1985/398 pages
**$4.95**
$6.45 postpaid from:
Bantam Books, Direct Response,
414 E. Golf Rd.
Des Plaines, IL 60016

*An excellent, down-to-earth explanation of the why's and how's of meditation.*

fascination. But they are best seen as markers along the way, signposts to be noticed, read, perhaps enjoyed, and then left behind as you go in.

There is no "best" or "right" kind of experience in meditation; each session is as different and unique as each day of your life. If you have ideas of what should happen, you can become needlessly disappointed if your meditation doesn't conform to these expectations. At first

meditation is likely to be novel, and it's easy to feel you are changing. After a while, there may be fewer dramatically novel experiences, and you may feel you're not making any progress. In fact, you may be making the most "progress" when you don't feel anything particularly significant is going on — the changes you undergo in meditation are often too subtle to detect accurately. Suspend judgment and let whatever comes come and go.

Some people find meditation boring. They feel as if nothing is happening. This is another way in which the old you holds on tight; and it is important to be able to persist even through the experiences of boredom. Set yourself a period of time to seriously try meditation, perhaps a period of two weeks or a month in which you say to yourself, "No matter what I experience in meditation I will continue to do it regularly." This will give you a chance to get through discouraging experiences in meditation such as boredom.

On the other hand, the initial reaction to meditation may be just the opposite of boredom — ecstasy. Many people find things happening after their first few meditative experiences that give them incredible enthusiasm and truly ecstatic states. This may lead them to proselytize, to want to tell others. I suggest that in the early stages you move gently and slowly. Don't overreact.

Positive experiences may well be followed shortly after by indifference. If you don't keep your experiences to yourself you may find yourself caught in a social situation in which you have created a monster of enthusiasm which you must pump up in a false way in order to be consistent. It is wise in all stages of meditation to be calm and not to make too much of any of your experiences, positive or negative. Merely notice them and keep on with your meditation.

Some people overreact to their experiences and go around saying that they're enlightened — they're the Buddha, they're the Christ. This is a self-deception. Others go to the other extreme and say they are nothing, they are unworthy. Both these positive and negative attitudes have to go.

Be open to whatever experiences come in your meditation. Don't get fixed on a model of what meditation is supposed to feel like. Set aside judging, being critical, having opinions. Meditation is giving up models and labels.

The less you expect, the less you judge, the less you cling to this or that experience as significant, the further you will progress. For what you're seeking is a transformation of your being far beyond that which any specific experience can give you. It is important to expect nothing, to take every experience, including the negative ones, as merely steps on the path, and to proceed.

*- Ram Dass*
*From* Journey of
Awakening

## How to Meditate
*The Acclaimed Guide to Self-Discovery*

By Lawrence LeShan
1974/162 pages
**$3.95**
$5.45 postpaid from:
Bantam Books
Direct Response
414 E. Golf Rd.
Des Plaines, IL 60016

*A classic meditation instruction guide that's simple and straightforward.*

# Breath Counting Exercise

Counting your breath is a meditation essentially designed to teach and practice the ability to do one thing at a time. It seems simple on the face of it, but do not let its apparent simplicity fool you. It is very hard, requires a great deal of practice, and — if worked at consistently — has definite positive psychological and physiological effects. `

Here, however, I suggest that you just try it for fifteen minutes in order to get a sense of what this work feels like. You start by placing yourself in a comfortable position so that you will get as few distracting signals from your body as possible. This may be either sitting, lying on the floor, or standing, depending on your particular wishes. Set an alarm or timer for fifteen minutes, or if this is not available, place a clock face where you can see it without moving your head. If you use an alarm clock or timer, use one with a gentle sound or muffle it with a pillow.

Now simply count silently each time you breathe out. Count "one" for the first breath, "two" for the second, "three" for the third, "four" for the fourth, and then start with "one" again. Keep repeating this procedure until the fifteen minutes are up.

The goal is to be doing simply that and nothing more. If other thoughts come in (and they will), simply accept the fact that you are straying from the instructions and bring yourself gently and firmly back to the counting. No matter what other thoughts, feelings or perceptions come during the fifteen minutes, your task is simply to keep counting your breaths, so keep trying to be

doing *only* that. Doing or being conscious of anything else during this period is wandering away from the task.

Do not expect to do well at it, to be able to succeed for more than a couple of seconds at a time in being aware only of your counting. That takes long practice. Simply do your best.

Now begin!

The road of meditation is not an easy one. The first shock of surprise comes when we realize how undisciplined our mind really is; how it refuses to do the bidding of our will. After fifteen minutes of attempting only to count our breaths and not be thinking of anything else, we realize that if our bodies were half as unresponsive to our will as our minds are, we would never get across the street alive. We find ourselves thinking of all sorts of other things rather than the simple thing we have just decided to think about. Saint Theresa of Avila once described the mind of man as an "unbroken horse that would go anywhere except where you wanted it to."

- *Lawrence LeShan*
*From* How to Meditate

## How to Meditate Deeply Now
*A Step-by-Step Guide to the Art of True Meditation*

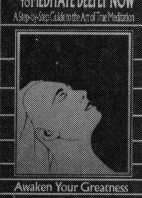

By Dr. Christopher Hills
1985/60 minute cassette tape
**$9.95**
$11.95 postpaid from:
University of the Trees
Box 66
Boulder Creek, CA 95006

*Side one of this tape shows you how to travel from a state of stress and even negativity through a step-by-step process of relaxation.*
*On side two Dr. Christopher Hills guides you into the depths of your own heart, until you meet your vaster unknown Self. You are compelled to let all fears and doubts go, and to free yourself for discovery of your greater being.*

## Very Practical Meditation

By Serene West
1981/102 pages
**$4.95**
$6.45 postpaid from:
The Donning Company,
5659 Virginia Beach Blvd.
Norfolk, VA 23502

*A very practical book that skillfully describes how to meditate. It then goes on to effectively illustrate how to use this skill to achieve positive results in your daily life from successful dieting to overcoming anger.*

## Meditation Made Easy
### An Edgar Cayce Learn-at-Home Course

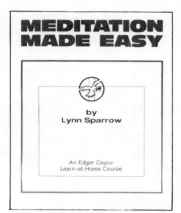

**MEDITATION MADE EASY**

by
Lynn Sparrow

An Edgar Cayce
Learn-at-Home Course

By Lynn Sparrow
1984/three 60-minute cassette tapes,
29 pages of instruction
**$24.95**
$26.95 postpaid from:
A.R.E. Press
Box 595
Virginia Beach, VA 23451

*This is a complete meditation course based on the Edgar Cayce readings. You'll learn meditation methods, techniques and exercises to help you get the most from your meditations.*

# Groups That Teach Meditation

### Ananda Marga
854 Pearl Street
Denver, CO 80203

*An international organization founded in 1955 by Sri Anandamurti. There are over 100 American centers offering meditation training and classes.*

### Integral Yoga Institute
227 West 13th St.
New York, NY 10011

*Founded by Sri Swami Satchindananda. Branches across America offering classes and teacher training.*

### Self Realization Fellowship
3880 San Rafael Avenue
Los Angeles, CA 90065

*Paramahansa Yogananda founded this group in 1920. Write for free literature.*

### Sivanda Yoga Vedanta Center
Eighth Avenue
Val Morin, Quebec J0T 2R0
Canada

*Offers classes, retreats and training. They also offer classes in the Bahamas.*

### Sri Chinmoy Center
Box 32433
Jamaica, NY 11431

*Sri Chinmoy holds meditation every week in Manhattan.*

### Sufi Order
Box 396
Lebanon, NY 12125

*Directed by Pir Vilayat Inayat Khan, this group offers training and classes at regional centers across America.*

### Theosophical Society in America
Box 270
Wheaton, IL 60187

*This nonsectarian group founded by H. P. Blavatsky and Annie Besant offers meditation correspondence courses. There are Theosophical Society study groups across America.*

### Transcendental Meditation
17310 Sunset Blvd.
Pacific Palisades, CA 90272

*There are hundreds of TM centers located in the United States and Canada.*

### Vipassana Meditation Center
Box 24
Shelbourne Falls, MA 01370

*Courses in the Vipassana method of Buddhist meditation is taught at centers worldwide.*

# Positions for Meditation

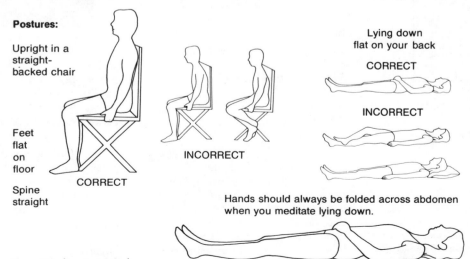

**Postures:**

Upright in a straight-backed chair

Feet flat on floor

Spine straight

CORRECT

INCORRECT

Lying down flat on your back

CORRECT

INCORRECT

Hands should always be folded across abdomen when you meditate lying down.

*- From* Meditation Made Easy

# Meditation Aids

## Astral Sounds
### A Natural High

By the American Research Team
1973/60-minute cassette tape
**$15.00**
$18.60 postpaid from:
Potentials Unlimited
4606-44th St. S.E., Box 891
Grand Rapids, MI 49518

## Songs of Seven Alloys
### The Divine Music of Tibetan Bowls, Bells and Gongs

By Ra Behl
1986/60 minute-cassette tape
**$9.95**
$11.95 postpaid from:
University of the Trees
Box 66
Boulder Creek, CA 95006

*This is a hauntingly beautiful tape with the simple, mystical sounds of gongs, Tibetan bells and bowls. It creates mystical background sounds that work well with the experience of meditation.*

## A Natural High?

As soon as a person begins to listen to Astral Sounds, the sound waves immediately stimulate the small bones of the inner ear and vibrate the fluids of the inner ear's labyrinth. Almost instantly the listener feels totally relaxed. The sounds automatically stimulate a pleasure center in the mind bringing about a feeling of physical relaxation and mental peace of mind. Warm, sensuous vibrations are sent throughout the entire body while certain sound waves begin to stimulate the rear portion of the brain. Known as the occipital region, it is this part of the brain which is responsible for creating what we see.

Each tone, pitch and sound wave was carefully patterned so that it faithfully duplicated the description of the sounds heard by our research subjects when they were in an unusually happy, healthy and blissful state of mind. After nearly two years of controlled testing of these laboratory created sound waves, the results far surpassed the researchers wildest expectations. Nearly all of the test participants reported entering into a natural deep rest where their body healed and was rejuvenated with additional energy and strength, where their stress, anxiety and worries disappeared while their physical pain was significantly reduced or vanished altogether. Some hallucinated beautifully, seeing colors, symbols, lights and faces pass before them as if in some magnificent and colorful parade. All test participants reported feeling better physically and emotionally after using the Astral Sounds tape cassette.

*– From the Astral Sounds Sales Literature*

## Rainy Day Meditation

By Dick Sutphen
1981/60-minute cassette tape
**$12.50**
$14.00 postpaid from:
Valley of the Sun
Box 3004
Agoura Hills, CA 91301

*This cassette tape's first side features the gentle sounds of the rain on a redwood deck, a sea gull's cry, brass windchimes and ocean surf. It provides a beautiful background for meditation. On side two, Sutphen guides you through a hypnosis-induced meditation to help you balance and harmonize with the same side-one sounds as a background.*

## The Meditator's Manual
### A Practical Introduction to the Art of Meditation

By Simon Court
1984/112 pages
**$12.95**
$14.45 postpaid from:
Sterling Publishers
2 Park Ave.
New York, NY 10016

*This is a how-to manual that combines a series of meditation exercises drawn from a number of different systems. It is designed to give the reader the experience of different fundamental techniques so he or she can choose what works best for them. It includes "feedback" sections for assessing progress, a mantra list, and guidelines for group work.*

# Dreamwork

## Tapping into Universal Knowledge

*By Joan Windsor*

I am Joan Windsor, licensed counselor by profession and teacher of parapsychology by choice. I have the privilege of introducing you to one of the most inspirational and life-transforming forces in the Universe. Properly used, it has the power to provide profitable business tips, comment on the body's physical condition, suggest treatment for its imbalances, enhance intuitive development, and teach us lessons in spirituality which inevitably culminate in soul evolvement. What is the source of this infinite wisdom? *Dreamwork* — or perhaps, it might more aptly be termed *Dreamplay* given the joy connected with the process.

"But," you exclaim, "only gifted clairvoyants and trained psychotherapists comprehend the significance of personal dreams. Mine make no sense!"

To these misguided statements I reply, "Nonsense!" I have heard such prattle repeatedly from my novice dream students. However, within six weeks, using the basic four-step method described below, 95% of them master the basic tenets of dreamwork. The formula my students have employed in interpreting their dreams with phenomenal success is comprised of these four components:

**Dream Incubation.** When you have been struggling in vain for solutions to seemingly irresolvable problems, the "incubated dream" either offers a unique solution to that problem in the dream state or intuition prompts the answer to spring forth in wakened consciousness. To incubate a dream one must formulate a specific question for which a response is anticipated or set forth a clearly defined problem, the solution of which has eluded you. When "response dreams" make their appearance (and they will), record

each and every pictorial or clairaudient impression received. "Response dreams" bestow specific and perfect answers for all involved. There are only given, however, to individuals who harbor the true intent of implementing higher guidance.

**Theme Identification.** Once having written down "incubated dreams," it then becomes the dreamer's responsibility to create some semblance of order out of the confusion and overlapping diversity of dream themes. The initial steps are (a) determining what life issue the dream is depicting (b) identifying and experiencing the feelings evoked (c) defining *in one sentence* its global theme. To these ends the Twelve Dream Classification system I've described in *The Inner Eye* provides a suitable reference. Categories include 1. *Dreams of Healing and Physical Health* 2. *Guidance and Creative Dreams for the Self and Others* 3. *Business Dream* 4. *Telepathic Dreams* 5. *Clairvoyant Dreams* 6. *Precognitive and Retrocognitive Dreams* 7. *Dreams of Local and World Events* 8. *Dreams of Death and the Departed* 9. *Past Life Dreams* 10. *Lucid Dreaming* 11. *Message Dreams* and 12. *Visionary Dreaming*.

**Theme Expansion through Dream Symbology.** The key to successful dream interpretation lies within the accurate assemblage and interlinking of "dream symbol puzzle pieces" to form a unified message of comprehensive import. This message should not only support but expand upon the theme identified in the previous step.

This requires translating the meaning of each dream symbol and its individual relationship to the global theme. Do not make the common mistake many beginning

students do by running to the nearest bookstore to purchase *10,000 Dream Symbols Interpreted for You* by A. Wise Guru. Your *own* dream associations will provide the most insightful and correct translations of these nocturnal commingues. Keeping a file box of personal dream symbology is a time-proven method for rapid expansion of dream interpretation skills.

**Dream Creativity.** The final step in our *Dreamwork* formula requires purposeful action on the part of the dreamer. Once the dream-coded message has been deciphered and internalized, the phenomenon of *dream creativity* comes into play. Dream creativity is the process whereby dream guidance is brought to fruition through its practical application within the life sphere of the dreamer. Dream creativity has as its ultimate goal a behavioral change in the life of the individual. Goal attainment is achieved through either an alteration in attitudinal focus or decisive action rendered. Initially, the dream student should determine what primary and secondary goals he desires to achieve and, upon that determination, formulate realistic courses of action which have seeded within them the highest probability of success. Adequate time should be allowed for the plan to manifest. Daily guidance should be sought through meditation. Once the goal is realized, identify the key factors responsible for its attainment. These will provide the impetus for the future employment of dream creativity at a continually high level of success. Conversely, if the plan results in failure, what flaws were concealed in your primary design which prevented materialization? In noting these fallacies you can avoid future catastrophies in dream creativity projects. After having recorded them, once again formulate a revised dream creativity project and begin with renewed faith. *Faith is the touchstone for God's promise of fulfillment.*

*Why study dreams?* Dreams are among God's original blessings for those who are visionary enough to attune their innate wisdom to Divine Direction.

*Joan Windsor*
*Personal Development Services*
*Box 1056*
*Williamsburg, VA 23187*

## Program Your Dreams

By Dick Sutphen
1981/60-minute cassette tape
**$12.50**
$14.00 postpaid from:
Valley of the Sun Publishing
Box 3004
Agoura Hills, CA 91301

*Side A is hypnosis programming, Side B is sleep programming designed to help you learn to actively program your dreams to work for you while you sleep. The hypnosis side helps you create a program and the sleep side reinforces the message.*

---

## Dream Network Bulletin
*A Newsletter for People Who Dare to Dream*

Edited by Linda Magallan
and Rob Trowbridge
**$18.00 for six issues/one year from:**
1083 Harvest Meadow Ct.
San Jose, CA 95136

*This magazine is devoted to experiential dreamwork and includes feature articles, how-to dream tips, personal experiences, dream organizations, and events.*

---

## Association for the Study of Dreams
P.O. Box 3121
Falls Church, VA 22043

*The ASD is a multidisciplinary, international forum to promote and disseminate recognition, study and research in dreamwork. They present seminars, workshops, and conferences. They also publish a monthly ASD Newsletter.*

## Dreams & Healing
*Expanding the Inner Eye*

By Joan Windsor
1987/320 pages
**$8.95**
$10.95 postpaid from:
Dodd, Mead & Co., Inc.
71 Fifth Ave.
New York, NY 10003

*Your dreams can be the key to accessing information about your health. Windsor provides examples and exercises to help you get the most from your dreams.*

# Advice Dreams for Maintenance of Personal Bodily Health

The most elementary type of healing dream focuses upon the refinement and maintenance of personal bodily health. Insights received from dreams may not involve major health issues or grandiose healing schemes but they do usually offer the dreamer statements designed to "tune-up" the body to the point where it will operate at peak efficiency. The advice given ranges from short "one-liners" or a mini-series of visual images, to rather extensive physical examinations of the bodily dysfunction. In either case the message is clearly transmitted along with the corrective measures to be adopted to assure physical improvement. If the advice is put into practice, changes begin to take place within several hours or a week or two at the most. Permit me to cite several prime examples of this subcategory to illustrate my point.

During the third week of March 1983, a minor back pain made its appearance across the small of my back. I could not recall how I hurt myself but began applying heat and massage to alleviate the condition. As if to assure me that no major disaster loomed on the horizon, on March 27th as I awoke, I received the following sentence of explanation and vote of confidence in my choice of treatment.

*"You hurt your back picking up the brown suitcase. You'll be ok."*

Another message received May 29, 1984, stated in no uncertain terms what my sedentary work life was accomplishing with regard to my circulatory system.

*"Your blood does not circulate well. You need to jog."*

- Joan Windsor
From Dreams & Healing

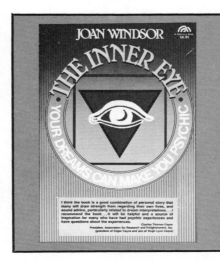

## The Inner Eye
By Joan Windsor
1985/240 pages
**$8.95**
$10.95 postpaid from:
Simon & Schuster
200 Old Tappan Rd.
Old Tappan, NJ 07675

*Is there a recurrent image in your dreams that seems to compel you to an unknown purpose? Have you ever had a vivid dream that came true?*
*Use your dreams to tap psychic powers you never knew you had.*

**Working with Dreams**
*Self-Understanding,
Problem-Solving, and
Enriched Creativity Through
Dream Interpretation*

By Montague Ullman, M.D.
and Nan Zimmerman
1979/334 pages
**$8.95**
$11.35 postpaid from:
J.P. Tarcher, Inc.
9110 Sunset Blvd.
Los Angeles, CA 90069

# Look at Dreams Positively!

Every psychiatrist, particularly one interested in dreams, owes a debt to Freud. Mine is an ambivalent debt. Certainly Freud's remarkable book on dreams established once and for all the therapeutic usefulness of dreams, and all psychotherapists since Freud have been the legatees of this heritage. There are, however, strings attached, and that is what bothers me. Freud's way of looking at dreams derived in large measure from his way of looking at neurotic symptoms. As a result people tend to link dreams and psychoanalytic theory and thereby to believe — wrongly, I feel — that only an expert can work effectively with dreams.

Of course dreams are useful in therapy, because they tell the truth about the dreamer. Confronting the truth about oneself and accepting it

without being defensive about it or frightened by it is the essence of psychological healing. Dream images derive from the feelings we have about issues that are of some importance to us. And feelings don't lie. They simply are. The images of the dream convey the source and context of these feelings in relation to our present as well as our past. When read correctly these images tell us who we are instead of who we think we are. They speak to us about our actual impact on others, not about what we would like that impact to be. In short they are honest, no-nonsense assessments of the immediate predicament in which we are at the time we are dreaming.

*- Montague Ullman, M.D.
From* Working With Dreams

**How to Interpret Your Dreams**
*Based on the Edgar Cayce Readings*
By Mark A. Thurston, Ph.D.
1978/192 pages
**$7.95**
$9.95 postpaid from:
A.R.E. Press
Box 595
Virginia Beach, VA 23451

*Edgar Cayce did many readings that mentioned dreams and their use in our lives. Here you'll learn how to find and use important information and get specific answers to your dreams.*

# How the Dream Themes Work

The hypothesis underlying the thematic approach to dream work is that our dream experiences reflect the basic patterns of daily life. This reflection may take the form of guidance, a warning, or simply a depiction of things as they are. The meaning or message of a dream may be a commentary on a particular theme being carried out in daily life. The commentary is sometimes contained in the symbology of the dream, although frequently the meaning of the dream is simply to *call attention* to the fact that a particular pattern of experience is going on in waking life.

The procedure for using the theme of a dream as an interpretation tool can best be explained by an illustration. In the diagram below,

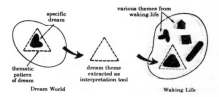

the contents of daily life experience are represented by various shapes — that is, patterns of behavior, of thinking and of feeling. In using the theme approach we try to identify the basic, overall "shape" of the dream, and then we look for the areas of waking life that it matches.

Once we discover an area of daily life that the theme matches, we are much more likely to be able to interpret properly the symbols contained in that dream. Occasionally we may not need to go back to the symbols because the meaning may simply be to call attention to the theme's applicability to daily life. However, when we do need to return to the symbology to extract a meaning, we have taken an important step forward: we have discovered the likely *context* in which the symbol is being used. Since many symbols have several possible interpretations, the knowledge of the context is extremely valuable.

*- Mark A. Thurston, Ph.D.
From* How to Interpret Your Dreams

## The Compleat Book of Dreaming

By Derek and Julia Parker
1985/224 pages
**$15.95**
$19.45 postpaid from:
Crown Publishers, Inc.
34 Englehard Ave.
Avenel, NJ 07001

*A beautifully illustrated and complete book of dreams and dreaming. It gives an in-depth look at dreams in history, current scientific knowledge and an extensive list of the meaning of dream symbols.*

### Snake

The snake symbol appears worldwide in most mythologies: in the west, the strongest reference is perhaps to the serpent in the Garden of Eden, which introduced Adam and Eve to sin (often believed by Christians to involve sex). Many other cultures also make a connection between a snake and the penis, although psychic and spiritual, as well as sexual, energy is symbolized by the snake. If the snakes in your dream frighten you, you should perhaps consider your attitude to sex, for your dream may be making a definite and important statement about your reaction to it. But there could also be a reference to some deep-rooted psychological problem. You must face up to the snake and tackle it. If you cannot reduce the element of fear to manageable proportions you may need counselling of some sort, especially if the dream recurs; your sex-life may well be not as fulfilling and rewarding as it could (and should) be. Remember, however, that a serpent creature has often been a symbol of wisdom and knowledge (the famous Oracle at Delphi was a snake-goddess).

*- Julia and Derek Parker*
*From The Compleat Book of Dreaming*

## Lucid Dreaming
### *The Power of Being Awake and Aware in Your Dreams*

By Steven LaBerge, Ph.D.
1987/288 pages
**$15.95**
$18.35 postpaid from:
Jeremy P. Tarcher, Inc.
9110 Sunset Blvd.
Los Angeles, CA 90069

*Lucid dreaming is "waking up" in your dreams without disturbing the dream state. This allows you to gain control over and determine the content of your dreams.*

## Controlling Your Dreams

By Steven LaBerge, Ph.D.
1987/60-minute cassette tape and 32-page manual
**$9.95**
$11.45 postpaid from:
St. Martin's Press
175 Fifth Ave.
New York, NY 10010

*This companion cassette to LaBerge's* Lucid Dreaming *teaches you the basics of lucid dreaming and how to control your dreams.*

**The Sun and the Shadow**
*My Experiment with*
*Lucid Dreaming*

By Kenneth Kelzer
1987/272 pages
**$9.95**
$11.95 postpaid from:
A.R.E. Press
Box 595
Virginia Beach, VA 23451

# Lucid Dreaming

According to the definition that is generally accepted by dream theorists and researchers today, *a lucid dream is a dream in which the dreamer is aware that he is dreaming while he is dreaming.* This process is distinct from an ordinary dream in which the dreamer is often thoroughly confined in the dream experience, so much so that he or she often believes the dream to be fully "real" as it is occurring. By contrast, the lucid dream contains a second level of awareness which emerges from and runs concurrently with the first level, that is, the ongoing content and process of the dreamscape. On this second level of awareness the dreamer, when fully lucid, knows with absolute certainty that what is seen and experienced around him or her is a dream, and this unusual certitude affords a level of freedom and personal power that is impossible to attain in an ordinary dream. In many lucid dreams the dreamer experiences a distinct transition point in which his consciousness shifts from the normal dream to the lucid state, a point that lucid dream researchers now refer to as the onset of lucidity. This shift of consciousness is sometimes felt very distinctly, like bursting out of the clouds in an airplane flight and feeling dazzled by the clear sunlight. Or sometimes it occurs so slowly and gradually as to be almost imperceptible to the dreamer. The lucid dream state is also frequently characterized by highly refined

energies that move about through the dreamer's body and mind, leaving a pleasant, tingling sensation that is often accompanied by gorgeous, vivid colors, intense and ecstatic feelings, or celestial, rapturous music that seems to come from another world. In short, the lucid dream can lead the dreamer into a whole new realm of human possibilities.

*Through lucid dreaming, a person can transfer the quality of mental lucidity into the waking state.*

- *Kenneth Kelzer*
*From* The Sun and
the Shadow

**The Dream House**
395 Sussex St.
San Francisco, CA 94131
415-239-6909

*This is a West Coast network of dreamers, dream workers, consultants, educators and therapists who come together to analyze the value of dreams. They offer an ongoing seminar/workshop program.*

**Lucidity Association**
c/o Dr. J. Gackenbach
Dept. of Psychology
University of Northern Iowa
Cedar Falls, IA 50614

*The Association is devoted to education and research into lucid dreaming and related phenomena. It publishes the biannual Lucidity Letter which disseminates research findings on lucid dreaming from researchers all over the world.*

# What Is an Out-of-Body Experience (OBE)?

We can formally define an OOBE* as an event in which the experiencer (1) seems to perceive some portion of some environment which could not possibly be perceived from where his physical body is known to be at the time; and (2) knows *at the time* that he is not dreaming or fantasizing. The experiencer seems to possess his normal consciousness at the time, and even though he may reason that this cannot be happening, he will feel all his normal critical faculties to be present, and so knows he is not dreaming. Further, he will not decide after awakening that this was a dream. How, then, do we understand this strange phenomenon?

First, OOBEs are a universal human experience, not in the sense that they happen to large numbers of people, but in that they have happened all through recorded history, and there are marked similarities in the experience among people who are otherwise extremely different in terms of cultural background. One can find reports of OOBEs by housewives in Kansas which closely resemble accounts of OOBEs from ancient Egyptian or oriental sources.

Second, the OOBE is generally a once-in-a-lifetime experience, seemingly experienced by "accident." Illnesses sometimes bring it about, especially illnesses which are almost fatal. Great emotional stress sometimes brings it about. In many cases, it simply happens during sleep without our having any idea of what might have caused it. In very rare instances it seems to have been brought about by a deliberate attempt.

Third, the experience of an OOBE is usually one of the most profound experiences of a person's life, and radically alters his beliefs. This is usually expressed as, "I no longer *believe* in survival of death or an immortal soul, I *know* that I will survive death." The person feels that he has directly experienced being alive and conscious without his physical body, and therefore knows that he possesses some kind of soul that will survive bodily death. This does not logically follow, for even if the OOBE is more than just an interesting dream or hallucination, it was still occurring while the physical body was alive and functioning and therefore may depend on the physical body. This argument, however, makes no impression on those who have actually had an OOBE. Thus regardless of what position one wants to take on the "reality" of the OOBE, it is clearly an experience deserving considerable psychological study. I am certain that our ideas concerning the existence of souls have resulted from early experiences of people having OOBEs. Considering the importance of the idea of the soul to most of our religions, and the importance of religion in people's lives, it seems incredible that science could have swept this problem under the rug so easily.

Fourth, the OOBE is generally extremely joyful to those who have it. I would make a rough estimate that between 90 and 95 percent of the people who have this experience are very glad it occurred and find it joyful, while 5 percent are very frightened by it, for the only way they can interpret it, while it is happening, is that they are dying. Later reactions of the person as he attempts to interpret his OOBE can be rather negative, however. Almost every time I give a speech on this subject, someone comes up to me afterward and thanks me for talking about it. They had had the experience sometime before, but had no way of explaining it, and worried that they were going "crazy."

Fifth, in some instances of OOBEs the description of what was happening at a distant place is correct and more accurate than we would expect by coincidence. Not the majority, by any means, but some. To explain these we must postulate either that the "hallucinatory" experience of the OOBE was combined with the operation of ESP, or that in some sense the person really was "there." The OOBE then becomes very real indeed.

*- Charles T. Tart*
*From the Introduction to*
*Journeys Out of the Body*
*By Robert A. Munroe*

\* *Current usage of this term has shortened to "OBE."*

2 Cassette Tapes  96 Page Manual

Dick Sutphen's
**Astral Projection**

By The Author Of
"You Were Born Again To Be Together"
& "Past Lives, Future Loves"

## Astral Projection

By Dick Sutphen
1980/two 60-minute cassettes,
96 page book
**$24.95**
$26.95 postpaid from:
Valley of the Sun
Box 3004
Agoura Hills, CA 91301

*You can condition yourself to leave your body!*

*Hypnosis is the ultimate technique to expand and alter consciousness, so it is the ideal methodology to explore the astral realms. Different people respond to different techniques and experience results in different ways. Thus the album is made up of an introduction/ preparation tape, followed by a controlled lift-out experiment and two lift-out techniques tapes.*

## Journeys Out of the Body

By Robert A. Munroe
1977/280 pages
**$7.95**
$8.64 postpaid from:
Doubleday & Co.
501 Franklin Ave.
Garden City, NY 11530

*This is Robert Munroe's first book describing his startling and spontaneous out-of-body experiences (OBEs). His search for answers to explain the strange phenomena leads him to self-experimentation and exploration.*

*A practical businessman, Munroe maintains objectivity and a cautious assessment of his out-of-body sojourns.*

*Munroe's first-hand descriptions and reactions allow the reader to experience the textures, sensations and subjective feeling of astral travel.*

# Dreaming?

Several months passed, and the vibration condition continued to occur. It almost became boring, until late one night when I was lying in bed just before sleep. The vibrations came and I wearily and patiently waited for them to pass away so I could go to sleep. As I lay there, my arm was draped over the right side of the bed, fingers just brushing the rug.

Idly, I tried to move my fingers and found I could scratch the rug. Without thinking or realizing that I *could* move my fingers during the vibration, I pushed with the tips of my fingers against the rug. After a moment's resistance, my fingers seemed to penetrate the rug and touch the floor underneath. With mild curiosity, I pushed my hand

down farther. My fingers went through the floor and there was the rough upper surface of the ceiling of the room below. I felt around, and there was a small triangular chip of wood, a bent nail, and some sawdust. Only mildly interested in this daydream sensation, I pushed my hand still deeper. It went through the first-floor ceiling and I felt as if my whole arm was through the floor. My hand touched water. Without excitement, I splashed the water with my fingers.

Suddenly, I became fully aware of the situation. I was wide awake. I could see the moonlit landscape through the window. I could feel myself lying on the bed, the covers over my body, the pillow under my head, my chest rising and falling as I breathed. The vibrations were still present, but to a lesser degree.

Yet, impossibly, my hand was playing in a pool of water, and my arm felt as if it was stuck down through the floor. I was surely wide awake and the sensation was still there. How could I be awake in all other respects and still "dream" that my arm was stuck down through the floor?

The vibrations started to fade, and for some reason I thought there was a connection between my arm stuck through the floor and their presence. If they faded away before I got my arm "out," the floor might close in and I would lose an arm. Perhaps the vibrations had made a hole in the floor temporarily. I didn't stop to consider the "how" of it.

I yanked my arm out of the floor, pulled it up on the bed, and the vibrations ended soon after. I got up, turned on the light, and looked at the spot beside the bed. There was no hole in the floor or rug. They were just as they always had been. I looked at my hand and arm, and even looked for the water on my hand. There was none, and my arm seemed perfectly normal. I looked about the room. My wife was sleeping quietly in the bed, nothing seemed amiss.

I thought about the hallucination for a long time before I was able to calm down enough to sleep. The next day I considered actually cutting a hole in the floor to see if what I had felt was there on the subfloor — the triangular chip of wood, the bent nail, and the sawdust. At the time, I couldn't see disfiguring the floor because of a wild hallucination.

- *Robert A. Munroe*
*From* Journeys Out of the Body

## Far Journeys

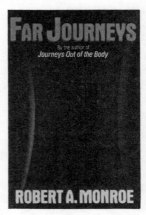

By Robert A. Munroe
1985/292 pages
**$9.95**
$10.64 postpaid from:
Doubleday & Co.
501 Franklin Ave.
Garden City, NY 11530

*This is Robert Munroe's second book detailing his out-of-body experiences (OBEs). After years of research and experimentation, Munroe's "abilities" have sharpened and expanded to encompass numerous levels of consciousness.*

*His first-hand experiences are as riveting as ever. In addition he provides a "flow chart" of astral levels and an extensive question and answer section for would-be astral travellers.*

It is as if one were to try to describe music, such as a symphony orchestra with choir, and do it in words without the use of such technical descriptions as notation, instruments, intervals, tonalities, and so on. One can use such words as "nice," "compelling," "frightening," "aweinspiring," "warm," "loving," "beautiful" — and be nowhere remotely near the actual description.

- *Robert A. Munroe*
*From* Far Journeys

### Monroe Institute

Rt. 1, Box 175
Faber, VA 22938

*The Institute was founded by Robert Munroe to study and make public research into OBEs and other phenomenon.*

Astral Travel
*Your Guide to the Secrets
of Out-of-the-Body
Experiences*

**ASTRAL TRAVEL**

Your Guide to the Secrets
of Out-of-the-Body Experiences

**Gavin and Yvonne Frost**

By Gavin and Yvonne Frost
1982/240 pages
**$6.95**
$8.45 postpaid from:
Samuel Weiser, Inc.
Box 612
York Beach, ME 03910

*A clear, detailed and comprehensive how-to book on astral travel with information compiled and coordinated by the Canterbury Institute in England and the American School of Wicca. Includes different types of astral travel, possible problems to anticipate/avoid and numerous charts and diagrams.*

# Is an OBE Experience Just Dreaming?

Most individuals do dismiss the experience when they encounter it as nothing more than a vivid dream. At most, it may be categorized by some as what is identified as a "lucid" dream. In the latter, the dreamer is apparently aware that he is dreaming, and can control the content of his dream, even to the point of changing the event, the participants, and the outcome.

In the OOBE,* the individual is near-totally conscious, as our civilization defines the state. Most if not all of your physical sensory perception is replicated. You can "see," "hear," and "touch" — the weakest seem to be smell and taste. Your perspective is from a position outside your physical body, near or distant. In a near state, it is usually from a location impossible for you to "be" with your physical body, such as floating against the ceiling. In a far location, it could be in Paris when you know you are in New York physically. You can observe events taking place, but you cannot change or significantly affect them. You can verify the authenticity of such events subsequently if you so desire. You cannot participate to any major degree in this physical activity because you are not "physical." It is the extreme reality of the OOBE that sets it apart from a dream. It is as "real" as any physical life experience.

# Why Should You Astral Travel?

Astral travel extends the scope of your life. Even today, when you are free of your body in dreams you can have experiences that in other circumstances would be considered beyond credibility. You can be a king in his palace or a sheikh in a harem. You can make love to the most beautiful women in the world; or as the queen of all you survey, you can be courted by the most romantic and attractive man it is possible to imagine. Whether you are rich or poor you can travel in time to see the past and the future. You can go at no cost to any place in the cosmos. We will also teach you to travel into other realms — realms and realities beyond the known cosmos, realms impossible to reach without this training. You can bring back knowledge about the future and about other ways that will be of inestimable benefit to you in your present life.

With the aid of the astral Little People (for little people really do exist) you will become able to find that proverbial pot of gold at the end of the rainbow. Age, upbringing, education — all totally irrelevant. Although we have found that it is slightly more difficult for a white Christian to accomplish all that others can, this difficulty is so easily overcome by the Institute's techniques as to be almost non-existent. If you devote a few of those Sundays you would normally spend in church to the practice of these techniques, you will find that you can accomplish just as much as any other citizen of the world.

- *Gavin and Yvonne Frost*
*From Astral Travel*

# Can Anyone OOBE?

Several studies made during the past ten years indicate that some 25 percent of adult humans remember having at least one spontaneous OOBE. Many were unaware of what had happened to them until the phenomenon was described to them.

... we believe that anyone can indeed consciously move into OOBE states.

- *Robert Monroe*
*From* Far Journeys

**The Parts of an Entity**

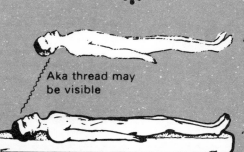

*

'I' – Consciousness or spirit
  can take on any shape
  can travel to upper
  spiritual realms

Astral double contains 'I'
  is double of 'Me'
  can astral travel most
  places may be too gross
  for spirit realms

Aka thread may
be visible

'Me' – in the mundane world

*Current usage of this term is now "OBE".

# Search for Consciousness

The past decade has seen an astonishing acceleration of the convergence of many disciplines of scientific study, all heralding our entrance into the New Age. The thought forms of science and metaphysics are merging into new theories of human potential. Science is discovering that our reality is not objective and concrete but subjective and relevant to the perspective of the viewer. New Age metaphysical literature is based on the premise that we create our own reality. Studies from the physical and natural sciences, as well as records from history and archaeology are pointing toward our continued and potential evolution as creative human beings. Does this potential ultimately include the creation of "ourselves"? Exciting new developments in consciousness research support these transcendent models of thought. Like the ever quickening approach at the end of a tunnel, physicists and psychologists alike are fast moving towards "consciousness" as the ultimate and only area of study which will crack the code of our universe.

## The Possible Human

By Jean Houston
1982/230 pages
**$9.95**
$12.35 postpaid from:

Jeremy P. Tarcher, Inc.
9110 Sunset Blvd.
Los Angeles, CA 90069

*A unique masterwork exploring the possibilities of the individual human. From kinesthetics to awakening the brain to spiritual exploration. This guidebook presents an informal perspective including creative exercises with discussions in easy to use format. A guidebook of the invisible possibilities of ourselves.*

## Uncommon Sense

By Mark Davidson
1983/240 pages
**$8.95**
$11.35 postpaid from:
Jeremy P. Tarcher, Inc.
9110 Sunset Blvd.
Los Angeles, CA 90069

*This is an easy to understand presentation of the thought of Ludwig Von Bertalanffy, recognized as the father of General Systems Theory. In spite of the General Systems Theory's ecological/holistic basis, it provides a new approach to personal and social problem solving as well.*

Common sense, which once assured humanity that the world is flat, now assures us that the world is the sum of its parts.

As a result, most of us deal with our environment by taking it apart — piece by piece, problem by problem — on the assumption that our efforts ultimately will add up to success.

The human race has gotten by with that piecemeal approach for centuries, just as it managed to get by for centuries with the pre-Copernican notion of a flat earth. But our age of innocence must now end. The unprecedented inter-connectedness of civilization compels us to face the fact that the world is greater than the sum of its parts. We therefore must begin paying attention to the fate of the whole earth rather than just the sum of its nations.

— *Mark Davidson*
*From Uncommon Sense*

# A Whole Earth

We arrive finally at our own time, when the human race can no longer afford the invidious comparisons and psychological imperialism that some "successful" cultures and nations impose upon others. In this time of planetary culture we need the full complement of human resources, wherever they are to be found. We need to bring forth and orchestrate all the Rhythms of Human Awakening that have ever been in humanity's search for what it can be.

As we have seen, previous cultures have tended to deny some areas of development while acknowledging and encouraging others. With the present convergence of the findings of anthropology, cross-cultural studies, psychophysical research, and studies into the nature and function of brain, we are beginning to have in hand a perspective on human possibility as profound as it is provocative. This perspective allows us to turn the corner on our humanity, exploring and experiencing the astonishing complexity and variety of the world of the possible human. It is virtually a new introduction to the human race.

`  ` ` ` ` ` `

We find ourselves in a time in which extremely limited consciousness has the powers once accorded to the goals. Extremely limited consciousness can launch a nuclear holocaust with the single push of a button. Extremely limited consciousness can and does intervene directly in the genetic code, interferes with the complex patterns of life in the sea, and pours its wastes into the protective ozone layers that encircle the earth. Extremely limited consciousness is about to create a whole new energy base linking together computers, electronics, new materials from outer space, biofacture, and genetic engineering, which in turn will release a flood of innovation and external power unlike anything seen before in human history. In short, extremely limited consciousness is accruing to itself the powers of Second Genesis. And this with an ethic that is more Faustian than godlike.

— *Jean Houston*
*From The Possible Human*

# Neurosis/Disease/Discontent

Terminology continues to be a problem. Since I can think of no one word that adequately expresses the common origin, nature and function of conditions often considered to be disparate, I must resort to the lamentable expediency of fabricating a single term, neurosis/disease/ discontent, or NDD, to use in the following discussion. I begin with a few preliminary points:

Civilization's most indispensable nonmaterial endowment to its children is some type of neurosis/ disease/discontent.

Each NDD, whatever its nature or origin, serves to keep the human individual in a state of dis-ease, to render each person's here-and-now being uncomfortable and distasteful. If properly programmed, the NDD also dulls the senses and cuts off the individual from nature and the cosmos. The best way of gaining temporary relief from dis-ease lies in forgetfulness of existence. This is generally achieved either by drugs or by the relentless getting and building that has characterized much of human life since the success of agriculture.

The NDDs do not necessarily result (as Freud would have it) from a conflict between humankind's primal sexual and aggressive *instincts* and the realities of social life. They are created by Civilization. *Even if humans had no sexuality or aggressiveness whatever yet were sensitive beings capable of joy and harmony with nature, they would still have to be afflicted with dis-ease in order for Civilization's work to be done.*

An NDD is more effective the more its origin is veiled. When one mode of programming dis-ease is widely revealed in a particular society, that mode loses much of its power. The society goes on to evolve a more subtle means of bestowing the Gift.

Up to a certain remarkably high breaking point, the NDDs are not maladaptive for the civilized individual but highly adaptive. A pre-ulcerous condition makes for success in this society; ulcers are a bit too much.

Whether seemingly physical or psychological, every NDD is actually both. As we shall see later in this chapter, every NDD leaves some physical scar. To that extent we are all maimed and we are maiming our children.

The NDDs are essentially incurable in any civilized society and perhaps in any society that has advanced as far as agriculture. Symptoms may shift and particular forms of dis-ease may be exchanged for others. The basic condition remains. Transformation of society is the only real cure.

- George B. Leonard
  From The Transformation

## Beyond Ego
### Transpersonal Dimensions in Psychology

Edited by Roger N. Walsh, M.D., Ph.D. and Frances Vaughan, Ph.D.
1980/272 pages
**$9.95**
$12.35 postpaid from:
Jeremy P. Tarcher, Inc.
9110 Sunset Blvd.
Los Angeles, CA 90069

Beyond Ego *provides a much needed and very useful integration of the major themes of transpersonal psychology as seen through the eyes of its masters. This volume serves as a comprehensive reference to this major field of the interconnectedness and interdependence of all things.*

## The Transformation
### A Guide to the Inevitable Changes in Humankind

By George B. Leonard
1972/260 pages
**$8.95**
$11.35 postpaid from:
Jeremy P. Tarcher, Inc.
9110 Sunset Blvd.
Los Angeles, CA 90069

*In its 3rd edition, and 15 years after its initial publication, The Transformation chronicles the events of our present deteriorating culture, exposing possibilities of a fascinating new adventure ahead of us.*

## Thinking Allowed
### Conversations on the Leading Edge of Knowledge and Discovery

315 Third St.
Suite 161
San Rafael, CA 94901
415-456-2532

*An exciting, innovative new series of 30-minute video taped programs featuring discussions with leading writers, researcher and explorers on all aspects of New Age culture. Some samples include Physics and Consciousness with Fred Alan Wolf, Creative Visualization with Shakti Gawain, Spiritual Channeling with Alan Vaughan, Developing and Applying Psychic Abilities with Kevin Ryerson and much more.*

## The Creative Imperative
### A Four-Dimensional Theory of Human Growth &

# THE CREATIVE IMPERATIVE

*A Four-Dimensional*

*Theory of*

*Human Growth &*

*Planetary Evolution*

CHARLES M. JOHNSTON, M.D.

By Charles M. Johnston, M.D.
1986/406 pages
**$14.95**
$15.95 postpaid from:
Celestial Arts
P.O. Box 7327
Berkeley, CA 94707

*The construction of breakthrough paradigm which focuses on the fact that "we are alive" as the central point in the human equation.*

Aliveness, just by what it is, confronts the key issues that now face us. At the personal level, the pivotal questions of our time concern purpose and identity: who are we — our roles, our beliefs, what we own, the images we get from media, parents, and peers? Aliveness is a direct statement about, and measure of, purpose. We feel purpose and "are" someone precisely to the degree we risk living from, and in relation to, what makes us most alive. Culturally, what we are wanting to do in each sphere is find ways of thinking and measuring that are sensitive to the place of that sphere in the larger living whole. From here, there becomes no more important task than learning to ask together the relative aliveness that different social options offer us.

In one sense, making the creative our referent is a radically new kind of motion; in another the creative is what we have been measuring all along. Each of our previous arbiters — the voices of nature spirits, moral canons, the laws of science — were also measures of the edge of creation. The difference with a creatively-based perspective is simply that now, in measuring creation, we are being conscious of the fact that this indeed is what we are measuring. We have moved far enough into creation that we are able to be not just creators of culture, but beings conscious of, and in, this process of creation.

- *Charles M. Johnston, M.D.*
*From The Creative Imperative*

## Star Wave
### Mind, Consciousness, and Quantum Physics

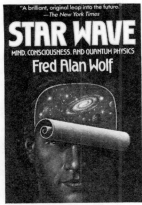

By Fred Alan Wolf
1984/340 pages
**$9.95**
$11.40 postpaid from:
Collier Books
MacMillan Publishing Co.
MacMillan Distribution Ctr.
Front and Brown Sts.
Riverside, NJ 08075

*Physicist Fred Alan Wolf applies the concepts of quantum physics to the study of human consciousness. This new model of the physics of the mind shows how our inner worlds of sensation, feeling, thought, and intuition are deeply connected to the physical processes of the universe.*

# The New Physics

It is 80,000 B.C. and you are there. It is time for foraging. Up ahead you come to a familiar landmark, but the scene has somehow changed. Perhaps it is the light on the tall grass. Even worse perhaps there is a dreaded bear about to pounce. Last time out you went to the right. Or was it to the left? You aren't sure. You must choose — the lives of your whole family depend on making the correct choice. You go left. You sense the danger as you move hurriedly along what appears to be a familiar track. Finally you reassure yourself. You are on the correct path. Suddenly, just as you relax, the great bear pounces. A sharp pain is all you remember as everything goes black. The scene is over. You are dead.

Hold it. Stop the action. Let's run that by again. Back to tall grass. But this time you go right. As you move cautiously along the path, a path that you cannot remember, you have a tingling feeling. It is somehow familiar and yet it is different. Ahead you see what you are searching for. You gather the firewood and return to your family. The scene ends. You have survived.

It seems cut-and-dried. Either you survived or you didn't. Right? Wrong. You survived and died back there on the prehistoric veldt. You took both paths. Yet you did choose a single path. You had to. How did you do both? The answer to this seeming paradox, indeed the realization of such a question, is a product of the "new physics." As fantastic as it may sound, the "new physics" called quantum mechanics posits that there exists, side by side with this world, another world, a parallel universe, a duplicate copy that is somehow slightly different and yet the same. And not just two parallel worlds, but three, four, and even more. No less than an infinite number of them. In each of these universes, you, I, and all the others who live, have lived, will live, will have ever lived, are alive.

- *Fred Alan Wolf*
*From Star Wave*

## The Institute of Noetic Sciences

475 Gate Five Rd.
Suite 300
P.O. Box 97
Sausalito, CA 94966
$35.00/year, Associate Member.
Additional membership plans
available.

The Institute of Noetic Sciences
was founded in 1973 to support
research and education on human
consciousness. A tax-exempt, non-
profit public foundation, its purposes
are to broaden knowledge of the
nature and potentials of mind and
consciousness, and to apply that
knowledge to the enhancement of
life on the planet.

In their current research, the
Institute continues to address what
are deemed to be the most promising
areas of the still unexplored frontiers
of the human mind and spirit.

The Institute sponsors and
conducts research and programs
categorized mainly into three
groupings: Exceptional Abilities,
Health and Healing, and Societal
Transformation.

Membership in the Institute of
Noetic Sciences includes a year's
worth of the most up to date
consciousness research material with
"Noetic Science Reviews,"
"Bulletins," "Investigations,"
"President's Letters" and other
quality publications; discounts on
books and related materials in the
annotated catalog, plus calendar and
lecture information.

Samples from the Past Projects List:

### Exceptional Human Abilities

Telepathy Research Project. SRI
International, Menlo Park,
California. Dr. Harold Puthoff and
Russell Targ. An investigation of
telepathic communications under
experimental conditions.

### Health and Healing

Near-Death Experiences and the
Dying Patient. Hospice of Palm
Beach County, Florida, and
International Association for Near
Death Studies. Dr. Kenneth Ring
and John Audette. An exploration of
possible connections between the
needs of dying patients and data
emerging from recent studies of near
death experiences.

### Societal Transformation

Hope for the Earth. Institute of
Noetic Sciences and United Nations
University for Peace. Dr. Willis W.
Harman. A program to explore the
relationship between consciousness
research and the global dilemmas.

### The Computer Analogy to Higher Centers

Living in the computer age, we
have an excellent analogy for this
situation. Each of us has a little
personal computer of our own. It
runs slowly, has only a small
memory for data, and very little data
stored in it. It uses three rather
primitive programming languages for
computing: Intellectual Basic,
Emotional Basic, and
Bodily/Instinctive Basic. It can
function very well for many of the
needs of ordinary life if we use it

efficiently. We rightly love and
admire this little personal computer,
for it is a marvelous, even if limited,
machine. Indeed, we have identified
with it: we think its thoughts are our
thoughts.

What we have forgotten, in our
attachment to and dependence on
our little personal computer, is that
there is a way of programming it so
that it will act as a terminal to
connect us with a giant supercomputer. This supercomputer runs
far faster than our personal
computer, has an enormous memory
full of vital facts ordinarily unknown
to us, and uses two very
sophisticated and powerful languages
for computing that solve all sorts of
important problems that can't be
adequately dealt with in Intellectual
Basic, Emotional Basic, or Bodily/
Instinctive Basic. These languages are
Higher Emotional and Higher
Intellectual.

## Brain/Mind Bulletin
### News From the Leading Edge

Published by Marilyn Ferguson
P.O. Box 42211
Los Angeles, CA 90042
**$35.00**/Subscription, 1 year
(12 issues) in US, Canada. Send a
business-size SASE for a
complimentary issue.

## Thinking and Destiny
### Being the Science of Man

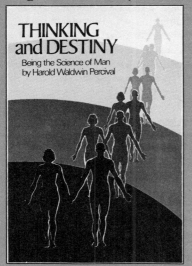

By Harold Waldwin Percival
1974/1020 pages
**$12.95**
$14.50 postpaid from:
The Word Foundation, Inc.
P.O. Box 18424
Dallas, TX 75218

*A mammoth encyclopedic edition of
Percival's wealth of information and
insights on the make-up of the human
being and consciousness. Complete with
30 pages of symbols, illustrations and
charts plus a comprehensive 400 subject
index.*

## Finding Him

Is it easier for children living today to learn how to play video games than it was for children a few years ago? Will adults of the next generation automatically be able to understand and operate computers faster than people learning how to operate them today? The answer to these questions, says Rupert Sheldrake, just might be *yes*. Just as the mechanistic approach fails to account for certain subatomic phenomena, Sheldrake believes it also leaves a number of disturbing and unsolved puzzles in his own field of biology. To explain these, Sheldrake proposes the existence of a new kind of field, a mysterious force that he says connects each individual with all other individuals in its species' past. Sheldrake further suggests that each species has a "group mind" that may provide a scientific basis for understanding certain psychic phenomena as well.

In the past decade quite a number of amazing coincidences in the laws of physics, coincidences that imply the universe was designed for the purpose of creating conscious entities capable of observing and understanding it, have come under scientific scrutiny, and currently there is an active debate about what these amazing coincidences mean. Some scientists believe that the human race, through billions of acts of observer-participancy traveling back through time, has actually had a major role in creating both the universe and the laws of physics. Others feel that the existence of such coincidences provides us with mathematical evidence of the existence of God.

- Michael Talbot
From Beyond the Quantum

## Beyond the Quantum
### God, Reality, Consciousness in the New Scientific Revolution

By Michael Talbot
1986/240 pages
**$9.95**
$11.45 postpaid from:
MacMillan Publishing Co.
MacMillan Distribution Ctr.
Front and Brown Sts.
Riverside, NJ 08075

*Age-old questions such as "What is reality?" and "What is consciousness?" are now being tackled by scientists, suggesting that the metaphysics of today may be the science of tomorrow. Beyond the Quantum explores the discourses and experiments that are creating an exciting new field.*

SUPPLEMENTARY MOTOR AREA

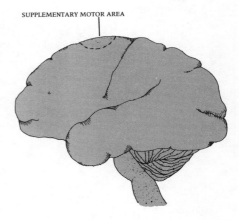

*The location of the supplementary motor area or SMA in the human brain. Neurophysiologist Sir John Eccles proposes that this is the site of interaction between mind and body.*

- Michael Talbot
From Beyond the Quantum

## Waking Up
*Overcoming the Obstacles to Human Potential*

By Charles T. Tart
1986/322 pages
**$17.95**
$19.70 postpaid from:
Shambhala Publications, Inc.
P.O. Box 308
Boston, MA 02117

*Waking Up is an original formulation of ancient teachings, many of them inspired by Gurdjieff, and clarified in the light of modern scientific understanding. With practical examples from daily life and simple in-the-moment techniques, it explores the process of moving from lifeless, mechanical habits of thought, perception, and behavior to the essential self of full human possibility.*

• • • •

The most important questions of our lives could be answered if the supercomputer worked on them in Higher Emotional and Higher Intellectual, drawing relevant knowledge from its vast data banks. But alas! We aren't connected. We try to solve these vital problems on our little personal computer, but we can't solve them in any of the

various Basic computer languages. Just as certain jokes in Hungarian may not translate into English without losing their essence, their funniness, certain things make sense only in Higher Emotional or Higher Intellectual. This is the kind of state-specific knowledge we talked about in Chapter 1.

- *Charles T. Tart*
*From* Waking Up

## What Is a Teacher?

A teacher is a person who is skilled at something you would like to learn. You respect his knowledge, are willing to pay or otherwise reimburse him for the time he takes instructing you, and, within reasonable limits, you will open yourself to unexpected and possibly painful methods of teaching if you are assured this is necessary. If you want to learn to speak a foreign language, for example, you select a teacher who speaks that language and has some credentials as a teacher.

You can learn enormous amounts from a teacher. How much more could you learn from a Teacher?

In reality, there may be Teachers, people who have so mastered themselves and attained such heights in the psychological/spiritual realms that they are indeed drastically different from ordinary people like you and me. Gurdjieff taught that there were indeed such people, those who were qualitatively as well as quantitatively beyond us, living at the third or fourth levels of consciousness. If you could be guided by such an awake person, have such a Teacher, you would be lucky indeed.

- *Charles T. Tart*
*From* Waking Up

## The Emergence of the Transpersonal Perspective

*We are what we think.*
*All that we are arises with our*
*    thoughts.*
*With our thoughts we make the*
*    world.*
*        - The Buddha*

In recent years it has become apparent that our traditional assumptions and thinking about who and what we are and what we can become may not have been generous enough. Evidence from a wide range of disciplines — psychological and nonpsychological, traditional and non-traditional, Western and non-Western — suggests that we may have underestimated the human

potential for psychological growth and well-being. Much of this new data is inconsistent with our traditional psychological models, and transpersonal psychology arose in response to these inconsistencies in an attempt to integrate suggestions of greater human capacity into the mainstream of the Western behavioral and mental health disciplines.

### Defining Transpersonal Psychology

Transpersonal psychology thus aims at expanding the field of psychological inquiry to include areas of human experience and behavior associated with extreme health and well-being. As such it

draws on both Western science and Eastern wisdom in an attempt to integrate knowledge from both traditions concerned with the fulfillment of human potentials.

The term *transpersonal* was adopted after considerable deliberation to reflect the reports of people practicing various consciousness disciplines who spoke of experiences of an extension of identity beyond both individuality and personality.

- *Edited by Roger N. Walsh*
*and Frances Vaughan*
*From* Beyond Ego

# Relationships
## Lovestyles

There's a pervasive myth in our society that there is a right and a wrong way to love. However, there's not much clarity about what the right way is. We all have difficulty with relationships, difficulty with love; therefore, we're liable to draw an uncomfortable conclusion: "Everyone knows how to love right except me." At times, when frustrated by a lover, you may indeed believe that everyone knows how to love "right" except you.

This attitude leads to blaming, defensiveness, accusing and a general shutdown of any loving feelings you *do* have. You feel helpless, betrayed, incompetent, angry and lost. You become defensive and withdraw from your beloved. It gets worse from there.

The truth is, there are as many ways of loving as there are people — and none of them is wrong. Some ways of loving do work better than others, but there are an infinite number of ways that work extremely well. This is good news, for it ends forever the fear that love can become boring, or that you can become bored with it. When looked at from this perspective, the object of relationships becomes to discover each other's way of loving (each other's lovestyle), to learn the style of loving your partner uses and to teach him/her the joys of your own style. In this way, each relationship adds to your options for love. Each new couple synthesizes a new lovestyle out of the two they bring together, one which is uniquely theirs and which can be restructured as their lifestyles change and grow.

> - Tina Tessina
> From Lovestyles

### Creative Listening
### How to Have Positive Relationships

By Dr. Christopher Hills
1985/60 minute cassette tape
**$9.95**
$11.95 postpaid from:
University of the Trees Press
Box 66
Boulder Creek, CA 95006

*A truly deep relationship that works requires communication. One of the most important components of the communications process in a relationship is listening effectively. This tape program is designed to help you work to become closer to your loved ones and avoid the pitfalls commonly found as a result of shallow communication. By listening creatively, it can help you to work to share more deeply, build trust, resolve differences and discover new levels of intimacy.*

### Love Styles
### How to Celebrate Your Differences

### The Lover Within
### Opening to Energy in Sexual Practice

By Julie Henderson
1987/114 pages
**$8.95**
$9.95 postpaid from:
Station Hill Press
Barrytown, NY 12507

Finally, salvation from sex-as-it's-supposed-to-be. Julie Henderson's delightful suggestions reach directly into the place of guarded habits where relationships wither and energy contracts to the point of pain. Her style is a relief: inviting, informal, confident, subtly ecstatic. Her exercises are energy excursions not technique mastery. Because of this her work feels very feminine. Its aim is awareness. Its effect is to charge. She encourages us, gives us heart for dissolving old, useless boundaries between and within us. I had the rare feeling when first reading it, that Julie Henderson's book could — dare I say it — change the world from the inside out.

> - Nor Hall
> A Review from The Love Within

By Tina B. Tessina
1987/276 pages
**$9.95**
$11.70 postpaid from:
Newcastle Publishing
Box 7589
Van Nuys, CA 91409

*Every relationship is unique. This book gives you the tools — by way of comparison and exercises — to identify your special differences and work with them to build a successful and satisfying relationship.*

## Two Hearts Are Better Than One
### A Handbook on Creating and Maintaining a Lasting and Loving Relationship

By Bob Mandel
1986/172 pages
**$8.95**
$9.95 postpaid from:
Celestial Arts
Box 7327
Berkeley, CA 94707

"I love you" are the three most powerful words I know.
- *Bob Mandel*
*From* Two Hearts Are Better Than One

## Soulmates

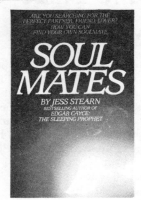

By Jess Stearn
1984/234 pages
**$3.95**
$5.45 postpaid from:
Bantam Books
Direct Response Dept.
414 E. Golf Rd.
Des Plaines, IL 60016

# Create-a-Mate

Many people read "how-to-do-it" books these days. There are books on how to fix your car, how to build your house, how to run a small business — to mention a few. But when it comes to the business of constructing a perfect loving relationship, people seem to be much more skeptical that such a thing can be designed.

Yet you have always designed your relationships, whether you know it or not. Your thoughts are creative, and your thoughts about relationships, based largely on conclusions you made watching your parents and siblings relate to each other and to you, become unconscious patterns that produce repetitive, compulsive behavior in your relationships. That is why you find yourself in similar situations, feeling similar feelings, with different people. You unconsciously project what is unresolved within your own mind onto your partner in any relationship. This is why people who insist upon "flowing with it," rather than being conscious of it, are often giving their unconscious programming a chance to have a field day.

Of course your thoughts are creative. If you want to stand up, you must think about it on some level. If you want to build a house, you must conceive of it first, plan it on paper. Moreover, if your conception is faulty, how can its realization be anything but flawed. It's the same with relationships. If your whole idea of what you want, expect, or think you deserve is limited, then your resulting relationship is bound to be full of shortcomings. The perfect execution of a misconceived plan is doomed to failure.

Conscious conception is an essential first step in creating a conscious relationship! You've *fallen* in love enough! It's time to stop falling, stop expecting your Knight in Shining Armor to come along, swoop you up, and rescue you from the cold, cruel world. It's time to stop looking for a parental surrogate, who will allow you to be the child you always wanted to be, who will take care of you, provide for you, and carry you through life so you never have to stand on your own two feet. It's time to stop *falling*. It's time for Romantic Realism.

*Bob Mandel*
*From* Two Hearts Are Better Than One

# How to Find A Soulmate

Because of my interest in the metaphysical I was besieged by those who thought I might have greater knowledge of the properties of the soul — and soulmates.

The questions put to me were naturally related to the individual interest:
- Firstly, what is a soulmate?
- How do you recognize him or her?
- Can one program a soulmate?
- How and why does it transcend any other human connection?
- Why is so much of it happening now?

This instinctual yearning for a soulmate was deep and sometimes obsessive, transcending any and all other relationships. The realization of love's dream often became its own justification, with normal prudence abandoned and convention ignored.

In the final analysis, the greatest authorities were the principals in this ongoing saga of love. This is their story, delving into the nature of a love that is as inevitable as it is deep and heartfelt, recasting lives in a moment of truth as it brought a depth and breadth of understanding they had never before achieved.
- *Jess Stearn*
*From* Soulmates

**Friends and Lovers**
*How to Create the*
*Relationships You Want*

By Marc Allen
1985/128 pages
**$6.95**
$7.45 postpaid from:
Good Living Catalog
Box 13257
Northgate Station
San Rafael, CA 94913

**A Conscious Person's**
**Guide to Relationships**

By Ken Keyes, Jr.
1979/145 pages
**$5.50**
$6.75 postpaid from:
Cornucopia Books
790 Commercial Avenue
Coos Bay, OR 97420

# Are Your Core Beliefs Getting in the Way of Your Relationship?

It's not always easy to discover core beliefs and express them in a simple, brief sentence that gets to the heart of the problems we're creating for ourselves. Core beliefs can be elusive, especially for those of us who tend to intellectualize a great deal — the "rampant rational mind" type — or for those who tend to become engulfed in overwhelming emotions — the "rampant emotional" type. While there is certainly nothing wrong with either our rational minds or our emotions, the two need to be balanced, in harmony. When one quality begins to dominate the other, we lose touch with our natural, innate clarity, and create far more problems for ourselves than necessary.

When we are emotionally upset, it is especially difficult for us to identify the core belief that is operating. We have developed a process, called the "core belief process," which is especially designed to identify these beliefs in the midst of an emotional problem, or following an emotional event that remains unresolved.

The process can be done either with a partner or alone. If done with a partner, one of you should ask the questions while the other answers, taking just a few minutes for each question. If you do it alone, you can write your answers to each question, or just answer them silently to yourself, or speak into a tape recorder and replay the tape afterwards.

To begin, sit silently for a moment, eyes closed.

Take a deep breath, and relax as you exhale. Then think of the particular situation, problem, or area of your life you want to improve.

Now proceed through the following steps:

1. Describe the nature of the problem, situation, or area of your life you want to work on. Take about three or four minutes to talk about it generally.

2. What emotions are you feeling? Name the specific emotion, i.e., fear, sadness, anger, guilt. (Do not describe the thoughts you are having about it, at this point.)

3. What physical sensations are you feeling?

4. What are you thinking about it? (What "conditioning" or "programming" can you identify? What negative thoughts, fears, or worries are you having?) Take a few minutes to describe your thoughts.

5. What is the worst thing that could happen in this situation? (What is your greatest fear?) If that happened, then what would be the worst thing that could happen? What if that happened? Then what would be the very worst thing that could possibly happen?

6. What is the best that could possibly happen? Describe the way you would ideally like it to be, your "ideal scene" for this area of your life.

7. What fear or negative belief is keeping you from creating what you want in this situation? Once you have explored this question, write your negative belief in one sentence, as simply and precisely as you can. If you have more than one, write down each of them.

8. Create an affirmation to counteract and correct the negative belief.

That's the entire core belief process. I've seen it have a very profound, positive effect on a great many people, including myself. All you need is the willingness to be honest with yourself. Your spontaneous answers to these questions may surprise you. After doing the affirmations, a lot of people, myself included, have felt a wave of relief, a feeling that can only be described as feeling a lot *lighter*. It is as if we were carrying around an emotional weight on our shoulders, which in many cases we weren't even fully aware of, and we've suddenly let it go. The result can be exhilarating. Try it and see.
- *Marc Allen*
*From* Friends and Lovers

## Birth & Relationships
### How Birth Affects Your Relationships

By Sondra Ray & Bob Mandel
1987/164 pages
**$8.95**
$9.95 postpaid from:
Celestial Arts
Box 7327
Berkeley, CA 94707

# How a Cesarian Procedure Can Affect You in Later Life

In a sense, "cesarians" have it easier. They don't have to plow through the birth canal to make it; nor do they have to be as guilty about causing their mothers pain. A simple incision does the trick. And nowadays, a c-section is a minor surgical procedure which makes birth quicker and easier for mother, doctor, and child.

In a sense!

The cesarian child, however, often suffers from interruption syndrome since his original direction in life was rudely interrupted by the obstetrician. (Nowadays, there is a proliferation of cesarians, often simply to please the doctor, fit his schedule, his golf game, whatever.)

He will often grow into a headstrong adult who insists on doing things his own way, often at his own expense. At the same time, the more he insists on going his own way in life, the more likely he is to attract unforeseen interruptions

blocking his path. He seems to want to make the journey through the birth canal he never made in the first place. He knows he knows how to do it, if only everyone else would leave him alone!

But they never do. People get in the way. Often, when cesarians are being rebirthed, they will create constant interruptions to upset themselves, evoking the confusion they experienced when coming out. A cesarian's relationships tend to be characterized by conflicts of will, changes of heart and mind, and constant disruptions. We've known several cesarian couples, and usually they are looking for someone outside the relationship to tell them which way to go in life, then resenting it and doing the opposite. If one partner is cesarian and the other is not, the latter can be set up to be the obstetrician — which happens in many relationships.

Support can be a major issue for cesarians. On the one hand, they want it desperately; on the other hand, they mistrust it and see all support as manipulation, interference, and opposition.

"I want to do it my way!" is the cry of the cesarian, at the same time thinking, "I better get some help or I'll never get out of this." The cesarian's double bind produces confusion at every crossroad of life. Let him drive a car, give him clear directions, and the journey will become a major obstacle course. You say "Turn left," and he'll turn right. You can bet on it. You say "North," and he'll go south.

Cesarians crave physical affection. Because they never received the initial massage the walls of the birth canal provide, they need a lot of extra hugging, holding, and cuddling as children. If they don't get it as children, they may still need what seems like an excess of caressing as adults.

Cesarians do have the potential for seeing the easy way out. When they relax into this knowledge, they are a vast storehouse for shortcuts in life. Once they get over their guilt for not doing it the hard way in the first place, they can enjoy the innocence of their own intuitive know-how. They can save us all a lot of time and energy.

*- Sondra Ray & Bob Mandel*
*From* Birth & Relationships

## Loving Relationships

By Sondra Ray
1980/174 pages
**$6.95**
$7.95 postpaid from:
Celestial Arts
Box 7327
Berkeley, CA 94707

*How to attract your ideal mate.*
*How to create the relationship the way you want*
*How to clear blocks that keep you from having a perfect relationship*
*How to prevent arguments and have good communications*
*How to use your relationship for enlightenment*
*How to prevent and handle jealousy*
*How to take out the difficulty in your relationship and have fun instead*
*How to have a relationship last as long as you want*
*How to create a "New Age" spiritual, exciting relationship*

### When you feel unloved, start loving yourself and then go out and love someone.

When you feel unappreciated start appreciating yourself and
 then go out and appreciate someone.
When you feel unacknowledged, start acknowledging yourself and
 then go out and acknowledge someone.
When you feel untouched, start touching yourself and
 then go out and touch someone.

*- Sondra Ray*
*From* Loving Relationships

# Rebirthing
# What is Rebirthing?

The purpose of rebirthing is to remember and re-experience one's birth; to relive physiologically, psychologically, and spiritually the moment of one's first breath and release the trauma of it. The process begins the transformation of the subconscious impression of birth from one of primal pain to one of pleasure. The effects on life are immediate. Negative energy patterns held in the mind and body start to dissolve. "Youthing" replaces aging and life becomes more fun. It is learning how to fill the physical body with divine energy on a practical daily basis.

Rebirthing is about 99 percent pleasurable. Some people call it fun! The one percent of rebirthing that is not enjoyable is due to your unwillingness to give up your misery. All discomfort in conjunction with rebirthing comes from holding on to negativity, misery or pain. The perfect divine energy that moves in your mind and body during rebirthing is your own pure life force cleaning the dirt from your soul and body. This energy frees you from all harm by making you aware of how you hurt yourself everyday (if you do) so that you can stop.

This perfect energy that flows into your body as a tingling sensation is God's healing power; the tingling or vibrating sensation is the cleansing action of God's love on the psychic "dirt" in your body and aura. God's energy does enter your body from the center of your cells. Rebirthing is an experience of opening your breath so that a special flow of spiritual energy washes your mind and body with a divine bath. This spiritual bath has many sensations. Some people feel fear or sadness or pain in the process of being freed from their unpleasantness, misery and sickness. But most people let go of their fear right from the beginning and love rebirthing.

It is impossible adequately to describe rebirthing. People usually tell us that "It is far more wonderful than anything you said." Obviously, God's energy can heal all human problems. Rebirthing is the science

of letting in God's energy, wisdom, and love. Rebirthing has been called an intuitive science, but all words are helpless and crude in the middle of the experience.

Rebirthing is a spiritual gift! In itself it is perfect and harmless. However, when you apply perfect spiritual energy to a mind that has been conditioned to know fear and pain and all kinds of negative things, then the conditioning is exposed and you can let go of it. You can let go of human misery to be a free and natural person. Your human personality can be filled with serenity, joy, health and spiritual wisdom. Rebirthing actually delivers more of these things than we can possibly promise. The reality of them is far more glorious than the words. We have not been able to say anything too good about rebirthing

because rebirthing, as we experience it, is God's power in your human form. Only your own personal divine goodness can feel it and know it. It has been called "a biological experience of religion."

To get the most out of a rebirthing experience, it is valuable to do it with a loving person who has been trained in the wisdom of how these spiritual energies work. It is also necesssary to raise the quality of your thoughts as you experience rebirthing, so that your mind is in harmony with your perfect divine energy. The more efficiently you raise your thoughts, the faster healings take place.

*- Leonard Orr and
Sondra Ray
From Rebirthing in the
New Age*

## Rebirthing in the New Age

By Leonard Orr and Sondra Ray
1983/286 pages
**$9.95**
$10.95 postpaid from:
Celestial Arts
Box 7327
Berkeley, CA 94707

*If you want a basic explanation of the Rebirthing process, this book by two of the founders of the Rebirthing movement is an excellent guide.*

## Loving Relationships Training (LRT)
Sondra Ray and Bob Mandel
145 West 87th St.
New York, NY 10024
212-799-7323

*This is the international headquarters for Rebirthing training by the LRT. Contact them for Rebirthers in your area.*

## Associated Integrative Rebirthers
1325 Springfield Pike
Cincinnati, OH 45215
800-641-4645, ext. 232

*This Association of Rebirthers has a toll-free number so you can find a professional in your area.*

## Open Heart Therapy

By Bob Mandel
1984/163 pages
**$7.95**
$8.95 postpaid from:
Celestial Arts
Box 7327
Berkeley, CA 94707

---

# What Is Open Heart Therapy?

This is a self-help book. In addition to the philosophy and psychology of love presented here, there are numerous "implants" and "by-passes" for you to do. The more you do your homework, the more these love lessons will work for you.

An "implant" is really a seed of transformation — a specific positive attitude that you plant in your subconscious mind through repetition in order to de-program negative patterns and replace them with positive ones. The result, if used properly, is a basic attitudinal change which affects your entire life. Sometimes implants are called *affirmations*.

A "by-pass" is an operation you perform on your own mind. It is a simple, safe structure in which you can locate thoughts, feelings and "stuck" points for the purpose of overcoming them. A by-pass can also be used for positive re-enforcement. While there are no panaceas prescribed in this book, there are shortcuts to an easier, happier life. A bypass is a way to cut your mind off at the pass — before it ambushes you later on!

*- Bob Mandel*
*From* Open Heart Therapy

# Rebirthing Supports Your Autonomy and Your Taking Responsibility

You cannot expect to get any kind of good results in life without first taking full responsibility for producing them. This is especially true of Rebirthing, because it is the nature of the Rebirthing process that *you* produce 100% of whatever results you get from doing it; Rebirthers can only teach you and guide you. Expecting your Rebirther to produce a result for you is like taking golf lessons and then expecting the golf professional to hit all your shots for you. Rebirthing itself is a tool that you can use to produce results for yourself. Expecting Rebirthing itself to produce results for you is like buying an ax and expecting the ax to chop your wood for you. Once you learn to Rebirth yourself you can produce the results for yourself whenever and wherever you choose; you do not become dependent on anyone, and you do not become dependent on the technique, either.

*- Jim Leonard*
*From* Rebirthing

## Rebirthing
*The Science of Enjoying All of Your Life*

By Jim Leonard
and Phil Laut
1983/290 pages
**$8.95**
$10.95 postpaid from:
Trinity Publications
Box 15608
Cincinnati, OH 45215

### How the Mind Works

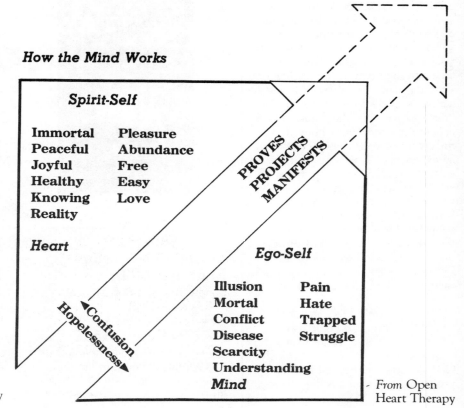

*- From Open Heart Therapy*

# Brain/Mind Technology

# Neuro-Linguistic Programming (NLP)

How do people who are acknowledged masters in communicating and effecting changes in others achieve their excellence? It was in pursuit of the answers to this question that NLP began because often such people cannot describe or teach how they do what they do so well.

In the early 1970's Dr. Richard Bandler and Dr. John Grinder through careful study of acknowledged masters of communication and change such as Drs. Milton Erickson, Virginia Satir, Gregory Bateson, and Fritz Perls, discovered what made these individuals so effective and in the process developed the field of Neuro-Linguistic Programming.

NLP enables the essential elements of excellence in any skill, "the difference that makes the difference," to be more easily discerned and organized and as a result made more teachable to others.

NLP also provides very effective techniques for achieving rapport with anyone more easily and for making the use of language and sensory acuity more effective in gathering information and establishing clear goals.

Additionally there is a growing body of patterns for accomplishing specific desired changes in emotions, beliefs, thinking strategies, and behavior. In accomplishing all of this NLP fosters an attitude of respectful fascination for the unique way in which each person creates his or her own experience.

NLP is recognized as a leading edge in communication and numerous books, papers and articles have been published about the field.

As Dr. Richard Bandler has said, "NLP teaches people to run their own brains instead of letting their brains run them." NLP is about understanding how your mind works, then getting into the driver's seat to "drive your own bus." And that means becoming more and more the resourceful person that each of us can be.

*- From the New England Institute of NLP*

### New England Institute of NLP
RFD 3, Pratt Corner Rd.
Amherst, MA 01002
413-259-1248

*NEINLP is dedicated to promoting quality certification training in NLP, Ericksonian Hypnosis and workshops all over the Northeast.*

## Ericksonian Hypnosis

Everyone has had the experience of driving in a car and having been so deep in thought that you missed the street or exit you were looking for.

During that time of concentration you were actually experiencing a light trance. Actually anytime you start to concentrate internally or focus inwards you change your level of consciousness. So, very naturally you go in and out of various levels of consciousness throughout every day. Hypnosis is the skilled and directed use of this naturally occurring state.

The person most responsible for advancing the field of hypnosis was Dr. Milton H. Erickson. This extraordinary person showed us how to use hypnosis to better meet

therapeutic goals. He taught us that we can communicate with the whole person by utilizing conscious and unconscious levels. Dr. Erickson also taught us how to utilize and bypass client resistance by embedding therapeutic interventions in seemingly casual conversation.

Perhaps most importantly he taught us that each person is an individual and psychotherapy should be more compatible with the way each person structures his or her own experience.

His legacy is a wealth of vital information for influencing behavior and for increasing your skills to better meet therapeutic goals.

*- From the New England Institute of NLP*

### Milton Erickson Foundation
3606 N 24th St.
Phoenix, AZ 85016
602-956-6196

*The Milton Erickson Foundation publishes a newsletter devoted to training and practices relating to Ericksonian Hypnotherapy.*

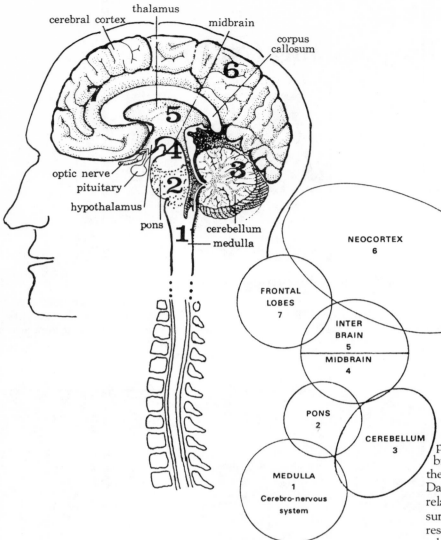

cerebral cortex — thalamus — midbrain — corpus callosum

7
6
5
4
3
2
1

optic nerve
pituitary
hypothalamus
pons
cerebellum
medulla

NEOCORTEX
6

FRONTAL
LOBES
7

INTER
BRAIN
5

MIDBRAIN
4

PONS
2

CEREBELLUM
3

MEDULLA
1
Cerebro-nervous
system

# Evolution of the Seven Brains

Since evolution has developed the brain not as a series of separate computers but with a wholistic purpose, the relationship between the brains is even more important than their separate specialized functions. Darwin's "survival of the fittest" relates mainly to the drive for survival in the first brain. The research of behavioral psychologists relates mainly to the second brain. Medical science focuses on the different brain lobes, and scientists in general study only the first three or four brains. Science knows very little about the fifth, sixth and seventh brains, yet these can be known by anyone willing to actually *use* them. Modern science may even deny the existence of more than four brains, but the science of tomorrow will confirm seven different levels of brain function which you can confirm by your own direct experience and observation right now. You don't need four years of study and a degree to know that doctors get just as sick as ordinary people do and that scientists have all the emotional hang-ups and egotism of ordinary people. The higher brain levels explain why.

        *- Dr. Christopher Hills*
        *From* How to Recharge
        Your Brain

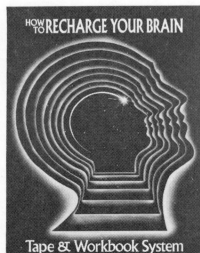

## How to Recharge Your Brain

By Dr. Christopher Hills
1984/60-minute cassette tape,
34-page workbook
**$14.95**
$16.95 postpaid from:
University of the Trees Press
P.O. Box 66
Boulder Creek, CA 95006

*Based on Dr. Christopher Hills 20 years of brain research,* How to Recharge Your Brain *presents a total system enabling you to develop your power to trigger brain hormones and experience heightened awareness of your psychic and spiritual potentials.*

    *- From* How To Recharge
    Your Brain

 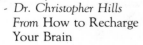

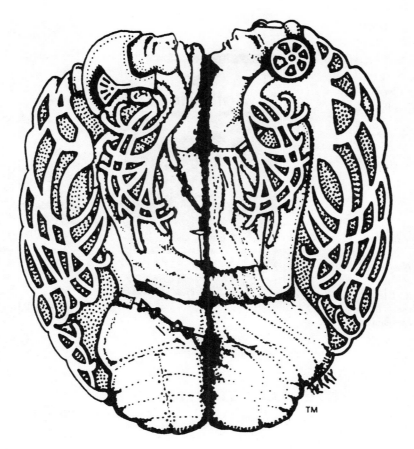

**Left Brain**
Linear
Mechanical
Analytical
Logical
Routine Memory
Verbal

**Right Brain**
Receiving
Creative
Meditative
Artistic
Spatial
Intuitive

™

## The John-David Learning Institute

2443 Impala Dr.
Carlsbad, CA 92008
619-931-0456

*John-David's training is based on left and right brain integration. The benefits include better personal organization, total concentration, increased reading speed and information retention and 90% recall of any previous event, book or other experience. Their intensives last from five to twelve days. They also have brain/mind and self-healing tapes.*

*Your Brain's Fitness Center™...*
# Brain/Mind Salons®

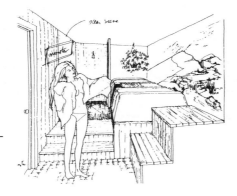

**FLOTATION TANKS** Place yourself inside a wonderful water chamber designed to free you of all outside distraction. You pleasantly float on 10 inches of water containing 800 lbs of epsom salts, the water is heated to skin temperature. Within minutes your left brain relaxes, you enter alpha or even theta brain wave patterns. You may remain in total silence to allow your brain to free associate, or our technicians will channel sound through underwater speakers or watch a video tape on memory, eliminating self-sabotage, ultra-intelligence, etc...all exclusively designed by the Institute and John-David.

**BRAIN SOUND ROOMS** Here a business person can dash over from the office for a brain/mind tuneup on subjects of concentration, peak performance, psychoimmunology, eliminating self-sabotage, memory improvement, reading rapidly, super sportspsychology, stop smoking, weightloss, better office relations or leadership. One merely sits inside a chair engineered to place sound back onto the body, numerous speakers surround the body. One can also watch a video geared to their interest: sports, memory, self-esteem. Both audio and video tapes are exclusively designed by the Institute and available no where else in the world.

**BRAIN/MIND INTENSIVES** Imagine yourself very slowly revolving on a platform immersed in sound coming from 32 specially engineered sound speakers hung from a geodesic dome. The sounds are the remarkable neuroscience breakthrough 'sound patterns' recently discovered by John-David. These sounds can speak to pre-designated areas of your brain, mind and body. A sound techncian, a graduate of the Institute and personally trained by John-David, directs and mixes these psycho-acoustical discoveries.

## Use Both Sides of Your Brain
*New Techniques to Help You Read Efficiently, Study Effectively, Solve Problems and Think Creatively*

By Tony Buzan
1983/156 pages
**$6.95**
$8.45 postpaid from:
E.P. Dutton, Inc.
2 Park Ave., 17th Fl.
New York, NY 10016

*This is a classic bestseller that gives step-by-step exercises to help you harness the long-neglected powers of the right side of your brain and use more of the left side. The integration of left/right brain is said to increase your brain power and mental skills immensely.*

# Advanced Reading Techniques

Apart from the general advice given above, some readers may be able to benefit from the following information which is usually practiced in conjunction with a qualified instructor:

**Visual aid techniques:** When children learn how to read they often point with their fingers to the words they are reading. We have traditionally regarded this as a fault and have told them to take their fingers off the page. It is now realized that it is we and not the children who are at fault. Instead of insisting that they remove their fingers we should ask them to move their fingers faster. It is obvious that the hand does not slow down the eye, and the added values that the aid gives in establishing a smooth rhythmical habit are immeasurable.

To observe the difference between unaided and aided eye movement, ask a friend to imagine a large circle about one foot in front of him, and then ask him to look slowly and carefully around the circumference. Rather than moving in a perfect circle, his eyes will follow a pattern more resembling an arthritic rectangle.

Next trace a circle in the air with your finger asking your friend to follow the tip of your finger as you move smoothly around the circumference. You will observe that the eyes will follow almost perfectly and will trace a circle similar to that shown below.

This simple experiment also indicates what an enormous improvement in performance there can be if a person is given the basic information about the physical function of the eye and brain. In many instances no long training or arduous practicing is necessary. The results, as in this case, are immediate.

The reader is not restricted to the use of his forefinger as a visual aid, and can use to advantage a pen or a pencil, as many naturally efficient readers do. At first the visual aid will make the reading speed look slow. This is because, as mentioned earlier, we all imagine that we read a lot faster than we actually do. But the aided reading speed will actually be faster.

- Tony Buzan
From Use Both Sides of Your Brain

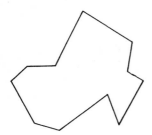

**Pattern showing unaided eye movement attempting to move around the circumference of a circle.**

**Pattern showing aided eye movement around the circumference of a circle.**

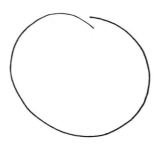

# Inspiration

## Seeds of Light
### Inspirations from My Higher Self

By Peter Rengel
1987/202 pages
**$9.95**
$11.45 postpaid from:
H. J. Kramer, Inc.
P.O. Box 1082
Tiburon, CA 94920

*A collection of pure and inspired poems created by the author during several weeks spent secluded in communication with his higher self.*

*Arranged in a dictionary format of 100 entries, each poem is a gem of enlightenment on its specific topic. Transcends poetry, even for traditional poetry-haters.*

## Meditation

Real Meditation has no techniques
  Because your mind would only
    Become attached to them.
There are no guided fantasies
  Because they only perpetuate
    imagination.
There are no solutions
  Because there are no problems.
There are no answers
  Because they make questions
    seem real.
There is only you
  Here
    In this moment
      With an opportunity to open
      your Heart
        And find inner Silence
        Where Love and
        Nurturance
          Await you.

       *- Peter Rengel*
       *From Seeds of Light*

## Choice

Your most profound choice
  Each new moment in time
    Is whether you are
    In your head
      Thinking
        Or in your Heart
        Being.

      *- Peter Rengel*
      *From Seeds of Light*

## Shakti-Hymns to Divine Mother

By Sita Stuhlmiller
1986/60-minute cassette
**$8.98**
$10.05 postpaid from:
Truth Consciousness
Gold Hill
Salina Star Rte.
Boulder, CO 80302

*Recorded live, this tape is one in a series of over 300 satsangs and chants to the Divine. Solo and group singing is accompanied by guitar, tabla, piano and tamboura.*

## Hinds' Feet on High Places
### An Allegory

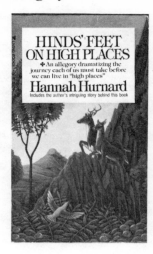

By Hannah Hurnard
1986/316 pages
**$3.95**
$4.95 postpaid from:
Living Books
Tyndale House Publishers, Inc.
P.O. Box 80
Wheaton, IL 60189

*A beautiful allegory dramatizing the yearning of God's children to be led to new heights of love, joy and victory.*

The Lord God is my strength, and he will make my feet like hinds' feet, and he will make me walk upon mine high places.
    - Habakkuk 3:19

She began to realize that, cowardly though she was, there was something in her which responded with a surge of excitement to the tests and difficulties of the way better than to easier and duller circumstances. It was true that fear sent a dreadful shuddering thrill through her, but nevertheless it was a thrill, and she found herself realizing with astonishment that even the dizzy precipice had been more to her liking than this dreary plodding on and on through the bewildering mist. In some way the dangers of the storm had stimulated her; now there was nothing but tameness, just a trudge, trudge forward, day after day, able to see nothing except for white, clinging mist which hung about the mountains without a gleam of sunshine breaking through.
    - Hannah Hurnard
      From Hinds' Feet on
      High Places

## Keepers of the Fire
### Journey to the Tree of Life

Story & paintings by
Eagle Walking Turtle
1987/128 pages
**$16.95**
$18.95 postpaid from:
Bear & Company, Inc.
P.O. Drawer 2860
Santa Fe, NM 87504-2860

*Inspired by the vision of Black Elk,
an Oglala Sioux medicine man,
Keepers of the Fire depicts the
medicine way on how to achieve peace,
harmony, and the healing and cleansing
of ourselves and the earth.*

*The artwork is inspirational and
archetypal.*

Blue Spotted Horse began to tell
of my vision and the bush people
understood and gave thanks to the
Great Mystery, the creator of all
creatures, and to our Earth Mother,
from whom they received all things
for living. They built four fires
between their sacred stones and it
was good, it was very, very good.

- *Eagle Walking Turtle*
  *From Retreat Into Eternity*

## The Day with Yoga

By Elizabeth Haich
1983/84 pages
**$4.95**
$6.95 postpaid from:
Aurora Press
P.O. Box 573
Santa Fe, NM 87504

*This is Elizabeth Haich's personal
collection of meditation quotes. Each has
been carefully selected to inspire and
attune us to the vibration of the day and
to release a deeper level of harmony and
inner peace within our lives.*

**SUNDAY**
*The Power of the Sun*
The light of your true being shines
from your center, illuminates your
whole body, just as the sun
illuminates the whole world from the
center of the solar system.
- **Maharishi**

**MONDAY**
*The Power of the Moon*
Truly blessed is the man to whom
woman is the representative of God's
motherhood.
- **Vivekananda**

**TUESDAY**
*The Power of Mars*
If your goal is great and your
resources small, act nevertheless.
Only through action will your
resources grow.
- **Aurobindo**

**WEDNESDAY**
*The Power of Mercury*
I am a born pupil. Everything that
exists is my master. I learn from
everything!
- **Keshab**

**THURSDAY**
*The Power of Jupiter*
Every sect has its truth, and every
truth has its sect.
- **China**

**FRIDAY**
*The Power of Venus*
Expansion means life, love is
expansion. Love is therefore the only
law of life. He who loves, lives.
- **Vivekananda**

**SATURDAY**
*The Power of Saturn*
Repayment for good and evil is
like the shadow that follows the
body.
- **China**

- *Collected by
  Elisabeth Haich
  From A Day With Yoga*

## Retreat into Eternity
### An Upanishad Book of Aphorisms

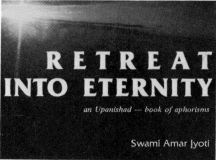

That's the way it should be
— your feet on earth,
your consciousness
with your Lord.

- *Swami Amar Jyoti*
  *From Keepers of the Fire*

By Swami Amar Jyoti
1981/128 pages
**$12.95**
$14.45 postpaid from:
Truth Consciousness
Gold Hill
Salina Star Rt.
Boulder, CO 80302

*An Upanishad is a Sanskrit literary
word meaning "sitting near (the master)
to listen." Retreat into Eternity is a
rich selection of thoughtful aphorisms
from the culture of Ancient India.
Complemented by beautiful and
inspiring photography.*

God has made us free. Be sure.

- *Swami Amar Jyoti*
  *From Retreat into Eternity*

# Creativity

## Higher Creativity
### *Liberating the Unconscious for Breakthrough Insights*

By Willis Harman, Ph.D.
and Howard Rheingold
1984/236 pages
**$8.95**
$11.35 postpaid from:
Jeremy P. Tarcher, Inc.
9110 Sunset Blvd.
Los Angeles, CA 90069

*A fascinating examination of the creative breakthrough experience in daily life, dreamwork, in metaphysical experience and in history. The authors suggest that we all are endowed with the capacity for insightful genius, and describes a simple sequence for triggering our own insightful mechanisms.*

## Writing the Natural Way

By Gabriele Lusser Rico
1983/286 pages
**$10.95**
$13.35 postpaid from:
Jeremy P. Tarcher, Inc.
9110 Sunset Blvd.
Los Angeles, CA 90069

*Expression and communication are vital to our everyday existence. This book presents innovative techniques and ideas for making our communications truly creative.*

## Writing the Natural Way Audio Tape

By Gabriele Lusser Rico
1987/60-minute cassette tape with interactive 32-page booklet
**$9.95**
$12.35 postpaid from:
Audio Renaissance Tapes, Inc.
9110 Sunset Blvd.
Suite 240
Los Angeles, CA 90069

*A "how-to" book of creative writing that can be put to work in less than an hour. A great companion to the original book.*

# Creative Clustering

To create a cluster, you begin with a nucleus word, circled, on a fresh page. Now you simply let go and begin to flow with any current of connections that come into your head. Write these down rapidly, each in its own circle, radiating outward from the center in any direction they want to go. Connect each new word or phrase with a line to the preceding circle. When something new and different strikes you, begin again at the central nucleus and radiate outward until those associations are exhausted.

The technique of clustering gives you access to the patterns and associations of your Design mind. It provides you with essentially two things: *choices* from which to formulate and develop your thought, and a *focus* meaningful enough to impel you to write. Facts or words in isolation are meaningless until they are brought into relationship by a consciousness that can create relationships. A word, filtered through the sieve of your unique consciousness, allows you to create something from nothing through the medium of words, and here you have the beginning of reawakening your natural writing powers.

> - *Gabriele Lusser Rico*
> *From* Writing the
> Natural Way

## An Experiment In Leisure

By Joanna Field
1980/240 pages
**$7.95**
$10.35 postpaid from:
Jeremy P. Tarcher, Inc.
9110 Sunset Blvd.
Los Angeles, CA 90069

## Drawing on the Right Side of the Brain

By Betty Edwards
1979/208 pages
**$9.95**
$12.35 postpaid from:
Jeremy P. Tarcher, Inc.
9110 Sunset Blvd.
Los Angeles, CA 90069

*This book is based on learning to acquire the artist's mode of seeing - from the right-hemisphere of the brain. The author's insights and techniques offer avenues for opening up the "creative gaze" which unlocks the doors to creativity in all aspects of life.*

# Seeing What You Believe

Most beginning drawing students have problems with proportion: parts of forms are drawn too large or too small in relation to other parts or to the whole form. The reason seems to be that most of us tend to see parts of a form hierarchically. The parts that are *important* (that is, provide a lot of information), or the

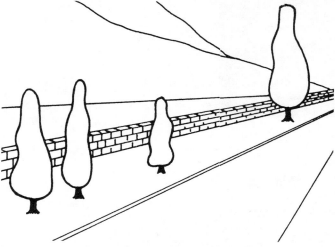

parts that we *decide are larger, or the parts that we think should be* larger, we *see* as larger than they actually are. Conversely, parts that are unimportant, or that we *decide* are smaller, or that we think *should be* smaller, we *see* as being smaller than they actually are.

Let me give you a couple of examples of this perceptual error. Above is a diagrammatic landscape with four trees. The tree at the far right appears to be the largest of the four. But that tree is *exactly* the same size as the tree at the far left. Lay a pencil alongside the two trees to measure and test the validity of that statement. Even after measuring and proving to yourself that the two trees are the same size, however, you will probably find that the tree on the right will still *look* larger.

The reason for this misperception of proportionate size probably derives from our past knowledge and experience of the effect of distance on the apparent size of forms; given two objects of the same size, one nearby and one at a distance away, the distant object will appear to be smaller. This makes sense, and we don't quarrel with the concept. But coming back to the drawing, even

after we have measured the two trees and have determined with irrefutable evidence that they are the same size, *we still wrongly see the right-hand tree as being larger than the left.* This is overdoing it! And this is precisely the kind of overdoing — of overlaying memorized verbal concepts onto visual perceptions —

that causes problems with proportion for beginning drawing students.

On the other hand, if you turn this book upside down and view the landscape drawing in the inverted orientation that the left brain rejects, thus activating your R-mode, you will find that you can more easily see that the two trees are the same size. *The same visual information triggers a different response.* The right brain, apparently less influenced by the verbal concept of diminishing size in distant forms, sees proportion correctly.

> *- Betty Edwards*
> *From* Drawing on the
> Right Side of the Brain

# Schools/Institutes/Retreats

The following schools and institutes are all directed toward helping people reach their highest potential. Each one will send you information about their programs upon request.

## Association for Humanistic Psychology

325 Ninth St.
San Francisco, CA 94103
415-626-2375

AHP provides publications, conferences, networking, and a community building to fost the "third force" — the work of humanistic psychologists like Maslow, Rogers and May. They publish a newsletter and The Journal of Humanistic Psychology.

## Association for Research and Enlightenment (A.R.E.)

Box 595
Virginia Beach, VA 23451
804-428-3588

This is the internationally respected organization founded by Edgar Cayce. His over 14,000 readings are stored here. They offer members a variety of services, publications and research facilities, conferences, workshops, and retreats.

## Astara

Box 5003
Upland, CA 91785

An organization that bases its teachings on the ancient mysteries. They offer correspondence courses for self-help and personal understanding.

## California Institute of Integral Studies

755 Ashbury St.
San Francisco, CA 94117
415-753-6110

This school offers advanced degrees in philosophy, psychology, and anthropology. Their educational philosophy combines eastern and western thought and recognition of the individual as a body-mind-spirit continuum.

## Camp Lenox

Route 8
Lee, MA 01238
413-243-2223

Summer programs are offered in a variety of New Age disciplines including nutrition, self-development, childrens' programs, music, and dance.

## Institute for Biogenetics and Gestalt

1307 University Ave.
Berkeley, CA 94702
415-849-0101

Activities of the Institute include training professionals, individual and group psychotherapy, and residential workshops. They use psychotherapeutic approaches incorporating bioenergetics, Gestalt therapy and Reichian therapy that "listen to the inner music of the body leading to depths and mysteries of our existence and more conscious and expressive living."

## Institute for Transpersonal Psychology

250 Oak Grove Avenue
Menlo Park, CA 94025
415-326-1960

The ITP offers graduate level education and research in transpersonal psychology — the investigation of evolution of consciousness and experiences that lie beyond the personal. Disciplines include dream analysis, meditation, spiritual psychologies, accupressure and transpersonal theory.

## Institute of Noetic Sciences

475 Gate Five Rd., Suite 300
Sausalito, CA 94965
415-331-5650

The INS was founded in 1973 by Edgar D. Mitchell, an Apollo 14 astronaut, to support research and education on human consciousness. They publish a newsletter (that now incorporates Charles Tart's Open Mind) and sponsor travel programs, lectures, and research intended to broaden knowledge of the nature and potentials of the mind and consciousness.

## Interface

552 Main St.
Watertown, MA 02172
617-924-1100

Interface is a holistic education center offering a wide variety of year-round educational and experiential events including healing, personal growth, consciousness issues, planetary vision and more. The emphasis is on integration of body, mind and spirit.

## Choices

Box 2238
Boulder, CO 80306
303-442-0566

Choices offers nationwide workshops and seminars nationally that help people discover what they really want and how to make it a reality. They also offer family workshops.

## Dialogue House

80 East 11th St.
New York, NY 10003
800-221-5844

National and international workshops are available to explore consciousness, creativity and refine abilities.

## Esalen Institute

Big Sur, CA 93920
408-667-2335

This 25-year-old center has explored New Age trends like philosophy, self-healing, behavioral sciences through seminars, workshops and residence programs.

## Harbin Hot Springs

Box 82
Middletown, CA 95461

This country retreat offers self-development programs in awareness, yoga, dance, macrobiotics and t'ai chi.

## Himalayan Institute of New York

At East West Books
78 Fifth Ave.
New York, NY 10011
212-243-5995

Classes in yoga, meditation, breathing, homeopathy, and vegetarian cooking are held at East West Books. The Center for Holistic Medicine offers courses on preventive medicine, shiatsu, biofeedback and psychotherapy.

## Hollyhock Farm

Box 127
Manson's Landing
Cortes Island, BC V0P 1K0
Canada
604-935-6465

During its five month summer season, Hollyhock hosts weekend and five-day workshops on dreams, painting, creativity, yoga, ritual and intimacy on its twenty-three acres in a western Canadian island near Vancouver.

# Joy Lake Mountain Seminar Center

Joy Lake Mountain Center offers weekend and five-day workshops from May through October with well-known leaders in personal growth and self-development. Designed especially to integrate mind, body, and spirit, this seminar series brings together educators, medical doctors, psychologists, spiritual teachers, holistic health practitioners, artists, and other visionaries of our time as presenters. Situated next to Toiyabe National Forest on the eastern ridge of the High Sierra mountain range, this New Age center contains an old western village, yurts, a four-acre lake ideal for swimming, a medicine wheel, and herbal gardens. Located between Reno and scenic Lake Tahoe, Joy Lake affords a singularly unique facility where human experience and the natural environment can interact creatively. Features presented have included former president of the Association of Humanistic Psychology Dr. Jean Houston; television author of *Journey's Out of Body*, philosopher Patricia Sun; psychologist Dr. Jean Shinoda Bolen; medicine men Sun Bear and Wallace Black Elk; Dr. Ken and Gloria Wapnick on "A Course in Miracles; shaman Dr. Michael Harner; internationally known parapsychologist Charles Tart; Brooke Medicine Eagle; Tibetan chanting teacher Jill Purce; and numerous others. Joy Lake offers a three-week, 135-hour certification program for a thorough and comprehensive knowledge of crystals. The Joy Lake Masters Program in Crystal Healing is designed to fulfill the need of those individuals who have a serious interest in enriching their therapeutic and scientific knowledge of quartz crystals. This program's teachers include Randall Baer, Oh Shinnah, Dr. Leonard Laskow, and Dr. Frank Alper.

- *Alan Morvay, Director*
*Joy Lake Mountain*
*Seminar Center*

## John F. Kennedy University

12 Altarinda Rd.
Orinda, CA 94563
415-254-6960

*JFK University offers graduate and undergraduate education in psychology, holistic health, arts and consciousness, transpersonal psychology, clinical psychology, counseling and much more. They also have the unique Graduate School for the Study of Human Consciousness. Class programs are offered year round.*

## John-David Learning Institute

Einstein Research Complex
2441 Impala Dr.
Carlsbad, CA 92008
619-931-0456

*High technology is the approach here. Audio and video is used to help teach people to reach their highest potential. Five-day workshops are offered in major U.S. cities.*

## Joy Lake Mountain Seminar Center

Box 1328
Reno, NV 89504
702-323-0378

*This mountain center has a May-October season with weekend and five day workshops with some of the New Age's best known teachers. Study areas include self-realization, native religions, music, intuitive development, and natural living.*

## Ken Keyes Center

790 Commercial Ave.
Coos Bay, OR 97420
503-267-6412

*This center provides from one day to three month residential programs designed to help foster personal happiness. They also offer weekend programs around the U.S., retreats, and literature.*

## Kushi Institute

P.O. Box 1100
Brookline, MA 02147
617-738-0045

*This institute is the educational center of the Kushi Foundation providing the greatest selection of courses in macrobiotics. Its courses include Macrobiotic Cooking, Order of the Universe, Health Evaluation and Oriental Diagnosis, Shiatsu and Body Energy Exercise, and Macrobiotic Health, Medicine, Nutrition, and Diet.*

## Life Integration Trainings

785 Centre St.
Newton, MA 02158-2599
617-965-7846

*Workshops are held regularly in the Boston area to help people reach their vision in life from Taking Your Next Step to Having it All!*

## The Light Ages Foundation

Box 278
Ashfield, MA 01330

*The Light Ages is an educational organization dedicated to promoting the development and evolution of the spiritual self. They present a regular series of national symposiums featuring New Age speakers and channelers.*

## Lorian Association

Box 663
Issaquah, WA 98027
206-641-3846

*This is a "community" of consciousness. The members do not live together, but rather explore spiritual understanding through classes, books and a newsletter. It is headed by David Spangler, one of the earliest members of the Findhorn Community in Scotland.*

## The Naropa Institute

2130 Arapahoe Ave.
Boulder, CO 80302
303-444-0202

*Naropa is the only accredited North American college whose educational philosophy is rooted in the Buddhist contemplative tradition. They offer a year-round schedule of classes.*

## New England Sound Healers

42 Baker St.
Lexington, MA 02173
617-861-1625

*NESH is dedicated to exploring the uses of sound for well-being. They sponsor monthly meetings with guest lecturers, seminars, and workshops.*

## New York Open Center

83 Spring St.
New York, NY 10012
212-219-2527

*A year-round program of lectures and workshops are offered by this Manhattan-based organization. Topics range from healing to philosophy and self-help.*

## Omega Institute for Holistic Studies

Lake Drive
RD 2, Box 377
Rhinebeck, NY 12572
914-266-4301

*Omega offers over 200 summer programs taught by some of the most respected people in the New Age field. Their season runs from May 15 to September 15 and features disciplines ranging from wellness to intuitive practices.*

## The Option Institute

RD #1, Box 174A
Sheffield, MA 02157
413-229-2100

*Learn to replace self-defeating beliefs with self-acceptance through special dialogue. They offer weekend, week-long and introductory seminars. Special programs are available for disabled children.*

## Outdoor Leadership Training Seminars

Box 20281
Denver, CO 80220
303-333-7831

*The wilderness is a powerful teacher of the inner and outer selves. This organization trains leaders through group weekly, monthly, and eight-month seminars in some of the toughest terrain America has to offer.*

## Parapsychological Services Institute

1502 Maple St.
Carrollton, GA 30117
404-834-1423

*William G. Roll, a Professor of Psychology and Psychical Research at West Georgia College heads this organization that offers counseling services for people experiencing paranormal phenomena. They also conduct workshops and publish Theta, a quarterly journal that focuses on the question of whether personality and consciousness extend beyond bodily existence.*

# Purpose of Rosicrucian Order, AMORC

The Rosicrucian Order, AMORC, is a worldwide educational organization of men and women. As a matter of fact, it is known as the world's oldest fraternal group, tracing its heritage to the mystery schools of ancient Egypt which developed and flourished circa 1400 B.C. Like most fraternal organizations, it functions on a lodge and chapter basis. In addition, it also offers its members a system of studies dealing with metaphysics, mysticism, philosophy, psychology, parapsychology, and science.

The purpose of the organization is to aid each individual in developing a personal philosophy based on a deeper understanding of natural laws and principles. Hopefully, this will be of benefit not only to the individual but also, ultimately, to the entire community.

## Worldwide Rosicrucian Membership

The Rosicrucian Order, AMORC, has approximately 250,000 active members in over 100 countries. The membership is comprised of representatives from every race, creed, culture, nationality, and profession. The Rosicrucian Order publishes its materials in 13 languages, including English, Spanish, Portuguese, Swedish, Danish, Norwegian, Finnish, Dutch, German, French, Italian, Greek, and Japanese. Because of its multilingual nature, the membership is divided into language jurisdictions and is served by separate administrative centers called Grand Lodges.

The administrative center at Rosicrucian Park in San Jose, California, houses not only the world headquarters of the entire organization but is also the Grand Lodge serving the Spanish-and English-speaking members. Out of this Grand Lodge, we currently serve approximately 90,000 active English- and Spanish-speaking members. Last year, almost three million pieces of mail left San Jose directly to all parts of the world.

Rosicrucian lodges and chapters exist in over 450 cities across the English-and Spanish-speaking world for those members who wish to participate at a local level. These local groups also offer interesting programs for the public throughout the year.

The Rosicrucian philosophy is very supportive of the principles and symbolism found in all religions. Members are encouraged to participate actively in their particular faiths. Indeed, after being involved in Rosicrucian studies, many members indicate that they turn to their respective religions with a renewed understanding of the import and significance of the principles inherent in each.

## Rosicrucian Egyptian Museum

In San Jose, the organization and its activities are housed in several Egyptian-style buildings in a park-like setting with broad lawns, many flowers, rose gardens, sparkling fountains, and statuary. Many trees and shrubs unusual to this area are also to be seen. The Park is spread over almost an entire city block near the downtown area of San Jose. In this setting several outstanding contributions are offered to the community.

The Rosicrucian Egyptian Museum in Rosicrucian Park is San Jose's largest tourist attraction, drawing approximately 200,000 people annually. The Egyptian Museum houses the largest collection of Egyptian, Babylonian, and Assyrian artifacts on the West Coast. In addition, it has the unusual distinction of being the only Egyptian museum in the world (including the Cairo Museum) which is housed in a building of authentic Egyptian architecture. The museum is offered as a cultural contribution to the community. There is a small admission charge for adults; children are free.

A M O R C

## Revis Mountain School of Self-Reliance

HCO2, Box 1534
Globe, AZ 85501
602-252-6019

*If you want to learn to get in touch with yourselves, the earth, and other people, try a wilderness retreat in the Superstition Wilderness area of Arizona. You'll learn survival skills and how to harmonize with nature.*

## Rosicrucian Order, AMORC

Rosicrucian Park
San Jose, CA 95191
408-287-9171

*This is the international organization that traces its roots to ancient Egypt. It is a fraternal group offering instruction via the mail.*

## The Sedona Institute

2408 Arizona Biltmore Circle,
Suite 115
Phoenix, AZ 85016
602-956-8766

*The Sedona Method taught by this organization is a technique for removing and releasing blocks that stop you from achieving what you want in life. Classes are held regularly in cities all over America.*

## The Self Center

7108 Remmet Ave.
Canoga Park, CA 91303
818-704-8464

*This is a local center serving the Los Angeles area. They offer classes, workshops, and training in a variety of New Age disciplines.*

## Shakti Center

Box 377
Mill Valley, CA 94942
415-927-2277

*Shakti Gawain is the well-known author of Creative Visualization. Her workshops at the Center include meditation, sharing, emotional clearing, and play ... to help you free yourself and begin creating the life you want.*

## Sierra University
### A University Without Walls

1020 Pico Blvd.
Santa Monica, CA 90405
213-452-3993

*Sierra goes beyond traditional classroom settings and offers one-to-one tutorial learning in traditional college-level disciplines, holistic studies and peace studies.*

## Spiritual Emergence Network

250 Oak Grove Ave.
Menlo Park, CA 94025
415-327-2776

*If you're having a spiritual crisis, the SEN can connect you with a "helper" to get you successfully through the experience. There are over 40 centers worldwide.*

## Three Mountain Foundation

Box 1180
Lone Pine, CA 93545
619-876-4702

*Richard Moss, M.D., is the founder and spiritual director of the Foundation. They offer classes, retreats, service programs and regional conferences in Lone Pine, CA. Moss has written extensively on the personal transformation process.*

## Transformation Arts Institute

Box 387
San Geronimo, CA 94963
415-488-4965

*TAI is a center of education, facilitation and research into the inner arts of shamanic power, healing and knowledge. They offer counseling and training that employs practical tools drawn from shamanic traditions including sacred law and elements of nature.*

## Windstar Foundation

Box 286
Snowmass, CO 81654
303-923-2145

*John Denver helped found this center that fosters global awareness, conflict resolution and ecology through seminars, concerts and retreats.*

## SIERRA UNIVERSITY

*A UNIVERSITY WITHOUT WALLS*

# Part 3: Transitions/Birth

I believe we choose certain things before we come onto this planet. Cristina chose a mother that was going to have a water birth. She was the type of soul that was open to a gentle entrance into the world. She knew that she wasn't going to have to go through the shock of a traumatic birth. The majority of adults in the U.S. right now did. We are fine. But it has taken us longer to get where we are. The new souls coming here are ready to BE. They are going to get on with it. It is not that there is no time — there is all the time in the world — but they don't want to take any more time to get on with things.

Birth and death are such a paradox. They both involve a major shift of energies into or out of a physical body. The energy is said to spiral into the physical body at birth. This energy continues as most babies turn while coming out the birth canal. People having near-death experiences and Full Body Channels are reported to say that they also experience a spiraling of energy while leaving and entering their bodies. The whole energy at birth is a huge vortex, and the energy of the baby to be born is going around like a tornado, going through the spiral tunnel that many people see in the near-death experience. Some people see it in the birthing experience when they are rebirthed. They feel their energy coming through that tunnel into their bodies, and then actually feel themselves being born. Who knows? Maybe dying is like going through a spiraling tunnel into a great vacuum of light where we stay until everything is in its proper timing for us to come out on the other side to who knows where?

- *Cai Inderhill*
  *Condensed from "The Divine Triangle," from*
  *Life Times Magazine*

## Conscious Conception
*Elemental Journey Through the Labyrinth of Sexuality*

By Jeannine Parvati Baker, Frederick Baker, and Tamara Slayton
1986/411 pages
**$16.95**
$17.95 postpaid from:
North Atlantic Books
2320 Blade St.
Berkeley, CA 94704

*A wonderful handbook illustrated with magical, mystical art and full of interesting information which the author describes as "an earthside manual to enrich our encounter with fertility."*

*Topics range from conscious menstruation to psychic birth control to the interaction of the intuitive arts and the fertility cycle.*

*A unique book in its field.*

Like attracts like on all planes of existence, and conception is a matter of magnetic attraction among three Souls. We cannot choose, as parents, but we are chosen.

- *Jeannine Parvati Baker,*
  *Frederick Baker, and*
  *Tamara Slayton*
  *From Conscious Conception*

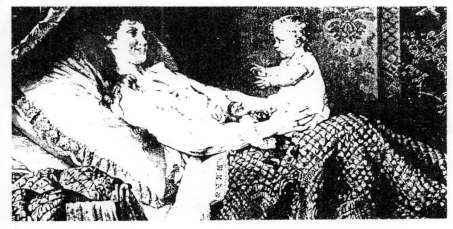

## Birth Without Violence

By Frederick LeBoyer
1975/114 pages
**$14.95**
$15.95 postpaid from:
Random House
400 Hahn Rd.
Westminister, MD 21157

*Forerunner of American conscious birth books. Birth Without Violence presents the LeBoyer method of birthing. LeBoyer's humanistic perspective focuses on the infant and its transition from the peaceful womb to the glaring stark reality of what can be immediately perceived as a violent world. Beautifully illustrated, this book shows us how we can achieve for our children a birth without violence.*

## The Secret Life of the Unborn Child

By Thomas Verny, M.D.
and John Kelly
1981/254 pages
**$8.95**
$10.45 postpaid from:
Dell Reader Services
P.O. Box 5057
Des Plaines, IL 60017

*This book examines current research information about fetal development and integrates this with holistic/humanistic ideas in parenting to create a workable model of the optimum environment for pregnancy and birth.*

*The startling evidence presented is sure to change any reader's current ideas of the possibilities of birth and development.*

# Extraordinary Infants

The Aquarian Age is bringing forth many child masters. There is a new cycle present in the last 25 years of the century enabling the collective vibrations of consciousness to be raised sufficiently so that many children can be born who are not ordinary infants. They are coming to set into motion a state of love and peace on the Earth plane. They are enlightened teachers and avatars with the potential for attaining Christ Consciousness. We must be prepared for them.

*I cannot stress enough the importance of listening to the baby as to how it would like to be born, how it would like to have things be, how it would like to grow up. And even when it would like to come out at delivery!*

Always acknowledging the fact that the baby is completely connected to Infinite Intelligence, and may be a being more enlightened than yourself, will produce wonders. Of this I feel certain.

*- Sondra Ray*
*From* Ideal Birth

## Ideal Birth

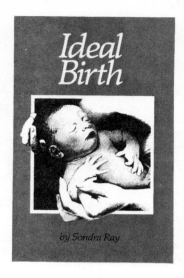

By Sondra Ray
1985/272 pages
**$8.95**
$9.95 postpaid from:
Celestial Arts
P.O. Box 7327
Berkeley, CA 94707

*An enlightened manual on conscious and loving pregnancy and childbirth with insight, clarity, and compassion.* Ideal Birth *includes personal accounts of some of the first underwater births in the U.S.*

*Sondra Ray illuminates how our choices made during conception, pregnancy and childbirth shape the emerging being.*

# Rebirthing Before and During Pregnancy

The supremely ideal birth to me would be where both parents had released their own Birth Trauma *before conception* of a child. This is my idea of perfection because there would be little or no psychic contamination to the fetus and little fear of the birth itself.

This could be done easily and pleasurably if both parents were willing to get rebirthed for at least a year prior to conceiving a child. The guidance of a Spiritual Master who is powerful enough to wash out Birth Trauma is also extremely helpful. It is interesting to speculate that the clearer they are of these factors, the more enlightened a soul the parent could attract to bring in.

As Rebirthers, we have seen mothers who have been rebirthed a lot during pregnancy, have an easier delivery. They tend to report that their babies "came out like butter." It was of course extremely helpful that the mother could do the Rebirthing breath during labor and delivery.

Throughout this book, Ideal Birth, I also have stressed the importance of conscious conception. I repeatedly stress how important it is to be clear as possible *before* conception. After years of Rebirthing, where I have taken people back to the memory of conception, I am more and more convinced of the importance of avoiding not only the Birth Trauma, but the Conception Trauma as well. There was a time when I did not believe one could remember one's conception! Now I have to laugh at my own ignorance. Just because one cannot consciously remember something does not mean it was not recorded, or not affecting one constantly. Just yesterday I rebirthed a woman whose whole life was stuck at her conception.

You may never have considered the fact that you chose your parents When you do, a lot will clear up for you because you will no longer blame them. You will begin to realize that you selected those parents to come through to teach yourself some lesson or complete some karma. Did you ever stop to think that if you want to get pregnant now, a soul is also picking you? It is important to exercise right thought, right speech and clear thinking if you want to attract high souls. Older, higher souls reject parents who are involved in any harmful acts because they do not want to be burdened by the karma of harmful actions.

*- Sondra Ray*
*From* Ideal Birth

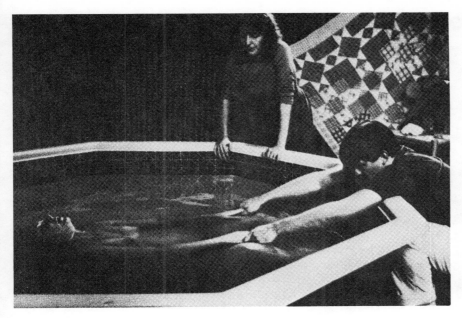

Laboring in the relaxing environment of
warm water enabled Robbie to birth Jason, a
ten-pound boy, after her previous daughter,
Peyton, was cesarean.

## The Healing Power of Birth

By Rima Beth Star
1986/146 pages
**$14.95**
$16.20 postpaid from:
Star Publishing
P.O. Box 161113
Austin, TX 78716

*Rima Beth Star chronicles her
personal growth through the births of her
three children, the last two of which
were underwater births. The sharing of
her own personal insights provide an
avenue for the reader to explore what
the birth transition means to the
emerging individual.*

## Water Birth Video

$60.00/VHS
$63.00 postpaid or
$25.00 for a 3-day rental from:
Star Publishing
P.O. Box 161113
Austin, TX 78716

Water Birth *is a 54-minute video of
the first water birth in the United States.
A moving visual experience, highly
recommended for any pregnant couple,
or person wishing to participate in a
water birth. Includes a thought-
provoking discussion of future
possibilities in human evolution. VHS
format.*

## Water Birth Information Packet

1986
**$9.95**
$11.20 postpaid from:
Star Publishing
P.O. Box 161113
Austin, TX 78716

*A collection of articles on water birth,
stories from other parents, bibliography,
and list of parents, midwives, and doctors
involved in water birth. The packet
continually grows as information from
others interested in integrating the use of
water in pre- and perinatal experience.*

## Moonflower Birthing Supply Catalog

P.O. Box 128
Louisville, CO 80027

*Books, supplies, medical equipment,
children's products, gifts, and videos all
offered in an attractive catalog for the
mother as well as the midwife.*

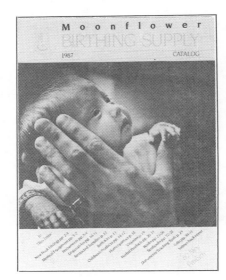

## Birth Reborn

By Michel Odent
1984/122 pages
**$8.95**
$10.45 postpaid from:
Pantheon Books
400 Hahn Rd.
Westminister, MD 21157

*This book's subtitle says it all: How
childbirth can be what women want it to
be — and how mothers and babies both
benefit. Dr. Odent combines his
experience in the field with holistic
thinking to provide a sourcebook of
knowledge and encouragement. Includes
underwater birthing discussions.*

# A Typical Near-Death Experience

The experience begins with a feeling of easeful peace and a sense of well-being, which soon culminates in a sense of overwhelming joy and happiness. This ecstatic tone, although fluctuating in intensity from case to case, tends to persist as a constant emotional ground as other features of the experience begin to unfold. At this point, the person is aware that he feels no pain nor does he have any other bodily sensations. Everything is quiet. These cues may suggest to him that he is either in the process of dying or has already "died."

He may then be aware of a transitory buzzing or a windlike sound, but, in any event, he finds himself looking down on his physical body, as though he were viewing it from some external vantage point. At this time, he finds that he can see and hear perfectly; indeed, his vision and hearing tend to be more acute than usual. He is aware of the actions and conversations taking place in the physical environment, in relation to which he finds himself in the role of a passive, detached spectator. All this seems very real — even quite natural — to him; it does not seem at all like a dream or an hallucination. His mental state is one of clarity and alertness.

At some point, he may find himself in a state of *dual awareness.* While he continues to be able to perceive the physical scene around him, he may also become aware of "another reality" and feel himself being drawn into it. He drifts or is ushered into a dark void or tunnel and feels as though he is floating through it. Although he may feel lonely for a time, the experience here is predominantly peaceful and serene. All is extremely quiet and the individual is aware only of his mind and of the feeling of floating.

All at once, he becomes sensitive to, but does not see, a presence. The presence, who may be heard to speak or who may instead "merely" induce thoughts into the individual's mind, stimulates him to review his life and asks him to decide whether he wants to live or die. This stock-taking may be facilitated by a rapid and vivid playback of episodes from the person's life. At this stage, he has no awareness of time or space, and the concepts themselves are meaningless. Neither is he any longer identified with his body. Only the mind is present and it is weighing — logically and rationally — the alternatives that confront him at this threshold separating life from death: to go further into this experience or to return to earthly life. Usually the individual decides to return on this basis, not of his own preference, but on the perceived needs of his loved ones, whom his death would necessarily leave behind. Once the decision is made, the experience tends to be abruptly terminated.

Sometimes, however, the decisional crisis occurs later or is altogether absent, and the individual undergoes further experiences. He may, for example, continue to float through the dark void toward a magnetic and brilliant golden light, from which emanates feelings of love, warmth, and total acceptance.

Or he may enter into a "world of light" and preternatural beauty, to be (temporarily) reunited with deceased loved ones before being told, in effect, that it is not yet his time and that he has to return to life.

In any event, whether the individual chooses or is commanded to return to his earthly body and worldly commitments, he does return. Typically, however, he has no recollection *how* he has effected his "reentry," for at this point he tends to lose all awareness. Very occasionally, however, the individual may remember "returning to his body" with a jolt or an agonizing wrenching sensation. He may even suspect that he reenters "through the head."

Afterward, when he is able to recount his experience, he finds that there are simply no words adequate to convey the feelings and quality of awareness he remembers. He may also be or become reticent to discuss it with others, either because he feels no one will really be able to understand it or because he fears he will be disbelieved or ridiculed.

— *Kenneth Ring*
From Life at Death

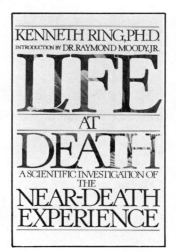

**Life at Death**
*A Scientific Investigation of the Near-Death Experience*
By Kenneth Ring, Ph.D.
1980/310 pages
**$7.50**
$9.00 postpaid from:
William Morrow & Co.
Wilmor Warehouse
39 Plymouth St.
Fairfield, NJ 07007

*The near death experience was explored scientifically for the first time in* Life at Death, *Ring's first, statistically-supported research. He documents the frequency of NDEs and their impact on a person's life.*

## Near-Death Experience Project

Prof. Howard Mickel, Director
Box 76
Wichita State University
Wichita, KS 67208
316-689-3108

*The NDE project is collecting written, audio and video interviews with people who have had NDEs and other mystical experiences. The Project provides public education, workshops, and support for people who have been on the brink of the death experience.*

## International Association for Near Death Studies (IANDS)

c/o University Health Center
Dept. of Psychiatry
Farmington, CT 06032

*Professionals and laypersons interested in the near death experience may join IANDS. They offer research, NDE experience support, seminars and publish the* Vital Signs *newsletter and* Anabiosis — The Journal for Near-Death Studies.

## Survival Research Foundation

### $2,000 Prize in Life After Death Experiment

The Survival Research Foundation (SRF) and its Committee of Judges remind readers that just one more year remains for the submission of the secret keys of the late Dr. Robert H. Thouless who left two messages in cipher as part of an ingenious test to prove his posthumous survival and ability to communicate. $1,000 will be given by the SRF to any charity designated by the first person who sends the SRF Committee of Judges the right submission which will allow one of Dr. Thouless's test messages to be made plausible, and another $1,000 will be given by the SRF to any charity designated by the first person who does the same for Dr. Thouless's second message. In one test message the deciphering key is the title of a literary work. For the second message he intended to communicate two words as the deciphering key.

This offer will be withdrawn one year from the date of this publication. The Committee will be the final arbiter of whether any submission indicates or supplies the right key.

Submissions, together with a description of how and where they were obtained, should be sent to:

Dr. E.L. Pattullo, Director, Center for the Behavioral Sciences, William James Hall, Harvard University, 33 Kirland Street, Cambridge, MA 02138.

## Heading Toward Omega
### *In Search of the Meaning of the Near-Death Experience*

By Kenneth Ring
1984/346 pages
**$6.95**
$8.45 postpaid from:
William Morrow & Co.
Wilmor Warehouse
39 Plymouth St.
Fairfield, NJ 07007

*Kenneth Ring took the initial research he had done in* Life at Death *and found much meaning in the near death experience. People who experienced NDE's often completely transform, their spiritual values change and they sometimes glimpse, during their otherworldly experience, the fate of planet Earth.*

# What NDE'ers Said About the Future in 1980 ...

Almost all these NDE'ers state or imply that the major geophysical and meteorological changes forecast will begin during this decade, though a few are inclined to believe it will be later. Probably most of them would agree that the changes have already begun and will be evident within a few years at most. The following sprinkling of brief quotations will convey the common timeframes used:

I believe the war will start in 1984 or 1985.

I think you can expect to see some of the most disastrous upheavals between now and 1988.

It is to be 1988 or was to be. That (would) be the year everything would be wiped away if we didn't change.

The seismic activity is going to be (be) within the next ten years.

(The war will) probably be in the next ten years.

I think around 1984, 1985, possibly even sooner (will see) the beginnings of droughts ... Anyway, by 1988, that will be when tensions finally grow to the point (of nuclear war).

I've been told we'll see signs of its approach ... There will be great natural catastrophes, an assassination attempt on the Pope, an intensification of the drug problem.

- *Ken Ring*
  *From* Heading Toward Omega

## International Institute for the Study of Death

Box 8565
Pembroke Pines, FL 33084

*The purpose of the IISD is to provide an international forum to explore the central questions raised by the death experience. They have a research division and publish multilanguage periodicals. The IISD also presents conferences and seminars.*

## Life After Life

By Raymond A. Moody, Jr., M.D.
1975/186 pages
$3.95
$5.45 postpaid from:
Bantam Books Direct Response Dept.
414 E. Golf Rd.
Des Plaines, IL 60016

*This is the pioneering NDE study by Dr. Raymond Moody, Jr. He interviewed more than one hundred subjects who experienced "clinical death." He found their stories to be remarkably similar, which led him to suspect that something we don't quite understand was going on with people who had been declared clinically dead, but somehow came back to life.*

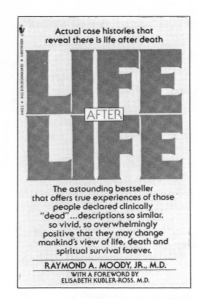

Actual case histories that reveal there is life after death

**LIFE AFTER LIFE**

The astounding bestseller that offers true experiences of those people declared clinically "dead"...descriptions so similar, so vivid, so overwhelmingly positive that they may change mankind's view of life, death and spiritual survival forever.

**RAYMOND A. MOODY, JR., M.D.**
WITH A FOREWORD BY
ELISABETH KUBLER-ROSS, M.D.

Isaiah 26:19: Thy dead men shall live, together with my dead body shall they arise. Awake and sing, ye that dwell in dust for ... the earth shall cast out the dead.

Daniel 12:2: And many of them that sleep in the dust of the earth shall awake, some to everlasting life, and some to shame and everlasting contempt.

*- Raymond A. Moody, Jr. From* Life After Life

## Reflections on Life After Life

Further investigation of an extraordinary phenomenon— survival of life after bodily death

**REFLECTIONS ON LIFE AFTER LIFE**

**RAYMOND A. MOODY, JR., M.D.**
The bestselling sequel to
Life After Life

By Raymond A. Moody, Jr., M.D.
1977/148 pages
$3.95
$5.45 postpaid from:
Bantam Books
414 E. Golf Rd.
Des Plaines, IL 60016

*In this sequel to* Life After Life, *Dr. Moody further examines the near death experience. He also talks about new elements he found to be woven through NDEs including "cities of light," "bewildered spirits," and "supernatural rescues."*

# The Only Judgment on "The Other Side" is Your Own

That's the part that has stuck with me, because it showed me not only what I had done but *even how what I had done had affected other people.* And it wasn't like I was looking at a movie projector because I could *feel* these things; there was feeling, and particularly since I was with this knowledge ... I found out that not even your thoughts are lost ... Every thought was there ... Your thoughts are not lost ...

*- Raymond A. Moody, Jr., From* Reflections on Life After Life

# What Is it Like to Die?

"All pain vanished."
"I went through this dark, black vacuum at super speed."
"There was a feeling of utter peace and quiet, no fear at all."
"I was in a very dark, very deep valley. Later I thought, 'Well, now I know what the Bible means by *the valley of the shadow of death* because I've been there.' "
"After I came back, I cried off and on for about a week because I had to live in this world after seeing that one."
"It opened up a whole new world for me ... I kept thinking, 'There's so much that I've got to find out.' "
"I heard a voice telling me what I had to do — go back — and I felt no fear."

*- Raymond A. Moody, Jr. From* Reflections on Life After Life

# Death & Dying

## Little Child, Big Soul

Know that this child is not a "poor little soul." This child is a resplendent acknowledgement of Life that can never die. The soul of a child is neither poor nor little. It is large, loving, beautiful, and healthy, just as the Source Itself.

The child came to teach and to learn. And, although it perhaps happened too quickly for you, the child has completed the mission. The child can now move on to even greater expressions of life and love. You and I have more to teach and more to learn.

Bless the child who graduates ahead of us.

Even if in tears, bless the child who finishes his or her mission before the rest of us finished ours.

Take heart that you have loved and been loved by a very special aspect of God. Your child is always a precious part of Infinite Life, and so are you.

Rest, and be assured.

*Today I carefully release any thoughts that God "took" my child. God gives, and my child accepts, a new and glorious morning.*

*- Elizabeth A. Johnson*
*From As Someone Dies*

*In my Father's House are many mansions.*
*I let go and allow my friend to step into another room.*

*- From As Someone Dies*

### As Someone Dies
### A Handbook for the Living

By Elizabeth A. Johnson
1985/80 pages
**$16.95**
$19.95 postpaid from:
Hay House
3029 Wilshire Blvd. #206
Santa Monica, CA 90404

*Inexpressible is the only word to describe the impending loss one feels when a loved one is about to go through the transition process.*

*This gem of a book talks to the grieving with understanding and caring. It helps.*

### Coming Home
### A Guide to Dying at
### Home with Dignity

By Deborah Duda
1987/300 pages
**$14.95**
$16.95 postpaid from:
Aurora Press
Box 573
Santa Fe, NM 87504

*Today in ever increasing numbers, terminally ill people are choosing to spend their last days at home, in the warmth of familiar surroundings rather than in the cold, impersonal sterility of a hospital or nursing home. With sky-rocketing hospital and nursing home costs, sometimes there is no choice.*

*If you, or a loved one is faced with this situation, here is an information source to support and assist your efforts and knowledge to ease the path of the terminally ill to a peaceful conclusion.*

### Death and Dying
### The Tibetan Tradition

By Glen H. Mullin
**$7.95**
$9.45 postpaid from:
Methuen, Inc.
29 W. 35th St.
New York, NY 10001-2291

*The Tibetans regard death and dying as vitally important. They have developed a wide range of materials on death, dying and the after-death experience including meditation to prepare for death, consciousness modes to facilitate transition and the famous Tibetan Book of the Dead.*

## On Dreams & Death

By Marie-Louise von Franz
1984/194 pages
**$12.95**
$14.70 postpaid from:
Shambala Publications, Inc.
314 Dartmouth St.
Boston, MA 02116

*Do your dreams warn you of your impending death? Von Franz has researched this idea, incorporated insights and examples from daily life and drawn from Jungian psychology, religious and cultural dogmas, and found that our dreams may mirror our fate. All we need do is recognize our own symbolism.*

# Dreaming of Death

The nearness of death is frequently represented in dreams by the image of a burglar, that is, by someone unfamiliar which unexpectedly enters one's present life. A businessman in his middle fifties wanted to undergo analysis with me, for he felt frustrated in his work and was looking for a deeper meaning in life. His first dream:

*He awakens in the middle of the night in bed, in a dark room halfway under the earth. A bright gleam of light streams in through the window. Suddenly he sees a stranger in the room, someone who fills him with such an inhuman, terrible fear that he awakens, bathed in sweat.*

The first dream in an analysis is often prophetic; it anticipates future developments which are being prepared, as it were, in the unconscious. I did not understand this man's dream and confined myself to the remark that something that is still very strange and fearful wants to come to him and that it would have some connection with light, that is, with illumination, with insight. After a couple of analytic hours the dreamer never showed up again; from time to time, however, he assured me by telephone that he wanted very much to continue the analysis but that he was overburdened with work. A year later I heard that he was about to die from cancer of the spinal cord. The sinister "intruder" of the initial dream had been clearly death itself.

*- Marie-Louise von Franz*
*From* On Dreams & Death

---

# The Family After Death Has Occurred

## On Death and Dying

Once the patient dies, I find it cruel and inappropriate to speak of the love of God. When we lose someone, especially when we have had little if any time to prepare ourselves, we are enraged, angry, in despair; we should be allowed to express these feelings. The family members are often left alone as soon as they have given their consent for autopsy. Bitter, angry, or just numb, they walk through the corridors of the hospital, unable often to face the brutal reality. The first few days may be filled with busywork, with arrangements and visiting relatives. The void and emptiness is felt after the funeral, after the departure of the relatives. It is at this time that family members feel most grateful to have someone to talk to, especially if it is someone who had recent contact with the deceased and who can share anecdotes of some good moments towards the end of the deceased's life. This helps the relative over the shock and the initial grief and prepares him for a gradual acceptance.

Many relatives are preoccupied by memories and ruminate in fantasies, often even talk to the deceased as if he was still alive. They not only isolate themselves from the living but make it harder for themselves to face the reality of the person's death. For some, however, this is the only way they can cope with the loss, and it would be cruel indeed to ridicule them or to confront them daily with the unacceptable reality. It would be more helpful to understand this need and to help them separate themselves by taking them out of their isolation gradually.

*- Elisabeth Kübler-Ross*
*From* On Death and Dying

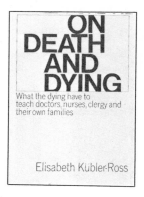

By Elisabeth Kübler-Ross
1969/260 pages
**$14.95**
$16.45 postpaid from:
MacMillan Publishing
Front and Brown Sts.
Riverside, NJ 08075

*This is the classic work on the process of dying. It established a new perspective on the terminally ill patient and helped open the door to a greater understanding of what might lie "on the other side" since the dying have a unique view of what lies ahead.*

## The Right to Die
*Understanding Euthanasia*

By Derek Humphry
and Ann Wickett
1986/372 pages
**$9.95**
$11.45 postpaid from:
Harper & Row Publishers, Inc.
2350 Virginia Ave.
Hagerstown, MD 21740

*The right to die is a thorny legal and moral issue. It also makes the question of our survival after death ever more compelling. The authors attempt to explain the complexities of the most controversial issue of this decade by contrasting it with historical and cultural precedents.*

# Religion and Euthanasia

Most Christian groups do not oppose passive euthanasia, and although they are less specific about it, neither do most Eastern religions. Allowing a hopelessly ill person to die by not imposing extraordinary measures is widely accepted today by the churches as being part of God's will. Only Mormons, Evangelicals, and other strict Gospel denominations are opposed to passive euthanasia in the West, while Islam is opposed in the East. Had any of these groups been asked about their position on euthanasia ten or more years ago, they probably would have been unable to give a ready answer. Public policy-making in this area has almost entirely followed the Karen Ann Quinlan case in 1976.

But active voluntary euthanasia — taking one's own life or helping another to die — is a different matter. No church hierarchy has endorsed the practice, although many would not condemn it, preferring instead to leave the matter to individual conscience and decision. Part of this lack of official policy is due to the nature of the reformed churches: They tend to eschew dogma and authoritarian figures, preferring their congregations to govern themselves according to a basic moral code. Another reason is the realization that active euthanasia is both a complex and an explosive question theologically.
- *Derek Humphry and*
*Ann Wickett*
*From* The Right to Die

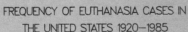

FREQUENCY OF EUTHANASIA CASES IN
THE UNITED STATES 1920–1985

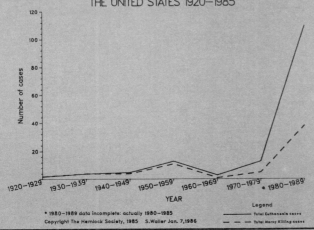

\* 1980–1989 data incomplete: actually 1980–1985
Copyright The Hemlock Society, 1985   S.Waller Jan. 7,1986

# Organizations That Deal With the Issue of Death

**Hemlock Society**
Box 66218
Los Angeles, CA 90066
*Deals with the issue of euthanasia*

**Concern for Dying**
250 West 57th St.
New York, NY 10107
*Information on death and dying*

**The Living/Dying Project**
Box 5564
Santa Fe, NM 87502
*This project consciously investigates living and dying. It is part of the Hanuman Foundation founded by Ram Dass.*

---

### The Unquiet Dead

Dr. Edith Fiore
1987/178 pages
**$15.95**
$16.89 postpaid from:
Doubleday & Co.
501 Franklin Ave.
Garden City, NY 11530

*Many people pass into spirit in a state of confusion, fear and disorientation. They have the potential to "hang onto" a living person and "possess" them. The result to the living person is often diagnosed as psychological or psychosomatic problems. Dr. Fiore has treated hundreds of these cases and found that about 70 percent of her patients were suffering from spirit possession. What was required was help for both the spirit entity and physical person to effect a successful release.*

# *Reincarnation*

# The Evolution of Reincarnation

Since the espousal of reincarnation and karma by the wisest spiritual and philosophical sages, the people of the East have remained in awe of the relentless revolutions of the "wheel of life." Not so their counterparts in the Western Hemisphere where reincarnation was buried alive more than fourteen centuries ago. The conspiring undertakers were the church and the state, fearful that their authority could be challenged by a doctrine that made individuals responsible for their own salvation. Since A.D. 553, when the "monstrous restoration" of rebirth was denounced by Emperor Justinian, the faithful have been taught to believe in eternal life while ignoring immortality's spiritual sister, reincarnation. Christians learn that eternity starts at birth. But, since only the beginningless can be endless, one might as well have faith in a table's ability to stand on only three legs!

Such quasi-immortality rendered materialism more attractive as a code by which to live. Consequently, with the growth of Western materialism indirectly ordained by the church, reincarnation's exile was confirmed. For materialism, which later bound fledgling science to its blinkered vision, sanctions no reality outside that which can be measured, weighed, heard, smelled, bought, and sold. Ironically, this trend also hastened the decline of ecclesiastical authority, which relied largely on the manipulation of the intangible.

The church was to remain all-powerful for centuries, even as it carried the seeds of its own decay. Many a rebel reincarnationist was put to death with vengeful fury as the bishops implicitly condemned the rebirth doctrine twice more at the councils of 1274 and 1439 with thunderous assertions about heaven, purgatory and hell. Yet the ancient belief that many lives are as essential to our spiritual evolution as a succession of years are to our physical development wouldn't be stamped out. When the Dark Ages retreated before the Renaissance,

society was reborn in a spontaneous exaltation of individuality. The hold of the papacy was finally broken and, in the Age of Enlightenment that followed, many of the great minds of Europe vented the conviction that reincarnation was an unalterable fact of life which tempered the chaos of an unfair world with justice, meaning and purpose. "After all," noted Voltaire, "it is no more surprising to be born twice than it is to be born once."

The masses, however, had other things to be surprised about as tremendous excitement was being generated by the rudimentary automation of the industrial revolution. Towards the end of the last century, the Theosophical movement challenged the prevailing mechanism of the times by rummaging around in the treasure chest of Hindu and Buddhist observance to retrieve reincarnation for adoption in the West. Pickled in fundamentalist concepts and skewered by the fear of death with its stark remuneration of either paradise or hellfire, most people weren't to be swayed.

Our own century witnessed the limited response, in the 1930s and 1940s, to the God-fearing mystic Edgar Cayce, who went into self-hypnotic trance to deliver — at first against his own wishes — startling revelations about past lives extending all the way back to the lost continent of Atlantis.

Not until the Bridey Murphy sensation of 1954 did the public imagination accept reincarnation as a reasonable hypothesis. Believers and unbelievers alike were captivated by accounts of how Colorado businessman Morey Bernstein had hypnotically regressed housewife Virginia Tighe to an obscure but historically plausible life in last-century Ireland as Bridey Murphy. Reincarnation-inspired movies and songs followed. So did pioneering studies that subjected past-life recall to scientific scrutiny. As files of intriguing cases grew, the mid-seventies saw past-life therapy

emerge as a dramatic way of curing physical and psychological disorders through the tapping of reincarnation memories under hypnosis. Belief in successive lives was not, however, enjoying its rebirth in isolation. Rather, it was taking place amid a widespread resurgence of spiritual awareness and a developing hunger for nonmaterial nourishment in what had become a highly technological world.

> *- Joe Fisher*
> *From* The Case for Reincarnation

---

## The Case for Reincarnation

By Joe Fisher
1984/178 pages
**$3.95**
$4.64 postpaid from:
Doubleday & Co.
501 Franklin Ave.
Garden City, NY 11530

*Joe Fisher has carefully researched the existing evidence relating to reincarnation and has come up with a strong case for the possibility that we come back again and again. He even provides "Magical Memory" exercises to stimulate that part of you that knows about your previous incarnations.*

## How to Remember Your Past Lives
*An Edgar Cayce Learn-at-Home Course*

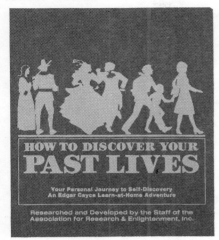

1984/three 60-minute cassette tapes, 94 pages of instruction
**$29.95**
$31.95 postpaid from:
A.R.E. Press
Box 595
Virginia Beach, VA 23451

*This highly recommended "home adventure" will take you through an extensive series of exercises that explore the many possibilities relating to your past incarnations. You'll learn the laws governing reincarnation as expressed in the Edgar Cayce readings and uncover present day behaviors and life's patterns that reflect your past lives.*

## Reincarnation: The Phoenix Fire Mystery

By Joseph Head & S. L. Cranston
1977/620 pages
**$10.95**
$14.45 postpaid from:
Crown Publishers, Inc.
34 Englehard Ave.
Avenel, NY 07001

*If you want to read about ancient civilizations and famous people and read some authentic case histories of people who could very well have remembered previous incarnations, this book is for you. It is the definitive work on reincarnation. Foreword by Elisabeth Kübler-Ross.*

# American Inventor Thomas Edison (1847-1931) on Reincarnation

As Thomas Edison was an early and lifelong member of the Theosophical Society, it is not surprising that during his last illness when reporters inquired if he believed in survival after death, he replied: "The only survival I can conceive is to start a new earth cycle again." On his eightieth birthday he was asked: "Do you believe man has a soul?" He answered that man as a unit of life "is composed of swarms of billions of highly charged entities which live in the cells. I believe that when a man dies, this swarm deserts the body, and goes out into space, but keeps on and enters another cycle of life and is immortal." In *The Diary and Sundry Observations of Thomas Alva Edison*, the inventor provides these further thoughts:

"I cannot believe for a moment that life in the first instance originated on this insignificant little ball which we call the earth ... The

particles which combined to evolve living creatures on this planet of ours probably came from some other body elsewhere in the universe ... The more we learn the more we realize that there is life in things which we used to regard as inanimate, as lifeless ...

I don't believe for a moment that one life makes another life. Take our own bodies. I believe they are composed of myriads and myriads of infinitesimally small individuals, each in itself a unit of life, and that these units work in squads — or swarms, as I prefer to call them — and that these infinitesimally small units live forever. When we "die" these swarms of units, like a swarm of bees, so to speak, betake themselves elsewhere, and go on functioning in some other form or environment."

- *Joseph Head & S.L. Cranston*
*From Reincarnation: The Phoenix Fire Mystery*

Colonial American architecture, 18th century

53 ☐ Like    ☐ Dislike

Comments _____

_____

_____

*Part of a past life memory test*
From How to Discover Your Past Lives

# Rudolf Steiner

Born in Austria in 1861, Rudolf Steiner received recognition as a scholar when he was invited to edit the Kurschner edition of the natural scientific writings of Goethe. In 1891 Steiner received his Ph.D. at the University of Rostock. He then began his work as a lecturer. From the turn of the century until his death in 1925, he delivered well over 6,000 lectures on the Science of Spirit, or Anthroposophy.

The lectures of Rudolf Steiner dealt with such fundamental matters as the being of man, the nature and purpose of freedom, the meaning of evolution, man's relation to nature, and the life after death and before birth. On these and similar subjects, Steiner had unexpectedly new, inspiring and thought-provoking things to say. Through a study of the transcripts of lectures like those contained in this book, one can come to a clear, reasonable, comprehensive understanding of the human being and his place in the universe.

*- From the Introduction to*
*Reincarnation and Immortality*

## Reincarnation and Immortality

By Rudolf Steiner
1970/204 pages
**$2.75**
$3.25 postpaid from:
Anthroposophic Press
Bell's Pond
Star Rt.
Hudson, NY 12534

## Life Between Life
### *Scientific Exploration into the Void Separating One Incarnation from the Next*

By Joel L. Whitton,
M.D., Ph.D.
and Joe Fisher
1986/198 pages
**$14.95**
$15.89 postpaid from:
Doubleday & Co.
501 Franklin Ave.
Garden City, NY 11530

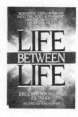

*Let's say we do reincarnate from one earth life to the next. What happens in between lives? What do we do between death and rebirth? During 13 years of study, Neurophysiologist Dr. Joel Whitton has determined that the period between lives, or bardo, is when we write our karmic script for our next incarnation.*

# In the Void Between Lives

... the extent to which the karmic script may be examined, and many other details. But in one fundamental aspect the privileged few who have visited the interlife receive the same unrelenting message: *We are thoroughly responsible for who we are and the circumstances in which we find ourselves. We are the ones who do the choosing.*

Total self-responsibility may be perceived as freedom on the edge of a razor, but the terror is mitigated by the knowledge that we are all partaking in an awesome evolutionary process that invests each thought, word, and deed with meaning and purpose. Having glimpsed how each succeeding incarnation is elected on the basis of one's past, travelers in the interlife are bound to return to this life with a heightened awareness of their responsibilities. But they also retain an acute appreciation of the moral sensitivity at work in the macrocosm, a sensitivity which pervades their own incredibly complex voyaging in and out of life incarnate.

*- Joel L. Whitton*
*and Joe Fisher*
*From Life Between Life*

## Reincarnation Explored

By John Algeo
1987/126 pages
**$6.95**
$7.95 postpaid from:
Quest Books
306 W. Geneva Rd.
Wheaton, IL 60189

*Algeo gives a clear, concise overview of the concept of reincarnation from methods of hypnotic past life recall to attempts to answer the question "Why be reborn?"*

# Why Do We Reincarnate?

In the theosophical tradition, the reason for reincarnation is to further human evolution, specifically the evolution of the human mind, for there is intellectual and spiritual evolution as well as the evolution of physical forms. Through reincarnation we develop our understanding of the universe and of our place in it. Our destiny is to become fully what we are now only potentially — centers of the authentic life, wisdom, and creativity of the ground of all being.

*- John Algeo*
*From Reincarnation Explored*

## Reincarnation Unnecessary

By Violet Shelley
1979/130 pages
**$5.95**
$7.95 postpaid from:
A.R.E. Press
Box 595
Virginia Beach, VA 23451

*Of the 1,200 people who received life readings from Edgar Cayce, 18 were told that when their lives ended, they could choose to not be reborn. What were the common factors that were woven through the many incarnations of these people in order to achieve perfection?*

## Edgar Cayce on Reincarnation

By Noel Langley
1967/286 pages
**$3.95**
$5.95 postpaid from:
A.R.E. Press
Box 595
Virginia Beach, VA 23451

*Edgar Cayce's readings provide much information on why we've lived before and why we don't remember past incarnations. It examines the question of whether or not the Bible condemns reincarnation and also the law of grace.*

## In My Next Life I'm Gonna Be the Princess!
*Cartoons on Reincarnation and Other New Age Stuff*

By Chuck Vadun
1984/96 pages
**$2.94**
$4.44 postpaid from:
Valley of the Sun
Box 3004
Agoura Hills, CA 91301

*Vadun's cartoons appear regularly in national magazines. Here he tackles the concept of reincarnation ... chuckling!*
> - Chuck Vadun
>   From In My Next Life
>   I'm Gonna be the
>   Princess

**I'm afraid our service doesn't extend to locating lovers from past lives.**

## Viewing Past Lives
### *The Ascension Technique*

2 Cassette Tapes · 96 Page Manual

Dick Sutphen's

**Viewing Past Lives**

The Ascension Technique

By The Author Of
"You Were Born Again To Be Together"
& "Past Lives, Future Loves"

By Dick Sutphen
1984/four 60-minute cassette tapes,
instruction book
**$39.95**
$43.70 postpaid from:
Valley of the Sun
Box 3004
Agoura Hills, CA 91301

*Ascension is a unique meditation technique used for past life regression. You experience your past incarnations through your inner eyes and become aware of your pre-birth decisions on the lessons to be learned in this life. You'll be able to learn about other people's past life relations with you and go through a process that uncovers past life problems being expressed in your present life.*

## Explorations Beyond Past Lives

By Dick Sutphen
1984/two 60-minute cassette tapes,
instruction book
**$24.95**
$26.95 postpaid from:
Valley of the Sun
Box 3004
Agoura Hills, CA 91301

*Once you've explored past lives, this tape program will help you learn about your future incarnations, parallel lives (others living right now on this planet who are expressions of your present self), and other realities where your soul may be experiencing. Fascinating.*

---

**Tape 3: Oversoul Awareness of Your Life Plan** — A Higher-Self expanded-state-of-consciousness session to explore your life from a multi-life perspective. The session goal is to explore your primary purpose and present level of awareness. You will become aware of what changes you need to make to advance according to your life plan, and about the primary unlearned lessons from previous lives. Also, how you can accelerate the evolutive process.

**Tape: Past-life Talents and Abilities** — A multi-life regression to seek out forgotten valuable knowledge from your former lives. This session, conducted in our seminars, has launched many people on to new careers, and for others it has opened the doors to latent abilities that were lying right below the surface. If you developed a particular talent or ability in your past, it should be exceptionally natural and easy to do it again.

## Past Life Therapy
### *Regression Album*

2 Cassette Tapes · 96 Page Manual

Dick Sutphen's

**Past·Life Therapy**

Regression Album

By The Author Of
"You Were Born Again To Be Together"
& "Past Lives, Future Loves"

By Dick Sutphen
1981/two 60-minute cassette tapes
**$29.95**
$32.20 postpaid from:
Valley of the Sun
Box 3004
Agoura Hills, CA 91301

*Past-Life Therapy has become widely recognized as an extremely valuable technique to eliminate problems. All of your feelings, anxieties, hangups, fears and phobias come from some definite event or series of events in your past. And it is our experience that the past includes prior incarnations. Even marriage and sexual problems are often related to previous lifetimes.*

## The Album Tapes

**Tape 1: Back-to-the-Cause Regression** — Structured for you to decide what you desire to investigate (e.g., a fear, a talent, a relationship, an affliction, an unusual situation). Dick directs you to focus upon it as he guides you back in time to the origin of the situation in your past — your current life or a past life. You are instructed to perceive the cause without pain or emotion, only as an observer. The investigation is approached from several different perspectives and you are awakened with the strong suggestion to release the past if it is negative.

**Tape 2: Wisdom Erases Karma** — Once you know the cause, this expanded-state-of-consciousness session guides you into your Higher-Self to achieve a karmic overview of the situation so you can fully understand the fear behind the problem and what you need to accept to completely eliminate the negativity from your life once and for all. Fear-based emotions are the cause of all problems between human beings.

## You Were Born Again to Be Together

By Dick Sutphen
1976/252 pages
**$4.50**
$6.50 postpaid from:
Simon & Schuster, Inc.
200 Old Tappan Rd.
Old Tappan, NJ 07675

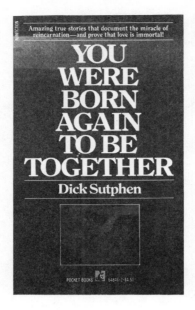

*If you love someone today, chances are you loved them in a past life.*

Johnathan Wells slid his gold pan into the creek bed in search of placer deposits. He spun away when he heard the unmistakable sound of a rattlesnake in the brush beside him. The snake struck, sinking its fangs into his wrist. Johnathan reeled backward, grabbed a rock, and quickly killed the large diamondback. He then sat down and cut open the wound and began to extract the poison.

A short time later a young Yavapai Apache woman found him lying unconscious, his wrist swollen and bleeding from his own incisions. She immediately took the blankets from his bedroll, made him comfortable, and began to treat the wound. Repeatedly during the night she changed the poultice used to draw out the poison and maintained the fire to keep him warm.

The time was the late 1800s near Wickenburg, Arizona. It was summer and the hills were filled with prospectors and mine workers.

Johnathan recovered, and the Indian woman remained with him. Together, for the next several years, they worked the rivers and creeks of central Arizona, making a living but never much more. A daughter was born, and they settled down in the desert foothills in an adobe house they built. They had a small herd of cows.

Then late in the summer, seven years after they first met, they were panning in a creek near their home. A flash flood from the mountains to the north rose as a wall of water and almost instantly engulfed them. Johnathan was able to swim to high ground, but he never saw his wife again ... until 1971, nearly one hundred years later, when they met at a party in Los Angeles, California. She was twenty-four and he was twenty-seven. They fell in love at first sight and soon were married.

Today they own a small riding academy and horse training center, living, working, and loving once more in the foothills of Arizona.

They were born again to be together.

*- Dick Sutphen*
From *You Were Born Again to be Together*

## The Search for Omm Sety

By Jonathan Cott
1987/256 pages
**$17.95**
$18.39 postpaid from:
Doubleday & Co.
501 Franklin Ave.
Garden City, NY 11530

*In 1907 when Dorothy Louise Eady was three years old, she suffered a near-fatal fall in her parents' London flat. It was an accident that would change her life forever. From that day forward, Dorothy insisted that England was not her "real" home. As she grew up, she began spending her days in the Egyptology wing of the British Museum — rooms filled with relics whose strange familiarity and attraction convinced her that Egypt was where she belonged. Dorothy recalled that in an earlier life, as a fourteen-year-old orphan named Bentreshyt, she had served in the temple at Abydos and fallen tragically in love with Pharaoh Sety the First. When Bentreshyt discovered she was pregnant, rather than reveal her secret, she commited suicide. Although Dorothy knew that she had lived in Egypt previously, no one — not even her family — believed her.*

*In 1953, Dorothy Eady left England forever and moved to Egypt.*

---

# What Is a Walk-in?

*By Ruth Montgomery*

The Guides, those mysterious pen-pals who communicate with me through automatic writing, describe Walk-ins as high-minded entities from the spirit plane who are permitted under certain circumstances to take over the unwanted bodies of other human beings. The motivation for the Walk-ins must be humanitarian, to help others along their spiritual path and to benefit all mankind. It cannot be for selfish ends, and therefore bears no resemblance to the many documented cases of "possession" in which multiple egos or malevolent spirits invade an inhabited body, creating havoc for all concerned.

The displaced Walk-out must be one who desperately wishes to depart, or who because of a clinical death or near-death experience is unable to keep his/her body alive. The Walk-in, coming directly from the spirit plane, is then able to re-energize the failing body, and because of high idealism and enthusiasm the personality of the "new" occupant often astounds friends and family members who had become accustomed to the discouraged, ineffectual mannerism of the body's original occupant.

I wrote about a number of such cases in *Strangers Among Us* and *Threshold to Tomorrow*. More recently, I asked the Guides for any new comments on the phenomenon, and they wrote: "Walk-ins are by no means perfected souls. They have similar faults to all the rest of us, but because of their highly developed awareness earned through previous lifetimes, they are able if they so wish to enter the body of one who desperately wishes to depart the earth plane or is unable to keep the body alive. They have assistance on this side to prepare for that step and then to make the substitution, sometimes after only a brief interval but more often after a rather lengthy preparation of several months or so.

They are required to pledge that they will work for the common good in helping people to fulfill their potential and are not permitted to interfere with the life plan of others while doing so. Sometimes their ego gets in the way, and when that occurs, Walk-ins, like anyone else, will retrogress and must return in normal fashion in future incarnations, if they wish to equalize their karma between good and bad and proceed on their pathway to eventual reunion with the Creator. We stress that they have human failings like anyone else, because they are as human as you or we are. It is just that they have adopted this

---

> WE STRESS THAT THEY HAVE HUMAN FEELINGS LIKE ANYONE ELSE, BECAUSE THEY ARE AS HUMAN AS YOU OR WE ARE.

---

course in order to avoid the lengthy years of earthly preparation for their life work — babyhood, childhood and school days — and get on quickly with their altruistic objectives.

"A few of those about whom you wrote in *Threshold to Tomorrow* have apparently retrogressed by allowing their own egos, perhaps as a result of the publicity they received from the book, to get in the way of their spiritual objectives. They are thinking more of self than of general uplift. It is an all too human failing, and they are not to be condemned more than others, except that having pledged on entry to work for the

common good they are sadly tainting their own karmic records. But others of them are soaring along beautifully and contributing greatly to the preparation for the New Age."

Since that book appeared I have been literally swamped by letters from readers who either believe that they themselves are Walk-ins or are convinced that they know one. Some who describe their complete alterations of personality, ideals and attitudes after a traumatic experience sounds to me like true Walk-ins, whereas others are probably cases of wishful thinking. Unfortunately I cannot give them positive verification. The Guides, because of so many thousands of requests, no longer identify Walk-ins or bring personal messages for the readers who beg to know their purpose in life. "No time and not our mission," the Guides explain, adding that the reason they took on the often onerous (I feel sure) task of writing through me is to reach a large segment of the population with spiritual truths that can help all humankind, rather than isolated individuals.

The Walk-ins say that many of our towering leaders of the past have been Walk-ins, and that others are currently in the citadels of power in various nations to help prevent World War III, to prepare us for the shift of the earth on its axis at the end of this century, and to usher in the peaceful New Age. They further assert that a Walk-in will be elected President of the United States in the decade of the 1990s, although they are not yet ready to divulge his identity. And they also stress that not all of today's Walk-ins are in positions of leadership or authority. Many splendid ones are going about their appointed rounds as taxi drivers, construction workers, business and professional people while quietly sowing seeds of spiritual thought that can make us all better human beings — if we try!

# Anwar Sadat: A Walk-in?

Like millions of others, I have long been a staunch admirer of Anwar Sadat, the late great president of Egypt who, in 1977, electrified the world by his historic visit to Israel. This dramatic bid for peace between warring Moslems and Jews in the volatile Middle East was unprecedented, and required incalculable bravery, since the other Arab states refused to recognize Israel's right even to exist as a nation. Thanks largely to the stunning actions of this Moslem leader, who was honored as *Time* magazine's Man of the Year in 1978 and awarded the Nobel Peace Prize together with Israeli Prime Minister Menachem Begin, the Camp David Accords came into being, and in 1979 a peace treaty between the two battle-scarred nations was signed on the south lawn of the White House.

The free world breathed a collective sigh of relief. Then came Black Tuesday, October 6, 1981, and while television cameras recorded Sadat's review of the troops on Egypt's Armed Forces Day, religious fanatics wearing the uniform of Egyptian soldiers assassinated that noble man.

Shortly before this despicable event, the Guides told me that Anwar Sadat was a Walk-in, and that the transferral of souls occurred while he was in prison.

Anwar Sadat, one of thirteen children of an Egyptian civil servant and his part-Sudanese wife, was born December 25, 1918, in a village on the Nile River Delta. The family moved to Cairo when he was twelve, and after the Abbassia Military Academy was reformed to admit lower-and middle-class applicants, young Sadat was accepted as a student. There he became friendly with Nasser, a fellow cadet. They graduated together in 1938 and were then stationed at the garrison town of Mankabad, where they and ten other young officers banded together to form a group that Sadat described as "a secret revolutionary society dedicated to the task of liberation." World War II broke out the following year, and British-controlled Egypt became a battleground, with

## Threshold to Tomorrow

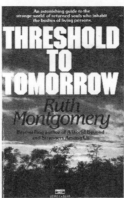

By Ruth Montgomery
1982/214 pages
**$3.50**
$4.50 postpaid from:
Random House
400 Hahn Rd.
Westminister, MD 21157

*You'll be introduced to 17 notable Walk-ins including Dick Sutphen, Anwar Sadat and Jason Winters. Ruth describes each person before, during and after the Walk-in process is completed.*

many patriotic Egyptians, including Sadat, viewing the possibility of German victory as a God-given means of ejecting the British overlords.

After his political arrest and escape into the underground, Sadat intensified his revolutionary activities and masterminded two assassinations, one of which was bloodily successful. In his autobiography, *In Search of Identity,* the title of which seems remarkably significant for a Walk-in, Sadat frankly told of his murderous intrigues, his lies and deceits in those days before the apparent transferral of egos.

From the aliens' jail where he had previously served time, Sadat was transferred to Cairo Central Prison, a dismal hole, where he was placed in solitary confinement in Cell 54; and according to the Guides it was there that the discouraged young revolutionary finally withdrew, to make way for a Walk-in of high ideals and love of mankind.

I asked the Guides for further comment on Sadat, and they wrote: "Sadat is now watching from this side (the spirit plane) and is pleased

## Strangers Among Us

By Ruth Montgomery
1979/256 pages
**$3.50**
$4.50 postpaid from:
Random House
400 Hahn Rd.
Westminister, MD 21157

*Are Walk-ins for real? Ruth is introduced to the concept of high-minded entities taking over bodies no longer wanted by the former owner who wished to return "home" to spirit. She names some famous Walk-ins including Moses, Christ, Lincoln and Gandhi.*

with the progress that his successor is making in his beloved Egypt. Before be became Anwar Sadat through the Walk-in process he had been an Egyptian of great renown. He loved every inch of that barren country, especially along the Nile, where life flowed through a desert land. When he became aware of the utter discouragement of the man in prison, and of his desire to leave that body and that stinking prison, he gladly stepped in, bringing with him awareness and a desire for peace. The transferral occurred in the darkest hour of that solitary prison confinement, and his Walk-in predecessor is here now, saying, "If I had devoted myself to love instead of hate and had sought peaceful ways to overthrow the British in my country, it would not have become necessary for me to leave. But I was deeply discouraged, hopeless and unwilling to face a longer time in incarceration, so I willingly stepped out so that a greater soul might have that body to help my homeland. Praise Allah!"

- *Ruth Montgomery*
*From* Threshold to Tomorrow

# What's So New Age About Religion?

I have read about the Buddhist concepts of karma and dharma. I even reviewed the 227 rules that Buddhist monks must follow, and then I realized how much I have to learn. But I came to the conclusion that what it is all about is self-awareness. Enlightenment starts within the individual. And if America is to cope with its current dilemmas, it must reach a higher level of consciousness than the level at which our problems were created. The belief of Tibetan Buddhism in the evolution of the individual is harmonious with the desire of a growing number of our citizens for spiritual growth to reach a higher consciousness. People involved with spiritual belief too often renounce politics and ordinary life. What His Holiness teaches is that one aspect of life connects with every other. Political solutions are linked directly with spiritual growth, and that is why this visit is so timely for America. The message of Tibetan Buddhism is entirely consistent with our Jewish and Christian heritage. The visionary humanism of His Holiness may even help us to find a more authentic expression of the religions with which we are familiar. All the world's religions lead along the same path.

> *- U.S. Congressman*
> *Charles G. Rose*
> *introducing His Holiness*
> *Tenzin Gyatso,*
> *the Dalai Lama*

` ` ` ` ` `

All religions have, generally speaking, the same motivation of love and compassion. Though there are often very large differences in the philosophical field, the basic goal of improvement is more or less the same. Still, each faith has special methods. Although our cultures are naturally different, our systems are coming closer together because of the world's becoming smaller and smaller with better communication, providing good opportunities for us to learn from each other. This, I feel, is very useful.

For example, Christianity has many very practical methods that are useful in the service of humankind, especially in the fields of education and health. Thus, for Buddhists there is much we can learn. At the same time, there are Buddhist teachings on deep meditation and philosophical reasoning from which Christians can learn helpful techniques. In ancient India the Buddhists and Hindus learned many points from each other.

Since these systems basically have the same purpose of benefit for humankind, on the negative side there is nothing wrong with learning from each other, and on the positive side it helps develop respect for each other; it helps promote harmony and unity.

> *- His Holiness Tenzin Gyatso,*
> *the Dalai Lama, from*
> *Kindness, Clarity and Insight*

---

## What Is Enlightenment?
### *Exploring the Goal of the Spiritual Path*
Edited by John White
1984/232 pages
**$8.95**
$11.35 postpaid from:
Jeremy P. Tarcher, Inc.
9110 Sunset Blvd.
Los Angeles, CA 90069

*A star collection of fifteen of the world's most respected spiritual teachers answer the question "What is Enlightenment?" This highly readable volume will assist every reader in their own personal quest for self-understanding and enlightenment.*

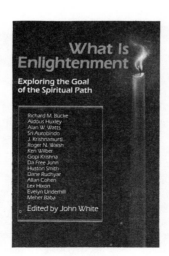

**Contributors include:**
Richard M. Bucke
Aldous Huxley
Alan W. Watts
Sri Aurobindo
J. Krishnamurti
Roger N. Walsh
Ken Wilbur
Gopi Krishna
Da Free John
Huston Smith
Dane Rudhyar
Allan Cohen
Lex Hixon
Evelyn Underhill
Meher Baba

## The Way Beyond

By William L. Mikulas
1987/150 pages
**$5.95**
$7.45 postpaid from:
The Theosophical Publishing House
306 West Geneva Rd.
P.O. Box 270
Wheaton, IL 60189-0270

*This is a book full of practical exercises you can use to maximize your potential for peak spiritual experience. Five basic practices create the focus of this examination: meditation, concentration, mindfulness, opening the heart and reducing attachments.*

Many people find that keeping a journal is a valuable aid in personal and transpersonal growth. The journal of writings and drawings can include many things, such as one or more of the following: a meditation log reporting daily perceptions, experiences, and thoughts about your meditation practice; an attachment log each day noting attachments of particular interest and significance and what you are learning about dealing with them; a dream diary kept by your bedside for recording dreams as soon afterward as they occur as possible; and a daily or weekly spiritual journal in which you note ideas, lessons, quotes, reminders, etc. about your spiritual practice. Keeping a journal can help you think more clearly about your practices and notice patterns and interrelationships you might otherwise overlook. It can also help you see progress where you think there is none. Reading over a journal you have kept for a while gives you a good perspective of yourself.

*- William L. Mikulas*
*From* The Way Beyond

# The Theory of Misdescription

Of course one can, on the ground of the contradictions, refuse to believe that the mystic has any such experience as he says he has. He is not suspected of telling an untruth, but he must be making a mistake. He may be unintentionally misdescribing his experience. He says that he experiences a total void which is yet a fullness, a light which is also darkness. But any such descriptions — like all descriptions of anything anywhere — include elements of interpretation. Just as it is impossible to obtain pure sense experience without interpretation, so it is impossible to obtain pure mystical experience. Any statements about it, even though apparently pure description, will include conceptual interpretations. And this might result in misdescription. If what the mystic experiences were described accurately and correctly, the contradictions might disappear. Let us consider this possible theory.

*- W.T. Stace*
*From* Mysticism and Philosophy

---

# Visions and Voices Are Not Mystical Phenomena

Let us begin by excluding from the class of mystical states certain experiences which popular opinion may perhaps tend to regard as mystical, but which are not genuinely so. The chief such occurrences to be excluded are visions and voices. Not only is this the opinion of most competent scholars, but it has also been the opinion which the great mystics themselves have generally held. They have often been subject to visions and voices, but have usually discounted them as of doubtful value or importance and at any rate as not to be confused with genuine mystical experiences.

A Catholic saint may have a vision

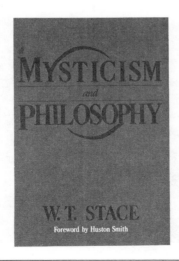

of the Virgin Mary or hear a voice which he attributes to Jesus. A Hindu may have a vision of the goddess Kali. Neither these nor the voices heard by St. Joan of Arc, Socrates, or Mohammed, are to be accounted as mystical phenomena, although it is quite possible that

## Mysticism and Philosophy

By W.T. Stace
1960/350 pages
**$11.95**
$14.35 postpaid from:
Jeremy P. Tarcher, Inc.
9110 Sunset Blvd.
Los Angeles, CA 90069

*The philosophical examination of the "mystical experience" presented in this book serves as a very useful tool in clarifying, through historical and contemporary analysis, the nature and value of this transcendent state for the individual and humankind.*

---

these persons may also have been the subjects of genuine mystical experiences.

*W.T. Stace*
*From* Mysticism and Philosophy

# Mystics & Masters
## Alice Bailey

The writings of Alice Bailey, based on teachings she received from a master (Djwhal Khul) referred to as "The Tibetan," comprise one of the most accessible sets of esoteric knowledge available to the Western world. She wrote a total of 24 volumes that address all areas of metaphysical knowledge, human spirituality and cosmic order.

# Extract from a Statement by the Tibetan
### *August, 1934*

... I live in a physical body like other men, on the borders of Tibet, and at times ... preside over a large group of Tibetan lamas, when my other duties permit ... Those associated with me in the work of the Hierarchy (and all true disciples are associated in this work) know me by still another name and office.

## Bailey's Pathway

I am a brother of yours, who has travelled a little longer upon the Path than has the average student, and has therefore incurred greater responsibilities. My work is to teach and spread the knowledge of the Ageless Wisdom wherever I can find a response, and I have been doing this for many years. I have told you much; yet at the same time I have told you nothing which would lead you to offer me that blind obedience and the foolish devotion which the emotional aspirant offers to the Guru and Master Whom he is as yet unable to contact.

> *- Alice Bailey*
> *quoting The Tibetan*
> *From* Ponder On This

## The Great Invocation

From the point of Light
    within the Mind of God
Let the light stream forth into
    the minds of men.
    Let Light descend on Earth.

From the point of Love
    within the Heart of God
Let love stream forth into
    the hearts of men.
    May Christ return to Earth.

From the centre where the
    Will of God is known
Let purpose guide the little
    wills of men —

The purpose which the
    Masters know and serve.

From the center which we
    call the race of men
Let the Plan of Love and
    Light work out.
And may it seal the door
    where evil dwells.

Let Light and Love and
    Power restore the Plan
    on Earth.

The Great Invocation is always presented with the Bailey writings.

## Ponder on This
### *From the Writings of Alice Bailey of The Tibetan, Djwhal Khul*

1971/432 pages
**$9.00**
$10.00 postpaid from:
Lucis Publishing Company
113 University Place, 11th Floor
New York, NY 10003

"Scattered through all my writings over the years is a mass of information which needs collating and bringing together as a basis for the instruction of disciples in training for an initiation."

> *- Alice Bailey*
> *quoting The Tibetan*
> *From* The Rays and
> the Initiations

The present compilation by a student is an attempt in this direction.

> *- Alice Bailey*
> *From* Ponder On This

## The Lucis Trust

113 University Place, 11th Floor
New York, NY 10003

*A nonprofit world service organization, the Lucis Trust is concerned with the establishment of human relations and world cooperation and sharing. In overseeing the Lucis Publishing Company, Lending Library and the Arcane School (found by Alice Bailey in 1923), the Trust publishes and promotes the writings of Alice Bailey.*

*Beacon magazine, published bi-monthly by Lucis Press, presents the esoteric philosophy and principles of universal Ageless Wisdom teachings as a contemporary way of life.*

# Christianity and the Western Tradition

## A Course in Miracles

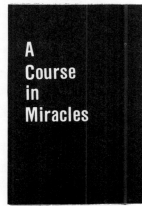

Channeled by Helen Schucman
1975/1110 pages
**$25.00** postpaid from:
Foundation for Inner Peace
Box 635
Tiburon, CA 94920

*As its title implies, the Course is arranged throughout as a teaching device. The curriculum is explained step-by-step at both the theoretical and practical levels.*

*Christian in statement, the Course opens our awareness to acknowledging Christ in all our brothers, and His Presence in ourselves. Forgiveness is recognized as the path to enlightenment for it reflects the law of Heaven where giving and receiving are the same. Acknowledging that there are many versions of the universal curriculum and they all lead to God. The Course specifically states "a universal theology is impossible, but a universal experience is not only possible but necessary."*

Lesson 158 - "Today I learn to give as I receive."

— A Course in Miracles

## Edgar Cayce's Story of Jesus

Selected and Edited by Jeffrey Furst
1968/414 pages
**$3.95**
$5.95 postpaid from:
A.R.E. Press
Box 595
Virginia Beach, VA 23451

*This book details what the Cayce readings say about the soul we call Jesus His birth as the man Jesus, His childhood, travels, initiation, ministry, crucifixion and resurrection. You will also discover what the readings say about the people surrounding Jesus as well as the world environment at that time and in Old Testament times.*

## Cayce on Christ

Q. What present printed version of the Bible gives the nearest to the true meaning of both Old and New Testaments?

A. The nearest true version for the entity is *that you apply* of whatever version you read *in your life*. It isn't that you learn from anyone. You may only have the direction. The learning, the teaching is within self. For where hath He promised to meet you? Within that temple!

There have been many versions of that which was purposed to have been written, and has changed from all those versions. But remember that the whole gospel of Jesus Christ is, "Thou shalt love the Lord thy God with all thy mind, thy heart and thy body; and thy neighbour as thyself. Do this and thou shalt have eternal life." The rest of the book is trying to describe that. It is the same in any language, in any version. (2072-14)

— *Edgar Cayce*
*From* The Story of Jesus

## Education in the New Age

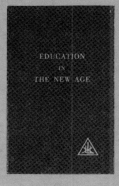

By Alice Bailey
1954/174 pages
**$7.00**
$8.00 postpaid from:
Lucis Publishing Co.
113 University Place, 11th Floor
New York, NY 10003

This presentation might be regarded as concerning itself with three different aspects of one general theme, which is that of the new and coming educational methods and ideas. The objective is to elucidate the cultural unfoldment of the race and to consider the next step to be taken in the mental development of humanity. Teaching, if true, must be in line with the past and must provide scope for endeavour in the present and must also hold out further enlightenment for those who have succeeded or are succeeding in attaining the indicated goals. There must be a spiritual future indicated. It is that which is required now.

— *Alice Bailey*
*From* Education in the New Age

### Speaking of Silence
### *Christians and Buddhists on the Contemplative Way*

Edited by Susan Walker
1987/336 pages
**$12.95**
$14.45 postpaid from:
Paulist Press
997 MacArthur Blvd.
Mahwah, NJ 07430

*For several years Christians and Buddhists have been meeting at the Naropa Institute in Boulder, Colorado, to share their understanding of meditation. As such, it has been an ongoing exchange among spiritual teachers. Despite some superficial differences, their experiences of the transcendent were very similar. Includes a complete resource of Christian and Buddhist contemplative centers in North America.*

### The Classics of Western Spirituality

Available from:
Paulist Press
997 MacArthur Blvd.
Mahwah, NJ 07430

This collection of Western mysticism includes the original writings of the Western tradition mystics, translated and introduced by internationally recognized scholars and religious thinkers. Sample titles include: *John of the Cross: Selected Writings, Pseudo Dionysius: The Complete Works, Meister Eckhart: Teacher and Preacher,* and the newly published *Angelus Silesius: The Cherubinic Wanderer.*

### Sources of American Spirituality

Available from:
Paulist Press
997 MacArthur Blvd.
Mahwah, NJ 07430

This new multivolume series presents the complete picture of American Spirituality from colonial times to the present. From mystics and clergymen to major themes and experiences, all are explored through letters, diaries, sermons and other original writings to paint a rich picture of the American experience of God. Some sample titles include: *Devotion to the Holy Spirit in American Catholicism, Elizabeth Seton, Alaskan Missionary Spirituality, William Ellery Channing* and the newest edition — *Eastern Spirituality in America.*

### The Christ Book
### *What Did He Really Say?*

By Christopher Hills
1980/214 pages
**$10.95**
$12.95 postpaid from:
University of the Trees
P.O. Box 66
Boulder Creek, CA 95006

*In this book, Christopher Hills talks with his students about the true meanings of many of Christ's mysterious parables and miracles. Hill's perspective has a certain air of truth and relevance about it in light of present New Age philosophy and scientific documentation of paranormal experiences and yogic mastery.*

# Ram Dass

*Ram Dass, a.k.a. Richard Alpert, is the embodiment of the 1960's society dropout who went on to effect spiritual enlightenment through study in India with his guru Neem Kanli Baba. His poignant, heartwarming, and sharing style provides the perfect vehicle for the integration of Eastern spiritual philosophy into the Western way of life. As a lecturer, writer, and founder of several service organizations, including his most recent, The Seva Foundation, Ram Dass has dedicated his life to service and the spread of enlightenment.*

## The Seva Foundation

108 Spring Lake Dr.
Chelsea, MI 48118

*This is a network of people drawn together in a common goal of service. Helping to raise and distribute funds, as well as create and staff various service organizations, Seva ("Seva" is the sanskrit word for service) workers also like to have fun doing it.*

---

## An Evening with Ram Dass
*Celebrating Spirit Through Service*

Produced and Directed by
Jack Herman
1987/90-minute videocassette, VHS
**$39.95**
$42.95 postpaid from:
ARC Audio Visual Enterprises, Inc.
500 West End Ave.
New York, NY 10024

*This 90-minute videotape was filmed on location in New York City during his 1985-86 "Celebrating Spirit with Service" tour. It's filled with anecdotes, personal accounts, and wisdom in Dass's personal, heartwarming style.*

## How Can I Help?
### Stories and Reflections on Service

By Ram Dass
and Paul Gorman
1985/244 pages
**$6.95**
$8.45 postpaid from:
Random House
400 Hahn Rd.
Westminster, MD 21157

*In his continuing tradition of bridge-building between Eastern enlightenment and the Western lifestyle, Ram Dass brings us a practical handbook of helping.*

*Anecdotes, insights, and practical guidelines are interwoven in a compassionate book for daily life.*

Many times ... the needs of others are what bring us to a state of sharp concentration. Whether it's because we feel very secure with those we're with or because we are functioning under conditions of extreme crisis, we find that in this state of intense concentration helpful insights arise on their own, as a function of our one-pointedness. In these experiences we meet a resource of remarkable potential. While we may be frustrated in not having access to it all the time, these experiences lead us to inquire whether there might be something we could do more regularly and formally to quiet the mind, strengthen its concentration, make available the deeper insights that often result, and bring them into closer attunement with the empathy and compassion of our heart. How immeasurably this might enhance our ability to help others.

- Ram Dass
From How Can I Help?

# Hindu/Indian Masters

Many masters of ancient Indian and Hindu wisdom, often called guru or swami, have made their way to the United States to share their enlightenment with an eager Western world. Occasionally, a master is of such caliber, radiating love, mastery and enlightenment, that he generates a devoted following of students who desire to celebrate, learn from and immortalize the master's teachings. Most everyone would be able to derive some gleanings of truth, if not the essential truth, from every authentic master's writings. Yet it is true, that there are as many paths and teachers to the Source as there are disciples to discover it.

# Swami Amar Jyoti

Born in India in 1928, Swami Amar Jyoti traveled to the Himalayas where his enlightenment was realized. He is the founder of many spiritual centers and ashrams, both in India and the United States.

## Truth Consciousness

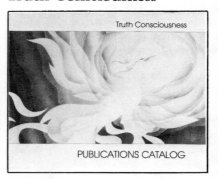

Gold Hill
Salina Star Rt.
Boulder, CO 80302

Truth Consciousness is a nonprofit organization which serves as a vehicle for Swami Amar Jyoti's work in America. The ashrams and community centers associated with Truth Consciousness provide a place for seekers to grow towards enlightenment under the guidance of the guru. All programs and information open to the public.

# Flight

Satyakam had never seen such a benevolent look on his Master's face — and what love! He wished to clasp the whole body of his guru, but etiquette prevented him from doing so. The ageless one approved of this control of emotion with satisfaction, and bade him good-bye. Satyakam watched him going, but lo! he too, like the swans, vanished suddenly in thin air. He had believed all along that his guru could do all this, but this was the first time he actually saw him doing it! The quick succession of the two vanishings jolted him to the core of his spine, waking him fully. Soon he settled into the new dimensions of his opening consciousness.

As he aimlessly turned back to walk on the grassy bank of the lake, he felt that his feet were not touching the ground! Curiosity compelled him to look down, but he couldn't bend his neck. He felt his body subject to a certain vibratory phenomenon where he could only stir the pupils of his eyes. From the corners of his eyes he visualized that his feet were a few inches above the ground. He was walking as usual, but on air! His whole body seemed light, in an unusual state of cheerfulness and inspiration. It simply floated as he walked more and more. Soon he came to the southeast corner of the lake where the mountain started towards the north. His eyes spontaneously looked up to the peak and a subconscious drive to reach there arose. All of a sudden his body flew up and, in the speed of a thought, he was standing on the peak! He became afraid and felt uncertain as he stood there, not knowing how to get down! Soon he gazed down on the northeast corner of the lake and saw his Master standing and looking up at him with amusement! Satyakam felt a vibratory pull, a sort of controlling computer, and, as if on wings, he descended slowly toward where his Master was standing. As he landed nearby, he felt secure. A teasing smile crossed the lips of his Master. Satyakam seemed neither ashamed nor mindful. He had enough self-control at his command. Each lesson that his guru had imparted to him, whether through words, example or actual happening, was grasped by him intelligently.

- Swami Amar Jyoti
From Spirit of Himalaya

## Spirit of Himalaya
### *The Story of a Truth Seeker*

By Swami Amar Jyoti
1985/124 pages
**$5.95**
$7.00 postpaid from:
Truth Consciousness
Gold Hill
Salina Star Rt.
Boulder, CO 80302

*A clear and inspiring story, full of beautiful nature images and the startling, yet heavenly, reality of enlightenment. The beautiful cover artwork is also available as a poster or as notecards from Truth Consciousness.*

"The quality of the goal you choose determines the quality of your life".
- *Swami Amar Jyoti*
*From* Spirit of Himalaya

## Spirit of Himalaya
### Notecards
### *with Quote by Master*

4" x 9" notecard/**$1.25**
6/**$6.25**
postage: 30¢ for one/17¢ each additional card

---

## Spirit of Himalaya
### Cover Art
### *with Quote by Master*

21" x 12" poster
**$3.95**
$5.50 postpaid from:
Truth Consciousness
Gold Hill
Salina Star Rt.
Boulder, CO 80302

## Satsang Notes of Swami Amar Jyoti

By Kessler Frey
1977/104 pages
**$2.95**
$3.75 postpaid from:
Truth Consciousness
Gold Hill
Salina Star Rt.
Boulder, CO 80302

*The term "Satsang" is a Sanskrit word meaning "Spiritual Communication with Truth." Collected here, by a devotee of Swami Amar Jyoti, is the essence of his satsang.*

# Kabbalah: A Definition

The literal meaning of the word Kabbalah is Receiving: thus, in the opening sentence of the Ethics of the Fathers, we read that "Moses received the Torah from Sinai" — the word used for "receive" being "kibel", the past tense of the verb "kabal". It was clear to the sages that the Torah received by Moses was unique in that it contained the knowledge necessary not only for the Jews of that time, but for all generations. Thus, when Rabbi Shimon came to reveal the mystical part of the Torah in the Zohar, he related it closely to the written Torah so as to demonstrate that Torah and Kabbalah are but different aspects of the same essential whole. The Torah itself represents the outer shell while Kabbalah is the inner core, concealed from sight — a relationship similar to that which exists between the physical body and soul. Torah reveals the word of God, while Kabbalah reveals the hidden and the revealed ... Kabbalah, then, may be understood as the study of wisdom.
- *Dr. Philip S. Berg*
*From* Kabbalah for the Layman

# Kabbalah

## *Kabbalah for the Layman*
By Dr. Philip S. Berg
1981/194 pages
**$9.95**
$10.95 postpaid from:
Research Centre of Kabbalah
83-15 124 Place
Kew Gardens, NY 11415

*A modern readable text on the development of Kabbalistic thought into the twentieth century. This book focuses on the understanding and use of the Kabbalah as a tool for spiritual growth and the understandings of the creation and purpose of existence.*

## Ramakrishna-Vivekananda Center of New York

17 East 94th St.
New York, NY 10128

Founded by Swami Nikhilananda in 1933, the center bases its teachings on the system of Hindu Vedanta especially as explained by Sri Ramakrishna (1836-1886) and his disciple Swami Vivekananda (1863-1902) and demonstrated in their lives.

Vedanta teaches that every soul is potentially divine and that its divinity may be manifested through worship, contemplation, unselfish work, and philosophical discrimination. The center offers membership, courses and publications seeking to stimulate the growth of the individual's innate spirituality.

# The Gospel of Sri Ramakrishna

Abridged Edition
Translated into English with an Introduction by Swami Nikhilananda
1942/640 pages
**$8.50**
$10.00 postpaid from:.
Ramakrishna-Vivekananda Center
17 East 94th St.
New York, NY 10128

This book is especially designed for daily devotional study.

He is born to no purpose, who having the rare privilege of being born a man, is unable to realize God in this life.
- Sri Ramakrishna
  From The Gospel of
  Sri Ramakrishna

# Objects of Desire

The next condition the disciple must fulfill is to conceive an extreme desire to be free.

We are like moths, plunging into the flaming fire of the senses, though fully knowing that it will burn us. Sense enjoyment only enhances our desire. Desire is never satiated by enjoyment; enjoyment only increases desire, as butter fed into fire increases the fire. Desire is increased by desire. Knowing all this, people still plunge into it all the time. Life after life they have been going after the objects of desire, suffering extremely in consequence; yet they cannot give up desire. Even religion, which should rescue them from this terrible bondage to desire, they have made a means of satisfying desire. Rarely do they ask God to free them from bondage to the body and senses, from slavery to desire. Instead they pray to Him for health and prosperity, for long life: "O God, cure my headache, give me some money or something!" The circle of vision has become so narrow, so degraded, so beastly, so animal! None is desiring anything beyond this body. Oh, the terrible degradation, the terrible misery of it! Of what little consequence are the flesh, the five senses, the stomach!

- Swami Vivekananda
  From Vivekananda: The
  Yoga and Other Works

## Raja-Yoga

By Swami Vivekananda Center
1956/320 pages
**$7.95**
$9.45 postpaid from:
Ramakrishna-Vivekananda Center
17 East 94th St.
New York, NY 10128

A clear presentation, in the swami's own words, of the practice and philosophy of Raja Yoga, a discipline in acquiring mastery over the mind.

Each soul is potentially divine. The goal is to manifest this divinity within by controlling nature: external and internal. Do this either by work, or worship, or psychic control, or philosophy — by one, or more, or all of these — and be free.

- Vivekananda
  From Raja-Yoga

# Vivekananda
## The Yogas and Other Works

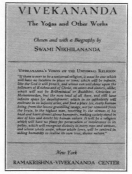

By Swami Nikhilananda
1953/1,018 pages
**$19.95**
$21.95 postpaid from:
Ramakrishna-Vivekananda Center
17 East 94th St.
New York, NY 10128

The selected materials from the complete works of Vivekananda are compiled here, presenting an accessible understanding of Hindu philosophy, as well as a portrait of the sensitive, profound and inspiring human that he was.

## The Flight of the Eagle

By J. Krishnamurti
1971/154 pages
**$3.95**
$5.45 postpaid from:
Harper & Row Publishers, Inc.
2350 Virginia Ave.
Hagerstown, MD 21740

"The eagle in its flight does not have a mark; the scientist does. Inquiring into this question of freedom, there must be not only scientific observation, but also the flight of the eagle that does not leave a mark."

- J. Krishnamurti
From The Flight of
the Eagle

## The Awakening of Intelligence

By J. Krishnamurti
1973/538 pages
**$12.95**
$14.45 postpaid from:
Harper & Row Publishers, Inc.
2350 Virginia Ave.
Hagerstown, MD 21740

# The Art of Seeing

We never see, or actually hear, what another is saying; we are either emotional, sentimental or very intellectual — which obviously prevents us from actually seeing the colour, the beauty of the light, the trees, the birds, and from listening to those crows; we never are in direct relationship with any of this. And I doubt very much if we are in relationship with anything, even with our own ideas, thoughts, motives, impressions; there is always the image which is observing, even when we observe ourselves ...

... Do please observe what I am talking about, not merely hear the words of the speaker, but observe yourselves, using the speaker as a mirror in which you can see

yourself. What the speaker has to say is of very little importance, and the speaker himself is of no importance whatsoever, but what you gather out of observing yourself is important. It is so because there must be a total revolution, a complete mutation in our minds, in our way of living, in our feeling, in the activities of our daily life. And to bring about such fundamental, deep revolution is only possible when we know how to look; because when you do look, you are not only looking with your eyes but you are also looking with your mind.

- J. Krishnamurti
From The Awakening of
Intelligence

## Jiddu Krishnamurti

*Jiddu Krishnamurti (1897-1986) is regarded internationally as one of the great educators and philosophers of our time. For over sixty years he traveled throughout the world giving public talks to large audiences. He published over thirty books and founded schools in the United States, England, and India. Information about his publications and recordings can be obtained from the Krishnamurti Foundation of America.*

## Krishnamurti Foundation of America

P.O. Box 216
Ojai, CA 93023
*The Foundation is dedicated to disseminating the Krishnamurti teachings in an undistorted or unspoiled manner.*

## You Are the World

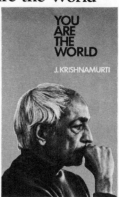

By J. Krishnamurti
1972/150 pages
**$4.95**
$6.45 postpaid from:
Harper & Row Publishers, Inc.
2350 Virginia Ave.
Hagerstown, MD 21740

What *is* important is not to follow anybody but to understand oneself. If you go into yourself without effort, fear, without any sense of restraint, and really delve deeply, you will find extraordinary things; and you don't have to read a single book. The speaker has not read a single book about any of these things: philosophy, psychology, sacred books. In oneself lies the whole world, and if you know how to look and learn, then the door is there and the key is in your hand. Nobody on earth can give you either that key or the door to open, except yourself.

- J. Krishnamurti
From You Are the World

## Hinduism Today

1819 Second St.
Concord, CA 94519
Monthly/**$15.00** for one year
**$25.00** for two years
*An international monthly newspaper "fostering Hindu solidarity among 650 million members of a global religion."*

# Sufism

Sufism is not confined to a religion or culture, it is essentially a way of living and seeing the world which honors the divinity in all life and the sacredness of all religious traditions.

The Sufi path represents those mystics who have sought the truth in all ages, however, time has associated certain teachings and disciplines with the Sufi name. Tales and parables provide the best vehicle for expressing Sufi teachings which instruct the inner self. Sufi teachings cannot be learned intellectually; they must be acquired experientially. Contemporary Sufi ideals recognize and foster planetary consciousness through Universal Worship Services.

## The Golden Words of a Sufi Sheikh

By His Holiness M. R. Bawa Muhaiyaddeem
1982/472 pages
**$15.95**
$17.95 postpaid from:
The Fellowship Press
5820 Overbrook Ave.
Philadelphia, PA 19131

*The essence of wisdom from his lifetime of truth questing is presented in the volume of stories and original sayings by M. R. Bawa Muhaiyaddeem.*

# What is Accomplishment?

It is through unity, through the unity of hearts, and through the brotherhood and friendship of people that true Sufism and true Islam are expressed. But if we are not a little conscious of ourselves and who we are, how we spend our time, then it is difficult to climb to a higher level and work from there.

A sultan once said, "I will give a bag of gold to anyone who has accomplished the most unusual thing." People came to the court with all kinds of accomplishments. One man had a friend hold a needle at one end of the courtyard. The man then took a thread and threw it a hundred feet through the air. It went through the eye of the needle. It was the most unusual thing, and the sultan gave him the bag of gold,

saying, "You've accomplished a feat that I learned has taken you twenty years to perfect, and it is truly a remarkable feat, but it is useless. And because you've spent twenty years of your life accomplishing such a useless thing, I also give you one hundred lashes."

What we do in our lives for ourselves is important. But in those lives, we can also have the ambition to help others. You can spend twenty years of your life doing something very good and accomplished, but it's of no real use if it only provides you bread and rent and a few pleasures. But if it does not provide for other greater possibilities, your time and your life will have been wasted.

*From* When You Hear Hoofbeats, Think of a Zebra

## Sufi Order in the West
P.O. Box 574
Lebanon Springs, NY 12114

*A non-profit organization promoting Sufism and providing information, home-study courses, publications of interest and support to Sufi communities in the U.S.*

The symbol of the Sufi Movement, which is a heart with wings, denotes its ideal. The heart is both earthly and heavenly. The heart is a receptacle on earth of the divine Spirit, and when it holds the divine Spirit, it soars heavenward; the wings picture its rising. The crescent in the heart symbolizes responsiveness. It is the heart that responds to the spirit of God which rises. The crescent is a symbol of responsiveness because it grows fuller as the moon grows fuller by responding more and more to the sun as it progresses. The light one sees in the crescent is the light of the sun. As it gets more light with its increasing response, so it becomes fuller of the light of the sun. The star in the heart of the crescent represents the divine spark which is reflected in the human heart as love, and which helps the crescent towards its fullness.

*— Sufi Order in the West*

## When You Hear Hoofbeats, Think of a Zebra
*Talks on Sufism*

By Shems Friedlander
1987/162 pages
**$5.95**
$7.45 postpaid from:
Harper & Row
2350 Virginia Ave.
Hagerstown, MD 21740

*This collection of stories and reflections by an American brings ancient Sufi wisdom and style within the reach of contemporary minds. His retelling of classic tales unfolds new significance in our daily lives.*

# Taoist/Buddhist Contemplation

Literally, the word *Tao* means "the Way," yet that word does not adequately designate all that lies within this complete statement of the ultimate reality. Thus, although the word *Tao* or "Way" symbolizes the ultimate, it is meant only to indicate. It does not encompass. The Tao is limitless. It is all that we can imagine and all that we cannot imagine. The Tao cannot be circumscribed by words and definitions. It cannot truly be discussed. It must be *perceived*.

Lao Tzu, the prominent Taoist sage who lived during the sixth century B.C., wrote in the *Tao Te Ching*,

> *There was something mysteriously formed,*
> *That existed before heaven and earth;*
> *Silent and void, dependent on nothing;*
> *Eternal;*
> *All pervading, unfailing.*
> *One may call it the mother of all under heaven.*
> *Its true name is unknown.*
> *Tao is the name we give it.*

We cannot name the Tao, only our narrow conception of it. The true, nameless, and limitless Tao is what is absolute.

Taoism became a complex, pluralistic system in the forty centuries since its legendary beginnings. It is concerned with four major areas: the philosophical (*Lao Tzu* and *Chuang Tzu*, for example), the ritualistic (temple worship of countless gods and goddesses), the talismanic (sorcery and magic to ward off evil), and the ascetic (the tradition of gaining immortality or spiritual enlightenment through elixirs or meditation).

— *Deng Ming-Dao*
*From* The Wandering Taoist

## The Wandering Taoist

By Deng Ming-Dao
1983/240 pages
**$7.95**
$9.45 postpaid from:
Harper & Row
2350 Virginia Ave.
Hagerstown, MD 21740

*The first of two volumes in the Chronicles of Tao series provide a colorful introduction into the fascinating world of Taoism. Biographical in nature and illustrated by the author, they provide an exhilarating, vicarious journey into mysticism, sorcery, and immortality. The Wandering Taoist concerns the initiation and making of Taoist master, Kwan Saihung.*

"Think, Little Brother. How much in life are we actually free to choose for ourselves? The seasons affect us. The stars direct us. Circumstances hamper us. Destiny guides us. You are the way you are because of what has come your way in life. You made selections, but usually there wasn't much real choice: Out of all the things that came your way, you decided to do what was right for you. Now think about me. A different flow of the Tao came my way. Women fall in love with me. Riches come easily to me. Martial prowess is strong in me. I did not ask for this. They came to me as part of my destiny. I accepted responsibility for it. We are both named Butterfly. We must fly free or die. Give me the chance to fly free. Let me pursue my destiny."

"It will lead to your death."

"That's a farmer's mentality. You and I should try to live like heroes. We will all die. And I know I must come back in future lifetimes. But this is my role now, just as you have yours. Let me continue to play out my role."

Saihung poured himself another cup of tea in a play for time. He agreed with Butterfly, and was impressed all over again with his elder brother's insight. He saw no reason to curtail such a special person's life. Butterfly was a unique and unusual person, Saihung thought. This grey and mundane world needed such spectacular humans.

Saihung stood up and faced his brother.

— *Deng Ming-Dao*
*From* The Wandering Taoist

## The Cycle of Day and Night
### *An Essential Tibetan Text on the Practice of Contemplation*

By Namkhai Norbu
Translated and edited by
John Reynolds
1987/126 pages
**$10.95**
$11.95 postpaid from:
Station Hill Press
Barrytown, NY 12507

*A contemporary guide to the ancient tradition of "Dzogchen," or Buddhist contemplation. Actual methods are given for entering into contemplation and integrating it with our activities during the twenty-four-hour cycle of day and night.*

## Kindness, Clarity and Insight
### *The Fourteenth Dalai Lama His Holiness*

By Tenzin Gyatso
Translated and edited
by Jeffrey Hopkins
1984/232 pages
**$10.95**
$12.45 postpaid from:
Snow Lion Publications
P.O. Box 6483
Ithaca, NY 14851

*In this collection of talks, the Dalai Lama addresses all areas of human spirituality and mental attitude with his characteristic warmth, wit and perception. Several chapters are devoted to the elucidation of Buddhist philosophy and practice. A timely book which meets the needs of New Age seekers.*

. . . .

**Question: How does one choose a teacher or know a teacher to be reliable?**

Answer: This should be done in accordance with your interest and disposition, but you should analyze well. You must investigate before accepting a lama or guru to see whether that person is really qualified or not. It is said in a scripture of the Discipline (*Vinaya*) that just as fish that are hidden under the water can be seen through the movement of the ripples from above, so also a teacher's inner qualities can, over time, be seen a little through that person's behavior.

We need to look into the person's scholarship — the ability to explain topics — and whether the person implements those teachings in his conduct and experience. A tantra says that you must investigate very carefully even if it takes twelve years. This is the way to choose a teacher.

> — *Dalai Lama*
> *From Kindness, Clarity and Insight*

## The Tao of Pooh

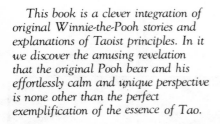

By Benjamin Hoff
1982/158 pages
**$4.95**
$6.45 postpaid from:
Penguin Books
Direct Mail Order
299 Murray Hill Pkwy.
E. Rutherford, NJ 07073

*This book is a clever integration of original Winnie-the-Pooh stories and explanations of Taoist principles. In it we discover the amusing revelation that the original Pooh bear and his effortlessly calm and unique perspective is none other than the perfect exemplification of the essence of Tao.*

# The Tao of Pooh

Literally, *Wu Wei* means "without doing, causing, or making." But practically speaking, it means without meddlesome, combative, or egotistical effort.

When we learn to work with our own Inner Nature, and with the natural laws operating around us, we reach the level of *Wu Wei*. Then we work with the natural order of things and operate on the principle of minimal effort. Since the natural world follows that principle, it does not make mistakes. Mistakes are

made — or imagined — by man, the creature with the overloaded Brain who separates himself from the supporting network of natural laws by interfering and trying too hard.

Not like Pooh, the most *effortless* Bear we've ever seen.

"Just how do you do it, Pooh?"

"Do what?" asked Pooh.

"Become so Effortless."

"I don't *do* much of anything," he said.

"But all those things of yours get done."

"They just sort of happen," he said.

"Wait a minute. That reminds me of something from the *Tao Te Ching*," I said, reaching for a book. "Here it is — chapter thirty-seven. Translated, it reads something like, 'Tao does not do, but nothing is not done.'"

"That sounds like a Riddle," said Pooh.

"It means that Tao doesn't force or interfere with things, but lets them work in their own way, to produce results naturally. Then whatever needs to be done is done."

"I see," said Pooh.

"In Chinese, the principle would be *Wei Wu Wei* — 'Do Without Doing.' From *Wei Wu Wei* comes *Tzu Jan*, 'Self So.' That means that things happen by themselves, spontaneously."

"Oh, I see," said Pooh.

> — *Benjamin Hoff*
> *From* The Tao of Pooh

## Snow Lion Publications
P.O. Box 6483
Ithaca, NY 14851

*Snow Lion Publications has been established to help further and protect Tibet's great religious and philosophic traditions. A newsletter and extensive selection of books and information is available.*

# Paramahansa Yogananda

*Paramahansa Yogananda (1893-1952) has long been recognized as a great world teacher on the truths of enlightenment. Through the example of his life and teaching, he has shown that the inner fulfillment we seek does exist and can be attained. In the more than thirty years that Paramahansa Yogananda lived in the West, he traveled extensively in the United States and abroad, lecturing and initiating thousands of students in the Science of Kriya Yoga. His teachings were transcribed and compiled through his direction to form the Self-Realization Fellowship Lessons.*

### The Divine Romance

By Paramahansa Yogananda
1986/468 pages
**$10.95**
$12.95 postpaid from:
Self-Realization Fellowship
3880 San Rafael Ave.
Los Angeles, CA 90065

*In this newest anthology of talks, the invisible, universal thread of love is illuminated as the metaphysical source of our limitless inner resources. Paramahansa Yogananda's easily understandable and compassionate style provide a practical source of inspiration on the ideals of love.*

## Autobiography of a Yogi

By Paramahansa Yogananda
1946/590 pages
**$3.95**
$5.95 postpaid from:
Self-Realization Fellowship
3880 San Rafael Ave.
Los Angeles, CA 90065

*Countless readers have been moved by the greatness of Paramahansa Yogananda simply through the reading of his autobiography. It is the account of a man's search for truth. Interwoven with this quest is a glimpse into the fascinating, scientifically documented world of the yogi who can perform "miracles" and ultimately attain complete self-mastery.*

### The Self-Realization Fellowship Foundation

3880 San Rafael Ave.
Los Angeles, CA 90065

*The Self-Realization Fellowship is an international organization headquartered in Los Angeles. The Foundation is based on the ancient science of Kriya Yoga, a step-by-step system of mental and spiritual discipline that enables one to achieve direct, personal experience of God through the practice of advanced techniques of meditation as taught by Paramahansa Yogananda. In addition, the foundation is responsible for the presentation and dissemination of the authentic writings of the master.*

# I Meet My Master

Together Habu and I set out for a distant marketplace in the Bengali section of Banaras. The ungentle Indian sun was not yet at zenith as we made our purchases in the bazaars. We pushed our way through the colorful medley of housewives, guides, priests, simply clad widows, dignified *Brahmins*, and ubiquitous holy bulls. As Habu and I moved on, I turned my head to survey a narrow, inconspicuous lane.

A Christlike man in the ocher robes of a swami stood motionless at the end of the lane. Instantly and anciently familiar he seemed; for a trice my gaze fed hungrily. Then doubt assailed me.

"The saint is magnetically drawing me to him!" With this thought, I heaped my parcels into the arms of Habu. He had been observing my erratic footwork with amazement, and now burst into laughter.

"What ails you? Are you crazy?"

My tumultuous emotion prevented any retort; I sped silently away.

"You are confusing this wandering monk with someone known to you," I thought. "Dreamer, walk on."

After ten minutes, I felt heavy numbness in my feet. As though turned to stone, they were unable to carry me farther. Laboriously I turned around; my feet regained normality.

The divine face was the one I had seen in a thousand visions. These halcyon eyes, in a leonine head with pointed beard and flowing locks, had oft peered through the gloom of my nocturnal reveries, holding a promise I had not fully understood.

"O my own, you have come to me!" My guru uttered the words again and again in Bengali, his voice tremulous with joy. "How many years I have waited for you!"

We entered a oneness of silence; words seemed the rankest superfluities. Eloquence flowed in soundless chant from the heart of master to disciple. With an antenna of irrefragable insight I sensed that my guru knew God and would lead me to Him. This was not the first sun to find me at these holy feet!

*Paramahansa Yogananda
From Autobiography
of a Yogi*

# Zen

Zen discipline consists in acquiring a new viewpoint for looking into the essence of things. The acquiring of this viewpoint is called satori. It is an experience which no amount of explanation or argument can make communicable to others. When a man's mind is matured for satori, it tumbles over one everywhere. An inarticulate sound, an unintelligent remark, a blooming flower, or a trivial incident such as stumbling, is the condition or event which will open his mind to satori. When conceptually understood, the lifting of a finger is one of the most ordinary incidents in everybody's life. But when viewed from the Zen point of view, it vibrates with divine meaning and creative vitality. Personal experience, therefore, is everything in Zen. Absolute faith is placed in man's inner being. No amount of reading, no amount of teaching, no amount of contemplation will ever make one a Zen master. Life itself must be grasped in the midst of its flow; to stop it for examination and analysis is to kill it, leaving its cold corpse to be embraced. When Zen is thoroughly understood, absolute peace of mind is attained, and a man lives as he ought to live.

> – *D. T. Suzuki*
>   *From* An Introduction to Zen Buddhism

---

## An Introduction to Zen Buddhism

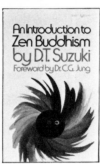

By D. T. Suzuki
1964; 132 pages
**$3.95**
$4.95 postpaid from:
Grove Press
400 Hahn Rd.
Westminster, MD 21157

*A basic text for the general reader seriously interested in understanding Zen. Clear and concise.*

An ancient master, wishing to show what Zen is, lifted one of his fingers, another kicked a ball, and a third slapped the face of his questioner. If the inner truth that lies deep in us is thus demonstrated, is not Zen the most practical and direct method of spiritual training ever resorted to by a religion?

> – *D. T. Suzuki*
>   *From* An Introduction to Zen Buddhism

## Zen Flesh, Zen Bones

Compiled by Paul Reps
174 pages
**$3.95**
$4.64 postpaid from:
Doubleday & Co.
501 Franklin Ave.
Garden City, NY 11530

*This book is a collection of Zen and pre-Zen writings, stories, and koans. An advanced student will delight in the rich source of Zen wisdom; the beginner may decide on deeper study.*

## The Way of Zen

By Alan Watts
1957/236 pages
**$4.95**
$5.95 postpaid from:

Vintage Books
400 Hahn Rd.
Westminster, MD 21157

*For both the general reader and the more serious student, Watts offers us the unique perspective of the Western mind which has successfully integrated Eastern thought.*

Zen is, above all, an experience, nonverbal in character, which is simply inaccessible to the purely literary and scholarly approach. To know what Zen is, and especially what it is not, there is no alternative but to practice it, to experiment with it in the concrete so as to discover the meaning which underlies the words.

> – *Alan Watts*
>   *From* The Way of Zen

## Zen Mind, Beginner's Mind

By Shunryu Suzuki
1985/138 pages
**$5.95**
$6.95 postpaid from:
Charles E. Tuttle Co.
P.O. Box 410
Rutland, VT 05701

Here is a book of profound and joyous reflection inspired by the practice of Zen. The approach is informal, drawing examples from ordinary events and common sense.

Nothing Special — If you continue this simple practice everyday (mindfulness) you will obtain some wonderful power. Before you attain it, it is something wonderful, but after you attain it, it is nothing special.

- *Shunryu Suzuki*
From Zen Mind, Beginner's Mind

## Is That So?

The Zen master Hakuin was praised by his neighbors as one living a pure life.

A beautiful Japanese girl whose parents owned a food store lived near him. Suddenly, without any warning, her parents discovered she was with child.

This made her parents angry. She would not confess who the man was, but after much harassment at last named Hakuin.

In great anger the parents went to the master. "Is that so?" was all he would say.

After the child was born it was brought to Hakuin. By this time he had lost his reputation, which did not trouble him, but he took very good care of the child. He obtained milk from his neighbors and everything else the little one needed.

A year later the girl-mother could stand it no longer. She told her parents the truth — that the real father of the child was a young man who worked in the fishmarket.

The mother and father of the girl at once went to Hakuin to ask his forgiveness, to apologize at length, and to get the child back again.

Hakuin was willing. In yielding the child, all he said was: "Is that so?"

- *Zen story*
From Zen Flesh, Zen Bones

## Nansen Cuts the Cat in Two

Nansen saw the monks of the eastern and western halls fighting over a cat. He seized the cat and told the monks: "If any of you say a good word, you can save the cat."

No one answered. So Nansen boldly cut the cat in two pieces.

That evening Joshu returned and Nansen told him about this. Joshu removed his sandals and, placing them on his head, walked out.

Nansen said: "If you had been there, you could have saved the cat."

Mumon's comment: Why did Joshu put his sandals on his head? If anyone answers this question, he will understand exactly how Nansen enforced the edict. If not, he should watch his own head.

*Had Joshu been there,*
*He would have enforced the edict*
*    oppositely.*
*Joshu snatches the sword*
*And Nansen begs for his life.*

- *Zen koan*
From Zen Flesh, Zen Bones

## How the Swans Came to the Lake

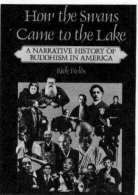

By Rick Fields
1981/446 pages
**$14.95**
$16.70 postpaid from:
Shambhala Publications Inc.
P.O. Box 308
Boston, MA 02117

*A fascinating and colorful account of the American Buddhist lineage.*

## Zen and the Art of Motorcycle Maintenance

By Robert M. Pirsig
1974/380 pages
**$4.95**
$6.45 postpaid from:
Bantam Books
414 E. Golf Rd.
Des Plaines, IL 60016

**"The real cycle you're working on is a cycle called 'yourself.' "**

"The study of the art of motorcycle maintenance is really a miniature study of the art of rationality itself. Working on a motorcycle, working well, caring, is to become part of a process, to achieve an inner peace of mind. The motorcycle is primarily a mental phenomenon."

- *Robert M. Pirsig*
From Zen and the Art of Motorcycle Maintenance

## Spiritualism

# Spiritualism in England and America

No one would deny that through the ages certain individuals have previewed the future, seen the so-called dead and heard spirit voices.

But it was not until 1848 that modern Spiritualism burst upon the earth.

Briefly, a certain John D. Fox became tenant of a house in Hydesville, Wayne County, New York State.

Inexplicable knockings took place all over the house and on the doors, while sentinels kept watch on either side.

Soon it was discovered that the knockings followed two of the Fox children from place to place.

John Fox, his wife and Catherine 12 and Margaretta, 15, were frequently disturbed at night.

The family discovered that if questions were put to the spirit rapper, intelligent answers came via knockings.

The communicator claimed to be a pedlar named Charles B. Rosna who had been murdered by a blacksmith, John C. Bell, who lived in the house at the time he disappeared. Rosna said his body had been buried in the building's cellar several years earlier.

So it was that in the summer of 1848, hair, part of the skull and some human bones were located.

However, roughly 50 years later, children playing in the now-deserted "Spook House" noticed human remains apparently embedded in the crumbling walls.

Later the then owner recovered a near-perfect skeleton ... and a pedlar's tin pack which had been commonly used in those parts half a century earlier.

News of the supernormal happenings spread rapidly. In Victorian Britain table-turning tea parties became a fashionable vogue. Indeed, the latter part of the 19th century saw the formation of the still somewhat august Society for Psychical Research, with leading liberal W. E. Gladstone declaring that psychical research was the "most important work being done in the world today."

Now — at least in the Free World — Spiritualism continues to enjoy popular support. Certain countries — such as Brazil — can boast millions of Spiritists, as they are known there, running orphanages, schools and other charitable institutions.

In Britain the picture is somewhat different. Over the last decade or so there has occurred a tremendous explosion in public interest. Radio, TV, newspapers and magazines regularly feature Spiritualism. Public opinion polls consistently show that millions of Britons accept life after death, have sat with a medium, believe in God or seen a ghost, etc.

It is against this backdrop that famous medium Doris Stokes's six books between them sold well over one million copies. Soon she became the celebrity that celebrities longed to meet.

British Spiritualism is roughly divided into two camps: those who accept the leadership of Jesus Christ, and the majority who maintain that he was an ordinary mortal displaying mediumistic gifts.

Currently a controversy is raging between the two main U.K. Spiritualist organizations on whether churches, for example, should display crosses and pictures of Jesus.

However, it is only since 1951 that Spiritualism in Britain has enjoyed a legal status. And it is astonishing to realize that as comparatively recently as 1944, materialization medium Helen Duncan was charged under the Witchcraft Act ... of 1735.

Today there are probably some thousands of Spiritualist churches in the U.K. Some are purpose-built, whilst others meet in rented accommodations.

The majority of mediums are non-professional in that they only practice their gifts after work hours. Unlike some countries, it is not a lucrative business. The average medium probably receives their travelling expenses and perhaps ten dollars on top for taking a church service. The average price for a private sitting is around twenty dollars.

Intriguingly, American Professor, Robert Morris, is the first holder of the Koestler Chair of Parapsychology at Edinburgh University. This seat was made possible by a bequest from writer Arthur Koestler and his wife, who both ended their own lives. The bulk of their estate was left to furthering the cause of parapsychology.

In America, Spiritualism is barely known to the general population except for Spiritualist Churches scattered across the continent. The national Spiritualist associations including National Spiritualist Association of Churches, the General Assembly of Spiritualists and the National Association of Spiritual Churches of Science and Revelation.

- *Tony Ortzen*
*Editor*, Psychic News
*London*

Tony Ortzen

**Psychic News**
20 Earlham St.
London, WC2H 9LW
England
Established 1932
Weekly/$39.00 for one year

*Tony Ortzen is the editor of this independent international Spiritualist weekly newspaper based in London. It offers news and feature articles on well-known spiritualist mediums, events, and related information.*

# Declaration of Spiritualist Principles

*Adapted by the National Spiritualist Association of Churches U.S.A.*

1. We believe in Infinite Intelligence.

2. We believe that the phenomena of nature, both physical and spiritual, are the expression of Infinite Intelligence.

3. We affirm that a correct understanding of such expression and living in accordance therewith constitute true religion.

4. We affirm that the existence and personal identity of the individual continue after the change called death.

5. We affirm that communication with the so-called dead is a fact, scientifically proven by the phenomena of Spiritualism.

6. We believe that the highest morality is contained in the Golden Rule: "Whatsoever ye would that others should do unto you, do ye also unto them."

7. We affirm the moral responsibility of the individual, and that he makes his own happiness or unhappiness as he obeys or disobeys Nature's physical and spiritual laws.

8. We affirm that the doorway to reformation is never closed against any human soul here or hereafter.

9. We affirm that the precept of Prophecy and Healing contained in the Bible is a divine attribute proven through Mediumship.

---

# What Spiritualism Is and Does

It teaches personal responsibility.

It removes all fear of death, which is really the portal of the Spirit World.

It teaches that death is not the cessation of life, but merely a change of condition.

It teaches, not that a man has a soul, but that man is a soul and has a body.

It teaches that those who have passed on are conscious — not asleep.

It teaches that the spark of divinity dwells in all.

Spiritualism is God's message to mortals, declaring that There Is No Death. That all who have passed on still live; that there is hope in the life beyond for the most sinful.

Spiritualism is a manifestation, a demonstration and a proof of the continuity of life and of the truth of the many Spirit manifestations recorded in the Christian Bible.

---

## National Spiritualist Summit

Box 30172
Indianapolis, IN 46320
Established 1919
Monthly/$7.00 for one year

*This is the official publication of the National Spiritualist Association of Churches. Each issue includes news about Spiritualist activities, teaching articles and features on Spiritualist concepts.*

## The Journal

International General Assembly of Spiritualists
1809 East Bayview Blvd.
Norfolk, VA 23503
Bimonthly/$15.00 for one year

*This is the official Journal of the IGAS, an international association of Spiritualist Churches. It publishes news about individual churches, Spiritualist doctrine and reader viewpoints. This group broke away from the National Spiritualist Association in 1931 because the NSA dropped the designation as a church upholding Christian doctrine.*

## Lily Dale Assembly

5 Melrose Park
Lily Dale, NY 14752
716-595-8721

*Spiritualist camps were very popular in the late 1800's. Today, just a few survive. One of these is Lily Dale, near Buffalo, New York. They offer workshops, training, and other New Age activities.*

## Two Worlds

Established 1887
Monthly/$14.00 for one year

An independent, international Spiritualist monthly that explores Spiritualist philosophy, healing, mediumship and psychic phenomena.

## Here and There

Established 1887
Monthly/$11.50 for one year

*Here and There* bills itself as "a monthly journal for Spiritualists." It reports detailed information on Spiritualist Church activities worldwide plus news and commentary.

*Two Worlds* and *Here and There* are available from:
The Headquarters Publishing
5 Alexandria Rd.
West Ealing, London W130NP
England

## The Spirits' Book

By Allan Kardec
1857/432 pages
**$6.95**
$7.95 postpaid from:
Starlite Distributors
P.O. Box 6750
Auburn, CA 95604

*Allan Kardec is the father of the Spiritist movement. This classic work said to be channeled from the spirit realms, details the basic doctrine of Spiritualism from the nature of the soul to existence in the spirit realms and how the spirit world interacts with the physical realm.*

# Spiritualist Organizations

### Church Associations

**General Assembly of Spirituality**
2107 Broadway
New York, NY 10023

**Independent General Assembly of Spiritualists**
1809 East Bayview Blvd.
Norfolk, VA 23505

**National Association of Churches**
Box 128
Cassadaga, FL 32706

**National Association of Spiritual Churches of Science & Revelation**
5618 Wilson Blvd.
Arlington, VA 22205

**Spiritualist Association of America**
19 Crofty Rd.
Lutchville, MD 21093

*Local Associations and Organizations*

**Cassadaga Spiritualist Campmeeting Assn.**
Box 130
Cassadaga, FL 32706

**Crystal Fountain Park Spiritualists Assn.**
Box 169
Sherwood, OH 43556

**Morris Pratt Institute**
11811 Watertown Plank Road
Wauwatosa, WI 53226
414-774-2994

*This is one of the primary education centers for Spiritualism in America today. It offers residence and correspondence courses in mediumship, counseling, healing and other disciplines to prepare students for certification as Mediums, Healers, Teachers or Ordained Ministers.*

**First American Spiritualist Assembly**
2276 E. Keys
Springfield, IL 62702

**Independent Spiritualist Assn.**
2138 11th St.
Niles, MI 49120

**Massachusetts State Spiritualist Assn.**
RR 3145 Herring Pond Rd.
Buzzards Bay, MA 02532

**National Colored Spiritualist Assn.**
1245 W. Watkins Rd.
Phoenix, AZ 85007

**Sun Spiritualist Camp Assn.**
Star Route 2, Box 596
Tonopah, AZ 85354

**Universal Spiritualist Assn.**
Maple Grove
5848 Pendleton Ave.
Anderson, IN 46011

**Universal Harmony Foundation**
5903 Seminole Blvd.
Seminole, FL 33542

## How to Be Healthy, Wealthy and Wise

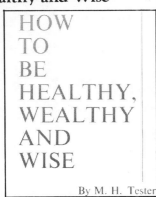

HOW
TO
BE
HEALTHY,
WEALTHY
AND
WISE

By M. H. Tester

By M. H. Tester
1972/192 pages
**$8.40** postpaid from:
Psychic News Bookshop
Freepost
London WCZB 5BR
England

*This is a simple, yet very profound self-help book that will inspire you. It is based on Spiritualist doctrine that fits right in with current New Age thinking on our place in the world and how to make some sense of it.*

## Mediumship Made Simple

Mediumship Made Simple

IVY NORTHAGE

By Ivy Northage
1986/108 pages
**$9.70** postpaid from:
Psychic News Bookshop
Freepost
London WCZB 5BR
England

*Ivy Northage is one of England's Spiritualist teaching mediums. She explains the Spiritualist's approach to mediumship, the intensive training required, and discusses each avenue recounted during mediumistic practice.*

# Do I Have Free Will or Is My Whole Life Mapped Out for Me?

Entire books, libraries of them, have been written on this subject. Are we pawns in the game, with every act and thought predetermined? Does our destiny stand there recorded, unalterable, whatever we do? In India you will find many who think this is so. The beggar sits in the gutter. He will do nothing to improve his lot. "It is written." In the West, too, there are many who believe that their fate is predetermined. One of the classic excuses for sexual intercourse is "we were fated to come together." Why such a pleasant experience should need an excuse is beyond me.

People reason that if we are all the object of a great and divine plan then it must encompass everybody, every animal, action and interaction. It says in the Bible that not a sparrow falls yet it is known to God. So it is argued that since the plan is based on an omnipotent and all-seeing power there is nothing we can do to alter it. This is fate.

It is patent that this explanation is false. Nobody can persuade me that Hitler and his murder of six million people were divinely inspired. Nobody can convince me that the horrors of the Holy Inquisition, which made Attila the Hun seem like a benign despot, were part of a great design. And the Church, remember, has been responsible for over twenty million deaths (though in all fairness it took them longer, so that Hitler's murder rate per annum is still the higher).

Well, what is the alternative? If there is no predestination then we must have free will. Is the whole universe one great accident? Is there no design? Does it really matter whether I do good as long as I have a terrific time and enjoy myself? If I am here as the result of a genetic chance, who can tell me what to do and not to do? I must just be an opportunist and make the most of things. Whatever happens to the rest, I'm all right, Jack!

Neither of these two extremes is correct. There is a plan, there is a design. Whether you like it or not you are part of it.

> – *M. H. Tester*
> From How to Be Healthy,
> Wealthy and Wise

---

# Transfiguration

Transfiguration is another form of physical mediumship requiring ectoplasm and combining with other areas of psychic centres in the process. It is well known that I demonstrated this phenomena with considerable success for many years. It is, nevertheless, in my opinion, an unsatisfactory form of presentation, at least to the degree that I was able to develop it. It requires a great deal of understanding co-operation from the sitters, which is too much to expect from an inquirer.

Transfiguration is operated by moulding an ectoplasmic mask over the face to a recognizable likeness of the communicating spirit. It requires, however, supporting evidence to prepare the sitter whom to expect and recognize. In my own case this was provided by my guide Chan giving facts and details of identity, then withdrawing while the spirit operators formed the face. The trance state in no way inhibited the release of ectoplasm. Without the formation of a larynx or voice box the spirit was unable to speak on his own behalf.

We made considerable progress in this, but the exhausting demands of public work, the ignorance of sitters who, in spite of all efforts to protect me, suddenly let in floods of light or made other disturbances causing me immense distress, caused my physical health to give way. Chan said I was not strong enough to develop it further, so this side of the work was discontinued.

> – *Ivy Northage*
> From Mediumship
> Made Simple

# Silver Birch

*Silver Birch, the spirit guide of England's Hannen Swaffer's home Spiritualist development "circle," is regarded by many as the world's most famous spirit mentor. For several* decades he gave, through his trance medium, Maurice Barbanell, teachings which covered a vast range of subjects concerned with life, death, and what follows in the next world.

---

## Light from Silver Birch
Compiled by Pam Riva
1984/218 pages
**$11.00** postpaid from:
Psychic News Bookshop
20 Earlham St.
London WC2H 9LW  England

We are engaged in a massive task all over your world where so many areas are engulfed in almost unique darkness.

Our progress is slow. The difficulties that have to be overcome are massive, but gradually we are breaking through. We are establishing bridgeheads in new areas. The power of the spirit is here to stay in your world. It will bring its benign influence to bear on millions.
- *Silver Birch*

## Silver Birch Companion

Edited by Tony Ortzen
1986/160 pages
**$11.00** postpaid from:
Psychic News Bookshop
20 Earlham St.
London WC2H 9LW
England

"We ask for no credit, no thanks, no gratitude. If we can serve; if we can see peace instead of war; smiling, happy faces instead of tears; healthy bodies instead of bodies racked with disease and pain; if we can see misery vanquished; if we can see all the despair that infests dispirited beings driven away, then we rejoice because we know that our mission is succeeding."
- *Silver Birch*
*From* Silver Birch Companion

---

# Healing — The Second Chance

*Spiritual healing, either by laying-on of hands or by mental contact over scores or thousands of miles, is a valuable part of the Other-Side plan.*

*Millions of sufferers, dismissed as medically incurable by hospitals and doctors, have found relief or permanent cures through healing mediums who channel divine power, sometimes being entranced, sometimes linking mentally with their spirit guides. These guides are often former surgeons or doctors still desiring to serve ailing humanity.*

*Always the aim is to touch the sick person's soul, awakening it to awareness of spiritual realities.*

The Great Spirit, with infinite wisdom and love, provides sufferers with a second chance when the people of the medical world say no more can be done.

What is important is to touch souls. Then the power of the spirit can quicken the flicker of divinity into a beauteous, lambent flame, so that the majesty of latent divinity shines through, enabling their bodies to become well, their minds to learn the lesson and their spiritual natures to unfold further as a result.

If a soul is touched because of the healing, then gratitude should be given to the Great Spirit for the privilege of the service the healer has rendered.

If a soul is not touched though the healing has cured the physical body, that is very sad. It means the sufferer has been given the opportunity of attaining awareness and unfortunately has failed to take it. A healer must do the best he can, and allow the fullest amount of spirit power to pour through and work its divine will wherever it possibly can.

Not all souls can be receptive because that is not possible. A healer cannot cure everybody who comes to him. If you can obtain results with the hopeless cases, then that should be the clearest evidence to any with the ability to think and reason that a power vastly superior to matter has been at work.

The healing power, which is divine in origin and in essence, is among the most important forces streaming into your world today. It is a very sick world. There are increasing numbers of diseases caused by the stresses and strains of the inharmonious conditions in which too many people live. Your so-called civilization has divorced man from nature which provides some of the sources of his energy.

Then the human battery, the soul, is depleted and has to be recharged by the power of the spirit. When that happens and the battery is working, then you achieve health, which is harmony between body, mind and spirit. The Great Spirit with infinite wisdom has created the human frame and all its concomitant parts in such a fashion that the spirit contains self-healing properties.
- *Silver Birch*
*From* Light from Silver Birch

# Native American

A veil hangs heavy around the Native concepts of medicine and vision. European philosophies would have us believe that Native medicine is comprised only of strange-looking sorcerers dressed in feathers and hides, shaking rattles, making remedies out of snake's tongues, frog's legs and other exotic ingredients that either kill or cure the poor ignorant patient. Others have taught that Indian medicine is "the work of the devil": evil, undermining, and dangerous to all the civilization that the white man has built. Medicine men have been painted as heartless savages, bound upon a course of human sacrifice, and as ignorant heathens who pray to the rocks and the trees. People of vision are often portrayed as dangerous lunatics.

Because many Europeans were determined to destroy all the medicine people and practices they could, Native people went underground with their medicine.

They had no choice. No one wanted to hear what medicine people really knew or practiced; they were killed if the European religious leaders found out that they practiced any medicine at all.

Medicine people (for both men and women served in this capacity) serve as healers of bodies, minds, souls and hearts. They fulfilled the functions of the people that we today call ministers, priests, rabbis, doctors, lawyers, psychologists, psychiatrists, midwives, family counsellors, teachers, masseuses, body workers, meditation teachers, and breath specialists. They also fulfilled some duties we have lost until recently: they designed and carried out rituals and ceremonies that marked the changes in the lives of people and of the planet.

During the first few years I spent working with Sun Bear, I watched everything with the loving eye of a new believer. He showed me how to see the earth as a living being. He taught me how to see the magic of all of her children — the rocks, the plants, the animals, the clouds, the waters — and I wondered how I ever lived before without seeing all of this beauty. I learned about Native American culture, and for a time, rejected my own background as a white, middle-class, educated writer.

After the first few years, I found my own balance and my own visions, and learned how to incorporate what I was learning from Sun Bear with the lessons I had already learned. I began to realize what a wonderful spirit path I was on, even though I knew it was fraught with danger. I had become, like Sun Bear, a bridge person, one walking between two cultures and looking for the connections that could bring unity and understanding.

> - Wabun (Marlise James)
> From the Introduction to
> Sun Bear, The Path
> of Power

---

## Sun Bear
### *The Path of Power*
As told to Wabun and
Barry Weinstuck
1983/268 pages
**$8.95**
$10.95 postpaid from:
Bear Tribe Publishing
P.O. Box 9167
Spokane, WA 99209

*Sun Bear, known to his traditional people as a practicing rainbow warrior and keeper of the Medicine Wheel, shares his vision of peace and unity for the whole earth as perpetuated through Native American culture. The Path of Power is a beautifully written work that details Sun Bear's personal path of power through an often conflicting, occasionally humorous, and sometimes beautifully revealing journey between two cultures.*

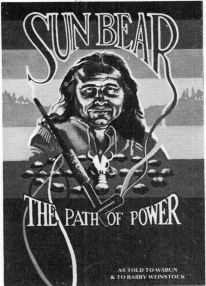

## Power Objects

Power objects, as I've said, have the ability to call in certain spirit forces, but you have to know how to call them in. That's why we say these objects, when they're sitting in museum cases, are asleep. The power doesn't come through them until you take power *over* them. For example, when a person comes to me for a blessing on his or her pipe, the blessing allows him to work with the power of the pipe. A pipe is a beautiful piece of artwork, but until it is awakened by a medicine person it isn't a power object. So when a person comes to me and asks me to bless his or her pipe, and I decide to do so, I'm giving that person power. Unless he or she knows how to tune into that power, it will do that person little good. Sometimes, for that reason, I'll tell a person to wait awhile longer, that I didn't feel he or she is ready to have that pipe awakened.

> - Sun Bear
> From The Path of Power

## Black Elk Speaks

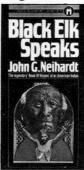

By John G. Neihardt
1932/238 pages
**$3.95**
$5.94 postpaid from:
Simon & Schuster, Inc.
Mail Order Dept.
200 Old Tappan Rd.
Old Tappan, NJ 07675

*Black Elk, warrior and medicine man of the Oglala Sioux, lived the life of the Plains Indians and saw the death of his people and their way of life.*

*This is the story of the Native American way that has been lost and the spiritual vision of a people.*

# Black Elk Speaks

It is the story of all life that is holy and is good to tell, and of us two-leggeds sharing in it with the four-leggeds and the wings of the air and all green things; for these are children of one mother and their father is one Spirit.

This, then, is not the tale of a great hunter or of a great warrior, or of a great traveler, although I have made much meat in my time and fought for my people both as boy and man, and have gone far and seen strange lands and men. But now that I can see it all as from a lonely hilltop, I know it was the story of a mighty vision given to a man too weak to use it; of a holy tree that should have flourished in a people's heart with flowers and singing birds, and now is withered; and of a people's dream that died in bloody snow.

But if the vision was true and mighty, as I know, it is true and mighty yet; for such things are of the spirit, and it is in the darkness of their eyes that men get lost.

> *- Black Elk as told to*
> *John G. Neihardt*
> *From* Black Elk Speaks

Peyote Religion

# Peyote Religion

## A HISTORY

## By Omer C. Stewart

By Omer C. Stewart
1987/464 pages
**$29.95**
$31.45 postpaid from:
University of Oklahoma Press
P.O. Box 1657
Hagerstown, MD 21741

*Long a subject of controversy, peyotism has become a unifying influence in Indian life, providing the basis for ceremonies, friendships, social gatherings, travel, and marriage, as well as comfort and healing. This research work provides a picture of the rise of peyotism and the Native American Church. Volume 181 in The Civilization of the American Indian Series.*

# The Peyote Plant

The Peyote plant is light green and segmented, about one to two inches across, growing singly or in clusters close to the ground from a long taproot. It is harvested by cutting off the exposed tops of the clusters, leaving the root to produce more "buttons," as the tops are usually called. The buttons are generally dried before being eaten, and they are extremely bitter to the taste, frequently producing vomiting. However, they also produce a warm and pleasant euphoria, an agreeable point of view, relaxation, colorful visual distortions, and a sense of timelessness that are conducive to the all-night ceremony of the Native American Church. To the church's members, peyote is the essential ingredient, the sacrament, in their well-established, unique ceremony. Peyote is not habit-forming, and in the controlled ambience of a peyote meeting it is in no way harmful.

> *- Omer C. Stewart*
> *From* Peyote Religion

## Spirit Song
### *The Visionary Wisdom of No-Eyes*

By Mary Summer Rain
1985/156 pages
**$7.95**
$9.45 postpaid from:
The Donning Company
5659 Virginia Beach Blvd.
Norfolk, VA 23502

*The great beauty and wisdom of the Native American philosophy and experience is set forth in this story about No-Eyes, a blind Chippewa medicine woman, living alone in the Rocky Mountains. No-Eyes takes Mary Summer Rain under her tutelage to impart to her eight decades of accumulated knowledge and ancient tradition. An inspiring tribute to reverence for the earth spirit in all its forms.*

## No-Eyes

Even though No-Eyes was totally blind, I knew she had a unique way of seeing everything she needed or wanted to see. She had seen me enter the still clearing around her house. She had seen my zombie-like approach and, worst of all, she had seen my sudden fright when she cleverly whipped open that one sightless eye of hers. I was naturally embarrassed and deeply mortified at having been the object of her questionable humor. Yet, No-Eyes never wasted her precious time or her valuable energies unless some vital lesson was involved. This I had come to learn just as I was to learn her special way of seeing without using my eyes.

- Mary Summer Rain
From Spirit Song

# Carlos Castaneda and the Lessons of Don Juan

*In a series of seven books on the lessons of Don Juan, Carlos Castaneda reveals his experiences while under apprenticeship to the sorcerer/warrior Don Juan. From perfecting the art of "seeing" and "stopping the world" to "dreaming" and "stalking," Castaneda gives a unique perspective on reality and mysticism on the path of personal power.*

### The Fire from Within

By Carlos Castaneda
1984/300 pages
**$4.50**
$6.50 postpaid from:
Simon & Schuster, Inc.
200 Old Tappan Rd.
Old Tappan, NJ 07675

*In this latest volume of the Don Juan series, Castaneda reviews and remembers more that he or his fellow apprentices have experienced while in another state of consciousness at the hands of Don Juan and his experienced group of sorcerers.*

### Journey to Ixtlan

By Carlos Casteneda
1972/268 pages
**$3.95**
$5.95 postpaid from:
Simon & Schuster, Inc.
200 Old Tappan Rd.
Old Tappan, NJ 07675

*This is the true story of an awesome journey through mind-bending reality. Many times over, Castaneda is challenged to suspend his beliefs in normal reality — he experiences a dead branch as a living animal, a talking coyote (bilingual), and a hat which transforms into a full-sized car before his eyes — as his teacher, Don Juan, leads him further into the world of the sorcerer.*

*Castaneda's journey is potentially transformative for any reader who wishes to understand.*

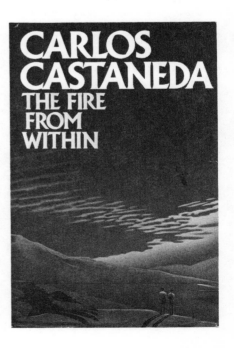

# Earth Religions

## The Spiral Dance
## A Rebirth
## of the Ancient Religion
## of the Great Goddess

By Starhawk
1979/218 pages
$10.95
$12.45 postpaid from:
Harper & Row Publishers, Inc.
2350 Virginia Ave.
Hagerstown, MD 21740

*The Spiral Dance demystifies the much misunderstood and maligned tradition of witchcraft as a religion. Rituals described include casting the circle, raising the cone of power, invoking the Goddess and God, and reaching trance states. The book also gives spells, chants, invocations, and advice on creating your own rites, and shows how these rituals and exercises are linked to psychological states.*

• • • •

# Visualizations

### Exercise 13: The Pentacle

Visualize a line of flickering blue flame, like a gas flame from a Bunsen burner. Now mentally draw a pentacle, a five-pointed star with one point up, in the invoking direction: starting at the top and moving down to the left. Watch it form out of the blue flame. Hold the image in your mind for a few moments.

Now retrace it in the banishing direction, starting at the lower left-hand corner and moving up. As you do so, watch it disappear.

Practice until it comes to you easily. This visualization is part of casting a circle.

### Exercise 14: The Knot

Visualize yourself tying a knot — any knot you can tie easily in reality. Try not to see a mental picture of yourself from outside; instead, put yourself in the picture. See your hands moving, and feel the string. Feel every moment you would make, then draw the knot closed, and feel the string pull taut.

This visualization is used to bind spells.

> — *Starhawk*
> *From* The Spiral Dance

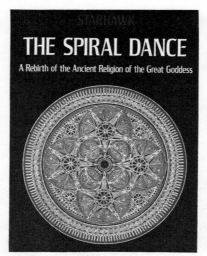

# The Coven

The coven is a Witch's support group, consciousness-raising group, psychic study center, clergy-training program, College of Mysteries, surrogate clan, and religious congregation all rolled into one. In a strong coven, the bond is, by tradition, "closer than family": a sharing of spirits, emotions, imaginations. "Perfect love and perfect trust" is the goal.

The coven structure makes the organization of Witchcraft very different from that of most other religions. The Craft is not based on large, amorphous masses who are only superficially acquainted; nor is it based on individual gurus with their devotees and disciples. There is no hierarchical authority, no Dalai Lama, no Pope. The structure of Witchcraft is cellular, based on small circles whose members share a deep commitment to each other and the Craft.

Finding a coven to join can be difficult. Witches are not listed in the Yellow Pages and rarely place classified ads. Often, however, they do give classes through Open Universities or metaphysical bookstores. Some universities are beginning to offer courses in Witchcraft in their religious studies departments. Occult shops sometimes also furnish leads. The best route, of course, is through personal contacts. Witches feel that when a person is internally ready to join the Craft she will be drawn to the right people.

> — *Starhawk*
> *From* The Spiral Dance

## Shaman's Drum
## *A Journal of Experiential Shamanism*

P.O. Box 2636
Berkeley, CA 94702
$15.00/5 issues
$25.00/9 issues from:

Shaman's Drum *is part of an informal network of people who practice and teach shamanism. This magazine offers multi-cultural exposure to new and traditional ways of tapping into the transformative magic of dreams, mythic arts, and sacred rituals. The experiential emphasis of each issue provides first-hand accounts, in-depth coverage plus a variety of viewpoints on shamanism.*

## Our Lady of Enchantment

Seminary of Wicca
Box 1366
Nashua, NH 03061

*In addition to a complete selection of courses in witchcraft, magic, and the occult arts at the seminary location in New Hampshire, Our Lady of Enchantment offers Home Study Courses. Fellowships, rituals and celebrations.*

## School of Wicca

Box 1502
Newbern, NC 28560

*Headed by Gavin and Yvonne Frost, the School of Wicca offers instruction and publications.*

# Women's Spirituality
## Womanspirit

In cultures throughout the world, woman has long been recognized as the creation maker. She has been revered for her ability to give birth, to create food with her own body, to provide a large part (in many cases, most) of her people's food through gathering, and for her contributions to the spiritual and everyday life of the community.

The dominance of man as creation maker is a relatively recent phenomenon; yet today we have all been raised in a culture created almost exclusively by men, a culture that recognizes a male god as the creator of all physical life. And now some of man's creations, in particular his technology, offer him the role of the destruction maker, as we face the possibility of nuclear annihilation of the planet. We also face the possible destruction of our souls; for competitiveness and separation of mind from body, and human from nature, have caused an alienation of the psyche greater than any previously known.

We have become too imbalanced. It is time for women to rediscover and fulfill our roles as creation makers if this planet is to survive and women and men are to be able to live creative, harmonious, and truly productive lives. We must bring back the power of women's wisdom. This strength is not a power over anything else, but a force emanating from deep within each of us, radiating out into the world and connecting and interacting with others, creating a new definition of strength.

... the synthesis of feminism and spirituality, called Womanspirit, is a major key to rediscovering this knowledge and power.

> - Hallie Austen Iglehart
> From Womanspirit

### Wise Women Center
P.O. Box 64
Woodstock, NY 12498

*A sacred space and classroom for the traditional studies of herbal medicine and various other forms of healing, the center offers seminars, intensives, and apprenticeships.*

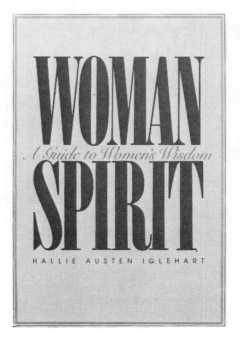

**Womanspirit**
***A Guide to Women's Wisdom***
By Hallie Austen Iglehart
1983/174 pages
**$7.95**
$9.45 postpaid from:
Harper & Row Publishers, Inc.
2350 Virginia Ave.
Hagerstown, MD 21740

*This is a meaningful and insightful integration of feminism and spirituality resulting in the emergence of* **Woman-spirit**. *This book outlines original techniques for divining the potential of the true woman wisdom heritage.*

## Space Meditation

For the first fifty thousand or more years of human existence, there were very few people on the planet Earth. In only the last few hundred years, that number has grown to such a degree that we are rapidly crowding ourselves out. In addition, we have a corresponding growth of buildings, machines, noise, and concrete. The ever-diminishing amount of space that each of us has affects our physical, emotional, and mental health. We forget about other forms of life. We become human chauvinists.

Find ways that you can develop more space — both inside and outside yourself.

● Spend a day in some open space alone.

● Meditate to open up your inner spaces.

● Consider carefully before contributing to the population explosion of humans and machines. Make space in your life for animals, plants, air, water, earth, and heavenly bodies.

● Meditate on the sky. Let it give you a perspective on yourself and the role of human beings in the universe. Sweep your eyes all along the horizon. Look straight above you. Look at other parts of the sky. What do you see? How is it different from yesterday? How does it make you feel? Do you remember what the sky looked like when you were younger? Do you have memories of special skies? What effect did it have on you? When there is a storm, sit and watch the clouds, snow, rain, hail, or lightning. Close your eyes and feel your inner space. How does it feel compared with the space that is out there?

● Night sky. Go somewhere where the air is relatively clear. Lie down on your back and watch the blackness, the stars, the clouds, the moon. How do they make you feel? Feel their expansiveness moving through your head, chest, belly, through your limbs. Feel the stars within you.

> - Hallie Austen Iglehart
> From Womanspirit

## The Great Cosmic Mother
### *Rediscovering the Religion of the Earth*
By Monica Sjöö
and Barbara Mor
1987/502 pages
**$16.95**
$18.45 postpaid from:
Harper & Row Publishers, Inc.
2350 Virginia Ave.
Hagerstown, MD 21740

*Well illustrated and documented, this passionate exploration of the Goddess reveals the true feminine origins of the basis of current civilization. The Great Cosmic Mother offers an inspiring vision in support of earlier times when communion with our planetary whole was the norm.*

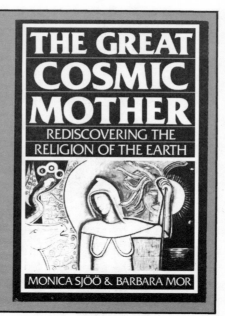

## Womanspirit Meditation
By Hallie Austen Iglehart
Music By Georgia Kelly
1984/60 minutes
**$9.95**
$11.95 postpaid from:
Womanspirit Catalog Co.
1442-A Walnut St. #184
Berkeley, CA 94709

*These meditations were adapted by Marcelina Martin and Hallie Iglehart from the Womanspirit book. The accompanying harp music is designed specifically for these meditations. A perfect companion to the book.*

## Women in Constant Creative Action (W.I.C.C.A.)
P.O. Box 201
Monmouth, OR 97361

*This national networking organization provides the means in which women can meet locally, in small groups called WINGS for supportive spiritual growth and metaphysical learning. A monthly newsletter connects all groups and provides suggestions for weekly meetings and the fulfillment of creative potential. Members also receive a study packet, and are informed of and invited to all classes, retreats and gatherings.*

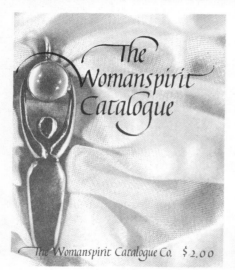

## The Womanspirit Catalogue
Compiled by Patrice Wynne
**$2.00** postpaid from:
The Womanspirit Catalogue Co.
1442-A Walnut St. #184
Berkeley, CA 94709

*Books, tapes, music, art, and gifts which celebrate womanspirit awakening and power.*

## Women in Spiritual Education (W.I.S.E.)
P.O. Box 697
Point Reyes Station, CA 94956
415-663-8280

*The Heart of the Goddess program offered at W.I.S.E. has emerged as an integration of the Womanspirit work of Hallie Iglehart and the Motherpeace work of Karen Vogel. In addition to individual sessions, classes and ritual celebrations and gathering, the nine-month Womanspirit Initiation program is offered in fulfillment of the vision of a women's mystery school.*

## Motherpeace
### *A Way to the Goddess Through Myth, Art, and Tarot*
By Vickie Noble
1983/276 pages
**$12.95**
$14.45 postpaid from:
Harper & Row Publishers, Inc.
2350 Virginia Ave.
Hagerstown, MD 21740

*Combining art, history, mythology, folklore, philosophy, science, astrology, and study of the tarot with an informed spiritual/feminist perspective, Motherpeace presents an inspiring avenue of exploration into the depths of our ancient Goddess unconscious — the heritage of all dwellers upon the Mother Earth. Included are 15 full-color plates of the companion Motherpeace Tarot Deck.*

## Motherpeace Tarot Deck
Designed by Vicki Noble
and Karen Vogel
**$24.95**
$27.95 postpaid from:
U.S. Games System, Inc.
179 Ludlow St.
Stamford, CT 06909

**The Lunar Calendar**
*Dedicated to the Goddess
in Her Many Guises*
1988/12-month wall calendar
**$12.00**
$14.50 postpaid from:
Luna Press
Box 511
Kenmore Station
Boston, MA 02215

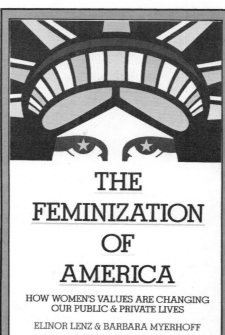

**The Feminization of
America**
*How Women's Values Are
Changing Our Public &
Private Lives*
By Elinor Lenz and
Barbara Myerhoff
1985/276 pages
**$9.95**
$12.35 postpaid from:
Jeremy P. Tarcher, Inc.
9110 Sunset Blvd.
Los Angeles, CA 90069

*A significant factor in the present
upheaval of American culture is the
move of women away from the domestic
home and out into the open world. The
Feminization of America explores the
changes this shift has brought from
opening up the doors to an enriched
experience of fatherhood for men to
encouraging energetic and open
communication in all aspects of daily
living.*

# Cinderella

The fairy tale of the cinder-maid
originated as an anti-ecclesiastical
allegory repeated by real "fairies" —
that is, pagans. Ella was *Hel*, or
Helle, daughter of Mother Earth, the
Goddess with her regenerative fires
reduced to cinders. Her ugly
stepmother was the new church. Her
ugly stepsisters were the church's
darlings, the military aristocracy, and
the clergy.

An early German version of the
story said Cinderella's real mother
the Earth, though dead, sent from
her grave a fairy tree in answer to her
daughter's prayer. This tree produced
golden apples, fine clothes, and other
gifts. Thus the "fairy godmother" of
later versions seems to have been a
ghost of the mother, the dispossessed
Great Goddess in retirement
underground.

Beautiful with her new riches,
Cinderella won the "prince"
(mankind), very easily impressed by
the display of finery. Their union
was symbolized by fitting her foot
into a shoe, a common sexual
allegory. The Eleusinian Mysteries
signified sacred marriage by working

a phallic object in a woman's shoe.
The glass slipper perhaps stood for
the Crystal Cave by which pagan
heroes entered the uterine
underworld.

- *Barbara G. Walker
From* The Woman's
Encyclopedia of Myths
and Secrets

**The Woman's
Encyclopedia of Myths and
Secrets**
By Barbara G. Walker
1983/1124 pages
**$29.95**
$31.45 postpaid from:
Harper & Row Publishers, Inc.
2350 Virginia Ave.
Hagerstown, MD 21740

*This encyclopedia, tastefully
illustrated and presented in convenient
"A to Z" style, is a compendium of
fascinating lore and well-researched
material. Drawing on sources from
mythology, anthropology, history, religion
and sexuality,* The Women's
Encyclopedia *reveals the stories behind
word origins, legends, superstitions and
customs, and can answer such questions
as: How did the custom of kissing begin?
Why was Cinderella's glass slipper so
important to the prince? Why was Jesus'
tomb attended only by women?
Compulsively readable!*

# Part 5: Wholistic Healing & Health
## Alternative Therapies
## Healing Is a Personal Choice

I always try to get patients to see standard medical treatments — such as radiation, chemotherapy, and surgery — as energy that can heal them. They buy time during which I can help the patient find the will to live, change, and heal. Many of the disagreements over the worth of alternate therapies arise because some people heal themselves no matter what external aids they choose, as long as they have hope and some control over the therapy. I support them as long as a patient has chosen them with a positive conviction, not out of fear. When a patient says, "I'm scared to death of surgery" and therefore chooses something else, I can't support that choice. Affirmation aids the body, fear is destructive. Treatment chosen out of fear is unlikely to be helpful.

I try to get patients to understand that the *body* heals, not the therapy. All healing is scientific. At a recent conference, someone told me he knew someone on a macrobiotic diet, someone else on a diet exactly the opposite, and a third person on chemotherapy and radiation. All three got well, and this person couldn't understand how the body could accomplish this or how the treatments made any sense. But the body can utilize any form of energy for healing — even Krebiozen or plain water — as long as the patient believes in it.

Let's say I recommended eating three peanut butter sandwiches a day to cure cancer. Some people would get well and claim it was the peanut butter that did it. Then even more people would have hope, eat peanut butter, and get better, too. But we know it's not the peanut butter. It's their hope and the changes they produce in their lives while they're on the new therapy.

The most important thing is to pick a therapy you believe in and proceed with a positive attitude. Each person must chart his own course. One may want a comprehensive nutritional supplement program, while another thinks taking dozens of pills a day is too much of a nuisance, and it becomes counterproductive. Some can just "leave their troubles to God" and be healed. Others need what I call the "football coach" method, in which the patient plans every detail. I thought of the phrase while working with Eileen, a patient who saw a hypnotherapist regularly, picked the date for surgery herself, and hired private-duty nurses. She made sure she was in control of the situation and ready for every eventuality. She is alive and well today, having recently celebrated a year cancer-free anniversary with a big party at her house. Her message to others with cancer is, "Here's the information. Go and *do it*."

- Bernie S. Siegel, M.D.
From Love, Medicine &
Miracles

---

## Love, Medicine & Miracles
### Lessons Learned About Self-Healing from a Surgeon's Experience

By Bernie S. Siegel, M.D.
1986/244 pages
**$15.95**
$17.05 postpaid from:
Harper & Row
2350 Virginia Ave.
Hagerstown, MD 21740

Many of Dr. Siegel's patients have cancer. Some of them survive. The key factor in curing this illness is examining the role illness plays in the patient's life and attitudes toward themselves. Exceptional patients — the ones who survive — take control and heal themselves, realizing they created their illness and have the power within to heal.

## Anatomy of an Illness
### As Perceived by the Patient

By Norman Cousins
1979/174 pages
**$5.95**
$7.45 postpaid from:
Bantam Books
414 E. Golf Rd.
Direct Resource Dept.
Des Plaines, IL 60016

*Anatomy of an Illness is the story of Norman Cousins and his successful fight against a crippling disease. It is the story of a partnership between a physician and a patient in beating back the odds. The doctor's genius lay in helping the patient use his own powers — laughter, courage, tenacity. The patient's talent was in mobilizing his body's own natural healing resources — in proving what powerful weapons all the positive emotions can be in the war against disease. Norman Cousins's story has been told in major medical and lay journals around the world. It gives a striking example of how one man responded to a challenge. It demonstrates what the mind and body, working together, can do to overcome illness.*

# Mind=Thought=Physical Reality

Understanding that the mind governs the body is the first vital step towards understanding the body and its functions. The mind uses the body to translate thought into physical reality. A sense of oneself as being small can, through physical tension, transform even a tall person into a stooped, slumped, cramped, "small" person. Likewise a sense of strength and power can cause a small person to move with such energy and expansiveness that his or her size becomes irrelevant and may even be unnoticed. The mind can reeducate the muscles in ways that are harmful or helpful. Through the mind, the process of physical degeneration can be reversed. We can eliminate the idea of the inevitability of disease. If we feel weak, small, or helpless, we can practice exercises - physical and mental - which give us a sense of expansiveness. If we notice any tendency in the body to improve, any sign that a process of degeneration is reversing, we should do everything in our power to encourage it. We can allow the body to become more at ease with itself, more flexible, and less stressed. Even if we have undergone damage to nerves or muscles, that tissue can be regenerated through a program of mental and physical exercises. To do this we have to work with both body and mind, so that the nonmaterial concept of health is manifested in our material being. This takes a lot of work. The loving hands of a friend, therapist, parent, or mate can help bring healthy stimulation to our muscles and nerves.

*- By Meir Schneider*
*From Self-Healing*

---

## Self Healing
### My Life and Vision
By Meir Schneider
1987/190 pages
**$9.95**
$11.45 postpaid from:
Metheun, Inc.
29 W. 35th St.
New York, NY 10001-2291

*Meir Schneider beat incredible odds and went from near blindess to being able to function visually once again. His healing process included exercise, movement, breathing and mental imagery. He now uses his system to help people with other illnesses including chronic headaches and muscular dystrophy.*

---

## The Mind as Healer
### The New Heresy
Edited by Onslow H. Wilson, Ph.D.
1987/233 pages
**$15.95**
$17.95 postpaid from:
Insights and Sources
201 West Main St.
Plainfield, IN 46168

*This book features the proceeds of the Metaphysiology Symposiums. The dialogue was based on self-healing and maintaining personal health. Speakers included here include Willis Harmon, Ph.D.; Kenneth Pelletier, Ph.D.; Martin Ressman, M.D.; Brendan O'Regan; Alan Brauer, M.D.; Onslow Wilson; Marilyn Ferguson; and Ray Gottlieb, Ph.D.*

# Holistic Medicine
## From Stress to Optimum Health

By Kenneth R. Pelletier, Ph.D.
1979/330 pages
**$8.95**
$10.45 postpaid from:
Dell Publishing
Box 5057
Des Plaines, IL 60017

*Pelletier focuses on three vital components of holistic health — stress control, nutrition, and exercises. He develops convincing evidence for changing our attitudes toward healing and health from the traditional point of view of the body as simply a machine that can be repaired.*

---

# Medical Self Care

Box 1000
Point Reyes, CA 94956
Monthly/$15.00 for one year

*This magazine is dedicated to presenting information you can use to help you keep your self healthy.*

# Heal Your Body
## The Mental Causes for Physical Illness and the Metaphysical Way to Overcome Them

By Louise L. Hay
1982/44 pages
**$3.00**
$5.00 postpaid from:
Hay House
3029 Wilshire Blvd.
Santa Monica, CA 90404

*Your thoughts create your entire existence — your reality. Your thoughts also create your illnesses. Louise Hay has come up with a list of physical problems and their associated mental attitudes and positive affirmations to negate the causal thought.*

# Cambridge Institute for Better Vision
## Natural Vision Improvement

79 Dana St.
Cambridge, MA 02138
800-372-3937

*The Institute teaches holistic, body/ mind methods to help people reduce, eliminate, or prevent poor vision and your need for eyeglasses or contacts.*

| PROBLEM | PROBABLE CAUSE | NEW THOUGHT PATTERN |
|---|---|---|
| Abdominal Cramps | Fear. Stopping the process. | I trust the process of life. I am safe. |
| Abscess | Fermenting thoughts over hurts, slights and revenge. | I allow my thoughts to be free. The past is over. I am at peace. |
| Accidents | Inability to speak up for the self. Rebellion against authority. Belief in violence. | I release the pattern in me that created this. I am at peace. I am worthwhile. |
| Aches | Longing for love. Longing to be held. | I love and approve of myself. I am loving and lovable. |
| Acne | Not accepting the self. Dislike of the self. | I am a Divine expression of life. I love and accept myself where I am right now. |
| Addictions | Running from the self. Fear. Not knowing how to love the self. | I now discover how wonderful I am. I choose to love and enjoy myself. |
| Addison's Disease | Severe emotional malnutrition. Anger at the self. | I lovingly take care of my body, my mind and my emotions. |
| Adenoids | Family friction, arguments. Child feeling unwelcome, in the way. | This child is wanted and welcomed and deeply loved. |
| Adrenal Problems | Defeatism. No longer caring to the self. Anxiety. | I love and approve of myself. It is safe for me to care for myself. |
| Aging Problems | Social beliefs. Old thinking. Fear of being one's self. Rejection of the now. | I love and accept myself at every age Each moment in life is perfect. |
| AIDS | Denial of the self. Sexual guilt. A strong belief in not being "good enough." | I am a Divine, magnificent expression of life. I rejoice in my sexuality. I rejoice in all that I am. I love myself. |

*- Louise Hay*
From Heal Your Body

# Natural Relaxation Is Better Than Drugs

The awareness that relaxation is important to the healing process is not new. Medical science shows us that relaxation can be produced in many ways. For example, there are drugs that quiet the nervous system, muscle relaxants and pain relievers that interrupt the pain-spasm cycle, and surgery that interrupts the nerve tracts.

*Natural* relaxation is produced by a change in the way we think and feel — by a change in our awareness of how maladaptive tension puts us into a state of imbalance. It's important to emphasize that we are talking about a process of relaxation that *you* create for yourself, rather than being the passive recipient of drugs or a surgical procedure. Moreover, by rearranging reflexes and nonconscious mechanisms that are maladaptive (rather than by imposing relaxation from the outside through chemical or physical means), the relief may be made permanent and the problem cured.

As you learn to relax yourself, you gain a great deal of power that can be used for maintaining your own health. Besides eliminating the painful symptoms produced by tension in the body, you can also enjoy the satisfaction of feeling independent and responsible for your own wellbeing. If you are motivated to do so, you can produce the state of relaxation efficiently so that your natural healing abilities keep your body balanced.

This point of view differs significantly from that held by many practitioners of medicine in our culture, where for many patients there is an almost complete feeling of dependence on the doctor. More and more people are beginning to see how they can rid themselves of lifelong physical and emotional ailments by becoming active participants in their own healing (rebalancing) processes.

- *Emmett E. Miller, M.D.*
*From* Self Imagery

## Self Imagery
### *Creating Your Own Good Health*

By Emmett E. Miller, M.D.
1986/272 pages
**$7.95**
$8.95 postpaid from:
Celestial Arts
Box 7327
Berkeley, CA 94707

*Miller tells us how we can create and maintain health through hypnosis, relaxation, and imagery. No illness is safe when you decide to create health.*

## Why Do You Want to Be Fat?

### Beyond Dieting
### *An Edgar Cayce Program for Permanent Weight Control*

By Linda Cochran
1983/128 pages
**$6.95**
$8.95 postpaid from:
A.R.E. Press
Box 595
Virginia Beach, VA 23451

*Your attitude and emotions can be your greatest ally in your war against weight. The author relies on Cayce's wisdom, her experience, humor, and innovative charts and guides to help you get in touch with your weight problem.*

## The Key to Getting Thin Is Finding Out Why You Want to Be Fat

Complete the following (and stop resisting — you might learn something):

I want to be fat because _____
_____

Permit me to share some conclusions to which others have come in working with this idea:

I want to be fat because — it makes my mother unhappy.

I want to be fat because — people expect less of me.

I want to be fat because — I feel more comfortable. If I'm too thin, I stand out from the crowd, and I feel self-conscious.

I want to be fat because — eating brings more satisfaction in my life than anything else.

I want to be fat because — I fear sexual confrontations with the opposite sex. This is the most common. In fact, as you continue to work with this idea of wanting to be fat, you may uncover other fears of which you were previously unaware.

- *Linda Cochran*
*From* Beyond Dieting

**The New Holistic Health
Handbook**
*Living Well in a New Age*

Compiled by the Berkeley
Holistic Health Center
Edited by Shepard Bliss
1985/430 pages
**$14.95**
$16.45 postpaid from:
Viking Penguin
40 West 23rd St.
New York, NY 10010

*This is a complete handbook for
holistic health care in the 1980's. It
features 65 articles from notables like
Norman Cousins, Molly Scott, Laurence
LeShan and James Gordon, M.D.*

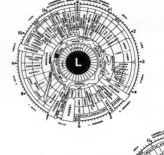

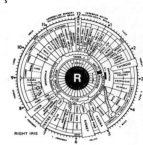

- *Iris Chart showing the body
part reflected in the iris of the
eye.*
From The New Holistic
Health Handbook

# Why Does Reflexology Work?

Reflexology refers primarily to
reflex points on the feet and hands,
but there are many other usable
reflex points throughout the body.

There are several theories on how
reflexology works. Some say that
each of the 72,000 nerve endings on
each foot connects to a different
body area.

Reflexology can assist the body
by relaxing it and stimulating the
blocked nerve endings, thereby
stimulating sluggish glands and
organs to regain their normal
functioning. Used frequently,
reflexology can give the body a
general toning to enhance vitality and
one's sense of well-being. It is also a
wonderful gift to give to a friend.

- *Lew Connor &
Linda McKim
From The New Holistic
Health Handbook*

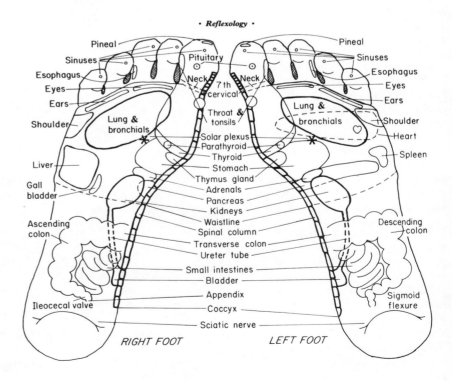

• *Reflexology* •

RIGHT FOOT      LEFT FOOT

## Headaches: The Drugless Way to Lasting Relief!

By Harry C. Ehrmantraut, Ph.D.
1987/138 pages
**$8.95**
$9.95 postpaid from:
Celestial Arts
Box 7327
Berkeley, CA 94707

*Once you realize headaches are not brain aches you can understand how acupressure, exercise, massage, relaxation, and/or breathing can cure them. Start with uncovering the cause, take appropriate action, and you may never need another aspirin again.*

# Headache Relief Through Proper Brushing

*Center brush is best type; others are quite useable.*

## What Is a Headache?

To understand this system of headache prevention, you need to understand the source of your headache pain: where, exactly, does the pain start?

The first thing to understand is that *the pain does not come from your brain.* The brain itself is insensitive and, in fact, even cutting it will not produce pain. Second, it is very unlikely that the pain comes from within the cranium at all. (The cranium consists of those skull bones surrounding the brain.) The only elements inside the cranium that can sense pain are parts of the blood vessels and the parts of the brain-covering membranes immediately adjacent to these blood vessels. Thus, only two problems *within* the cranium can cause headache pain, and neither of these is the cause in even 1 percent of the headaches of the general population.

One of these problems is a brain tumor that is sufficiently advanced in size to actually pull or press on a sensitive part of the membrane or blood vessel. Usually by this time, the tumor will have produced other effects, such as vision problems, dizziness, etc., long before it produces headaches. The second source is sudden and violent accelerations of the head, especially in rotation, so that the mass of the brain, continuing to turn slightly after the skull has stopped, will pull on the main arteries at its base.

In over 99 percent of headaches,

the pain comes from outside of your skull. In fact, it originates in the tissues lying outside of the skull and under the skin, namely the muscles and blood vessels of the scalp and neck. The actual source of pain is the end of the pain nerve. That pain nerve terminates in one of three structures: the large and small skeletal muscles of the neck; the small muscles making up the scalp; or the very small muscles comprising the walls of the arteries and veins of the scalp, forehead, and neck. *All of your headache pain comes from nerve endings in muscles.*

This is an extremely fortunate fact for headache victims. If the pain arose from the brain, it would be very difficult to reach, to manipulate, and to control. But as this pain arises totally from muscle tissue which we clearly *can* reach and manipulate, we *can* control it. The pain is sensed because the bare ends of the pain nerves are irritated. Any irritation will give rise to pain, since that is the only message these nerves can convey, but the usual irritation is either *mechanical* or *chemical.*

- Harry C. Ehrmantraut, Ph.D.
From Headaches

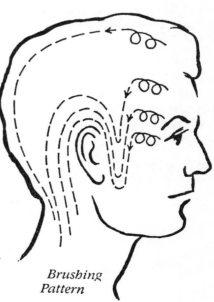

*Brushing
Pattern*

## Natural Vision Improvement

By Janet Goodrich, Ph.D.
1986/218 pages
**$12.95**
$13.95 postpaid from:
Celestial Arts
Box 7327
Berkeley, CA 94707

*The choice is yours: either continue looking through glass to see clearly or gradually improve your sight by working with your inner self through movement, visualization, and exercises.*

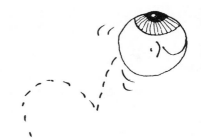

# Natural Vision Is Ours to Keep

Natural vision is seeing with every part of ourselves. From our physical eyes right through our feelings, thoughts, dreams, creative insights, and spiritual unfolding, vision permeates all our life experiences. And it is ours to keep.

If we regard vision in this broadened wholistic way it gives us the doorway, the inspiration and the knowledge to maintain and improve our seeing ability. If vision is all these inter-related parts, we might ask 'Why must it only roll downhill and then be irretrievable? Don't we have within us somewhere the power not only to recover and maintain our eyesight, but also to develop it even further?' There we stand, scratching our heads, either straining through glasses, or fending them off, muttering, 'There must be a better way'.

Fortunately for those of us who want our visual experience to be progressive throughout our life, to be full of excitement and beauty, replete with 'aha' and 'I see that clearly now', there are answers. We are able to keep, improve, develop and expand our vision through our own actions.

*- Janet Goodrich, Ph.D.
From* Natural Vision Improvement

# Holistic Health Organizations

**American Holistic Medical Association**
2727 Fairview Ave. E
Seattle, WA 98102
206-322-6842

*They offer education for a variety of holistic/alternative disciplines and a holistic physician referral network.*

**American Association of Holistic Nurses**
205 St. Louis St.
Springfield, MO 65806
417-864-5160

*This group helps educate nurses in holistic methods and philosophy. They publish a newsletter and support networking for nurses.*

**Association for Holistic Health**
Box 12407
La Jolla, CA 90237
619-535-0101

*They provide networking and information through seminars, publications and a directory.*

**Biofeedback Institute of San Francisco**
3428 Sacramento St.
San Francisco, CA 94118
415-921-5455

*The BISF offers biofeedback training, evaluation and therapy services for stress related problems ranging from migraine headaches to asthma. They also offer books, tapes, videos and biofeedback equipment.*

**Holistic Dental Association**
974 North 21st St.
Newark, OH 43055
614-366-3309

*If you want to locate a holistic dentist, this organization can help.*

**International Association of Holistic Health Practitioners**
3419 Thom Blvd.
Las Vegas, NV 89106
702-873-4542

*The IAHHP provides a referral service for holistic centers and practitioners plus seminars and publications.*

**International Chiropractors Association**
1901 L St. N.W.
Washington, DC 20036
202-659-6476

*For information and chiropractor referrals, contact the ICA.*

---

**The Health Resource**
209 Katherine Drive
Conway, AR 72032
501-329-5272

*If you have a medical problem and you would like to know everything you can about it, this organization can help. They provide 40-to-100 page reports on a particular health problem including the latest advances in medical technology, the treatment alternatives and physicians who are specialists in a particular condition.*

# Glossary of Holistic Health Terms

**Acupuncture:** An Oriental system that involves stimulating points on the skin with fine needles.

**Acupressure:** An Oriental practice of applying finger pressure to certain places on the skin to affect healing. Also called Shiatsu massage.

**Biofeedback:** A technique for controlling biological processes by using a machine that reads body measurements.

**Body Cleansing:** A program of fasting and elimination of toxins to maintain body health.

**Bodywork:** The use of a number of therapies for healing that employ physical regimens.

**Chiropractic:** A therapy treatment bases on the manipulation of the spinal chord.

**Flower Essence Therapy:** The use of extracts from flowering plants as a healing method.

**Herbology:** The use of herbs to promote healing and health.

**Homeopathy:** A system based on the theory of "like cures like." It is meant to stimulate the body's healing ability.

**Macrobiotics:** A dietary wellness system based on whole grains, vegetables, and fish.

**Polarity Therapy:** A therapy that attempts to remove energy blockages in the body by applying hands on certain places on the body surface.

**Reflexology:** A system that stresses manipulation of reflex points on the soles of the feet for healing.

**Reiki:** A "laying on of hands" therapy.

**Rolfing:** A stringent muscular realignment therapy. It is used mainly for back and neck problems.

**Visualization and Imagery:** The process of forming positive thoughts as a means of creating wellness.

**Yoga:** An Eastern system that stresses exercise for attaining bodily or mental health.

# Edgar Cayce on Healing & Health

Over half of the 14,000 Edgar Cayce readings were devoted to health and healing. His approach was holistic, since he always dealt with the human being as a whole entity — body, mind, and spirit.

In 1970, the Association for Research and Enlightenment (A.R.E.) Clinic was founded in Phoenix, Arizona, by Drs. William and Gladys McGarey. They are dedicated to healing the physical, mental, and spiritual aspects of the individual. Series include biofeedback, acupuncture, massage, hydrotherapy, counseling, music, movement, osteotherapy, diet, and meditation.

Contact the A.R.E. Clinic at 4018 N. 40th St., Phoenix, AZ 85018.

A.R.E. headquarters can be contacted at P.O. Box 595, Virginia Beach, VA 23451, 804-428-3588.

## The Edgar Cayce Remedies

By William A. McGarey, M.D.
1983/272 pages
**$3.95**
$5.95 postpaid from:
A.R.E. Press
Box 595
Virginia Beach, VA 23451

*This is an outline of Edgar Cayce's philosophy and methods of healing including suggestions for treating specific illnesses.*

• • • •

"Know that there is within self all healing that may be accomplished for the body. For all healing must come from the Divine, for who healeth thy diseases? The source of the Universal Supply."

*- Edgar Cayce*
*reading #4021-1*
*From* The Edgar Cayce Remedies

## Preventive Measures

Edgar Cayce said many things while asleep that challenge one's imagination. For instance, we all have heard of ragweed, one of the most troublesome allergens. It is found everywhere, it seems, and the manufacturers of the desensitivity serums would be at a loss were it not for dust and ragweed. Cayce often referred to ragweed by its more romantic name, *Ambrosia* weed; and he saw in this remarkably bothersome plant a tremendously therapeutic ability.

Thanks to some careful research by Bob Clapp at the A.R.E. Headquarters in Virginia Beach, we find that this plant, when made into a tonic or a tea, can — according to Mr. Cayce — acts to bring the entire intestinal tract into a better functioning condition. It can help the functioning of the liver, improve eliminations, and do all manner of remarkable things. Listen to this extract from the readings:

If there will be taken in the system, at regular intervals, those properties that are not habit forming, neither are they effective towards creating the condition where cathartics are necessary for the activities through the alimentary canal — whether related to the colon or the jejunum, or ileum — yet these will change the vibrations in such a manner as to keep clarified the assimilations, and aid the pancreas, the spleen, the liver, and the hepatic circulation, in keeping a normal equilibrium. The properties would be found in those of the Ambrosia weed made in this manner: To 6 oz. of distilled water, add 3 oz. of the *green* ragweed, or Ambrosia weed. Steep for sufficient period to reduce to half the quantity. Then strain, adding to this 2 oz. of simple syrup, with 1 oz. of grain alcohol. Shake the solution before the dose is taken. The dose would be half a teaspoon twice each day, when the period for taking has arisen — or take it about once a month, for three or four days. This will aid the digestive system, will aid the whole of the eliminating system.

*- Edgar Cayce Reading*
*William McGarey, M.D.*
*From* The Edgar Cayce Remedies

# Acid-Alkaline Food Combinations

Cayce stressed the value of certain food combinations and the harm in others in relation to the acid-alkaline balance. Many of his theories have been validated by important research since he advanced them. Others seem to work, although just why they do is a job for further research. Here are a few examples:

Q-3. What foods should I avoid?
A-3. Rather it is the combination of foods that makes for disturbance with most physical bodies, as it would with this ... Do not combine the (alkaline) reacting acid fruits with starches, other than *whole wheat bread*. That is, citrus fruits, oranges, apples, grapefruit, limes or lemons or even tomato juices. And do not have cereals (which contain the greater quantity of starch than most) at the same meal with the citrus fruits. (416-9)

This, as you will see, radically alters the usual pattern of the American breakfast. It suggests that citrus juices — such as orange juice — should be taken between meals or at least one to two hours before breakfast. However, it can be combined at breakfast with an egg and toast, not cereal.

And while we are still talking about breakfast it would be well to point out that Cayce felt very strongly about coffee, which he suggested was a food when taken alone, but should never be taken

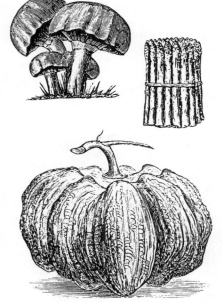

with milk or cream and sugar, since the milk transformed itself into a leathery curd blocking the digestive process. The research of British scientists has confirmed this in recent years.

Coffee, taken properly, is a food; that is *without* cream or milk. (303-2)

If coffee is taken, do not take milk in same. If tea is taken, do not take milk in same. This is hard on the digestion ... (5097-1)

Q-20. Is [the use of] tea and coffee harmful to the body?
A-20. Tea is more harmful than coffee. (303-2)

## CITRUS FRUITS SHOULD BE MIXED WITH LEMON OR LIME JUICE

Four parts orange juice should be combined with one part lime or lemon. Grapefruit juice may be prepared the same way.

And to the question, "Is the quart of milk a day, and orange juice, helpful?" Cayce answered, "Orange juice and milk are helpful, but these would be taken at opposite ends of the day; not together." (274-9)

## AVOID EATING MEAT AND STARCH AT THE SAME MEAL

Rather is it the combination of foods that makes for disturbance with most physical bodies ... ... avoid combinations where corn, potatoes, rice, spaghetti or the like are taken all at the same meal ... all of these tend to make for too great a quantity of starch — especially if any meat is taken at such a meal ... for the activities of the gastric flow of the digestive system are the requirements of one reaction in the gastric flow for starch and another for proteins, or for the activities of the carbohydrates as combined with starches of this nature ... Sweets and meats taken at the same meal are preferable to starches and meats. (416-9)

## COMBINATIONS OF VEGETABLES

A. Have at least three vegetables that grow above the ground to one that grows under the ground.

B. Have at least one meal each day that includes a quantity of raw vegetables such as cabbage, lettuce, celery, carrots, onions, and the like. Tomatoes may be used in their season. Have at least one leafy vegetable to every one of the pod vegetables taken.

C. Do include often in the diet raw vegetables, prepared in various ways, not merely as a salad, but scraped or grated and combined with gelatin.

- *Dr. Harold Reilly and Ruth Brod*
  *From The Edgar Cayce Handbook for Health Through Drugless Therapy*

# The Role of Imagery in Healing

Imagery, or the stuff of the imagination, affects the body intimately on both seemingly mundane and profound levels. Memories of a lover's scent call forth the biochemistry of emotion. The mental rehearsal of a sales presentation or a marathon race evokes muscular change and more: blood pressure goes up, brain waves change, and sweat glands become active. Because of this pronounced effect the image has on the body, it yields power over life and death, and plays a key role in the less dramatic aspects of living as well.

In primitive societies, the witch doctor shakes the bones and utters a curse. The victim's heart flutters, his temperature drops, and death comes quickly. An autopsy would show that the hex had the effect of causing the body to shut down — a parasympathetic nervous system death, the physiologists might call it. The victim dies, not from fright, but from hopelessness, from the vivid working of the imagination.

A terminally ill cancer patient goes to the shrine at Lourdes, France. A woman with severe rheumatoid arthritis crosses the border into Mexico to get therapy that is unproven according to U.S. authorities and therefore illegal in this country. A couple, long childless, pays a first visit to a famous medical school's infertility clinic. In each of the cases, positive changes in the condition in question have been documented that either preceded treatment or accompanied what might be classified as medically worthless intervention. Patients all over the world are administered placebos of one kind or another. Often they show decreases in pain, nausea, anxiety, and even in tumor cells. It is not just their attitude that changes; their biochemistry has also undergone a transformation. Far from being the duping of innocents and malingerers, placebos and the power of suggestion tend to work best in people who need and want to get well.

*Jeanne Achterberg*
*From* Imagery in Healing

## Imagery in Healing
### *Shamanism and Modern Medicine*

By Jeanne Achterberg
1985/254 pages
**$9.95**
$11.70 postpaid from:
Shambhala Publications, Inc.
P.O. Box 308
Boston, MA 02117

*Mental Imaging can help patients through painful events like childbirth and burn treatment and can have a positive influence on diseases. Jeanne Achterberg draws parallels between the work of the ancient shaman and modern medicine and draws them together under the powerful healing force called imagery.*

## The Realms of Healing
### *A Scientific Exploration of Non-Medical Healing*
By Stanley Krippner and Albert Villoldo
1986/212 pages
**$9.95**
$10.95 postpaid from:
Celestial Arts
Box 7327
Berkeley, CA 94707

If there are paranormal phenomena involved in the Spiritists' sessions, they may be only indirectly involved with the healing itself. It is my suspicion that much of the healing that occurs is self-healing, inspired by the healer's pyrotechnical displays. Therefore, medicine could learn a great deal from what was going on in the Spiritists' centers, even if they remained skeptical about the psychic nature of the incidents.

- *Stanley Krippner and Albert Villoldo From* The Realms of Healing

*This is a unique study into psychic and paranormal healing of the Spiritists of Brazil, Filipino healers and others. They also tackle the age-old question of how healing occurs.*

## Psychic Surgery

I stood by Sison's table as an elderly man was placed on his back. He was blind in both eyes. As Sison rubbed the right eye, red fluid poured down the side of his face. She repeated the procedure with his left eye then thrust a wad of oil soaked cotton in his left ear. As she poked it in his ear, it appeared to disappear completely. Moving her hands, she seemed to pull a wad of cotton from his right ear. The cotton had the same shape and size as the wad which had apparently entered the left ear; the oil could not be seen and there were red streaks on the cotton. Sison predicted that sight would begin to return to his left eye in three weeks.

- *Stanley Krippner observing Filipino Psychic Surgeon Sison From* The Realms of Healing

# Nutritional Approaches to Healing

## Gerson Institute

Dr. Max Gerson developed nutrition therapies that they claim has helped many people cure "incurable" diseases like cancer and multiple sclerosis. They do not sell or distribute healing substances or operate any hospitals. They offer information and educational materials. They do operate the Gerson Therapy Center in Mexico to teach people how to use Gerson dietary methods to help with physical conditions.

For information write:
Gerson Institute
Box 430
Bonita, CA 92002

## Silver Dental Fillings
### *The Toxic Time Bomb*

By Sam Ziff
1984/202 pages
**$10.95**
$12.95 postpaid from:
Aurora Press
Box 573
Santa Fe, NM 87504

*Can the mercury in your silver dental fillings kill you? This pioneering book on a rather scary topic — since most of us have silver dental fillings — discusses the history, uses, and possible problems associated with mercury in the human body.*

## A Cancer Therapy
### *The Cure of Advanced Cancer by Diet Therapy*

1986/432 pages
**$2.00**
$3.00 postpaid from:
Gerson Institute
Box 430
Bonita, CA 92002

*This is a complete and detailed explanation of Gerson's dietary therapy designed to re-activate the body's healing mechanism. It also presents 50 documented cases of people with terminal diseases who recovered for at least 5 years. Many were still alive at the time of the last update 30 years later.*

# How Can Mercury Get in Your Body?

Mercury from the dental filling can travel down through the tooth into our bodies. Once the dentist has cleaned out the decay in the cavity, he prepares it for the filling material by first placing a liner and base into the cavity. This is a resin material that is supposed to seal the cavity and prevent any of the metals in the amalgam filling material from working their way into the pulp and subsequently down through the root into the bone and surrounding tissues.

The protective effectiveness of the seal is quite controversial. Early investigations claimed that they were effective and prevented any passage of the metals into the pulp. However, later studies using radioactive mercury amalgam fillings have shown, by tracing the radioactive mercury, that it does migrate into the pulp. Another study, done by O'Brien and Ryge in 1978, concluded that the sealer will only delay the entry of the mercury into the pulp. The pulp canal extends to the end of the root and has a restricted opening at the very end. This opening permits the body to provide blood and nutrients to the pulp (which is composed of tissue, blood, and nerves) and to the tooth, which in effect keeps the tooth "alive."

If mercury or any of the other metals in the amalgam get into the pulp, they then have a way of getting out of the tooth and into the alveolar bone and the surrounding tissues that support the teeth, where they can then easily migrate to other locations in the body.

Mercury is cytotoxic. This means it acts as a toxin or an antibody and has a specific poisonous effect on the cells. Bleeding gums and alveolar bone loss, which results in loosening of the teeth, are both classic signs of mercury toxicity. Of course these conditions can also be caused by germs or bacteria but according to Till in 1978, who used germ free animals in his experiment, mercury in amounts released from amalgam fillings could produce the same signs plus inflammation of the tissues surrounding a tooth. (This is sometimes called gingivitis, pyorrhea, or periodontitis).

- *Sam Ziff*
*From* The Toxic Time Bomb

# Reiki
# What Is Reiki?

Reiki (pronounced "ray-key") is an Oriental word meaning "universal life energy." The term "Reiki" has been applied to a specific technique for restoring and balancing your natural life-force energy. Reiki is neither a dogma nor a religion but is a complete, scientific method for self-healing and for maintaining your health and sense of well-being physically, emotionally, mentally, and spiritually. Reiki is an effective technique for prevention of diseases and energy imbalances on all levels of your being. Reiki is also a unique, highly effective tool for personal transformation, growth, and change. Reiki is a natural energy-balancing and renewing method that can be used in conjunction with any other technique of health-care treatment as well as with any other personal growth therapy. Reiki does not conflict with traditional medicine but can be used with it or as an additional source for restoring vital energy and promoting health and well-being.

*- Barbara Weber Ray*
*From* The Reiki Factor

## The Reiki Factor

By Barbara Weber Ray, Ph.D.
1983/142 pages
**$8.00**
$9.50 postpaid from:
Exposition Press
P.O. Box 2120
Smithtown, NY 11787

*The Reiki Factor is written to introduce you to what Reiki is and what it can do. There are case histories and plenty of history. Don't look for a section on how to do Reiki; they left that out. You must go to an authorized Reiki teacher for therapy.*

## American-International Reiki Association

Box 13778
Atlanta, GA 30324
404-874-9142

*This is the international headquarters for the Reiki association and where you can be directed to a certified Reiki practitioner.*

## The Cancer Prevention Diet
*Michio Kushi's Nutritional Blueprint for the Relief and Prevention of Disease*
By Michio Kushi with Alex Jack
1983/460 pages
**$9.95**
$11.45 postpaid from:
St. Martin's Press
175 Fifth Ave.
New York, NY 10010

*Michio Kushi is revolutionizing America's understanding of health and treatment of disease. Drawing on cancer and heart disease research, including studies of his methods at Harvard Medical School, he presents in* The Cancer Prevention Diet *a groundbreaking dietary program that can be implemented in the American home at a fraction of the cost of usual meals and medical care. Not until now has there been an integrated theory on why different cancers develop and how various foods affect the body.*

# Diet and the Development of Cancer

To understand how cancer develops, use the analogy of a tree. A tree's structure is opposite to that of the human body. For example, the leaves of a tree have a more open structure and a green color, while the cells of the human body, which correspond to the leaves of a tree, have a more closed structure and are nourished by blood, which is red in color. A tree's sustenance comes from the nutrients absorbed through the external roots. The roots of the human body lie deep in the intestines in the region where nutrients are absorbed into the blood and lymph and then distributed to all of the body's cells. If the quality of nourishment is chronically poor in the soil or in the food that is consumed, the leaves of the tree or the cells of the body eventually lose their normal functional ability and begin to deteriorate. This condition results from the repeated intake of poor nutrients and does not arise suddenly. While it is developing, many other symptoms might arise in other parts of the tree trunk and branches or in the body.

Cancer develops over a period of time out of a chronically precancerous state. In my estimation, as many as 80 to 90 percent of Americans, Europeans, Japanese, and other modern people have some type of precancerous condition. The repeated overconsumption of excessive dietary factors causes a variety of adjustment mechanisms in the body which progressively develop toward cancer. Since the body at all times seeks balance with the surrounding environment, the normal process is for this excess to be eliminated or stored when it exceeds the body's capacity for elimination. Eventually, the overaccumulation will be stored in the form of excessive layers of fat, cholesterol, and the formation of cysts and tumors.

*- Michio Kushi with*
*Alex Jack*
*From* The Cancer
Prevention Diet

## Minding the Body, Mending the Mind

By Joan Borysenko, Ph.D.
1987/240 pages
**$14.95**
No postage
Addison Wesley Publishers
Jacob Way
Reading, MA 01867

*How do we heal? According to Joan Borysenko, it is through the integration of biology along with deep personal and spiritual understanding. It is this mind/body relationship that she urges you to understand and work with to attain wholeness and peace, which is true healing.*

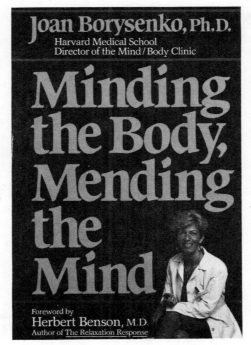

Joan Borysenko, Ph.D.
Harvard Medical School
Director of the Mind/Body Clinic

# Minding the Body, Mending the Mind

Foreword by
Herbert Benson, M.D.
Author of The Relaxation Response

## SHOULDER SHRUGS

*To Relieve Stress*

**A. INHALE**
Shoulders up

**B. CONTINUE TO INHALE**
Roll shoulder blades together

**C. EXHALE**
Shoulders down

## AWFULIZING THOUGHTS

narrowed perspective
one-track thinking
regressive coping

**AUTONOMIC NERVOUS SYSTEM RESPONSES**

increased blood pressure
increased heart rate
sweaty palms
dry mouth
enlarged pupils
goose bumps
fast, shallow breathing
sinking feeling

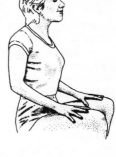

**MUSCLE TENSION**

face
neck
chest
back
arms and legs

**The Anxiety Cycle**

*- Joan Borysenko, Ph.D.*
*From Minding the Body, Mending the Mind*

# Psychospiritual Nature of the Disease AIDS

We believe that the AIDS virus particularly strikes individuals and groups who have been isolated by the dominant culture — *culturally isolated minorities* who are forced to express their emotional, physical, and spiritual nature apart from the community at large — and individuals within those isolated communities who experience undue psychological and/or socioeconomic hardship. Societal isolation places unusually heightened degrees of stress upon the individual and collective mind, body, and spirit of its outcasts. It is this isolation, often internalized as self-hatred or lack of self-acceptance, which allows the AIDS virus to begin to incubate once it has entered the system.

The place in the physical body where a disease manifests can help us discover the deeper disease which resides on mental and spiritual levels. The concept of "psychosomatic ailments" evidences an understanding of the connection, for example, between suppressed feelings or unresolved emotional trauma and subsequent physical disease.

The physical key to understanding AIDS lies in its association with the complete collapse of the thymus gland. The thymus is the central factor of the immune system, and is responsible for producing those T-cells we hear so much about. From a metaphysical perspective, it is associated with the heart chakra, the spiritual energy center that radiates harmony and love within and without our being. The thymal dysfunction which lies at the heart of AIDS is connected to the deeper disharmony at the core of this disease, the lack of love from without internalized as a lack of self-love.

North American gay men and Haitian refugees are the two culturally isolated minorities hit hard by AIDS in the United States, with gays accounting for 75% of the reported cases. Gays in particular, whose current wave of liberation began with the 1969 Stonewall Rebellion, have seen the blossoming and growing tolerance of their lifestyle threatened by the rise to power of the fundamentalist Christian right and conservative political administrations. Fostered by John Briggs, Anita Bryant, Jerry Falwell, and Lyndon LaRouche, social pressures upon the gay community have increased to the point where fear can be felt in the air. It is no coincidence that the rise of AIDS has to a large extent coincided with the recent upsurge of right-wing political and religious repression of gays.

- *The Holistic Group*
From Psychoimmunity and the Healing Process

## Northern Lights Alternatives

2303 Bronson Hill Dr.
Los Angeles, CA 90068
213-877-4846

*NLA is an AIDS networking organization created for people who wish to become aware of literature, centers, social issues, support organizations, workshops, seminars, and health care alternatives related to AIDS.*

## Tools for Change

*T o o l s • f o r • C h a n g e*

Box 14141
San Francisco, CA 94114
415-861-6838

*Margo Adair is director of this organization that provides information, workshops and tools for people who need to work with life-threatening conditions like AIDS. Her work focuses on personal empowerment through consciousness development which includes visualization, applied meditation, and cultivating wellness.*

## AIDS: A Positive Approach

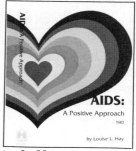

By Louise L. Hay
1983/60 minute cassette tape
**$10.00**
$12.00 postpaid from:
Hay House
3029 Wilshire Blvd. #206
Santa Monica, CA 90404

*Louise Hay offers counseling and awareness for her listeners with AIDS. She teaches how to create self-love, change negative attitudes and turn them into positive ones. Hay says her counseling, combined with nutrition and support of a physician, has helped several of her students with AIDS to enter a state of disease remission.*

# Healing AIDS

**Psychoimmunity & the Healing Process**
*A Holistic Approach to Immunity & AIDS*
Edited By Jason Serinus
1986/344 pages
**$9.95**
$10.95 postpaid from:
Celestial Arts
Box 7327
Berkeley, CA 94707

**PSYCHOIMMUNITY & THE HEALING PROCESS**

A HOLISTIC APPROACH TO IMMUNITY & AIDS

*What is the healing process? How can we access it? Serinus has collected a series of essays by the best-known experts on healing. He focuses this material on the current AIDS crisis, but the principles detailed here are for every human ailment. Contributors include Elisabeth Kübler-Ross, Jack Schwartz, Kevin Ryerson, and Paul Lee.*

### AIDS: From Fear to Hope
*Channeled Teachings Offering Insight and Inspiration*
By Spirit Speaks
1987/270 pages
**$12.95**
$14.95 postpaid from:
Spirit Speaks
Box 84304
Los Angeles, CA 90073

*This is a collection of channeled material from spirit entities who regularly appear in Spirit Speaks magazine.*

**AIDS:**
*Spirits Share Understanding and Hope from the "other" Side.*

### Serenity
### *Challenging the Fear of AIDS — From Despair to Hope*

SERENITY
Challenging
the fear
of AIDS—
–from despair
to hope.
PAUL REED

By Paul Reed
1987/96 pages
**$5.95**
$6.95 postpaid from:
Celestial Arts
Box 7327
Berkeley, CA 94707

*This is a thoughtful and profound book that incorporates practical information, philosophy and AIDS resources.*

# Memory

Memory can play a dirty trick on us. It can render past experience as the most blissful and peaceful of times. It can select only the very best — and eliminate the worst or even the slightly shoddy.

In the midst of a crisis like AIDS — where our entire focus has shifted, our world has fallen away — we are strongly tempted to dredge up old memories and play with them like childhood teddy bears. They comfort us, reminding us that no, we haven't missed out, we *were* there, we *did* enjoy it.

This can be a healthy indulgence, or it can be a foul trap. It depends on the approach. To settle oneself comfortably with a cup of tea and reminisce, to sit cozily in a booth at the cafe with friends and remember, to open the trunk of fun times past and handle those memories with fondness can be momentarily satisfying and enriching.

But to become obsessed with the past — to feel that the best times are over, to do nothing but yearn for a time that has come and gone and will never return — can render life meaningless and moody.

*- Paul Reed*
*From Serenity*

# Will There Be a Cure for AIDS?

When it is no longer necessary to have a disease such as AIDS upon the Earth plane, when no one needs that experience anymore, then someone from the Spirit side may very well pass the idea to someone on the Earth plane and a so-called "cure" will come forward. But there will always be some other illness waiting in the wings, some other way to exit for the human being who is choosing to leave the Earth plane. *Cures come when the disease is no longer necessary.* There are no accidents. As long as there are those who need to have the experience of leaving the Earth by AIDS or have the need for the experience of the communication of AIDS (and changing their lives because of it), it will stay upon the Earth plane. Always. Those within the Spirit dimension will not interfere in *any way* with the Earth plane. It is always the choice of those on the Earth as to their needs and their path.

As more and more individuals go within and discover their own inner guidance, work on themselves, take responsibility for their own lives, then less and less is their need for what some would see as catastrophe or tragedy. There will be those who chose to leave through Earth changes, volcanic eruptions, airplane crashes, all forms of departure. And when there is no further need for those experiences, then there will be no further need for that illness or experience to be manifest and it will go away.

*- Soli, a Spirit Entity Speaking Through Rev. Neville Rowe From AIDS: From Fear to Hope*

## Oriental Medicine

### Health Through Balance
*An Introduction to Tibetan Medicine*

By Dr. Yeshi Donden
1986/252 pages
**$10.95**
$11.45 postpaid from:
Snow Lion Publications
Box 6483
Ithaca, NY 14851

*Tibetan medicine restores and maintains balance through diet and behavior therapy. This system has been used in Tibet for over 1,000 years.*

# The Secret of the Inner Smile

When you smile at someone it makes them feel good about themselves. When you smile at your plants they feel your loving energy and they grow. When you go home, pat your dog on the head and smile at him, your dog will wag his tail to show you he's happy. But if you go home, yell at him and kick him, he'll cower, growl, or bite. If you scream at your loved ones they'll feel defensive and unloved.

A true smile is a sign of love, a transmitter of energy which has a warming, healing effect. It is a vehicle for music. A person who does not smile is like a guitar which is not played: the guitar sits in the corner, begins to warp, it's strings stretch out, and gradually the guitar cracks and decays. The non-smiler, likewise, does not develop his ability to give and receive love. His dark countenance and serious approach to life is often coupled with ulcers and other medical disorders as his life slowly crumbles for lack of care and love.

On the other hand, the guitar that is polished and played has its strings changed regularly, the bow adjusted and is kept safely in a case. A well-loved and tended guitar brings life and light to the musician, and often outlives its owner. The smiler, too, brings joys to people's lives, and leads a happy healthy life that may be soundly remembered long after physically passing away.

- *Mantak Chia*
*From Awaken Healing Energy*

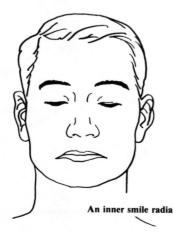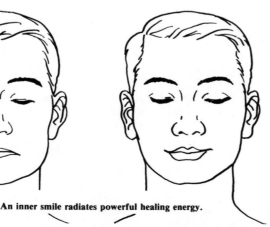

**An inner smile radiates powerful healing energy.**

*Aurora Press © 1983*

# Disease Classification in Tibetan Medicine

Disorders can be classified by different methods in terms of location in the body, type, environmental factors, and so forth. Here, by considering four classes of these one hundred and one diseases, there come to be four hundred and four:
(1) 101 disorders that are under the strong influence of actions (*karma*) in previous lifetimes
(2) 101 disorders of this lifetime — which have their causes in an early period of the life and manifest later in this same lifetime
(3) 101 disorders involving spirits
(4) 101 superficial disorders, so called because by simply following proper diet and behavior patterns one can correct them without having to resort to medication and accessory therapy.

- *Dr. Yeshi Donden*
*From* Health Through Balance

### Awaken Healing Energy Through the Tao

By Mantak Chia
1983/194 pages
**$10.95**
$12.95 postpaid from:
Aurora Press
Box 573
Santa Fe, NM 87504

*Taoist Esoteric Yoga is an ancient, powerful system of physical, psychological and spiritual development encompassing meditative and external energy practices. This book describes how to open energy channels, kundalini, and proper wiring of the etheric body.*

# Ayurveda

## The First Life Science

Ayurveda is a holistic system of medicine that is indigenous to and widely practiced in India. The word Ayurveda is a Sanskrit term meaning "science of life." Ayu means "life" or "daily living," and Veda is "knowing." Ayurveda was first recorded in the Vedas, the world's oldest extant literature. This healing system has been practiced in daily life in India for more than 5,000 years.

## Ayurveda and Human Potential

Ayurveda teaches that man is a microcosm, a universe within himself. He is a child of the cosmic forces of the external environment, the macrocosm. His individual existence is indivisible from the total cosmic manifestation. Ayurveda views health and "disease" in holistic terms, taking into consideration the inherent relationship between individual and cosmic spirit, individual and cosmic consciousness, energy and matter.

According to the teachings of Ayurveda, every human being has four biological and spiritual instincts: religious, financial, procreative and the instinct toward freedom. Balanced good health is the foundation for the fulfillment of these instincts. Ayurveda helps the healthy person to maintain health, and the diseased person to regain health. It is a medical-metaphysical healing life-science, the mother of all healing arts. The practice of Ayurveda is designed to promote human happiness, health and creative growth.

Through studying the teachings of Ayurveda, the practical knowledge of self-healing may be acquired by anyone. By the proper balance of all energies in the body, the processes of physical deterioration and disease can be impressively reduced. This concept is basic to Ayurvedic science: the capability of the individual for self-healing.

## Ayurveda, Yoga and Tantra

Ayurveda, Yoga and Tantra are the ancient life-disciplines that have been practiced in India for centuries. They are mentioned in the scriptures of the Vedas and Upanishads. Yoga is the science of union with the Divine, with Truth; Tantra is the most direct method of controlling the energy that creates the ultimate union with Truth; and Ayurveda is the science of life.

The purpose of each practice is to help the individual to achieve longevity, rejuvenation and self-realization. The object of the practices of Yoga and Tantra is liberation, although only certain disciplined individuals are able to achieve this ultimate goal through these practices. However, Ayurveda can be practiced successfully by anyone for the achievement of good health and longevity.

In the spiritual evolution of a man, Ayurveda is the foundation, Yoga is the body and Tantra is the head. It is necessary first to understand Ayurveda in order to experience the practices of Yoga and Tantra. Thus, Ayurveda, Yoga and Tantra form an interdependent trinity of life. None of these practices stands alone. The health of the body, mind and consciousness depends on the knowledge and practice of these three in daily life.

- Dr. Vasant Lad
From Ayurveda: The Science of Self Healing

## Ayurveda
### *The Science of Self-Healing*

By Dr. Vasant Lad
1984/176 pages
**$9.95**
$11.70 postpaid from:
Lotus Press
Box 6265
Santa Fe, NM 87502-6265

*This book clearly explains the principles and practical applications of Ayurveda, which is said to be the oldest healing system in the world.*

## Ayurveda Video
### *Elizabeth Clare Prophet Interviewing Dr. Vasant Lad*

1986/87-minute videocassette, VHS
**$29.95**
$31.45 postpaid from:
Summit University Press
Dept. 268, Box A
Livingston, MT 59047

*Elizabeth Clare Prophet interviews Dr. Lad who provides an overview of Ayurveda, the 5,000 year old science. He talks about applications you can use in a process of self-rejuvenation and how to bring your physical, mental and emotional bodies into alignment with the inner self.*

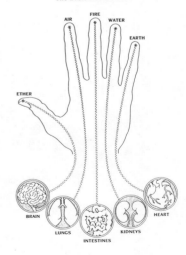

## The Ayurvedic Institute
Box 23445
Albuquerque, NM 87192

*The Institute is a private educational institution devoted to teaching Ayurvedic principles. They offer courses, a wellness program and the Ayurvedic Wellness Journal.*

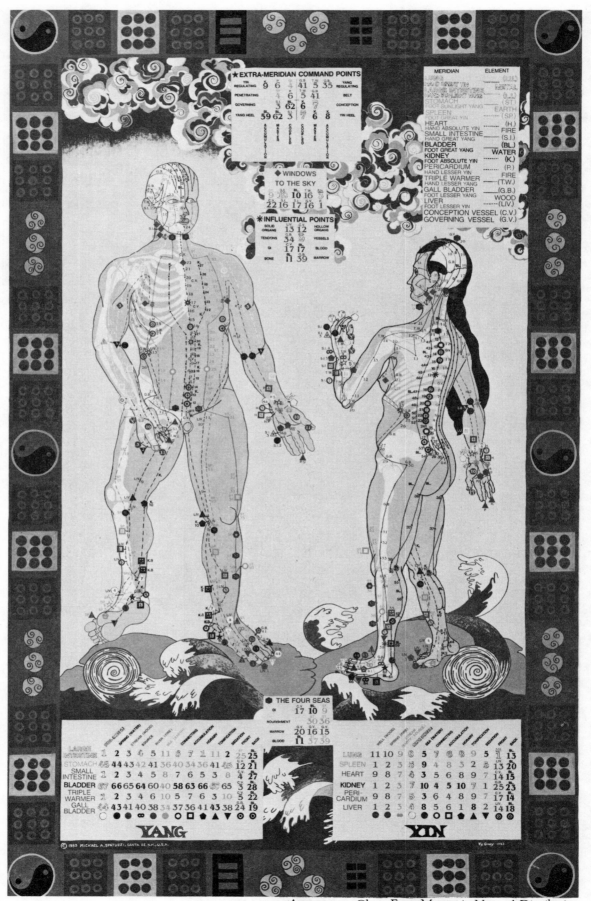

Acupuncture Chart From Mountain Natural Distributing

# Acupuncture

## The Complete Book of Acupuncture

By Dr. Stephen Thomas Chang
1976/240 pages
**$8.95**
$9.95 postpaid from:
Celestial Arts
Box 7327
Berkeley, CA 94707

*Acupuncture is one of the most important Chinese healing arts and one that stresses prevention and naturalness. This book details the basics of acupuncture. Part one discusses the theory of the flow of body energy, meridians, needling, and diagnostic procedures. The second part illustrates common acupuncture points on the body. Part three shows specific treatment for selected diseases.*

## Acupuncture

Acupuncture is a therapy used for the prevention of disease or for the maintenance of health. The practice consists of either stimulating or dispersing the flow of energy within the body by the insertion of needles into specific points on the surface of the skin, by applying heat (thermal therapy), by pressing, by massage, or by a combination of these. Acupuncture was developed by the Chinese, and its origins date back almost 6,000 years.

### *NEEDLES*
### Style and type of needles:

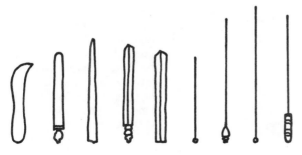

*Dr. Stephen Thomas Chang
From* The Complete Book of Acupunture.

◀**Acupuncture Chart**
**$16.95**
$19.95 postpaid from:
Mountain Natural Distributing
Box 24275
San Diego, CA 92124

## Academy of Chinese Culture & Health Sciences

420 14th St.
Oakland, CA 94612
415-763-7787

*This a fully accredited educational institution that grants two year degrees in acupuncture therapy. There is a permanent faculty of twenty four, and a fully staffed clinic.*

## San Francisco College of Acupuncture
## California College of Oriental Medicine

2051 Market St.
San Francisco, CA 94114
415-863-3500

*They offer undergraduate and graduate level degrees in acupuncture.*

# Homeopathy
## Homeopathic Medicine

Homeopathic medicine offers an alternative. Instead of giving one medicine for a person's headache, another for his constipation, another for his irritability, and yet another to counteract the effects of one or more of the medicines, the homeopathic physician prescribes a single medicine at a time that will stimulate the person's immune and defense capacity and bring about an overall improvement in that person's health. The procedure by which the homeopath finds the precise individual substance is the very science and art of homeopathy.

Most Americans today know little or nothing about homeopathic medicine, despite the fact that 15 percent of American physicians at the turn of the century considered themselves to be homeopaths, and despite the fact that homeopathy is so popular throughout the world today. Homeopathic medicine is a natural pharmaceutical system that utilizes microdoses of substances from the plant, mineral, or animal kingdom to arouse a person's natural healing response. Homeopathy is a sophisticated method of individualizing small doses of medicines in order to initiate that healing response. Unlike conventional drugs, which act primarily by having direct effects upon physiological processes related to a person's symptoms, homeopathic medicines are thought to work by stimulating the person's immune and defense system, which raises his or her overall level of health, thereby enabling him or her to re-establish health and prevent disease.

Homeopathy, of course, cannot cure everything or everybody, but it does offer the real possibility of cure for various deep-seated acute, chronic, and hereditary diseases. Some research (which will be discussed in other chapters) has begun to verify this claim, though certainly more scientific investigation is necessary to determine how effective homeopathy is and how to make it even more effective.

> *- Dana Ullman*
> *From* Homeopathy:
> Medicine for the 21st
> Century

## Everybody's Guide to Homeopathic Medicine

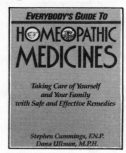

By Dana Ullman, M.P.H., and Stephen Cummings, F.N.P.
1984/312 pages
**$8.95**
$11.35 postpaid from:
Jeremy P. Tarcher, Inc.
9110 Sunset Blvd.
Los Angeles, CA 90069

*This book on Homeopathy is an excellent guidebook/manual describing the basics of this ancient healing concept.*

## Homeopathy: The Royal Medicine

Great Britain's Royal Family has utilized homeopathic medicines since the 1830s, and since then, homeopathic care has become as much a tradition of the British Royalty as has been the passing of the crown. In the 1930s King George V was so enthused by his experiences with homeopathy that he named one of his racing horses Hypericum, the name of a popular homeopathic medicine. Today, Queen Elizabeth II is the patron to the Royal London Homeopathic Hospital, and it is widely known that the Queen and Prince Charles carry homeopathic medicines with them whenever they travel.

Other "royalty" who have advocated for this little known medical specialty include: Mahatma Gandhi, Mark Twain, William James, John D. Rockefeller, Tina Turner, Lindsay Wagner, Yehudi Menuhin, and Dizzy Gillespie.

> *- Dana Ullman*
> *From* Homeopathy:
> Medicine for the 21st
> Century

**Homeopathy:**
*Medicine for the 21st Century*

By Dana Ullman, M.P.H.
1987/300 pages
**$12.95**
$14.95 postpaid from:
Homeopathic Educational Services
2124 Kittredge St.
Berkeley, CA 94704

*A updated companion to Everybody's Guide to Homeopathic Medicine.*

## Homeopathic Medicine at Home

### Natural Remedies for Everyday Ailments and Minor Injuries

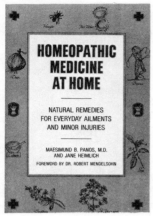

By Maesimund B. Panos, M.D., and Jane Heimlich
1980/288 pages
**$6.95**
$9.35 postpaid from:
Jeremy P. Tarcher, Inc.
9110 Sunset Blvd.
Los Angeles, CA 90069

*A practical home guide to homeopathic remedies for everyday medical concerns. It also includes a detailed infant and children's health section and homeopathic advice for pregnant women.*

# Homeopathic Organizations

## Foundation for Homeopathic Education and Research

5916 Chabot Crest
Oakland, CA 94618
415-420-8791

*This organization is dedicated to scientific inquiry into the use of natural medicine. They publish Homeopathic Research Reports.*

## Homeopathic Educational Services

Dana Ullman, M.P.H., Director
2124 Kittredge St.
Berkeley, CA 94704
415-653-9270

*This organization offers homeopathic information, medicines, books, tapes and even a veterinary homeopathy kit for animals.*

## The National Center for Homeopathy

1500 Massachusetts Ave., N.W.
Washington, DC 20005
202-223-6182

*The NCH offers seminars, information, a magazine called Homeopathy Today and access to the latest research on natural remedies.*

## International Foundation for Homeopathy

4 Sherman Ave.
Fairfax, CA 94930

*Offers information and homeopathic sources for treatment and medicine.*

# Major Study of Homeopathy: Positive Results with Hay Fever Patients

Recent research published in the *Lancet* (October 18, 1986) showed that the microdoses utilized in homeopathic medicine were effective in treating hay fever. This new research verifies that the placebo response is not the primary factor in the action of the homeopathic medicines.

An impressive double-blind trial was conducted in Glasgow and London hospitals on 144 patients suffering from hay fever. The authors of the study included two representatives of the Glasgow Homeopathic Hospital, representatives from departments of statistics and immunology at the University of Glasgow.

Each hay fever patient was given extremely small doses (30c) of a mixture of twelve different species of grass pollens. The research results showed that those given a homeopathic medicine experienced six times as much improvement as did those who were given a placebo. The subjects were allowed to take an antihistimine if it seemed their symptoms warranted it. However, by the end of the study, those under homeopathic treatment only needed to take this conventional medication half as much as did those on a placebo. The results from this experiment were considered statistically highly significant.

The results of this trial are particularly impressive in light of the fact that it can be assumed that the results would be even better if the homeopaths were able to individualize medicines according to each sick person's unique symptoms.

*- From Homeopathic Research Reports Summer, 1987*

## Herbology

# The Philosophy of Herbal Use

The most important issue in herbal use is why are they different? What is it that sets herbs apart from any other healing agent? To the herbalist, herbs are unique because they are not just a group of chemicals. Each herb has its own nature which, for want of better word, we call its personality. The concept of herbal personality is the basis of herbology and has played a major role in herb use for thousands of years.

Most of the world's people continue to use herbs as their primary form of medication. While various cultures may not have our knowledge of biochemistry of plants or the same perspective on the structure of the human body, all herb using cultures have an appreciation for the 'personality' of herbs. A herb is a living substance and has its own constellation of energy. We don't think of ourselves or our pet dog as being merely a conglomeration of physical parts. We have emotions, mental concepts and spiritual feelings. It would be silly to assume that herbs don't have patterns of energy beyond mere molecules. North American Indians believe that the spirit of the herb is directly involved in a battle with an illness when herbal healing takes place. Other cultures (e.g. the Chinese and East Indian) choose their herbs by taste, smell and colour along with energies related to fire, metal, water, wood and earth — features which we might not think were important for healing. A first step in understanding herbology lies in appreciating the fact that we should focus just as much on the essence or 'personality' of the herb as on the scientific descriptions.

- *Terry Willard*
  *From* Helping Yourself
  With Natural Remedies

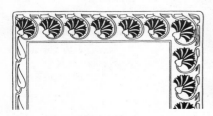

## Helping Yourself with Natural Remedies

By Terry Willard, Ph.D.
1986/126 pages
**$9.95**
$11.95 postpaid from:
CRCS Publications
Box 1460
Sebastopol, CA 95472

*This is an encyclopedic book that lists common herbal formulas and their application with physical problems like constipation, obesity and nervous tension.*

# Herbs to Bolster Your Memory

The cerebral cortex of the brain controls memory function. Arteriosclerosis in the arteries leading to the brain, along with inorganic mineral deposits in the brain cells themselves, results in ischemia (cell starvation from lack of oxygen and nutrients). This interferes with the thinking processes and produces what is usually recognized as senile behavior.

### Recommended Action

Drink large amounts of steam-distilled or reverse osmosis water to leach out the inorganic deposits. Ensure that the brain receives proper nourishment to rebuild the deteriorating cells. Maintain and promote good circulation.

**Single Herbs:** Blue Vervain, Gotu Kola, Fo-ti-teng, Blessed Thistle (specifics for the brain).

**Synergistic Vitamins and Minerals:** Vitamin B formula (two, twice daily), Vitamin C (500 mg. three times daily), Glutamine, Tyrosine, Lecithin (1200 mg. twice daily).

### Gotu Kola For Memory

Probably the best herb for memory is Gotu Kola. It has the ability to aid both circulation and the oxygen content of the blood circulating to the brain, thus stimulating the metabolism of protein to start the memory process.

- *Terry Willard*
  *From* Helping Yourself
  With Natural Remedies

# Glossary of Herbal Terms

*Alterative* - Producing a healthful change without perception.

*Anodyne* - Relieves mild pain.

*Anthelmintic* - A medicine that expels worms.

*Antibilious* - Acts on the bile, relieving biliousness.

*Antiemetic* - Stops vomiting.

*Antiperiodic* - Preventing regular recurrences.

*Antilithic* - Prevents the formation of stones in the urinary organs.

*Antirheumatic* - Relieves or cures rheumatism.

*Antiscorbutic* - Cures or prevents scurvy.

*Antiseptic* - A medicine that prevents putrefaction.

*Antispasmodic* - Relieves or prevents spasms.

*Antisyphilitic* - Having effect of curing or relieving syphilis.

*Aperient* - Gently laxative without purging.

*Aromatic* - A stimulant, spicy, anti-griping.

*Astringent* - Causes contraction and arrests discharges.

*Carminative* - Expels wind from the bowels.

*Cathartic* - Evacuates the bowels (a purgative).

*Cephalic* - Pertaining to the head.

*Cholagogue* - Increases the flow of bile into the intestine.

*Condiment* - Improves the flavor of foods.

*Demulcent* - Soothing, relieves inflammation, especially for skin and mucous membranes.

*Deobstruent* - Removes obstruction.

*Depurative* - Purifies the blood.

*Detergent* - Cleansing.

*Diaphoretic* - Produces perspiration.

*Discutient* - Dissolves and heals tumors.

*Diuretic* - Increases the secretion and flow of urine.

*Emetic* - Produces vomiting.

*Emmenagogue* - Promotes menstruation.

*Emollient* - Softens and soothes inflamed parts when locally applied.

*Eculent* - Edible.

*Exanthematous* - Pertaining to skin eruptions and diseases.

*Expectorant* - Facilitates expulsion of mucus or phlegm from the lungs and throat.

*Febrifuge* - Abates and reduces fevers.

*Hepatic* - Pertaining to the liver.

*Laxative* - Promotes bowel action.

*Lithotriptic* - Dissolves calculi (stones) in the urinary organs.

*Mucilaginous* - Soothing to all inflammations.

*Nauseant* - Produces vomiting.

*Nervine* - Acts specifically on the nervous system, stops nervous excitement, tonic.

*Parturient* - Induces and promotes labor at childbirth.

*Pectoral* - A remedy for chest afflictions.

*Refrigerant* - Cooling.

*Resolvent* - Dissolves boils, tumors, and other inflammations.

*Rubefacient* - Increases circulation and produces red skin.

*Sedative* - Quiets nerve action and promotes sleep.

*Sialogogue* - Increases the secretion of saliva.

*Stomachic* - Excites the action of the stomach, has the effect of strengthening it and relieving indigestion.

*Styptic* - Arrests hemorrhage.

*Sudorific* - Produces profuse perspiration.

*Tonic* - A remedy which is invigorating, strengthening, and toning.

*Vermifuge* - Expels worms from the intestines.

- *Terry Willard*
From Helping Yourself
With Natural Remedies

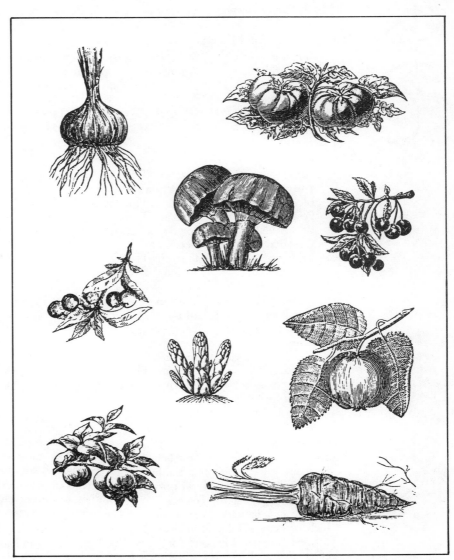

# Dandelion

*(Taraxacum officinale)*
Part Used: leaf and root
Properties: Cholagogue, Diuretic, Hepatic, Lithotriptic, Stomachie;
      alterative, astringent, galactogogue
Body Parts Affected: liver, kidneys, gall bladder, stomach, pancreas,
      intesstines and blood
Preparation and Dosage:

| | |
|---|---|
| Infusion: | Steep 30 minutes. Three to four cups daily, hot or cold |
| Decoction: | Simmer root 30 minutes. 6 oz. frequently or three to four times daily, hot or cold |
| Tincture: | 30 to 60 drops (½ to 1 tsp.) frequently |
| Powder (leaves) | 10 to 20 #0 capsules (60 to 120 grains) frequently |
| Powder (root): | 5 to 10 #0 capsules (30 to 60 grains) frequently |

Indicated Uses:

Internal

| | |
|---|---|
| Acne: | Tincture, Fluid Extract, Decoction |
| Anemia: | Decoction, Powder |
| Blood purifier: | Tincture, Fluid Extract, Powder, Decoction |
| Boils: | Tincture, Fluid Extract, Powder, Decoction |
| Bronchitis: | Powder, Decoction |
| Constipation: | Decoction |
| Cramps: | Tincture, Fluid Extract |
| Diabetes: | Infusion, Decoction |
| Gall stones: | Decoction |
| Indigestion: | Infusion of leaves |
| Jaundice: | Infusion, Decoction |
| Kidney diseases: | Decoction |
| Kidney stones: | Decoction |
| Low blood sugar: | Infusion, Decoction |
| Psoriasis: | Tincture, Fluid Extract, Infusion, Decoction |
| Skin diseases: | Tincture, Fluid Extract, Infusion, Decoction |
| Spleen, pancreas, gall bladder obstructions, liver: | Decoction |

Dandelion is both a nutritive herb
and one of nature's best medicines.
Its main influence is upon the liver
and it is an excellent blood purifier
for conditions such as eczema,
dropsy and diabetes. Because of its
high content of mineral, it is used
to treat anemia. It is good for
enlargement of liver and for pancreas
and spleen problems. Always use
dandelion root when treating
hepatitis and jaundice. It will increase
the flow of urine and is good in
kidney formulas. The roasted root is
a coffee substitute.

    - *Humbart Santillo*
    *From* Natural Healing
    With Herbs

## Back to Eden

By Jethro Kloss
1983/680 pages
**$6.95**
$8.70 postpaid from:
Back to Eden Books
Box 1439
Loma Linda, CA 92354

*Jethro Kloss is a pioneer in the use of herbs and other natural products of the earth in maintaining health and personal welfare. He developed many of the herbal therapies used today.*

## The Yoga of Herbs

By Dr. Vasant Lad and
David Frawley
1986/248 pages
**$11.95**
$13.70 postpaid from:
Lotus Press
Box 6265
Santa Fe, NM 87502-6265

*This book has detailed explanations and classifications of herbs, based on the ancient system of Ayurveda. Over 250 herbs are listed along with their application for all types of physical and mental conditions.*

# Hay Fever

*Causes* — We hear all kinds of theories about the causes of hay fever, but the general belief is that it comes from the pollen of various plants and weeds. It usually occurs from June until October and depends somewhat upon the section of the country and the climate where one lives. I have known men to get hay fever every summer while making hay and loading it. Many believe the ragweed is at fault, and is the cause of this disease. This may all be true, as far as I know, but it is also true that it would be a rare thing for anyone to have hay fever who had good digestive organs and whose nose membrane was in a healthy condition. Wrong eating habits have much to do with it.

*Symptoms.* — Hay fever usually comes on suddenly, and at about the same time every year with many people. There is a tickling in the nose, sneezing, and irritation down into the bronchial tubes. The mucous membrane is swollen in the nose and mouth, and there is coughing. At times there may be distress in breathing, with smothered feelings, much the same as in asthma. The eyes are filled with tears, and the nose runs continually. These conditions exist as a rule until colder weather returns.

*Treatment* — You may greatly relieve the irritation in the nose at once, by snuffing salt water up the nose. For this purpose, dissolve one heaping teaspoonful of salt in a pint of warm water. Gargle with this solution, and blow the nose entirely clear of mucus, before snuffing this up.

In addition to this, make a solution, using a rounding teaspoonful of golden seal and a heaping teaspoonful of borax in a pint of boiling soft water. Shake well. Let stand an hour or two, shaking occasionally; it is then ready for use. Pour some into the hand and snuff up the nose. Repeat this a number of times until the nose is entirely clean. This is very healing and soothing to the membrane and should be repeated four or more times a day.

I have had good success in treating hay fever with ragweed and golden rod. Use one teaspoonful of each, and one teaspoon each of skunk cabbage, and calamus root. Mix thoroughly, and take a teaspoonful in a glass of warm water an hour before each meal and one upon retiring.

Put one tablespoonful of ephedra in one pint of boiling water. Let steep one-half hour, strain through a cloth, then snuff up the nostrils, drawing it through into the throat. Repeat this several times until relieved, using the same treatment three or four times a day. This treatment is also excellent for other nasal troubles.

Take one heaping teaspoonful of powdered bayberry bark and pour over it one pint of boiling water. Steep twenty minutes. Let settle and snuff up the nostrils four to six times a day. This is also good to take internally, one half glassful three or more times a day.

- *Jethro Kloss*
  *From* Back to Eden

# Herbal Sources of Vitamins

**Vitamin A:** Alfalfa, Watercress, Parsley, Nettles, Violet leaves, Cayenne, Paprika, Eyebright, Raspberry leaf, Grape leaves, Dandelion, Comfrey, Chicory, Elderberries, Lamb's Quarters, Nori, Yellow Dock.

Depleted by: fluorescent lights, mineral oil, liver "cleansing," coffee, alcohol, cortisone, chemical drugs, excessive intake of iron, lack of available protein in the body.

**Vitamin B Complex:** Comfrey, Red Clover, Parsley.

Depleted by: sulfa drugs, sleeping pills, insecticides, estrogen, sugar, alcohol.

**Thiamine, Vitamin B1:** Dandelion, Alfalfa, Red Clover, Fenugreek, Grape leaves, Parsley, Raspberry leaf, Seaweeds such as Nori and Kelp, Catnip, Watercress.

Depleted by: alcohol, coffee, sugar, tobacco, narcotic drugs, raw oysters.

**Riboflavin, Vitamin B2:** Rose hips, Parsley, Saffron, Dandelion, Dulse, Kelp, Fenugreek.

Depleted by: alcohol, coffee, sugar, tobacco, narcotic drugs, raw oysters, plus restricted diets.

**Pyridoxine, Vitamin B6:** Produced by healthy intestines; found in all whole grains.

Depleted by: constipation, fasting, oral contraceptives, tobacco, radiation, pregnancy, lactation, coffee, narcotic drugs, aging, heart problems, alcohol.

**Vitamin B12:** Alfalfa, Comfrey, Miso, Seaweeds such as Kelp and Dulse, Catnip.

Depleted by: alcohol, coffee, tobacco, narcotic drugs, laxatives.

**Niacin, Vitamin B Factor:** Burdock root and seed, Dandelion, Alfalfa, Parsley.

Depleted by: sugar, antibiotics.

**Vitamin C:** Elderberries, Rose hips, Watercress, Pine needles, Parsley, Cayenne, Dandelion greens, Chicory, Violet leaves, Red Clover, Burdock, Coltsfoot, Paprika, Comfrey, Plantain, Nettles, Primrose, Wormwood, Alfalfa.

Depleted by: antibiotics, aspirin and other pain relievers, coffee, cortisone, sulfa drugs, smoking anything, baking soda, mental and physical stress, infections, injuries, DDT, inhalation of petroleum fumes, aging, burns, high fevers.

**Vitamin D:** Alfalfa, Nettles, Sunshine.

Depleted by: mineral oil.

**Vitamin E:** Watercress, Alfalfa, Rosehips, Raspberry leaf, Dandelion, Seaweeds.

Depleted by: mineral oil, oral contraceptives, sulfates.

**Vitamin K:** Alfalfa, Nettles, Kelp.

Depleted by: frozen foods, rancid fats, radiation, x-rays, aspirin, air pollution, antibiotics, mineral oil, enemas.

  - *Susun S. Weed*
    *From* Wise Woman Herbal for the Childbearing Year

## Wise Woman Herbal for the Childbearing Year

By Susun S. Weed
1986/172 pages
**$6.95**
$8.95 postpaid from:
Ask Tree Publishing
Box 64
Woodstock, NY 12498

*Weed has compiled a complete herbal guidebook for woman to refer to from conception to birth. It also included herbal gathering and preparation instructions.*

# How to Deal with Depression

Have a pizza with lots of oregano. If you don't have the oregano, forget the pizza. In fact, forget the pizza and just have the oregano. Oregano may ease that depressed, heavy-hearted feeling.

If you have a juicer, whip up half a glass of watercress and half a glass of spinach. Throw in some carrots to make the juice sweeter. Then, bottoms up and spirits up.

Eat 2 ripe bananas a day to chase the blues away. Bananas contain the chemicals serotonin and norepinephrine, which are believed to help prevent mental depression.

While running a warm bath, prepare a cup of camomile tea. Add the used teabag to the bath, along with a new one. If you use loose camomile, then wrap the herb in cheesecloth before putting it in the tub to avoid messy cleanup. Once the bath is ready, take pen and paper along with your cup of tea and relax in the tub. Make a list of a dozen wishes as you sip your tea. Be careful ... the things you wish for may come true.

Cheer yourself up by wearing rose colors — pink and scarlets. The orange family of colors are also picker-uppers.

Making love can help people overcome feelings of depression — unless, of course, they have no one to make love to and that's why they're depressed.

*- Joan Wilen and*
*Lydia Wilen*
*From Chicken Soup &*
*Other Folk Remedies*

## Chicken Soup & Other Folk Remedies

By Joan Wilen and Lydia Wilen
1984/210 pages
**$5.95**
$6.95 postpaid from:
Random House
400 Hahn Rd.
Westminster, MD 21157

*Its been medically proven that chicken soup can help cure the common cold. If that folk remedy was effective, what about all the others your grandmother used to talk about? This book lists hundreds of folk remedies from all types of sources. Every ingredient can be bought at the corner store. They're safe, too.*

## More Chicken Soup & Other Folk Remedies

By Joan Wilen and Lydia Wilen
1986/286 pages
**$5.95**
$6.95 postpaid from:
Random House
400 Hahn Rd.
Westminster, MD 21157

*Here are plenty more folk remedies to add to the ones brewed up in the Wilen's first book.*

# The Seven Dhatus and Ojas

Ayurveda categorizes herbs according to the *dhatus* or tissues upon which they work. It also contains a knowledge of special herbs and substances (minerals and metals) that work on the subtler tissues, including the nerve and reproductive tissues.

*- Dr. Vasant Lad &*
*David Frawley*
*From The Background of*
*Ayurvedic Medicine*

## Herbal Energetic Chart

Edited by David Frawley
1987/13" x 11"
**$4.95**
$6.70 postpaid from:
Lotus Press
Box 6265
Santa Fe, NM 87502

*A detailed herbal reference chart for determining the use of 53 herbs, based on the Ayurvedic (Indian) system of healing-which corresponds to Western herbal applications.*

### The Flower Essence Society
Box 459
Nevada City, CA 95959
916-265-9163

The Society was founded by Richard Katz in 1979 to serve as an international network for over 10,000 practitioners who employ flower essences as part of their therapies. They provide a research and networking base for the work that Dr. Edward Bach had done until his death in 1936. At that time he had discovered 36 remedies using English wildflowers. To date 72 more flower-based remedies have been discovered. The Society provides training and certification, workshops, literature, and publishes a member newsletter.

---

# Herbal Sources

### The Heritage Store
314 Laskin Rd.
Virginia Beach, VA 23451
800-862-2923

During his lifetime, Edgar Cayce gave over 14,000 readings. The majority of them had to do with the health of the person the reading was done for. Often Cayce would recommend specific natural remedies and therapies for the individual to use. Many of these products have been formulated and are sold by the Heritage Store, which is located a short distance from Cayce's legacy, the Association for Research and Enlightenment (A.R.E.) in Virginia Beach, Virginia.

The Cayce products include Aura Glow Massage Oil — a formula recommended in hundreds of Cayce readings — a wide variety of skin treatments, hair care formulas, cough syrups, digestive aids, castor oil packs, soaps, cosmetics, and tinctures.

### Native Herb Company
Box 742
Capitola, CA 95010

The founder of Native Herb Company is Christopher Hobbs, a third generation herbalist. They offer high potency herb extracts, booklets on the uses of herbs, herbology teaching aids and an information search service.

### Alive Energy Formulas
### Auro Trading Co.
Box 2525
Aptos, CA 95003

Auro Trading has created a unique line of herbal formulas. These herbs are superconcentrated whole foods. Specific herbal formulas have been created for your specific needs. These herbal combinations come in specially formulated tablet form for "clear thinking," "female energy," "drive," "mind expansion," and many more. They offer a chart of the human energy system and how to select the right "Alive Energy Formula" for your needs.

### Platonic Academy
Box 409
Santa Cruz, CA 95061
408-423-7923
Paul A. Lee, Ph.D., Director

The Platonic Academy offers a correspondence course in herbology. The 10 lesson program includes traditional medicine, how to propagate and cultivate herbs, herbal history, and legal ramifications of what the Academy calls the "herb renaissance".

---

# What Are Flower Essences?

Flower essences are liquid, potentized preparations, which carry a distinct imprint of a given flower. They address health in a broader sense, recognizing a relationship between soul and body. Carrying only an insignificant material component, flower essences are not chemical agents or drugs. They can most accurately be regarded as *catalysts* which carry a formative or etheric pattern of the plant species used. Each archetypal plant essence speaks in a subtle language that can be received by the inner self, much as we "hear" a musical composition, or "see" a painting or sculpture.

The essences pioneer a new modality of health enhancement based on the insight that the human soul is a microcosm within the macrocosm of Nature. It is a modality that correlates the outer flowering language of Nature with the inner constellations of the human soul. Essences work most effectively as part of an over-all program of health enhancement, including exercise, nourishing diet, stress reduction, inner development, appropriate medical care and other natural therapies as needed.

-From The Flower Essence Society

# Macrobiotics: Eat Your Way to Health

*By Michio Kushi*

Macrobiotics. The Great Life. A traditional and universal way of life including a way of eating that was practiced by many cultures and civilizations and is as vital and modern as today.

The word "macrobiotics" provides the best explanation of what it is all about. Macrobiotics is composed of two Greek words, "macro" meaning great or large and "bios" meaning the science of life. It is a healthful way to live life according to the largest possible view, the natural Order of the Universe. Macrobiotics recommends how to apply this order to daily life through the selection, preparation, and consumption of specific foods which affect the whole person — physically, mentally and emotionally — resulting in peaceful and happy lives.

While it is true that the macrobiotic diet and lifestyle has helped people prevent and often recover from cancer, heart disease, and other degenerative disease, the major focus of macrobiotics is the attainment of good health, well-being, peace of mind, and eventually to realize One Peaceful World.

Ancient wisdom and many aspects of modern science have discovered that within the changing cycles and seasons of the earth, a natural order existed. All energy in the universe moved harmoniously between and over two basic and opposite directions. Common sense beliefs were that all phenomena were composed of contrasting opposites in harmony — like winter and summer, night and day, male and female.

Those who have studied and lived with macrobiotics have found that the same basic principle of complemental forces can be applied to harmonize different combinations of food in their diets. The Chinese call these opposing forces YIN and YANG (pronounced "een" and "yahn").

Foods in a macrobiotic diet can be classified into these two headings to offer a balanced menu. An unbalanced diet of extreme foods results in ill health and a feeling of disharmony.

Yin foods are usually more expanded or larger, softer in texture, more moist than dry, higher in potassium and they thrive in warmer weather. Yang foods are the opposite.

The standard macrobiotic dietary approach for people who live in temperate climates recommends whole grains as the principal food, constituting 50 to 60 percent of the daily diet by volume. Between 20 and 30 percent of the diet should consist of fresh vegetables (about two thirds cooked and one third or less salad or pickles). Five to ten percent should consist of beans, bean products, and a small amount of sea vegetables. Moderate servings of fish or seafood, temperate-climate fruit in season, seeds and nuts, and naturally sweetened desserts may also be eaten. Condiments and non-aromatic, nonstimulant beverages, such as mild teas and natural fruit juices, can also be served after meals.

Although a large portion is vegetarian-based, the macrobiotic diet includes all the important nutrients such as protein, calcium, and vitamin C. Protein is supplied by whole cereal grains, various legumes and bean products, seeds and nuts, and fish. Recent trends in nutritional advice have decreased the amount of protein and fat, especially animal-based food, in the average diet.

Common sources of calcium in the diet are green and yellow hard vegetables, leafy greens, beans and bean products, as well as sea vegetables. Vitamin C is found in broccoli, brussels sprouts, most leafy greens, and cauliflower.

A macrobiotic diet should be flexibly adapted to changing activities and individual differences like physical activity, age, and general health. It is a natural foods diet because the recommended foods are to be grown without chemicals and used as much as possible in their natural organic state.

It is a holistic way of eating which not only helps to maintain and improve physical health, but also promotes the development of a clear mental and sound emotional state. The macrobiotic diet and way of life helps people gain control of their lives and gives them the key to understanding their own natures.

Practicing macrobiotics includes regular daily exercises and an individual spiritual practice of meditation, prayer, or solitary relaxation. Respect for self, elders and others; expression of gratitude; and appreciation of nature are all as important as eating well.

Education is the key to practicing macrobiotics, and The Kushi Foundation in Boston offers programs to this end. It teaches students from all over the world how to apply the macrobiotic principles and balance to daily life activities. The Foundation also serves at the international headquarters for associated centers; provides the greatest selection of courses to train macrobiotic counselors and teachers; and offers comprehensive two-day Way of Life Seminars, one-week residential experiences, intensive cooking classes, and a series of spiritual development seminars as well as public education events.

Macrobiotics is common sense in today's world because it offers the answers to so many vitally important questions about diet, health, and peace — for the individual and humankind — toward the realization of One Peaceful World.

For more information about macrobiotics, call or write to: The Kushi Foundation, P.O. Box 1100, Brookline, MA 02147, (617) 738-0045.

## The Kushi Foundation and Institute

P.O. Box 1100
17 Station St.
Brookline, MA 02147
617-738-0045

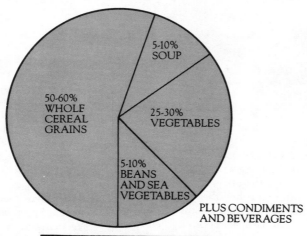

5-10% SOUP

50-60% WHOLE CEREAL GRAINS

25-30% VEGETABLES

5-10% BEANS AND SEA VEGETABLES

PLUS CONDIMENTS AND BEVERAGES

FOR OCCASIONAL USE
Fish and seafoods
Seasonal fruits
Nuts, seeds & other natural snacks

The Kushi Foundation was established in 1981 by Michio Kushi to promote macrobiotic education, research and counseling. The Kushi Institute offers an internationally known training program for teachers as well as students. General programs open to the public include macrobiotics, way-of-life seminars, cooking lessons and dietary counseling. The Kushi Foundation is dedicated to the resolution of global problems of degenerative disease, hunger, crime, and the abuse of natural resources.

Michio Kushi is an internationally respected authority on the macrobiotic way of life. In addition to the Kushi Foundation, he is the founder of numerous organizations, centers and restaurants as well as an internationally respected author, lecturer and research consultant.

## One Peaceful World
## Michio Kushi's Approach to Creating a Healthy and Harmonious Mind, Home, and World Community

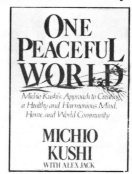

By Michio Kushi with Alex Jack
1987/370 pages
**$16.95**
$18.45 postpaid from:
St. Martin's Press
175 5th Ave.
New York, NY 10010

A milestone book of Kushi's lifelong dedication to macrobiotics and a peaceful way of life, One Peaceful World, presents a comprehensive program for building world peace through a sane and orderly way of eating. Menus and recipes, reference sources, illustrations, and a wealth of information guide us all on a new approach to diet and thought, based on Kushi's conviction that world peace begins in the kitchen and radiates outward from the individual to families, friends, communities and nations.

# The Standard Macrobiotic Diet

# Three Types of Civilization

|  | Spiritual and Aesthetic | Material and Social | Comprehensive |
|---|---|---|---|
| Ruled by | Idea | Law | Understanding |
| Backed by | Truth | Power | Love |
| Authority | Moral Code | Constitution | Natural Order |
| Food | Vegetable Quality | Animal Quality | Balance |
| Environment | Rural | Urban | Natural |
| Lifestyle | Agricultural | Industrial | Holistic |
| Orientation | Spirit Intuition | Matter Analysis | Energy Synthesis |
| Center | Church | State | Family |
| Social Unit | Tribe/Clan | Nation | Geographical, Climatic, Ecological Region Planet |
| Occupation | Rest | Work | Play |
| Direction | East South | West North | Global |

- *Michio Kushi with Alex Jack From One Peaceful World*

# Cooking Better

*With today's emphasis on healthy eating, meal planning and preparation has taken on a new importance and significance. We have become aware of the effect of our diets on our overall physical and mental well-being. Time and again, scientific research has confirmed to the old adage, "You are what you eat." Naturally, the increased importance of nutrition has given rise to personal anxiety over our eating habits. Is our food devoid of nutrients due to poor cooking techniques? Can we purchase vegetables that have not been coated with chemicals or exposed to radiation? What about the metal content in our food due to packaging, canning, and freezing materials? Now that we have become aware of these concerns, our attention is focused on learning ways to successfully adapt our thinking, cooking, and eating habits to reflect the essentials of true nourishment.*

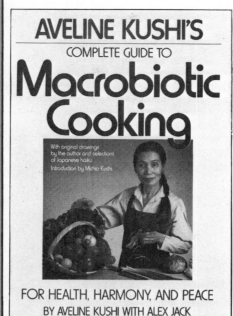

## Complete Guide to Macrobiotic Cooking For Health, Harmony and Peace

By Aveline Kushi with Alex Jack
1985/414 pages
**$13.95**
$14.95 postpaid from:
Warner Books
P.O. Box 690
New York, NY 10019

*In this from-the-heart handbook of macrobiotic cooking, Aveline Kushi explains how to use intuition and create balanced whole food meals for the whole family. Truly a holistic manual, this book addresses such topics as harmonizing diet with the seasons. The medicinal energies of different foods, festive menus and how to select and buy the highest quality whole grains, vegetables and seafood. Beautifully, illustrated with original drawings by the author and selections of Japanese haiku.*

# Noodles and Pasta

Noodles are delicious, offer endless variety, and are more digestible than flour prepared in baked form. In Japan, noodles are a way of life. There are restaurants that serve only noodles. Some serve only *soba*, the hardy buckwheat noodles that have been enjoyed in the Far East for centuries. These restaurants are called *sobaya* or *soba* houses. Others serve only *udon*, or whole wheat noodles, and are called *udonaya*. Vendors sell homemade noodles from pushcarts on the street corners, and some of them play flutes to attract customers.

Today, most noodles and pasta in the East and West are made with refined flour, chemical preservatives, and other artificial ingredients and are produced by automated machinery.

*- Avelina Kushi with Alex Jack From the* Complete Guide to Macrobiotic Cooking

## Practically Macrobiotic

By Keith Michell
1987/240 pages
**$12.95**
$14.95 postpaid from:
Thorsens Publishing House
P.O. Box 1534
Hagerstown, MD 21741

*This book includes the ingredients, preparation and cooking instructions of more than 200 delicious macrobiotic recipes. Very attractively presented, with color pictures, it explains the "yin/yang" balance of foods, and gives suggestions for seasonal menus.*

*Rotating the mill stones,*
*I grind flour*
*With my mother.*

—Yoshie

## Nourishing a Happy Affair
### Nutrition Alternatives for Individual and Family Needs

By Leslie Cohen
1982/150 pages
**$8.95**
$10.45 postpaid from:
Larson Publications, Inc.
4936 Route 414
Burdett, NY 14818

*This is an excellent healthy-eating and living guide for just about anyone interested in true nutrition, particularly for beginners and families. The information is common sense and practical, taking into account the differing needs of the various age groups in a family. Many flavorful, yet healthy and easy to prepare meatless recipes are included.*

Nourishing a Happy Affair

Nutrition Alternatives For Individual And Family Needs

Leslie Cohen

Larson

## The California Nutrition Book
### A Food Guide for the '90s

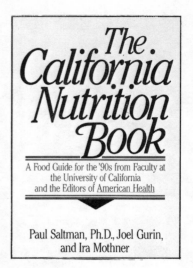

The California Nutrition Book

A Food Guide for the '90s from Faculty at the University of California and the Editors of American Health

Paul Saltman, Ph.D., Joel Gurin, and Ira Mothner

By Paul Saltman, Joel Gurin, and Ira Mothner
1987/324 pages
**$17.95**
$19.45 postpaid from:
Little, Brown & Co.
200 West St.
Waltham, MA 02254

*This practical nutrition book supplies the most current medical information (in layman's terms) on food and nutrient values, how the body uses food and the effect of diet on health. General nutritional concerns such as cholesterol, weight, stabilization, food allergies and other such issues are addressed thoroughly and informatively. Many areas of specific interest are highlighted for in-depth discussions such as fiber, profiles of all the vitamins and essential minerals, and nutrition as a cure for disease.*

Chives—useful anywhere one would use onions. Especially good in salad dressings and omelettes. Chop fine.

Dill—good in salad dressings and cucumber and yogurt salad. Indispensable for flavoring pickles.

Fennel—has a licorice flavor. Use sparingly in tomato dishes. Makes a nice tea.

Basil—adds incredible zest to any tomato dish. Use generously. Wonderful in soups and salad dressings. Essential to pesto.

Marjoram or oregano—useful in almost any vegetable dish. Use generously. Good in soups, salad dressings, casseroles.

Parsley—leaves can be tossed in salad, or added to salad dressing. Good in soups, casseroles, Italian sauces—almost anywhere. Don't forget parslied potatoes.

Sage—use in sautéed vegetables, bean soups, Use sparingly. Makes a useful tea (see p. 81).

Thyme—good for almost anything. Delicious in salad dressings, tomato dishes, sautéed vegetables, soups, omelettes, loafs.
   *- Leslie Cohen*
   *From* Nourishing A Happy Affair

## National Food Associates
P.O. Box 210
Atlanta, TX 75551
Membership:
**$15.00**/1 year
**$40.00**/3 years

*Offers monthly magazine* Natural Food and Farming *and the NFA Educational Program.*

## Confessions of a Kamikaze Cowboy

By Dirk Benedict
1987/228 pages
**$9.95**
$11.70 postpaid from:
Newcastle Publishing Co., Inc.
P.O. Box 7589
Van Nuys, CA 91409

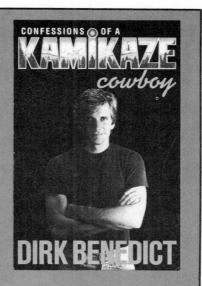

*This is the true story of this "A-Team" actor's courageous battle against prostate cancer resulting in victory through meditation and macrobiotics. Very candid and informative,* Confessions of a Kamikaze Cowboy *presents real-life macrobiotics.*

## Forget the Hamburger and French Fries, I'll Take Dandelion

There were days in New Hampshire when I felt weak beyond belief. I couldn't climb the stairs to the upstairs room where I was sleeping, so I slept on the floor of the living room. This would be followed by tremendous bursts of energy: I would be up for eighteen hours and sleep for only four or five before arising again, ready to take a hike down the road on a dandelion hunt.

And I had dreams. Mostly of food. Night after night I had a recurring dream in which two hamburgers would come and talk to me. They would tell me how much they missed me. Ask what was wrong with me. Finally they would plead for me to take a bite of them. I never responded to them in my dream, but simply sat and watched as they went through their routine: sometimes talking among themselves, sometimes getting angry and threatening when I would have nothing to do with them. My later experiences with people who would try to force me to just try a piece of steak or hot dog or hamburger would be a word-for-word replay of my New Hampshire hamburger nightmares. Offering, pleading and finally trying to coerce me into validating their own dietary choice by joining in.

The cowboy in me became Kamikaze as I stuck to the task of restructuring my body and my life while enduring countless attacks over the years by those who saw my "off-beat" way of eating as an attack on their own dietary habits. Time and again I was told that my quack diet was going to kill me, that there was nothing wrong with meat or sugar and it wouldn't be long before I would see the error of my ways.

No matter how many times this happened — and it occurred virtually every time I was trapped in a social gathering where there was food being served and someone noticed I wasn't eating my share of hamburgers or guzzling any Coca-Cola — I was always astonished by the ferocity of the attack. I constantly wondered, and sometimes asked, why it mattered to them what I ate? I have yet to get an answer, other than the fact that they are concerned for my welfare. Can you begin to understand what goes through my mind when an overweight, balding individual with blood-shot eyes, five to ten years my junior, starts to lecture me on the evils of my choice in food?

*- Dirk Benedict*
*From* Confessions of a Kamikaze Cowboy

## The Complete Book of Steam Cookery
*Tasty and Healthful Dishes from Around the World*

By Coralie Castle
1985/248 pages
**$9.95**
$12.35 postpaid from:
Jeremy P. Tarcher, Inc.
9110 Sunset Blvd.
Los Angeles, CA 90069

*Over 200 creative recipes from all over the world are compiled in this cookbook of healthful, nutritious easy and delicious low-calorie meals. The easy to follow section on utensils and techniques makes steam cookery even easier.*

## Marinated Vegetables

This section, like the one on vegetable purees, does not give full recipes. These directions are designed to help you turn your deliberately undercooked vegetables into a main-meal or side-dish salad. There are a few recipe suggestions following a list of suitable vegetables and how to prepare them. Dressings and toppings that appear with capitalized initial letters can be found in Basic Savory Sauces and at the end of this chapter, respectively.

Steam the vegetables *just* until beginning to soften, remove from heat, and immediately immerse in ice water to retard further cooking. Drain and refrigerate, covered, up to 3 days. Some cooks recommend dressing vegetables while they are hot. I find that the vegetables stay crisper and have a cleaner taste and brighter color if the cooking is halted and the vegetables chilled. They will still absorb the dressing.

*- Coralie Castle*
*From* The Complete Book of Steam Cookery

## Hunger Foods, Inc.

345 32nd St.
Boulder, CO 80303

A planet/profit organization marketing non-meat, frozen/non-perishable health food items for sale or for distribution through franchises. Their food labels are designed as a networking and message service with clever product names and slogans. All profits go toward service and global healing organizations.

## Sun Chlorella

$18.15/300 tablets
$20.15 postpaid from:
Sun Chlorella, Inc.
4025 Spencer St.
Suite 103
Torrance, CA 90503

Chlorella is a green algae which has been prized for years as one of the major health foods of Japan. Each chlorella cell is a self-sufficient organism with all of the plant's necessary nutrients and life functions taking place inside the cell. The result is an extremely high concentration of important nutrients DNA and RNA in the whole chlorella plant, which translates into a superior source of naturally occurring nutrition for human consumption. Available in tablets or extract granules.

## Changes
### The Microbiotic Center of Baltimore

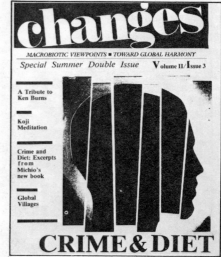

604 E. Joppa Rd.
Towson, MD 21204
301-321-21204
$12.00/Bimonthly, six issues

Changes is the bimonthly magazine of the Macrobiotic Center of Baltimore offering macrobiotic viewpoints toward global harmony.

## Vegetarian Times
### The World's Leading Magazine for Vegetarians

$19.95/Monthly — 12 issues from:
Vegetarian Times
P.O. Box 446
Mt. Morris, IL 61054-9894

Vegetarian Times covers topics of interest to vegetarians such as natural foods, holistic health, cooking, celebrity vegetarians, natural lifestyles and related spiritual issues.

## Royal Jelly

**$17.95**/100 capsules
**$19.95** postpaid
**$14.95**/11-oz. jar, 25-mg. per
teaspoon
**$16.95** postpaid from:
Premier One Products, Inc.
7171 Mercy Rd.
Suite 135
Omaha, NE 68106

Royal Jelly is a glandular secretion
made by worker bees for the queen bee
to feed on. Even though a queen bee
will live 40 times longer and grow to
1½ times the size of a worker bee, the
only difference between the two classes is
the royal jelly which only the queen eats.
Thus it is generally thought, through the
backing of moderate scientific research,
that royal jelly increases energy, mental
alertness, and general well-being. One of
the world's richest sources of pantothenic
acid, it is said to combat stress, fatigue
and insomnia. Naturally preserved and
available as an additive to honey, Royal
Jelly is also available in tablets.

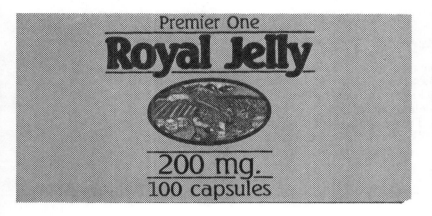

## The Secrets of Spirulina
## Medical Discoveries of
## Japanese Doctors

By Christopher Hills
1980/218 pages
**$6.95**
**$8.95** postpaid from:
University of the Trees
P.O. Box 66
Boulder Creek, CA 95006

The Japanese doctors and scientists
who originally published this book in
Japan have spent fifteen years studying
the remarkable benefits of Spirulina
plankton. This book reveals their
discoveries that Spirulina is highly
nutritious and completely digestible as
well as an effective treatment in many
diseases including diabetes, ulcers,
cirrhosis, and other chronic disorders.

## Wheat Grass

**$5.50**/75 tablets
**$8.00** postpaid
**$9.75**/250 tablets
**$12.25** postpaid from:
Pines International
The Wheat Grass People
P.O. Box 1107
Lawrence, KS 66044

Formed in 1976, Pines specializes in
growing, dehydrating, and packaging
cereal grasses and other green foods.
Grass contains the perfect balance of
fiber and nutrients for the digestive
systems of land-based mammals.
Dehydrated and pressed into tablets,
cereal grass is a convenient way to add
the essential nutrients of deep green,
leafy food which is so often lacking in
our diets.
Pines offers general and research
information about cereal grass as well as
an extensive variety of products in tablet,
liquid, and powder form.

## Spirulina

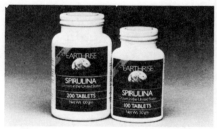

**$7.75**/100 tablets
**$10.00** postpaid
**$14.99**/200 tablets
**$17.24** postpaid from:
Earthrise Company
P.O. Box 7796
San Rafael, CA 94915

Earthrise began researching and
cultivating Spirulina, a blue-green micro-
algae, in 1975 with the goal of ending
world hunger. Spirulina has been found
to be a concentrated source of vitamins,
minerals, protein, amino acids, and
beta-carotene, and as such is highly
valued as a superior nutrition source.
Spirulina is available in powder and
tablets as well as in combination with
diet and enhanced immunity formulas.
Earthrise currently supports village
Spirulina projects in Third World
countries combating hunger and
promoting village self-sufficiency.

# Part 6: Bodywork/Movement

From all the time and money Americans have lavished on physical fitness in the past decade, it would seem that what is important about bodywork would be well established in our national thinking. But this is not the case. Our efforts at exercise are well-intentioned in that they strive to improve the functioning of certain body systems — especially our large-muscle groups and cardiovascular systems — and some of them certainly benefit some people sometimes. But frequently, physical fitness programs are more concerned with building up our armor, our images, and our self-protective attitudes than they are with providing any lasting physical value. Many programs concentrate on developing the outer musculature, for instance, which, as Don Johnson writes, "is useful for rapid defense. But its speed and strength are not as useful for more refined sensitivity,

for subtler forms of movement, or for making love."

Nor can the outer musculature alone — or in conjunction with the cardiovascular system — maintain the kind of balance that makes for easy living. Indeed, the speed and aggressiveness encouraged by many fitness programs stand in direct contrast to the major efforts of bodywork, which aim to reduce the muscular tensions that both hold and produce physical and psychological armor, to make immaterial the images we have learned to carry around with us, and to free us psychically and somatically from the habits of our attitudes. In short, it is by seeking to balance us, rather than tighten us, that the bodywork traditions seek to free us.

There are dozens of different kinds of bodywork, for the most part based in the common theme that people live fundamentally through

their bodies, and that emotional, mental, and spiritual health depend on the organism's ability to function well through what Joel Kovel calls "the wisdom of the body and instinct."

Some approaches to bodywork are concerned directly and solely with the flesh, some seek to reach the mind, and some work with the projected energy of the spirit. However a discipline seeks to bring a person to balance, its work is predicated on a plan to enable the body to express itself as well as possible according to its innate design; for while every aspect of a person expresses his or her entire being, "no words are so clear as the language of body expression once one has learned to read it."

*- Joseph Heller and*
*William A. Henkin*
*From Bodywise*

---

## Bodywise
### *Regaining Your Natural Flexibility and Vitality for Maximum Well-Being*

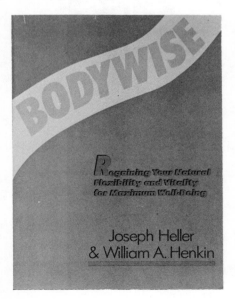

By Joseph Heller and
William A. Henkin
**$10.95**
$13.35 postpaid from:
Jeremy P. Tarcher
9110 Sunset Blvd.
Los Angeles, CA 90069

*Joseph Heller is the founder of Hellerwork, bodywork designed to restore the body to its maximum state of well-being by reversing the negative effects that physical and emotional traumas*

*have had on the body in the course of a lifetime. Heller says it's not enough to just work with the body, you need to reach the mind and spirit as well to effect permanent change.*

*- Joseph Heller and*
*William A. Henkin*
*From Bodywise*

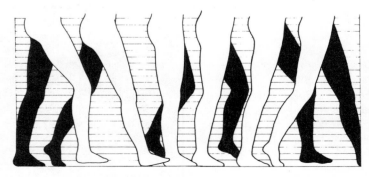

**Figure 7-10.** Proper movements of the leg in simple walking.

## Job's Body
### A Handbook for Bodywork

A Handbook for Bodywork

JOB'S BODY

Deane Juhan
Foreword by Ken Dychtwald

By Deane Juhan
1987/400 pages
**$29.95**
$30.95 postpaid from:
Station Hill Press
Barrytown, NY 12507

*Job's Body* gives a detailed and vivid picture of how the body responds to touch and why therapeutic manipulation effects so many apparently miraculous cures. Easily accessible to the general reader and student of human potential, while offering a veritable reference library on the workings of the body-mind, it provides a tool and practical guide for the health professional, bodyworker and movement instructor. Aiming to meet the needs aroused by a renaissance of bodywork in America, Deane Juhan synthesizes scientific, historical and experiential data to support many of the claims of a wide variety of distinctly different techniques, such as Feldenkrais, Tragering, Rolfing, Shiatsu, Alexander, Rebirthing, Neo-Reichian/Bioenergetics, Zero-balancing, Trigger-point, as well as the various schools of massage.

*- Deane Juhan*
*From* Job's Body

## Trager Mentastics
### Movement as a Way to Agelessness

Whenever I use the word "feeling,"
I am referring to the unconscious mind.
  The conscious mind does not feel.
The unconscious mind is the part of our mind
that is not conscious.

Mentastics is a coined expression meaning
  "mental gymnastics."
They are mentally directed movements that
suggest to the mind feelings of
lightness, freedom, openness,
grace and pleasure resulting in
  an ageless body.

---

## Trager Mentastics
### Movement as a Way to Agelessness

**Trager Mentastics**
movement as a way to agelessness

**Milton Trager, M.D.**
with Cathy Guadagno, Ph.D.
Foreword by Turnley Walker

By Milton Trager, M.D.
1987/176 pages
**$19.95**
$20.95 postpaid from:
Station Hill Press
Barrytown, NY 12507

Mentastics is an approach designed to restore and maintain this agelessness of body and mind. The term is a coined expression meaning "mental gymnastics" — very gentle gymnastics that are mentally directed to free the body from tensions.

One of the most pleasing and natural aspects of Mentastics is the way the body's own weights are used to open and move each part. For example, the arm can hang and swing freely, joining — not resisting — the effects of gravity. Movements done in this manner can bring us into a deeply relaxed and peaceful state that Dr. Trager calls "hook-up."

Hook-up is the same as meditation. Dr. Trager describes its process as blending and becoming one with the energy force that surrounds all living things. Science has been able to observe and even measure this energy. We can see and study it through the use of scientific instruments, such as Kirlian photography, illustrated later in this book. Most important, we can experience hook-up. When in hook-up, we can enjoy a renewed and enhanced sense of well-being.

*- Milton Trager, M.D.*
*From* Trager Mentastics

Mentastics can reverse the ageing process.
It begins very early in life, usually around age 10.
As we age, it is not the tissues of the body
that are at fault.
The rigidity that one feels as one gets older
is from the effects of the many adverse experiences
that have occurred during one's life.
These experiences can include trauma,
illnesses and disappointments.

The tensions, restrictions and rigidities
responsible for the ageing process
  are not physical patterns,
  but are mental patterns.

*- Milton Trager, M.D.*
*From* Trager Mentastics

---

### The International Center for Release and Integration

450 Hillside Ave.
Mill Valley, CA 94941
415-383-4017

*The ICRI offers training programs for those who want to become certified professional practitioners of deep bodywork, postural integration. They have affiliated centers across the United States, Europe, Australia and Canada.*

# The Body as the Self

If you were to take a close look at me, you might comment on how healthy and well-proportioned I am. If you were a physician, you would probably say that I am in good health and that I am lucky to have such a vital, well-toned body. When I examine myself closely, however, I notice that there are all sorts of imbalances, confusions, and rough edges alive within my tissue as surely as they are alive within my soul, conflicts that have come to form my physical body as definitely and as distinctly as they have also served to mold my character and life.

In fact, my body is incredibly lopsided. My right leg is longer than my left; my left hand is smaller than my right; my right shoulder is lower than my left; the top half of my body is more muscular than the bottom half; my pelvis is rotated a bit in a clockwise fashion; my neck is angled slightly to the right; my spine is not as straight as it is supposed to be; my feet are somewhat archless; my right hand is more coordinated than my left hand; my left leg is tighter than my right leg ... and on and on. There is an infinity of asymmetries and imbalances within my body.

I am not smooth, for my life has not always been smooth. I am not perfectly balanced, for my feelings are not always balanced. I am not symmetrical, for my actions are not symmetrical. My muscular strength is not equally proportioned throughout my body, as my interests are not equally distributed throughout my life. In a way, my body is like the body of the earth, which with its mountains, valleys, riverbeds, and uneven topography tells the story of its history and creation as surely as my body expresses the trials and creative changes that I have experienced throughout my lifetime. Every aspect of my body reflects a distinct aspect of my self, which, extending outward from my psyche and embodied in flesh, encounters the passions and challenges with which I am continually engaged.

In my attempt to explore the terrain of my own life and being, I have discovered that my body and my mind are reflections of each other and that the emotions and experiences which have formed my personality have affected the formation and structuring of my muscles and tissue. As I have become more aware of my own history and the realm of possibilities that it reveals, I have also come to appreciate some of the ways that these body/mind relationships can be discovered, examined, and improved upon.

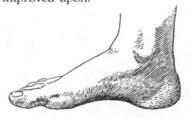

*Healthy, Well-Grounded Foot*

- Ken Dychtwald
From Bodymind

## Bodymind

By Ken Dychtwald
1986/302 pages
**$8.95**
$11.35 postpaid from:
Jeremy P. Tarcher, Inc.
9110 Sunset Blvd.
Los Angeles, CA 90069

*This classic work on the body/mind connection takes you to higher self-awareness and the complex connection of body type, personality, and experience.*

# What Does a Receeding Jaw Signify?

A receding jaw usually reflects withheld sadness or anger, or an urge to cry or scream. This blockage may hamper an individual's ability to express any of his emotions and beliefs orally, whether they relate to the emotion that caused the freeze in the body's growth or not. This person might tend to have a great deal of difficulty speaking up in groups, defending himself, and voicing his opinion.

*Receding Jaw*

- From Bodymind

# What Is Polarity Therapy?

Polarity Therapy is a wholistic health care program designed by Dr. Randolph Stone, D.O., D.C., D.N. over a sixty-year career. It incorporates a set of principles of energy flow, and the Polarity Therapist evaluates the ways in which the individual's energy is imbalanced, using a variety of procedures (whatever is indicated) to aid the individual in establishing balance and harmony physically, emotionally, and mentally. Diet and nutrition, stretching postures, exercise, manipulation, and the role of lifestyle and individual thought patterns are all included. In addition to orthodox anatomy and physiology, Dr. Stone directs his attention to the "energy anatomy" of the human body and seeks to release and balance the energy that is blocked and causing pain and disease. Dr. Stone seemed to have "x-ray" hands, which immediately located where the energy was blocked, and he knew what to do to give relief.

*- Randolph Stone*
*From* Polarity Therapy

## Touch for Health
### A New Approach for Restoring Our Natural Energies

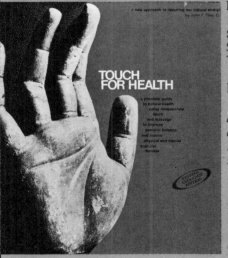

By John F. Thie, D.C.
1973/132 pages
**$13.95**
$15.45 postpaid from:
T.H. Enterprises
1200 N. Lake Ave.
Pasadena, CA 91104

*A system of body checks and balances are used in this bodywork system designed especially for doing it yourself. Lavishly illustrated with explicit, step by step instructions*

If the muscle goes weak when the middle finger pulse alone is held lightly, for example, we know it is the gall bladder meridian which is over-energized.

*- John F. Thie, D.C.*
*From* Touch for Health

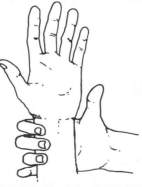
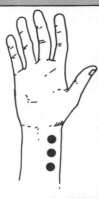

**LEFT HAND**

**LIGHT TOUCH**
Small Intestine
Gall Bladder
Bladder

**DEEP TOUCH**
Heart
Liver
Kidneys

**RIGHT HAND**

**LIGHT TOUCH**
Large Intestine
Stomach
Triple Warmer

**DEEP TOUCH**
Lung
Spleen
Circulation -sex

## Polarity Therapy, Volume I & II
### The Complete Collected Works

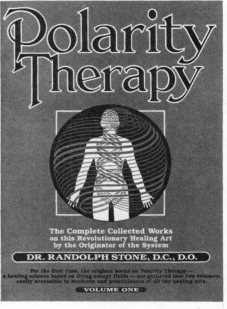

By Randolph Stone, D.O., D.C., D.N.
1986/112 pages
**$25.00** each
$27.00 postpaid from:
CRCS Publications
Box 1460
Sebastopol, CA 95472

*These volumes contain the original books written about Polarity Therapy, a healing science based on living energy fields.*

# Massage

## The Book of Massage
### *The Complete Step-by-Step Guide to Eastern and Western Techniques*

THE BOOK OF MASSAGE
*The Complete Step-by-Step Guide to Eastern and Western Techniques*

By Lucinda Hall
1984/192 pages
**$10.95**
$12.95 postpaid from:
Simon & Schuster
200 Old Tappan Rd.
Old Tappan, NJ 07675

*A beautifully photographed and illustrated guide to massage, shiatsu, and reflexology. Great for the beginner or advanced practitioner.*

**Position for Working on Face**
*You remain sitting or standing at your partner's head for the whole of this sequence. Keep your pressure even as you work down from forehead to chin.*

## The Face
You don't need to oil your hands to massage the face, as what you already have on your fingers will be enough for this relatively small area. Before giving a face massage for the first time, practise on your own face to see how it feels. The face is bonier and less fragile than it looks and you may be surprised to find that you can apply quite deep pressure without discomfort. Thresholds of comfort vary, however, so you should be sure to get feedback on your pressure from your partner. Before beginning, check whether your partner is wearing contact lenses; if so, refrain from working over the eyelids. In this sequence, you work gradually down the face, stroking across it in strips from the centre to the sides. Make your movements slow and "clean" and keep your awareness in your fingers.

**Forehead**
*Place your thumbs at the centre of the forehead, just above the brows, anchoring your hands on the sides of the head. Moving up a strip at a time, draw your thumbs apart slowly, coming out over the hair and off the sides of the head. Cover the whole forehead in this way, travelling up as far as the hairline.*

- Lucinda Hall
From The Book of Massage

## Sense Relaxation

By Bernard Gunther, Ph.D.
1968/102 pages
**$9.95**
$11.70 postpaid from:
Newcastle Publishing
Box 7589
Van Nuys, CA 91409

*Bernard Gunther originated the massage program at the Esalen Institute at Big Sur. This book celebrates awakened, conscious massage. Although it was first published 20 years ago, its message remains as strong as ever. Fully illustrated.*

## Institute of Psycho-Structural Balancing
*The Fine Art of Body Therapy*

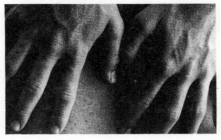

4502 Cass St.
San Diego, CA 92109
619-272-4142

*The IPSB is a private school devoted to the art and science of professional massage and bodywork.*

### Instructions for touching others:

1) See-feel relate to the person-area that is to be touched.

2) Let your hands take the contour of the area to be touched.

3) Touch slowly-gently, move both in and away with sensitivity; take at least 10 seconds.

4) Give your partner plenty of time in between touches.

5) Don't move your hands or fingers around once you have established contact.

6) The touch is firm-light; don't push down or squeeze your partner.

7) Stay with what you're doing, touching, rather than letting your mind wander elsewhere.

### Suggestions for being touched:

1) Keep your eyes closed during the entire experience unless instructed otherwise.

2) Be open in your organism and let the effects of the touch move through you.

3) Allow whatever wants to happen.
Don't make anything happen or keep anything from happening.

4) Let your partner know if he is not touching right.

5) Keep breathing.
- *Bernard Gunther*
*From Sense Relaxation*

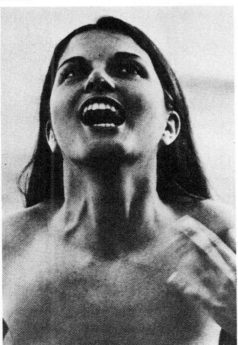

## Acupressure Institute

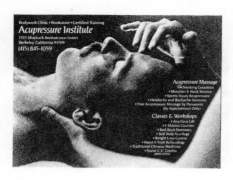

Michael Reed Gach, Director
1533 Shattuck
Berkeley, CA 94709
415-845-1059

*Acupressure is finger-pressure therapy. The Institute offers acupressure and certification training, therapy, classes, workshops, acupressure products and reflexology.*

## The Bum Back Book

By Michael Reed Gach
1983/134 pages
**$7.95**
$8.95 postpaid from:
Celestial Arts
Box 7327
Berkeley, CA 94707

*Have a bum back? Millions of Americans do. This book illustrates practical techniques to relieve tension for yourself and others. These include massage, yoga, acupressure and exercise.*

. . . .

# Shoulder and Neck Tension

Many of the Acupressure meridians travel through the neck and shoulder region. This is often the first area of the body where tension accumulates when someone is under stress. Anyone with

| BENEFICIAL EXERCISES | PAGE |
|---|---|
| Upper Back Opener | 22 |
| Pelvic Raise | 23 |
| Dollar Pose | 34 |
| Elbow Lift | 49 |

pressures, such as deadlines, obligations and taxing responsibilities, usually suffers from shoulder and neck tension to some degree. A "pain in the neck" is often the body's literal response to these frustrating situations.

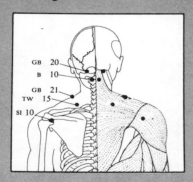

The release of shoulder and neck points improves circulation and is especially good for cold hands, fatigue, irritability, shoulder pains and stiffness of the neck. Traditionally, these points are also considered useful for hypertension.

| Acu Points | Traditional Associations |
|---|---|
| Triple Warmer 15 | Shoulder and neck pain, arm and elbow painful and cannot be raised, stiff neck. |
| Gall Bladder 20 | Alternately hot and cold, eyes foggy, nervousness, painful shoulder, rheumatism, stiff neck, upper parts of the body feel heavy or hot. |
| Gall Bladder 21 | The major point where shoulder tension collects. Traditionally used to release stiff neck, regulate hyperthyroidism, and relieve rheumatism. |
| Bladder 10 | Head heavy, spasm of the neck muscles, limbs and body not coordinated, throat sore or swollen. |
| Small Intestine 10 | Muscular pain, numbness, swelling or arthritis in the shoulder—scapula region. |

*- Michael Reed Gach*
*From The Bum Back Book*

# Flash Cards
## 30 *Acupressure* Points

(30 cards per set)

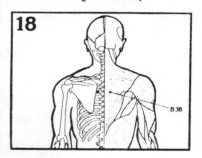

**$6.95** postpaid from:
Acupressure Institute
1533 Shattuck Ave.
Berkeley, CA 94709

# Yoga

Yoga is an Eastern science of living — a system of physical and mental exercises for you to stay in top physical condition.

## Yoga
### *The Art of Living*

By Renee Taylor
1986/48-minute videocassette, VHS or Beta
Volume I: Beginning Yoga
**$42.95** postpaid
Volume II: Intermediate Yoga
**$42.95** postpaid from:
Spectrum Video
18121 Napa St.
Northbridge, CA 91325

Learning yoga exercises is easy when someone is demonstrating for you. Renee Taylor explains and demonstrates yoga in this video series to help you build a healthier, happier body and promote physical and mental well-being.

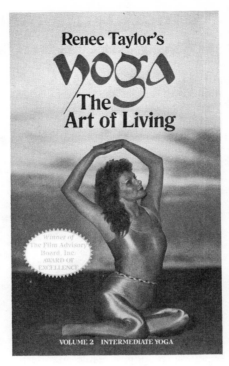

Renee Taylor's
**YOGA / The Art of Living**

*Winner of The Film Advisory Board, Inc. AWARD OF EXCELLENCE*

VOLUME 2   INTERMEDIATE YOGA

## Yoga Society of San Francisco
2872 Folsom St.
San Francisco, CA 94110
415-285-5537

Offers yoga classes, meditation practice, teacher training, and massage therapy.

## Sivananda Yoga Vedanta Centers
243 West 24th St.
New York, NY 10011
212-255-4560

Swami Vishnu Devananda came to the United States from India in 1957 to spread the word about the science of yoga. Today there are centers in Quebec, Canada; Woodbourne, NY; Nassau, Bahamas; Grass Valley, CA; Kerals, India; and in New York, Los Angeles, Chicago, Ft. Lauderdale, and Ft. Pierce, Florida. They offer yoga retreats, teacher training, kids' camps, and personal yoga training.

---

# Ceiling Walk

**BENEFITS:** Because the back is flat, the strain of postural alignment is eliminated, making the ceiling walk safe for even the student with a weak, problem back. This is basically an abdominal strengthener, but the muscles which flex the hip joints and raise the thighs are also toned. Abdominal muscles do more than hold the stomach in. Functions include balancing the opposing muscles in the back which hold the spine straight, moving the bowels, urinating, childbirth, even exhalation requires contraction of these diverse muscle groups.

**TECHNIQUE:** Lie flat on a mat as you raise both legs perpendicular to the floor. Check your back at the waistline. It should be flat and pressed into the floor. With feet flat and knees straight, simulate a wide stride across the ceiling. Watch the breath and coordinate it with the alternate movements. Work until you feel a quivering sensation or grow tired. Then rest, with knees bent.

- *Lorna Bell, R.N., and Eudora Seyfer*
  *From Gentle Yoga*

## Gentle Yoga

GENTLE YOGA

Yoga for people with arthritis, stroke damage, multiple sclerosis, in wheelchairs, or anyone who needs
A Guide to Gentle Exercise
Lorna Bell, R.N. & Eudora Seyfer

By Lorna Bell, R.N., and Eudora Seyfer
1987/143 pages
**$7.95**
$8.95 postpaid from:
Celestial Arts
Box 7327
Berkeley, CA 94707

Gentle Yoga is for those with physical limitations like arthritis who need to practice gentle exercise. This program was developed so you can adapt these exercises for your special needs.

## Fundamentals of Yoga
### A Handbook of Theory, Practice, and Application

By Rammurti S. Mishra, M.D.
1987/224 pages
**$12.95**
$16.45 postpaid from:
Crown Publishers, Inc.
34 Englehard Ave.
Avenel, NJ 07001

*This is an authoritative handbook that details the basic principles of Yoga. It also contains 30 step-by-step lessons on yoga to control physical and mental states.*

## Tai Chi Ten Minutes to Health

By Chi Siew Pang
and Goh Ewe Hock
1985/132 pages
**$12.95**
$14.95 postpaid from:
CRCS Publications
P.O. Box 20850
Reno, NV 89515

# Richard Hittleman's Yoga Video Course

For many centuries, countless millions of people have found Hatha Yoga to be the perfect system for maintaining a high level of lifelong fitness. Ancient in origin and universally respected, it is recognized today by numerous health authorities as a comprehensive, holistic approach to well-being: it cultivates not only the health of the body, but also that of the mind and emotions. Additionally, its techniques are being effectively applied in a variety of physical and psychological problems.

Always be aware that much more than "exercising" is inherent in Hatha Yoga. In addition to the numerous physical benefits, serious practice of the postures and breathing techniques results in a deep quieting of the mind and emotions. The profound state of tranquility and inner peace that is then experienced is beyond description. This state is one of the major objectives of Hatha Yoga.

Richard Hittleman has been an instructor of Yoga for more than thirty five years. Through his books, recordings and television programs, he has taught Yoga to more people throughout the world than any living authority.

### Richard Hittleman's Video Yoga Course

Course 1 & 2, VHS
45 minute video cassettes
**$39.95** each
$40.95 each postpaid from:
Clear Lake Productions
Box 3007
Santa Cruz, CA 95063

*Course #1 is a beginning Yoga Workshop. Course #2 is intermediate level.*

# What Is Tai Chi

Tai chi, an ancient martial art based upon Taoist philosophy, probably developed in China during the Sung dynasty. It was initially taught and practiced only in northern China. The Japanese invasion in the twentieth century stimulated its spread to other parts of the country while the communist takeover of the nation was largely responsible for its dissemination to Taiwan, Hong Kong and the countries of Southeast Asia. From these overseas centers the art was propagated even further.

Paradoxically, despite its popularity, there exists a good deal of misconception about tai chi. Some view it as a mild exercise. Yet those who practice other forms of martial art recognize it as a martial art that takes a long time to learn and even longer to perfect. Many will attest to its effectiveness, but just what makes it effective as a martial art no one seems to know.

This is not surprising. Relatively few people have mastered tai chi; fewer are willing to pass on knowledge of it. Most of those who do often describe only the basic tenets on which it is based, and even those in very vague and general terms.

*- Chi Siew Pang and*
*Goh Ewe Hock*
*From Tai Chi, Ten Minutes to Health*

## Aikido and the New Warrior

Edited by Richard Strozzi Heckler
1985/230 pages
**$12.95**
$14.45 postpaid from:
North Atlantic Books
2320 Blake St.
Berkeley, CA 94704

edited by
**Richard Strozzi Heckler**

# Aikido

Master Ueshiba established Aikido as an effective, even awesome, self-defense form. At the same time he concluded that the emphasis on winning at any cost, and the domination of others through physical force and manipulation, was anachronistic to the spiritual needs of contemporary society. Searching for a martial art that would meet the needs of the modern age the Founder stayed true to the original vision of budo: the cultivation and perfection of the spirit. Asserting that Aikido was not a competitive sport, with the accompanying divisions of winners and losers, Master Ueshiba developed a martial form that empowered human beings from the inside out, without categories and contests to determine who is best. He said that the "opponent is within" and that we must first work with our own minds and bodies instead of trying to correct others. He established dignity and integrity as a priority to greed and the acquisition of fame and power.

> - *Richard Strozzi Heckler*
> *From* Aikido and the
> New Warrior

## Living Aikido

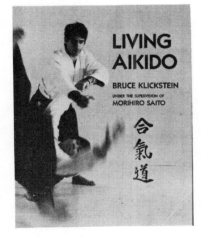

By Bruce Klickstein
1987/158 pages
**$16.95**
$18.45 postpaid from:
North Atlantic Books
2320 Blake St.
Berkeley, CA 94704

*This is an illustrated guide to Aikido for beginners or more advanced practitioners who wish to improve their technique.*

## T'ai Chi Ch'uan
### A Simplified Method of Calisthenics for Health & Self Defense

### Cheng Man-ch'ing
## T'AI CHI CH'UAN

By Cheng Man-ching
1981/135 pages
**$8.95**
$10.45 postpaid from:
North Atlantic Books
2320 Blake St.
Berkeley, CA 94704

# Shadow Boxing

T'ai-chi Ch'uan, as it is practiced in China today, is a system of physical exercise based on the principles of effortless breathing, rhythmic movement, and weight equilibrium. It is also designed to serve as a method of self-defense. As such, it can be practiced by an individual alone in a limited space. It can also be practiced by two opponents, one taking the offensive and the other defensive. It requires no equipment, except a loose-fitting garment which permits continuous rhythmic bodily movements. T'ai-chi Ch'uan has often been referred to, perhaps facetiously, by Westerners as "shadow boxing." When performed by an expert, its rhythmic movement reaches such a state of harmony that it can be likened to a form of dancing.

The essence of T'ai-chi Ch'uan lies in the maintenance of perfect body balance at all times. It illustrates most conclusively that in the case of any physical object, the larger its base and the lower its center of gravity, the greater is its stability. For this reason most of the movements of T'ai-chi Ch'uan are executed in a semi-crouch in order to achieve the maximum nature of stability, while offering the opponent the smallest possible target area. In this posture you are trained to attain the closest and nimblest coordination between the movement of the waist, the arm and the hand, and the movement of the legs in a series of continuous turns and shifts of footwork and bodily position. Of particular importance is the method of breathing required in these exercises which, I am told, gives the practitioner a continuous sense of relaxation so that he is never out of breath.

> - *George K.C. Yeh*
> *From the Introduction to*
> T'ai Chi Ch'uan

揽雀尾左
起勢
預備式

# The Chiropractic Alternative

## How the Chiropractic Health Care System Can Help Keep You Well

**NATHANIEL ALTMAN**

*Foreword by Mary Jane Newcomb, D.C., Ph.D.*
*Cleveland Chiropractic College*

By Nathaniel Altman, D.C., Ph.D.
1981/206 pages
**$5.95**
$8.35 postpaid from:
J.P. Tarcher
9110 Sunset Blvd.
Los Angeles, CA 90069

*This is an excellent introduction to chiropractic procedures. The author details what a chiropractor can and cannot do, how to choose the right practitioner and how to enhance the benefits of regular chiropractic care.*

- *Nathaniel Altman, D.C., Ph.D.*
  *From* The Chiropractic Alternative

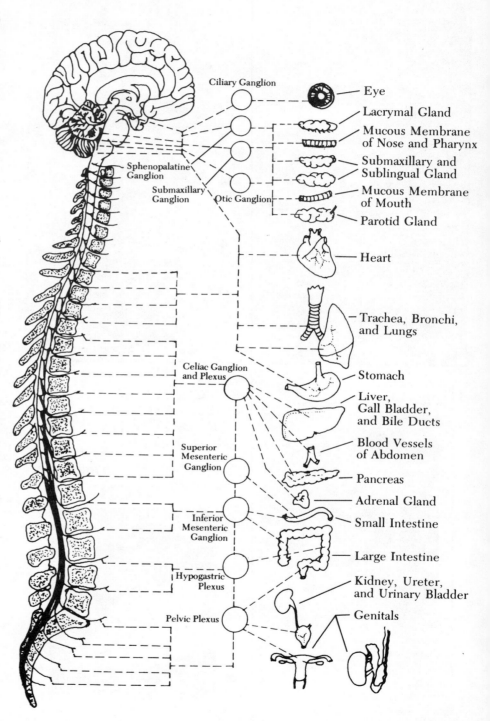

The nervous system, revealing two divisions: central and autonomic. From Schafer, *Chiropractic Health Care.* Reprinted courtesy of The Foundation for Chiropractic Education and Research.

# Sports Self-Help

**The Warrior Athlete**
*Self-Transformation Through Total Training*
By Dan Millman
1979/172 pages
**$9.95**
$11.95 postpaid from:
Stillpoint International
Box 640
Mettinghouse Rd.
Walpole, NH 03608

*There is a natural "athlete" within you. This is the blending of body, mind, and spirit to enhance your natural abilities. This isn't an exercise book, but rather an opportunity for you to discover your full potential.*

## The Illusion of Difficulty

"Difficulty" has no absolute meaning; it is only relative to your preparation. If you're prepared — if you've developed all the necessary physical, mental, and emotional qualities — then nothing will be difficult for you.

A common experience for the usual athlete is to find learning easy at first but more difficult as time passes. This increasing difficulty is such a common pattern that we accept it as normal. Yet it is not the natural pattern; it is only a reflection of insufficient preparation.

The natural athlete is one who has developed his talent from the outset, making learning easier as time passes.

In order to avoid falling onto path A, that of the usual athlete, we might take a look at the primary reasons anyone chooses this way:

● He might not appreciate the importance of thorough preparation.
● He might not know what thorough preparation consists of.

● He may be in a hurry, seeking shortcuts, because he lacks a realistic map of understanding.
● Lacking confidence, he may avoid a path that appears slower at first and promises few immediate rewards.
● He may have a teacher who falls into one of the above categories.

Many coaches and teachers allow or even encourage shortcuts in order to "keep the students interested" or because it's "more practical." Immediate competitive pressures and deadlines aggravate this tendency.

Beginning students cannot be expected to have a complete understanding of the training process and priorities. Therefore, an intelligent and patient teacher is one of the most important aspects of your training. Choose with great care.

*- Dan Millman*
*From* The Warrior Athlete

## Every Athlete Must Deal with a Combination of Pressures

The various pressures you feel in sports don't just act by themselves; they mix. They come at you from different directions and you are caught in the middle. One pressure makes you feel and act one way, while another says to act in the opposite way. For example, consider what may be happening in your head when you're lining up that short putt and you start thinking, "If I make this one, I'll be par and maybe break 90 for the first time in my life."

First, you came to the golf course with certain personal needs — to relax, of course, but also, let us say, to be sociable with a new business associate. But you're playing better than your usual game and are giving the other player a sound beating. While you feel good about winning, you also feel a bit embarrassed that he may think you lied about your handicap and worried about how he may take your really beating him.

Your personal needs, which already have an element of conflict in them, now run up against the societal pressures, for you are culturally conditioned to be a strong competitor and to go for the big one whenever you can. When you started the game, you expected to shoot no better than a 93. But now you realize you have a chance at an 89, your best score ever. Even if you miss, you could congratulate yourself on carding 90, but you want to go for the big one, too. Now it has become 89 or a washout. So, instead of feeling good about how well you have done, you now have cause for worry about how well you will have done after the putt.

Caught up in a welter of conflicting thoughts provoked by contradictory personal and social conditioned needs, is it any wonder that your palms get a little sweaty and your vision begins to blur just a little?

*- Thomas Tutko and*
*Umberto Tosi*
*From* Sports Psyching

## Sports Psyching
*Playing Your Best Game All of the Time*

How to overcome the tensions, fears, and frustrations that undermine your game and keep you from winning.

# SPORTS PSYCHING

## Playing Your Best Game All of the Time

"For the past twelve years I have worked with thousands of professional athletes on the psychological techniques they use to reach their full athletic potential. Whatever your sport, these techniques will help you repeat the best day you ever had."

**THOMAS TUTKO, Ph.D.**
Co-founder, Institute of Athletic Motivation, and Professor of Psychology, San Jose State University

**AND UMBERTO TOSI**

By Thomas Tutko, Ph.D.
and Umberto Tosi
1976/230 pages
**$6.95**
$9.35 postpaid from:
Jeremy P. Tarcher, Inc.
9110 Sunset Blvd.
Los Angeles, CA 90069

*Why do we sometimes "choke" when the pressure is on? Why do we miss easy shots? How can we change this? The authors are sports team consultants who have helped thousands of athletes replace stress-related habits with constructive, winning behavior.*

## The SyberVision Catalog
*Audio and Video Achievement Programs*

6066 Civic Terrace Ave.
Newark, CA 94560
Send $2.00 for catalog.

# Success Comes from Mastery of the Fundamentals

What do the best athletes ... the most successful business people ... super achievers in general ... all share in common? Complete and total mastery of the fundamentals. With a solid grounding in the fundamentals, there is literally no limit on what can be achieved.

And that's what you get from all SyberVision programs. There are four easy steps to how SyberVision works.

1. We identify models. At SyberVision we go out and find those people who have mastered the fundamentals better than anyone else. In skiing, golf, speaking a

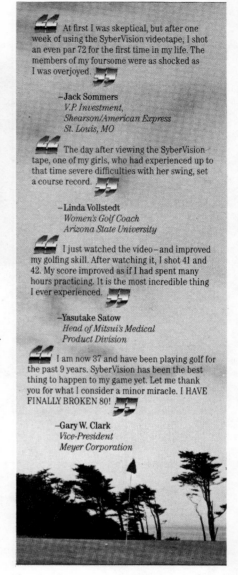

foreign language, just to name a few.

2. We isolate key fundamentals, show them, and explain them. determine what characteristics the top group in any activity or endeavor possess. We then bring these common characteristics to you on either audio or video cassettes.

3. We give you a system for learning the fundamentals.

4. We give you a system for performing the fundamentals when and where needed.

*- From* The Sybervision Catalog

# Part 7: New Lifestyles/Communities
# The Meaning of Community

There is something in the human condition that eternally yearns for a greater sense of connectedness, yearns to reach out and deeply touch others, throwing off the pain and loneliness of separation to experience unity with others. In all times and all places people have consciously reached out to feel their connectedness with a larger whole. This is the experience of *community*.

The word "community" contains the word "unity" and, on the deepest level, community is the experience of unity or oneness with all people and with all of life. We can be in community with our family, our friends, our clubs, our co-workers, our neighbors, and with our fellow humans — as long as we are feeling a sense of connectedness and unity with them. Social researcher Daniel Yankelovitch describes community in this way:

> Community evokes in the individual the feeling that "Here is where I belong, these are my people, I care for them, they care for me, I am part of them, I know what they expect from me and I from them, they share my concerns. I know this place, I am on familiar ground, I am at home."

Community is not a static structure; rather it is an ongoing process of unfoldment of the wholeness of a person on all levels — physical, emotional, mental, spiritual. Community is the context for actualizing potentials within the individual and between the individual and others, for connecting with others and experiencing oneness. It is a sense of brother/sisterhood, beyond separation, where we recognize ourselves in the "other." At times, this experience of unity bursts upon us spontaneously, revealing the wonder and mystery of life — a taste of the Divine. And yet we also can create a sense of unity consciously, building it patiently, step by step, as we get to know each other, revealing more of our deeper selves, trading vulnerabilities, developing trust, keeping our hearts open as we work out conflicts and differences. As this process extends beyond the human world, we develop a sense of community with all other life forms who share the earth with us.

*- Corinne McLaughlin and*
*Gordon Davidson*
*From* Builders of the Dawn

## Builders of the Dawn

By Corinne McLaughlin and
Gordon Davidson
1985/372 pages
**$12.95**
$14.45 postpaid from:
Sirius Publishing
Baker Rd.
Shutesbury, MA 01072

Builders of the Dawn *presents an overview of the new communities of the 1980's. It offers workable guidelines for building new communities based on the experience of many successful community founders such as Peter and Eileen Caddy, Swami Kriyananda, Stephen Gaskin, Sun Bear, and Ken Keyes. The benefits and problems of community living are explored in depth, as well as*

*innovative approaches to governance, economics, relationships, and spirituality being pioneered in today's communities. A resource listing of the 100 communities.*

## The Different Drum
*Community Making and Peace*

By M. Scott Peck, M.D.
1987/334 pages
**$16.95**
$18.95 postpaid from:
Simon & Schuster
200 Old Tappan Rd.
Old Tappan, NJ 07675

*The experience of true community is a unique way of communicating, of sharing our deepest thoughts and feelings without fear or guilt. Writing with the insight and immediacy of his pioneering work in creating communities in every part of the country, Dr. Peck describes the exhilarating process by which we join together, whatever our cultural backgrounds and religious beliefs, overcome our prejudices, transcend our differences, and learn to accept and love ourselves and each other. With fascinating stories and case histories, he reveals that the steps we must take toward achieving community are surprisingly similar to the steps we must take toward achieving wholeness and maturity in our human growth.*

- M. Scott Peck, M.D.
From The Different Drum

## Communities Magazine
*Journal of Cooperation*

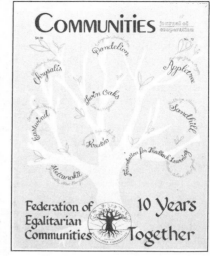

105 Sun St.
Stelle, IL 60919
$16.00/One year/four issues

This is a national forum for communities. Issues include news, commentary, organization trends and community history.

## The New Age Community Guidebook
*Community Referral Service*

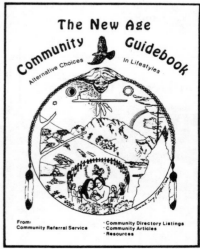

Box 2672
Eugene, OR 97402
$8.00 postpaid/Annual

A directory of hundreds of North American Communities. This is a must if you're thinking of joining a community. Each issue includes articles on individual communities and reader commentary and networking section.

# Stumbling into Community

We tend to speak of our hometowns as communities. Or of the churches in our towns as communities. Our hometowns may well be geographical collections of human beings with tax and political structures in common, but precious little else relates them to each other. Towns are not, in any meaningful sense of the word, communities. And sight unseen, on the basis of my experience with many Christian churches in this country, I can be fairly confident that each of the churches in your hometown is not likely to be much of a community either.

While on one hand we bandy about the word "community" in such a shallow, meaningless way, many of us simultaneously long for the "good old days" when frontier neighbors gathered together to build one another's barns. We mourn the *loss* of community. I am not enough of a historian to know whether back then our forefathers did indeed enjoy the fruits of genuine community more than we do today or whether we are simply yearning for an imaginary "golden age" that never existed. Still, I know of some hints that indicate we humans may once have known more of community than we currently experience.

- M. Scott Peck, M.D.
From The Different Drum

## Natural Products

# What Are Natural Products?

Along with an increased awareness of the unpleasant effects of hidden toxins in processed and chemically grown foods comes the realization that many household cleaners, personal care products, and home furnishings contain lethal ingredients. Beyond the potential health hazards, however, is the question of personal responsibility in terms of the testing of cosmetics on animals and the polluting effects of chemical waste on the environment.

Natural products provide an alternative to toxic chemical ingredients which may pollute the home as well as the surrounding environment. Cosmetics are made of natural ingredients which often take advantage of the healing, restorative properties of herbal formulas, and are never tested on animals. Fabrics for clothing and bedding are made from natural fibers, particularly cotton, and are free of irritating synthetic material. Household cleaners are simple but effective and return to the environment without toxic waste tagging along with the dirt.

These products are a "natural" extension of the growing interest in natural foods and lifestyles. Their popularity is evidenced by the increasing number of companies formed to provide an alternative market for the enlightened consumer.

# ChiPants: Room to Move

These pants incorporate a very simple concept: a gusset instead of a standard seamed cross in the crotch. It's a simple, freeing idea. These pants allow you to move freely. They are extra comfortable without knotting and binding even if you just do normal movement. They come in 100% cotton fabric in a variety of styles.

Chi Pants
Box 7400
Santa Cruz,
CA 95061

# A Clean Home Isn't "Clean"

The average "clean" home is a mine field of toxics. From cleansers to personal care items to food and clothing, researchers are linking harmless-looking products to headaches, depression, sterility, diseases of the nervous system, cancer, birth defects, and genetic changes. It's enough to make you sick.

*The Nontoxic Home* is the concerned consumer's guide to safe household products. From tap water to pesticides, from talcum powder to asbestos, and from nail polish to alcoholic beverages, this book explains how toxic substances enter your system and the immediate steps you can take to avoid the harmful effects. Also included is advice on how to minimize the dangers caused by video display terminals, second-hand smoke, and a variety of hard-to-avoid environmental poisons.

Surprisingly enough, making a nontoxic home for your family is less expensive than living with the chemicals that now surround you.
- The Nontoxic Home

# The Futon

The Futon is the traditional sleeping mat of the Orient made of layers of batting that can be used either as a bed, folded into a couch or rolled up and stored away. Essential Alternatives of Vermont offers a choice of natural battings, sizes, frames and fabric covers.

**The Nontoxic Home**
*Protecting Yourself and Your Family from Everyday Toxics and Health Hazards*

By Debra Lynn Dadd
1986/214 pages
**$9.95**
$12.35 postpaid from:
Jeremy P. Tarcher, Inc.
9110 Sunset Blvd.
Los Angeles, CA 90069

Learn About the Health Effects of and Safe Alternatives to

THE
NONTOXIC
HOME

Protecting Yourself and Your Family
from Everyday Toxics and Health Hazards

DEBRA LYNN DADD
author of NONTOXIC & NATURAL

Essential Alternatives
38 Center St.
Rutland, VT 05701

# "Natural" Furniture Polish

It's easy to make your own furniture polish. The active ingredient in most polishes is plain mineral oil, which you can purchase at a drug store and apply sparingly with a soft cloth. Mineral oil is a petrochemical product that is relatively safe to use; its only real danger comes from repeated, regular ingestion. It's odorless and is absorbed right into the wood. Many polishes contain mineral oil — you'll just be using the same active ingredient without all the extra solvents and perfumes. If you like lemon-scented polish, you can add 1 teaspoon of lemon oil to 2 cups mineral oil.

The idea behind furniture polish is to get an oil absorbed into the wood, but it doesn't matter what kind of oil you use. It could be any oil, even one right in your kitchen cabinet. I just use plain mayonnaise. Just open the bottle, put a little on a soft cloth, and rub it in. Your furniture will smell like a sandwich for a few minutes, but the odor disappears quickly and the mayonnaise leaves a soft, non-sticky finish.

You can also mix your own "salad dressing" polishes:

• 1 teaspoon olive oil, mixed with the juice of one lemon, 1 teaspoon brandy or whiskey, and 1 teaspoon water. (Make fresh each time.)

• 3 parts olive oil mixed with 1 part white vinegar.

• 2 parts olive or vegetable oil mixed with 1 part lemon juice.

• For oak: Boil one quart beer with 1 tablespoon sugar and 2 tablespoons beeswax. Cool, wipe onto wood, and allow to dry. Polish when dry with a chamois cloth.

Don't worry about the odors any of these natural polishes might leave. The food smells quickly dissipate, and they don't become rancid.

*- Debra Lynn Dadd*
*From* The Nontoxic Home

## Non-Toxic Mail Order Sources

**Charles W. Jacobsen**
401 S. Salina St.,
Syracuse, NY 13201
315/422–7832
315/471–6522
*Free catalog*

**Charles Webb**
28 Church St.
Cambridge, MA 02138
617/491–2389
*Free catalog*

**Cheese Junction**
1 W. Ridgewood Ave.
Ridgewood, NJ 07450
800/631–0353
*Free catalog*

**The Chef's Catalogue**
725 County Line Rd.
Deerfield, IL 60015
312/480–9400
*$1 catalog*

**The Cherry Tree**
PO Box 361
Sonoma, CA 95476
707/938–3480
*Free catalog*

## Nontoxic and Natural
*How to Avoid Dangerous Everyday Products and Buy or Make Safe Ones*
By Debra Lynn Dadd
1984/290 pages
**$9.95**
$12.35 postpaid from:
Jeremy P. Tarcher, Inc.
9110 Sunset Blvd.
Los Angeles, CA 90069

*An excellent, comprehensive source-book for companies carrying natural products of all kinds.* Nontoxic and Natural *provides an alphabetical listing of over 300 categories — from "afgan to yoghurt" — of household items. Each listing describes possible toxic dangers of commonly used products, a list of sources carrying natural alternative products and, if appropriate, do-it-yourself recipes for making your own household products.*

# Do-It-Yourself

**Antiperspirant**
• Mix ½ cup vodka, 2½ cups pure water, 1 tablespoon alum, and 1 tablespoon powdered zinc oxide in a blender or food processor. Place in spray bottle. Shake before using.

**Deodorants**
• Apply pure, dry baking soda or white clay directly to underarm.
• Mix baking soda with cornstarch, wheat starch, rice starch, or white clay. Apply to underarm.
• Mix 2 teaspoons alum into 1 pint warm pure water. Place in spray bottle.

*- Debra Lynn Dadd*
*From* Nontoxic and Natural

**Everything Natural**
$18.00 per year/Bimonthly
from:
Everything Natural
P.O. Box 390
Inverness, CA 94937

*This 24-page newsletter serves as a clearing house for new information of household toxics and natural products. A typical issue contains a letters column (questions, answers, and sharing), bits and pieces from the news media. In-depth articles on products and alternative methods. Interviews with experts, book reviews, new brand-name products and mailorder catalogs, and much more.*

# Resources for Natural Products

This list is only a representative sample of the many natural product companies in existence. Catalogs are available from these companies for mail order purchases.

## Bedding

**The Futon Company**
412 W. Franklin
Chapel Hill, NC 27514

**Portable Products**
428 Stinson Blvd.
Minneapolis, MN 55413

## Clothing

**Deva**
P.O. Box F83
Burkittsville, MD 21718

**Erlander's Natural Products**
P.O. Box 106
Altadena, CA 91001

**Meditation & Spiritual Creations**
Box 4483
Bay Terrance, NY 11360

## Personal Care/Cosmetics

### Aubrey Organic Products

4419 North Manhattan Ave.
Tampa, FL 33614

### Clearly Natural Products
31 Pamaron Way
Novato, CA 94947

### Heritage Store

P.O. Box 444
Virginia Beach, VA 23458

### Nature's Gate Herbal Cosmetics
9183-5 Kelvin Ave.
Chatsworth, CA 91311

### New Age Creations
219 Carl St.
San Francisco, CA 94117

### Paul Penders D & P Products
P.O. Box 878
Old Canning Plant Rd.
Seffner, FL 33584

### Weleda

1986 Mail Order Catalog

P.O. Box 769
Spring Valley, NY 10977

## Household Products

### Livos Plant Chemistry
*The Natural Choice*

614 Agua Fria
Santa Fe, NM 87501

### Naturall Brand Products
P.O. Box 28
Walled Lake, MI 48088

## Business & Investing

The Golden Egg
*The Spiritual Renaissance of Business*
By Christopher Hills
1979/374 pages
**$9.95**
$11.95 postpaid from:
University of the Trees Press
P.O. Box 66
Boulder Creek, CA 95006

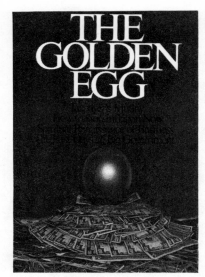

# Modern Industry

*The Golden Egg* is a scathing expose' of big government, big business, big oil and utilities companies. Not only has the author openly confronted these powerful vested interests who grow fat on the public wealth and even manipulate the government of the land, but he has unmasked the love affair between big government and big business. Christopher Hills challenges the American people to see that a financial crash is coming in this country very soon and that we must act *now* if we are to prevent it. *The Golden Egg* supplies practical workable solutions to our soaring taxes, our tottering Social Security system and the encroaching cancer of inflation, provided the people have enough spiritual fiber left to rise up and put the new principles into practice.

- *Christopher Hills*
*From* The Golden Egg

# Unimaginable Inefficiency

The most striking thing about modern industry is that it requires so much and accomplishes so little. Modern industry seems to be inefficient to a degree that surpasses one's ordinary powers of imagination. Its inefficiency therefore remains unnoticed.

An industrial system which uses forty percent of the world's primary resources to supply less than six percent of the world's population could be called efficient only if it obtained strikingly successful results in terms of human happiness, well-being, culture, peace, and harmony. I do not need to dwell on the fact that the American system fails to do this, or that there are not the slightest prospects that it could do so *if only* it achieved a higher rate of growth of production, associated, as it must be, with an ever-greater call upon the world's finite resources.

- *E. F. Schumacher*
*From* Small Is Beautiful

**Small Is Beautiful**
*Economics As If People Mattered*

By E.F. Schumacher
1973/306 pages
**$5.95**
$7.45 postpaid from:
Harper & Row Publishers, Inc.
2350 Virginia Ave.
Hagerstown, MD 21740

*Schumacher creates a people-oriented economic model that could help us survive into the 21st century. Things are going reasonably well right now. They might not go so well a few years from now. Maybe we ought to listen to this economic visionary.*

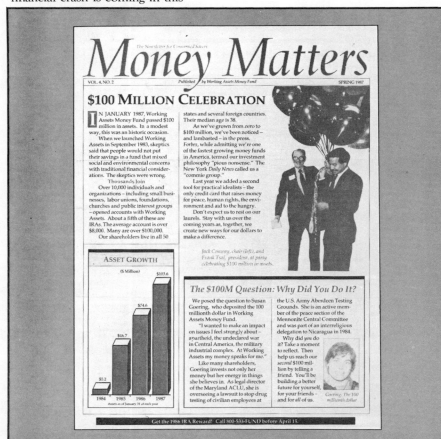

# Responsible Investing

There is a whole new consciousness when it comes to investing in the New Age. Socially conscious investing is the commonly used terminology. The method is to invest only in companies, countries and industries that care for the Earth and everything that lives on it. This generally means not investing in South Africa, the nuclear industry, in companies who don't hire minorities, have little concern for the environment or social concerns, and companies involved in the defense industry.

The following companies offer conscious investment opportunities. We suggest you contact these firms directly for their investment criteria. Many can accommodate your particular requirements.

**Affirmative Investments**
59 Temple Place
Boston, MA 02111
617-350-0250

**Anchor Investments**
110 E. Main St.
Madison, WI 53703

**The Calvert Group**
4550 Montgomery Ave.
Bethesda, MD 20814
301-951-4864

**Conscious Investments**
93 Saturn St.
San Francisco, CA 94114

**The Financial Advocates**
2328 Nebraska Ave. N.W.
Washington, DC 20016
202-364-8660

**Co-op America**
2100 M St. N.W.
Washington, DC 20036
202-871-5307
800-424-2667

They're helping to build an alternative marketplace that aligns buying habits with political and social concerns. Membership provides alternative health insurance, biannual shopping catalogs, alternative investing opportunities, and a quarterly magazine titled Building Economic Alternatives.

**New Alternatives Fund**
295 Northern Blvd.
Great Neck, NY 11021
516-446-0808

**Pax World Fund**
224 State St.
Portsmouth, NH 03801
603-431-8022

**The Pioneer Group**
60 State St.
Boston, MA 02109
617-742-7825
800-225-6292

**Strategic Investment Advisors**
142 Lincoln Ave.
Santa Fe, NM 87501
505-983-9370

**Thomas McKinnon Securities**
126 College St.
Burlington, VT 05402

**The Windmill Group**
530 Main St.
Armonk, NY 10504
914-273-1700

**Working Assets**
230 California St.
San Francisco, CA 94111
415-989-3200
800-223-7010

# Investing Information Sources

**Clean Yield Publications**
Box 1800
Greenboro, VT 05842
802-535-7178

This is a stock investment newsletter that reports on companies who are socially and environmentally responsible.

**Energy Investment Research**
Box 73
Greenwich, CT 06831
914-937-6939

An energy and environmental investment newsletter published every two weeks.

**Franklin's Insight**
711 Atlantic Ave.
Boston, MA 02111
617-423-6655

"The advisory letter for concerned investors" is their motto. They deal with only socially responsible companies, even rating them according to this newsletter's special rating system.

**Good Money Publications**
Box 363
Worcester, VT 05612
802-223-3911

Publishers of a group of socially responsive investment newsletters, investor guides and reports on companies and their track records relating to social, environmental and political concerns.

**Investment Ethics**
2980 College Ave.
Berkeley, CA 94705
415-845-9651

If you need to know a particular company's record on minorities, South Africa, its concern for the environment, the nuclear industry and other social concerns, this organization can provide updated reports.

**Renewable Resource and Conservation Report**
311 Miramar Rd.
Rochester, NY 14624
716-247-8197

Published every other month, this guide details investments in industries focused on renewable resources.

# Media

The New Age has spawned its share of media including magazines, newspapers, newsletters, and broadcast programs. This is a sampling of what we feel are the best and have an excellent chance of being in existence for a while.

Fact is, there are thousands of New Age publications being published at any given moment.

Check your local bookstore, natural products retailer, or New Age Center and you'll undoubtedly find some being distributed for free. These New Age networking devices are an excellent way to see what's going on nationally and in your community, from channeling sessions to New Age radio shows.

## Common Boundary
### *Between Spirituality & Psychotherapy*
7005 Florida St.
Chevy Chase, MD 20815

*Explore the boundary between psychotherapy and spirituality. This magazine also serves as a networking tool for people interested in these issues.*

## Body, Mind & Spirit Magazine
*Formerly Psychic Guide*

Box 701
Providence, RI 02901
**$15.00**/One year/six issues

*We're the people who created the book you now have in your hands. We're America's best read New Age magazine featuring a broad spectrum of New Age topics from spirituality to healing and natural products.*

*If you like this book, you'll love Body, Mind & Spirit.*

## Balance Magazine
359 Walden Green
Branford, CT 06405
**$15.00**/One year/six issues

*A slick magazine devoted to balanced, holistic living. Includes articles on wellness, spirituality, movement, and mysticism.*

## Beyond Avalon
93 Jackson Ave.
Bridgeport, CT 06606
**$9.00**/One year/four issues

*An eclectic mix of New Age topics including channeling, book reviews, personal experience and whatever else the editor, John Chambers, feels like writing about.*

## Brain/Mind Bulletin Newsletter
Box 42211
Los Angeles, CA 90042
**$35.00**/One year/12 issues

*Marilyn (The Aquarian Conspiracy) Ferguson is editor and publisher. They feature the results of brain/mind research.*

## Common Ground

305 San Anselmo Ave.
San Anselmo, CA 94960
415-459-4900
Distributed free in northern California.

## Earth Star/New England
Box 1597
Meredith, NH 03253
603-279-7429
Distributed free in New England.

## East West Journal
Box 6769
Syracuse, NY 13217
**$18.00**/One year/12 issues

*The Kushi Foundation is America's center for macrobiotic dietary studies. This magazine is a forum for macrobiotic news and information and other New Age topics.*

## The Essential Whole Earth Catalog
27 Gate Five Rd.
Sausalito, CA 94965
**$15.00**/Annual

*Includes an array of objects, books and publications on subjects ranging from psychological self-care to mysticism and desktop publishing. An encyclopedia of excellence for today's world.*

## Fate Magazine
170 Future Way
Marion, OH 43305
**$11.95**/One year/12 issues

*This is the original psychic magazine first published in 1948. Fate regularly features UFOs, strange happenings and ancient mysteries.*

## Free Spirit
137 Sixth Ave.
Brooklyn, NY 11217
718-638-6990
Distributed free in the New York Metro area.

## Greater Cincinnati Resource Directory

3514 Burch St.
Cincinnati, OH 45208
513-871-4950
Distributed free in Ohio.

## Harmonist Magazine

One Almaden Blvd.
San Jose, CA 95113
$7.90/One year/four issues

Published by the National Organization for Public Awareness, this magazine offers alternative thought and culture.

## Holistic Health

Box 955
Mill Valley, CA 94942
$8.00/One year/four issues

This journal of holistic health care has a decidely Eastern flavor.

## Life Times

Box 4129
Santa Barbara, CA 93140
$16.00/One year/four issues

Features New Age topics like channeling, birthing, Eastern religions, philosophy and relationships.

## The Light Connection

Box 578
Cardiff-by-the-sea, CA 92007
$15.00/One year/12 issues

A New Age newspaper serving souther California.

## The Loving Brotherhood Newsletter

Box 556
Sussex, NJ 07461
$18.00/One year/12 issues

This is a gay spiritual newsletter with articles, networking and activities listing.

## Magical Blend

Box 11303
San Francisco, CA 94101
$12.00/One year/four issues

A very mystical magazine that features spirituality, channeling, mystics, poetry, and visionary art.

## Meditation Magazine

17510 Shermay Way
Van Nuys, CA 91406
$8.00/One year/four issues

This magazine explores and promotes meditation as a consciousness expanding activity.

## Mighty Natural Directory of South Florida

Box 415137
Miami Beach, FL 33181
305-866-5259

## The Monk

2966 Diamond St.
San Francisco, CA 94131
$10.00/One year/four issues

This is a magazine of "health and humor." It is "the relationship between two men, their two cats and their Macintosh Computer, as they roam the continent reporting on the extraordinary people and things they meet along the way."

## National New Age Yellow Pages

Box 5491
Fullerton, CA 92635
$14.95/Annual

This is a California-dominated directory that has yellow colored pages of advertisers. Contains a broad spectrum of New Age listings.

## New Age Exchange

80 Rising Trail Drive
Middletown, CT 06457
$19.00/One year/six issues

This newsletter circulates in the Connecticut area. It includes channeled material, listings of local New Age events and local advertisers.

## New Dimensions Radio Network

Box 410510
San Francisco, CA 94141

A nationally syndicated radio network offering a fine selection of New Age voices speaking on topics ranging from intuition to addictions. They offer a program guide and tapes of their broadcasts.

## New Frontier Magazine

129 N. 13th St.
Philadelphia, PA 19107
$12.00/One year/12 issues

This magazine focuses on the Philadelphia area, featuring news and articles from well-known people in the field of human consciousness.

## New Frontiers Newsletter

Fellowship Farm, Rt. 1
Oregon, WI 53575
$15.00/One year/four issues

New Frontiers is a New Age center. Their newsletter contains international news and information on the more controversial and unusual research going on in this field. Edited by Walter Uphoff.

## New Age Journal

Box 853
Farmingdale, NY 11735
$24.00/One year/six issues

New Age is written for people who are searching for better ways to achieve a satisfying balance in their lives. This magazine explores relationships, health, food, technology, media, and leisure.

## New Realities

4000 Albemarle St. N.W.
Washington, DC 20016
$18.00/One year/six issues

New Realities *features a variety of New Age topics including channeling, consciousness research, spirituality and personal development.*

## The New Times

Box 51186
Seattle, WA 98115
$7.50/One year/12 issues

*The Northwest's monthly New Age newspaper.*

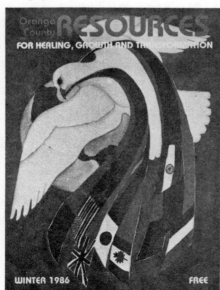

## Orange County Resources

228 20th St.
Huntington Beach, CA 92648
714-969-1371
Distributed free in Orange County California.

## Reflections

Box 13070
Portland, OR 97213
501-281-4486
Distributed free in the Pacific Northwest.

## Vegetarian Times

Box 570
Oak Park, IL 60303
$19.95/One year/12 issues

*More than six million people follow a vegetarian diet. This magazine provides vegetarian news and information plus vegetarian recipes.*

## Whole Again Resource Guide

Box 6767
Santa Barbara, CA
$24.95/Annual

*A national directory of New Age/ alternative media including magazines, newspapers, newsletters, sourcebooks, directories and bibliographies.*

## Whole Life Magazine

89 Fifth Ave.
New York, NY 10003
$20.00/One year/eight issues

*This is the New York metro piece of what was once a national Whole Life Magazine. Features New Age material, events calendar and practitioner listings.*

## Whole Life Monthly

409 Santa Monica Blvd.
Santa Monica, CA 90401
$15.00/One year/12 issues

*This is the L.A. portion of what was once the national Whole Life magazine. Offers a mix of New Age topics and listings.*

## Yoga Journal

Box 6076
Syracuse, NY 13217
$15.00/One year/six issues

*Published by the California Yoga Teachers Association, this publication regularly features yoga news, information, teaching articles and an annual directory of yoga teachers, centers and programs.*

# *Fiction*

When people think of New Age literature, they tend to look at it as mostly nonfiction self-help or experiential books.

But there is a fiction side to the New Age as well that has been showing itself more prominently in the last few years.

We've selected some interesting examples ...

## The Eye of the Child

By Ruth Mueller
1985/226 pages
**$7.95**
$9.45 postpaid from:
New Society Publishers
4722 Baltimore Ave.
Philadelphia, PA 19143

"Ah! Of all the creatures to whom the great mother had given birth all were a part, not apart, but one. Yes all but one flowed as she had flowed, born of her womb, dying in her bosom, struggling, true, but never against their own life support. One, only one, capable of standing apart, imagining self above and outside, turning to rend, turning to overpower, to subdue, to conquer the vessel of life itself, creation's own embodiment. Had she not labored for aeons to give birth to a triumph of joy and beauty as fair as dawn, a creature of light to share the glowing consciousness of the whole, one of understanding as deep as her deeps are deep, of laughter as divine as tears and of tears as cleansing as laughter, one who was not alien to mercy, capable of new visions above predation, a familiar to the art of healing, above all a creature of tongues, creation itself no longer mute to express — to express —

"What had gone wrong?"
- Ruth Mueller
From The Eye of the Child

## The Essential Colin Wilson

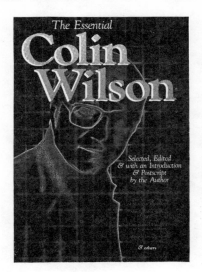

By Colin Wilson
1986/274 pages
**$8.95**
$9.95 postpaid from:
Celestial Arts
Box 7327
Berkeley, CA 94707

When Colin Wilson's critical study The Outsider was published in 1956, it was greeted with instant international acclaim. Ever since then, Colin Wilson has continued to build his reputation with an output of astonishing diversity. He is the author of over fifty books, both fiction and nonfiction, whose subjects range from mysticism and the occult to criminology.

This anthology of fiction and nonfiction shows the depth and vision of Wilson's writing, with excerpts from his most famous titles, such as The New Existentialism, The Occult, Mysteries, The Mind Parasites, and, of course, The Outsider. His writings explore how man can achieve those curious moments of inner freedom, the sensation of sheer delight.

## The Golden Dream

By Heather Hughes-Calero
1987/294 pages
**$16.95**
$17.95 postpaid from:
Coastline Publishing
Box 223062
Carmel, CA 93922

"Life Is a Dream but the Dream Has Become so Commonplace That We Cannot See It"

You are invited to explore the reality of dreams, to realize through the eyes of Milarepa that life is a result of our day-dreams, that it is woven by the private fantasies of our imaginations.

Set in Tibet, 1040-1143 A.D., The Golden Dream is a true story of Milarepa's plight to unlock the bonds of consciousness and to free himself from the invisible chains of a fate steeped in black magic.

In The Golden Dream, at the demand of his mother, Milarepa leaves his boyhood home to study with the evil sorcerer Lama Yungtun-Trogyal and returns with the power to avenge his family. After destroying his village, he wanders alone in the mountains, where he begins to become aware of dream-like sensations. Finally, naked and self-starved, he stumbles into the village of Nar where he meets Marpa, his life-long guru and teacher. With Marpa, Milarepa begins the process of spiritual awakening.

## Twelve

By Elaine Kittredge
1981/74 pages
**$6.95**
$8.95 postpaid from:
Optext
100 East Ohio
Chicago, IL 60611

Twelve is a metaphysical story especially for preteens, describing the deeper feelings and experiences of a young boy from nine to twelve. His discovery of the inner life of a tree combines with his love of the starry skies and what is beyond — a mystery perhaps best fathomed by a child's eyes and heart ... a lovely, sensitive tale of a child's awareness of two realities.

## The Silver Bird
### A Tale for Those Who Dream

By Joyce Petschek
1981/174 pages
**$9.95**
$10.95 postpaid from:
Celestial Arts
Box 7327
Berkeley, CA 94707

*We are such stuff as dreames are made on and our little life is rounded with sleep.*
   *- William Shakespeare,*
      *The Tempest*

The Silver Bird *is a book of teachings, disguised in the form of a fantasy for all ages. At first it appears as a child's book and, indeed, its simplicity, sensitivity, and beautiful illustrations speak to the child within us all.*

*This is the story of Aisling, a child whose memories of distant times and other places are exceedingly clear. Guided by Whisper, her inner voice, Aisling and the reader embark on a journey through such esoteric realms as in-and-out-of-the-body experiences, the spiritual meaning of colors, archetypes of the super conscious, the power of crystals, as well as Tibetan teachings concerning far memory, dream practices, karma and reincarnation.*

*The excitement of this beautiful, intimate book is that at the end of it one is left with a sense that the "lost treasures" of innocence can be recaptured to nourish and give meaning to our lives.*

## The Anointed

By Z'ev Ben Shimon Halevi
1982/240 pages
**$9.95**
$11.45 postpaid from:
Methuen, Inc.
29 West 35th St.
New York, NY 10001-2291

*In a small, remote town in fifteenth-century Spain, a group made up of Christians, Jews, and a Moor meets to study spiritual matters. Against a background of religious intolerance and persecution, this esoteric group of necessity meets in secret, able for a while to maintain its quiet purpose in the precarious calm of the time. It is led by Don Immanuel, a Jew whose conversion to Christianity enables him to carry out his self-appointed task of religious and political peacemaker more effectively, although as a converso he has enemies among Jews and Christians alike.*

*One day this quiet backwater is disturbed by the arrival of the Inquisition, come to seek out apostates. Their chief target is Don Immanuel, although before the drama is done it touches everyone in the town, including his daughter Rachel who falls in love with one of the officers of the Inquisition. As the story unfolds it becomes clear that Don Immanuel is ordained to become the Anointed or Messiah of the time, acting out with the Inquisition the same issues that Christ did with the Sanhedrin.*

## Way of the Peaceful Warrior

By Dan Millman
1984/210 pages
**$9.95** postpaid from:
H. J. Kramer, Inc.
Box 1082
Tiburon, CA 94920

Way of the Peaceful Warrior *is based on the true story of Dan Millman, a world champion athlete who journeys into realms of flesh and spirit, romance and terror, light and darkness, laughter and magic. Guided by a powerful old warrior named Socrates, tempted by an elusive, playful woman named Joy, Dan is led toward a final confrontation which will deliver or destroy him. Join Dan as he learns what it means to die — and live — like a warrior.*

# Transformational Travel

Travel can be a lot more than visiting some faraway place. It can be insightful and enlightening whether its reaching out to a foreign culture or setting off on a mountain retreat to find peace within yourself.

There are a number of travel organizations offering specialized travel opportunities that can be truly transformational.

## Specialty Travel Index

9 Mono Ave.
Fairfax, CA 94930
415-459-4900
**$5.00**/Biyearly, two issues
**$3.00**/Single issue

If you're looking for specialized, transformal travel opportunities, the Index contains hundreds of trips, destinations, travel companies and specialty tours accompanied by famous lecturers. It includes a reader service card for easy contact for up to 50 listees.

## Earthwatch

680 Mount Auburn St.
Watertown, MA 02272
617-926-8200

Members of this organization which sponsors field research around the world receive the quarterly Earthwatch magazine. They sponsor efforts to preserve the world's endangered habitats and species, explore cultures, and promote world health and cooperation.

## Above the Clouds Trekking

Box 398
Worcester, MA 01602
617-799-4499
800-233-4499

Visiting Nepal in the vicinity of Mount Everest can be one of the most enchanting experiences on Earth. This organization is based in Nepal and specializes in taking people "off the beaten path."

## The Spa Finder

784 Broadway
New York, NY 10003
212-475-1000
800-255-7727
**$4.00**/Refundable if you book a spa vacation.

This is the first time any one has searched out the over 200 spas, fitness-related resorts and health vacations packages at destinations worldwide. A questionnaire can be filled out by the reader, then sent to Spa-Finders, who will send you a list of the destinations best suited to your particular needs. The travel agency that sponsors Spa-Finders — Jeffrey Joseph's Travel — will take care of everything from helping you select the perfect spa to travel arrangements.

## The Four Winds Foundation

Box 948
Sausalito, CA 94966
415-332-1306

This group leads study retreats to Mexico, Peru and Brazil. Trips include transformation studies based on the culture being experienced.

## Travel Companion Exchange

Box 833
Amityville, NY 11701
516-454-0880

If you're traveling alone and would rather have a companion, this organization can help with linking you up with a well-matched traveler.

## University Expedition Program

University of California
Berkeley, CA 94720
415-642-6586

The university sponsors field research expeditions around the world in archaeology, zoology, and marine research.

- From Spa Finder

# New Age Music
## What Is New Age Music?

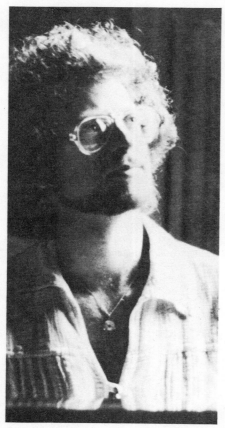

*By Steven Halpern*

The past decade has seen an exponential rise in the visibility, viability, and availability of what is commonly known as New Age Music. Although the definitions may vary, one thing is clear: for the first time since the birth of the blues, jazz, and rock, a new genre of music has manifested on our planet.

The Age of Aquarius (the "New" Age) is a time of personal and global transformation, and an opportunity for all of us to open to new levels of awareness. At its best, New Age music reflects our times, and encourages the integration of the inner and the outer being, offering an audio portrait of world peace.

For thousands of years, people around the world have honored and acknowledged the healing and ceremonial, uplifting and healing art of music. On one level, New Age music is really a return to roots, an existential exegesis to the primordial

power of sound. The fact that certain New Age recordings are used in meditation, relaxation, hospitals, and executive boardrooms represents a long overdue reversal of the trend that limited the role of music to that of "entertainment," dancing, or advertising soundtracks.

So just what is New Age music?

That depends on whom you ask. But consider: If you ask "What is classical music?" you'd receive a wide range of answers, from Baroque to Romantic, sonata to symphony.

The same goes with rock. Is it hard rock, soft rock, heavy metal, golden oldies, etc.?

That which underlies any musical genre is a school of thought — a collective consciousness that might best now be understood in terms of Rupert Sheldrake's theory of morphogenetic resonance, or the "hundredth monkey" paradigm ... but that goes beyond the scope of this introduction.

Suffice it to say that research has proven that music is a carrier wave for consciousness. It's not just the music itself, in other words, but the vibrational state of the artist when he or she is composing or recording to which we respond.

When you understand that basic "sound principle," you understand an essential aspect of this art form that has eluded most critics. It is generally recognized that a higher percentage of New Age musicians are into various forms of meditation/holistic health/cosmic awareness than other genres. This is not to say that it's better, but it *is* different. A composer who has "composed" him/herself through meditation, yoga, communing with nature, etc. has raised his/her own vibrational rate, and we resonate to this as well as the notes themselves.

Many New Age recording artists freely admit a significant amount of "channeling" as a source of their inspiration, when they are accessing co-operative, co-creative wavelengths and dimensions, networks of an ongoing cosmic symphony.

Such music makes us feel good. It uplifts our life energy and elevates our consciousness.

As Stephen Hill so eloquently states in "Music from the Hearts of Space:" "Such music creates a way to enter a space that is always there, as close as the heart, a slightly

different frequency ... a breath away ... we enter the space by allowing it to enter us."

"There are sounds of other dimensions, aural fragrances, radiant liquid pools of sound, shimmering and pulsing, crystal essences that seem like seeds of vast galactic swirls of hidden music ... taking us beyond ourselves and through ourselves, in which we seem to melt."

This is music based on harmony and consonance, rather than dissonance and percussive rhythms. It "sounds" and "feels" different than what you hear when you play "radio roulette."

And as such, the best of New Age music can be used as a form of sonic psychospiritual technology. It provides, as Lee Underwood describes, "emotional, psychological, and spiritual nourishment. It offers peace, joy, bliss, and the opportunity for all of us to rediscover in ourselves our own highest nature."

The rapid rise of New Age music has inevitably resulted in a variable glut on the marketplace. Many musicians, with good intentions but limited musicianship, have released the New Age equivalent of "garage band" cassettes, often made even worse by nonprofessional recording and duplication quality.

If that weren't bad enough, the record industry took notice of the astronomic economic tangent of growth, and jumped on the bandwagon, often hyping their own rock and jazz artists as "closet" New Agers, as a ploy to take advantage of the new marketing possibilities.

Widespread exposure, then, has been a two-edged sword. It has resulted in an exploitation and dilution of the original thrusts of New Age music, but it has also yielded an expansion and extension of its audience. As Underwood articulates, "New Age Pop" has emerged as a natural extension of art and commerce. It now exists on its own, doing what pop music has always done: It stimulates our emotions, and our intellect, and in the process, entertains us."

What New Age music means to you, and how it can contribute to your life, are open-ended questions that clearly require your participation and experience. The possibilities are as endless as the variety in the music.

So stay tuned, and enjoy!

## Whales Alive

By Paul Winter
**$9.98**/cassette or LP
$11.48 postpaid from:
Moss Music Group, Inc.
200 Varick St.
New York, NY 10014
800-422-4869
(Catalog available)

*Paul Winter's work is famous for his unique blending of unusual sounds of nature with brilliant instrumentals. This album features the voices of the humpback whales.*

## Sweet Baby Dreams

By Steven Bergman
**$9.98**/cassette
$10.98 postpaid from:
Steven Bergman Enterprises
220 De La Vina
Monterey, CA 93140
800-626-2720
(Catalog available)

*Steven Bergman carries a novel line of children's tapes as well as mainstream New Age titles.*

*This tape provides calming music for expectant mothers, new babies, and children. The heartbeat used is a pregnant mother's, recorded while resting for maximum effectiveness. Side 1 is composed by Steven Bergman, Side 2 is Pachelbel's Canon in D. Arranged and conducted by William Bolthouse. Illustrated by Tauna Caulson.*

# New Awareness

While many today unquestioningly consume whatever noise, sounds and music are being fed to them by the sound producers, others are beginning to ask questions. A new trend of sound health inquiry is starting, one that will ultimately make all of us conscious and concerned about the ways in which we nourish our bodies with sound.

Many people today are aware that it is now possible to satifying our sound needs in ways that were not possible ten years ago. The science of sound health has come a long way.

On the one hand, researchers are discovering how *certain kinds of music and sounds may contribute to stress, tension, headache, nausea, hearing loss, disturbed sleep, poor digestion, irritability, lack of concentration, and hyperactivity.* On the other hand, people are listening to — and composing — music to enhance their health and life. They are learning how to choose and create music to *facilitate such things as relaxation, concentration, learning, creativity, meditation, muscle response, digestion, mood change, psychotherapy, and self-healing.*

With the growth of sound awareness focused on health, we now have the opportunity to begin paying attention to sound as it affects our total health. In taking care of our own sound health, we may experience new vistas of self-discovery and aliveness that we never knew existed.

— *Steven Halpern*
*From Sound Health*

## Sound Health
### *The Music and Sounds That Make Us Whole*

By Steven Halpern with
Louis M. Savary
1985/210 pages
**$8.98**
$10.48 postpaid from:
Harper & Row
2350 Virginia Ave.
Hagerstown, MD 21740

*This is Halpern's pioneering work on the effects of sound on the body and the positive, healing qualities of music.*

## A New Vision
### A New Age Sampler

**$5.98**/LP or cassette
$7.93 postpaid from:
Gramavision
100 Seaview Dr.
Secaucus, NJ 07094
201-863-6120
(Catalog available)
or Body, Mind & Spirit Book Shop

*Gramavision carries a small but select line of New Age musicians. This sampler includes the work of Terry Riley and The Kronos Quartet, Yas Kaz and Steven Halpern.*

## The Spirit Music Sampler

**$6.00**/cassette
$7.00 postpaid from:
Spirit Mail Order
42 Baker Ave.
Lexington, MA 02173
617-861-1625
(Catalog available)

*This is a small, independent label that carries some unique, hard-to-find titles as well as New Age.*

*The sampler includes the work of Don Campbell, Sam McClellan, Laraaji & Lyghte, and Kano.*

# How to Select New Age Music

Chances are you won't hear New Age music being played anywhere on your radio dial.

So how can you hear the music before you buy a New Age album or cassette?

The solution is New Age Music Samplers. Most of the major New Age music companies offer sampler tapes featuring the sounds of their stable of artists. That way you can listen and decide if you want to take the next step and buy a particular artist's album or cassette.

We have listed a selection of New Age Music Samplers featuring some of the best-known New Age music artists. We suggest that you contact each of the companies we've included and ask for their latest catalog.

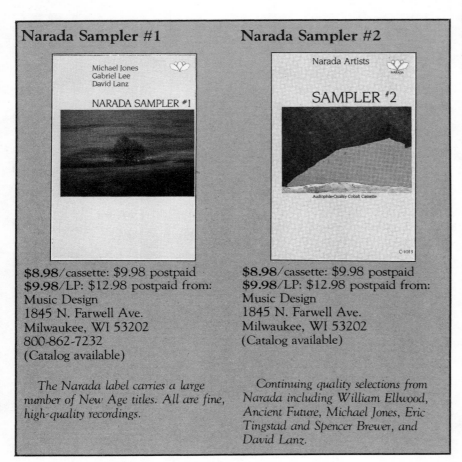

## Narada Sampler #1

**$8.98**/cassette: $9.98 postpaid
**$9.98**/LP: $12.98 postpaid from:
Music Design
1845 N. Farwell Ave.
Milwaukee, WI 53202
800-862-7232
(Catalog available)

The Narada label carries a large number of New Age titles. All are fine, high-quality recordings.

## Narada Sampler #2

**$8.98**/cassette: $9.98 postpaid
**$9.98**/LP: $12.98 postpaid from:
Music Design
1845 N. Farwell Ave.
Milwaukee, WI 53202
(Catalog available)

Continuing quality selections from Narada including William Ellwood, Ancient Future, Michael Jones, Eric Tingstad and Spencer Brewer, and David Lanz.

## The Rising Sun Collection

**$8.98**/cassette: $9.98 postpaid
**$9.98**/LP: $12.98 postpaid from:
Music Design
1845 N. Farwell Ave.
Milwaukee, WI 53202
800-862-7232
(Catalog available)
or Body, Mind & Spirit Book Shop

Rising Sun is the music division of Whatever Publishing, Inc. which carries a popular line of New Age music. The sampler includes the work of Marcus Allen, Teja Bell, Jon Bernoff, Dallas Smith and David Nowlin.

## Windham Hill Records Sampler '86
### Selections from the Windham Hill Records Album Catalog

**$10.00**/cassette or LP
$11.00 postpaid from:
Windham Hill Products
P.O. Box 9388
Stanford, CA 94305
415-329-0647
(Catalog available)

Windham Hill was one of the earliest companies to begin carrying music that would come to be known as New Age. It has an extensive line of musicians, many of them pioneers in new musical forms.

This sampler includes the work of: Philip Aaberg, The Montreux Band, Scott Cossu with Eugene Friesen, Malcolm Dalglish, Interior, Mark Isham, Michael Manring, Mike Marshall and Darol Anger, Shadowfax, Ira Stein and Russel Walder, and Liz Story.

## Heartsong Review
### Resource Guide for New Age Music of the Spirit
**$5.00**/Biannual-for 2 issues from:
Heartsong Review
P.O. Box 1084
Cottage Grove, OR 97424

This independent biannual review magazine is an excellent resource for New Age music information in all forms, from Ancient and Traditional to Folk and instrumental. Each review includes a description of the musical content, "Tech Notes" on sound quality, length, etc. and ordering information.

Also included are catalog listings, interviews, short articles, and a handy index.

# The True Spirit of New Age Music

*By David & Steve Gordon*

There's no question about it now — New Age music is emerging into the mainstream. New artists, record labels, and even radio stations are appearing on the scene each day. People everywhere are discovering the need for peaceful nonhectic music. A new form of music has arrived, and it holds the promise of bright future possibilities.

The origins of New Age music can be found in the instrumental progressive music from Europe in the seventies. More recently in the eighties, its development has been fueled by increased interest in metaphysical concepts and the new spiritual awakening.

Actually New Age music has been around for quite a while. For over ten years New Age music could mostly be found in small metaphysical book stores and mail order catalogs. Most of the recordings were created by musicians on small New Age record labels, or by artists who distributed their own music directly to the stores as a small home cottage business.

The music which these people created in a real picture of their own aspirations and consciousness. Their music reflects the inner peace and expanded awareness they have discovered during meditation or through contact with the natural environment. These dedicated musicians were much more concerned with sharing these inner spiritual feelings with others than with fame and a number one record.

As New Age music gains in popularity, many musicians, radio programmers, and business people are hopping on the bandwagon, hoping to cash in on the next big thing. Many large record labels have hired the same people who make the jingles for soft drink commercials and TV shows to create "New Age Music" for them. The result has been a huge number of recordings released — everything from acoustic to electronic to light jazz to classical, even some with vocals — all billed as "New Age Music."

At the same time, the musicians who originated New Age music are continuing to produce inspiring new recordings while enjoying the increased popularity of their work. And they have been joined by a variety of aware new artists who are also creating music of the spirit. Some of these artists have been picked up for distribution by larger record companies, but most sell their music at the grass roots level through word of mouth and small metaphysical book stores.

With this wide spectrum of music being called "New Age," how can an interested listener know where to start? This leads us to ask the question, "What exactly is New Age music, really?"

In New Age music, intent is more important than form. It may be acoustic or electronic, or a combination of both; it may contain jazz, classical, or folk elements, or it may be a totally free-form ambient exploration. It may even contain vocals! True New Age music is created with the intent of affecting the very consciousness of the listener; inspiring the mind and uplifting the spirit. If the only intent of the music is to be mellow and non-intrusive that doesn't make it New Age. New Age music is not just another kind of musical entertainment, but an important tool for rediscovering our own highest nature.

As life becomes more complicated and fast-paced, people are discovering the need for peaceful sounds which they can use to create a more healing tranquil environment. They use New Age music not just as background but as an integral part of their personal reality. It becomes interwoven with the fabric of their day to day lives, helping them to be more centered, energized and loving. Listening to New Age music is a way they can leave behind the surface intellect for a few moments and feel the unlimited peace and joy of their inner being.

The essence of New Age music lies in the power of sound to actually vibrate the body's psychic energy centers and transform our awareness. To awaken within us that spark of universal love and oneness with all that is. New Age music is becoming popular now because more and more people are starting to move beyond bitterness and fear. They are daring to dream of a future of global harmony, full of light and compassion — a world of abundance for everyone, not just a privileged few. This is the true spirit of New Age music: helping us remember that a New Age is not only possible but is unfolding right now, more and more every minute.

## Astral Journey

By David and Steve Gordon
**$8.98**/cassette
$10.98 postpaid from:
Sequoia Records
Box 280, Dept. PH80
Topanga, CA 92090
818-992-0880
(Catalog available)

*Soar beyond the skies, into a luminous new reality. Reflective melodies, celestial keyboards, flutes, bells, gongs, and tranquil guitars transport you to new levels of awareness ... a wonderfully relaxing musical meditation.*

## A Store Selling Just New Age Music?

*Only New Age Music is located in Los Angeles under the ownership of musician Suzannet Doucet and her husband James Bell.*

*The shop features a listening bar where customers can put on earphones and sample the sounds. There is a TV monitor that continuously screens New Music videos.*

*An audio gallery is also featured where patrons can commission musicians and visual artists for original works. They also feature New Music networking seminars, workshops.*

*If you're in Los Angeles, visit them at 648 North Fuller Avenue, Hollywood, CA 90036, 213-934-2221.*

## Beside the Laughing River

By Steve and David Gordon
**$8.98**/cassette
$10.98 postpaid from:
Sequoia Records
Box 280
Topanga, CA 92090
818-992-0880
(Catalog available)

*Come to your special place beside the peaceful river — let the soothing sound of the water and the enchanting music carry you away. Subtle swells of keyboards, piano, and sustained guitar melodies float gently on the bubbling laughter of the flowing river.*

## Healing Sounds
### The Power to Rejuvenate Yourself

By Dr. Christopher Hills
1985/60-minute cassette
**$9.95**
$11.95 postpaid from:
University of the Trees Press
P.O. Box 66
Boulder Creek, CA 95006

*The special vocal music on this tape is unique and unusual. It is comprised of a spontaneous vocal song without words, designed to soothe and rejuvenate.*

*On Side One, Bruce Cryer explains techniques for recreating the sounds and how to get the most out of listening to them.*

# New Age Music Sources

*(Write for their latest catalog)*

**Ananda**
14618 Tyler Foote Rd.
Nevada City, CA 95959

**Glen Canyon**
P.O. Box 2191
Santa Cruz, CA 95963

**Fortuna Records**
P.O. Box 1116
Novato, CA 94947

**Heartsong Productions**
1775 Old Country Rd.
Belmont, CA 94002

**Hyperion Records**
P.O. Box 11445
Phoenix, AZ 85061

**Invincible Recordings**
P.O. Box 13045
Phoenix, AZ 85002

**Ladyslipper**
P.O. Box 3124
Durham, NC 27705

**New World Productions**
295 Dennison Dr.
Torrington, CT 06790

**Wind Sung Sounds**
P.O. Box 880
Willis, CA 94590

# Visionary Art

## Visionary Art of the New Age

Visionary art has existed for thousands of years, predating one of its first recognized forms, the Thangka Art of the Far East. The works of Bosch and Blake certainly are an integral part of what is called Visionary. However, the works of most of the Great Masters (though given differing names based upon time and technique) are also part of the elusive Visionary Movement.

To define Visionary Art, we must first consider the manner of expression and then the message expressed. The manner of expression is most simply defined as the incorporation of two or more disparate realities in the same image when these disparate realities are represented naturalistically. The message expressed is both positive and looking to the highest ideals of humankind. The message is a message of optimism above all others. Therefore, to be Visionary Art, a work must include at least two distinctly unique paradigms of reality represented naturalistically and expressing an uplifting message — containing a spiritual content.

Contemporary Visionaries are also pioneers as they reach beyond our technologically hectic world into the worlds of imagination which lie beyond. They bring back "pictures" of what the future frontiers hold. They similarly blur the boundaries suggesting that we can have the best of either or both worlds. The contemporary Visionaries speak to people of hope, peace, and of greater possibilities and grander realities. With all the individual and global changes in our world, Visionary Art brings light to an often dark perspective — a light which may not be necessary for our physical survival, but which is essential for our mental, emotional, and psychic well-being. It is essential for our spiritual nurturement.

- *Peny Prestini*
*From* Illuminations

**Illuminations**
*The Visionary Art of Gilbert Williams*
1986/40 color plates
**$14.95**
$16.95 postpaid from:
Visionary Publishing, Inc.
P.O. Box 2440
San Anselmo, CA 94960

*This book contains 40 color high quality plates (suitable for framing) by one of the most important artists of the New Age.*

Gilbert Williams is in many ways the quintessential Visionary painter. His canvases are filled with the imagery of transcendence — moons and temples, goddesses and gateways, groves and guardians, lakes and light beings — and a brilliance of light, color, intricacy, and beauty virtually unknown in contemporary painting. In paintings that range from ancient Celtic ring stones to Greek temples floating in space, each image points toward a deeper knowledge and even more beautiful possible realities.

- *Peny Prestini*
*From* Illuminations

ILLUMINATIONS
The Visionary Art of Gilbert Williams

Wall of Temple Mysteries

Causal Plane

Passage

- Gilbert Williams
From Illuminations

# Visionary Notecards

*Visionary Publishing, Inc. carries an extensive line of full color prints, notecards and postcards of the paintings of Gilbert Williams and many other New Age artists.*

**$17.50** Box of 10 (same design)
Include $2.85 postage for each
order from:
Visionary Publishing, Inc.
P.O. Box 2440
San Anselmo, CA 94960

Notecards/$1.75 each from:

**Shell Landscape**
*Gage Taylor*

**Lazaris**
*Gilbert Williams*

**The Immortal Light**
*Jeffrey Bedrick*

**Playmates**
*Scott Thom*

**Gateway**
*Gilbert Williams*

**Twin Moons of the Proper Dawn**
*Clayton Anderson*

**Dry-Docked**
*Gage Taylor*

**Ancient Shores**
*Gilbert Williams*

**Song of the Nature Spirits**
*Gilbert Williams*

# The Conspiracy Continues

*By Marilyn Ferguson*

After reading galleys of *The Aquarian Conspiracy* on an airplane in late 1979, a fellow writer called to say, "This isn't your book — it's ours." He echoed my sense of joint authorship. Many times I had felt like a spider spinning a web from a community of ideas and people, and the diarist of a vast emigration.

Perhaps for that reason, *The Aquarian Conspiracy* has proven to be more a phenomenon than a book, a statement that helped catalyze support for the shifts it described. As the conspiracy was mapped and named, as the web became visible, it gathered strength. In that sense, I was not so much an author as a midwife.

Even before publication, the reaction to the manuscript was reassuring. Four or five Xeroxed copies given to friends turned into twenty or thirty in the hands of strangers. Within weeks after publication, leaders of the Solidarity Movement in Poland had ordered ten copies. The book became a text in a variety of college courses. It was published in the United Kingdom, France, Germany, the Netherlands, Sweden, Japan, Portugal, and Spain. Discussion groups were started in prisons, churches, government agencies, and even in a South African village.

Beyond the conspiracy I had described, there was a community of respected leaders scanning the horizon for helpful new ideas. This community was a dynamic counterpart to the traditional power structure. I found myself talking to — and learning from — such diverse groups as health educators, nuclear physicists, school counselors, Canadian farm wives, members of Congress, data processing managers, hotel executives, state administrators, medical librarians, college presidents, and international gatherings of youth and business leaders.

There were thousands of letters, whose common motif was relief: "Thank God, I'm not alone." People said they were strengthened by knowing that change is not only possible but under way. One woman wrote, "The voices are no longer crying in the wilderness."

More hearts harbored the dream of a better world than I had imagined in my wildest moments. The impact of the vision continues to surprise me.

Certainly these headlong years have seen the erosion of tradition and an escalation of chaos and rebellion. Yet here and there, as promised, we can see a rising force of creative organizers, some even drawn from the ranks of ex-rebels. We are beginning to realize — or remember — that ours is a common fate. And that may be the biggest news.

We need not know the outcome of these stories to play a part in them. Because there are always forces and countervailing forces, each day we choose which wave to support. Will we contribute to the problem or the solution? Will we see possibilities or impossibilities? From the perspective of critics, we will focus on what can't be done. From the perspective of creators, we will know what must be done.

The time of spectators is fast coming to a close. Let us choose, sooner rather than later, to be masters of construction.

"The New Age watershed classic" *American Bookseller*

WITH A NEW AFTERWORD AND UPDATED RESOURCE LIST

# The AQUARIAN CONSPIRACY

### Personal and Social Transformation in Our Time

**MARILYN FERGUSON**

Foreword by John Naisbitt

**The Aquarian Conspiracy**
*Personal and Social Transformation in Our Time*
By Marilyn Ferguson
1980/448 pages
**$9.95**
$12.35 postpaid from:
Jeremy P. Tarcher, Inc.
9110 Sunset Blvd.
Los Angeles, CA 90069

*This book is a powerful and wide-ranging view of human possibility. Marilyn Ferguson addressses each area of daily living — from home to school to health to politics — with an illumination of the possibilities for expansion and renewal. For millions of "underground Aquarian" networkers who have read it,* The Aquarian Conspiracy *remains a source of inspiration and encouragement for continued striving toward renewal of ourselves, our society, and our planet.*

# Nostradamus

Nostradamus (Michel de Nostradamus 1503-1566) has acquired a unique place in history by predicting, in minute detail and with astonishing accuracy, the future of the world. Throughout history, his ten recorded volumes of prophecy, called The Centuries, have defied explanation by consistently forseeing future events. His volumes have constantly remained in print, although to this day, his magnificent ability and mystical experience are still shrouded in mystery.

## Nostradamus and the Millennium
### *Predictions of the Future*
By John Hogue
1987/208 pages
**$16.95**
$17.89 postpaid from:
Doubleday & Co.
501 Franklin Ave.
Garden City, NY 11530

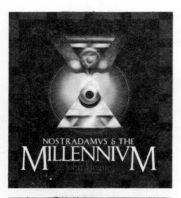

A book for our times, this beautiful volume presents Nostradamus and his works alongside fully documented pictorial material.

The main thrust of this clearly presented book, however, is the much prophecized events surrounding the year 2000 A.D. Along with popular prophesies of doom and apocalypse, Nostradamus also illuminates the other possible path of conscious enlightenment which is included in our predictive future, if man so chooses that road.

## Nostradamus' Diary

A great famine through a pestilent wave.
(It) will extend its rain over the length of the arctic pole,
Samarobrin, one hundred leagues from the hemisphere,
They shall live without law, exempt from politics.

Two recent discoveries of anti-AIDS test drugs bring another of Nostradamus' quatrains to the forefront of interest. As so often with this remarkable prophet, it is not possible to detect his meanings until actual new words appear in our languages. The two drugs in question are suramin and ribavarin. In the quatrain ... the name *"Samarobrin"* appears — a word that has had interpreters of the prophet scratching their heads for years! Whatever it is, it is hovering above us some two hundred and seventy miles high — perhaps a Soviet satellite — "samo" means self and "robrin" means operator in Russian — self-operator?

In the past this quatrain was applied to the Spanish Influenza of 1918 which followed World War I. But we may now apply it more readily to AIDS — a disease which belongs to the family of lentilviruses found in sheep, goats, and horses — capable of taking a mutated form which would eventually rain on us from the air.

But then we can also return from this macabre interpretation of the quatrain naming *"Samarobrin"* to the first suggested meaning of the two anti-virus drugs suramin and ribavarin. Perhaps Nostradamus is trying to tell us the combination effect of these two drugs, in some way related to zero-gravity laboratories in satellite space. Such work already happens and it may be that a time will come, however extreme it may seem now, when scientists fight to produce a remedy for a plague-torn Earth in labs high above the planet.

- John Hogue
From Nostradamus and the Millennium

## Nostradamus Comments on Soviet/U.S. Alliance in the Middle East

One day the great powers will become friends
Their great power will be seen to increase.
The new land (America) will be at the height of its power.
To the man of blood (the anti-christ) the number is reported.
The two will not remain allied for long,

Within the thirteen years they surrender to barbare and Iranian leaders
There will be such a loss on both sides, that one will bless Petrus Romanus (the end of millennium Pope).

- John Hogue
From Nostradamus and the Millennium

## A Vision of the Aquarian Age
### The Emerging Spiritual World View

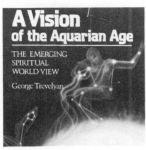

By George Trevelyan
1984/172 pages
**$6.95**
$8.95 postpaid from:
Stillpoint Publishing
Box 640
Meetinghouse Rd.
Walpole, NH 03608

*Trevelyan gives us a vision and hope for what is possible in the emerging world view of complete spirituality. His enlightened interpretation of human, social, and planetary trends awakens in us the full significance of the Age of Aquarius.*

## Time for Changes

We have stressed that we are living in apocalyptic days. We must expect changes — social, psychological, and even in the outer world. Many think that man's treatment of the living earth has been such that this great sentient being will strike back in protest. Whether that be literally true or not, we are in any case in an epoch for which we have no precedent in history. What then should we do? Often we feel helpless and revert to brain tracks or habits which lead us back into old anachronistic reactions and an opportunity is therefore thrown away. How often we "kick ourselves" for doing this! But how *do* we move forward into change? One clue may lie with the Chinese, in whose language there is no word for "crisis." The closest Chinese approximation is "opportunity for important decisions."

> - *George Trevelyan*
> *From A Vision of the Aquarian Age*

## The Evolutionary Journey
### A Personal Guide to a Positive Future

By Barbara Marx Hubbard
1982/178 pages
**$7.95**
$8.95 postpaid from:
Mindbody Communications
3339 Kipling Street
Palo Alto, CA 94306

*In truly optimistic and visionary style, Barbara Marx Hubbard awakens and then ignites the creative and transformative spark in each of us. She integrates the vision of the potential human on planet Earth with the practical reality of where we stand now. This book charts a course of how we might proceed.*

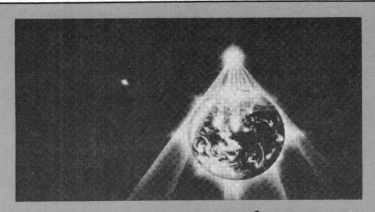

# Take the Perspective of a More Mature Species. What Might We Be Like When We Grow Up, Stop Fighting, and Start Using All Our Capacities Harmoniously?

In order to understand ourselves at this early phase of our universal history, take a moment to envision Humanity as we can become as we mature through this critical transition from Earth-only to universal life. What would it be like if everything we now know we can do, worked? This would include education, health, communications, productivity, systems planning, space, cybernetics, genetics, spirituality, psychic abilities, etc.

We assume that the future is not predetermined but prepatterned. The fifteen billion year process of transformation is continuing in our age. We have learned to expect synthesis, newness, a rise in consciousness, freedom, and beauty at every step of the spiral. The process is prophetic and we are the product of the process. The story of creation is written in our blood and bones. In some sense, then, we already "know" the next step for our species, as a young child "knows" it will grow. Try to trigger your "memory of the future."

> - *Barbara Marx Hubbard*
> *From The Evolutionary Journey*

## The Mayan Factor
### Path Beyond Technology
By Dr. José Argüelles
1987/222 pages
**$12.95**
$14.95 postpaid from:
Bear & Co.
P.O. Drawer 2860
Santa Fe, NM 87504-2860

*In this currently much quoted and reviewed text, especially in relation to the Harmonic Convergence (August 16-17, 1987), Dr. Argüelles interprets the philosophy and science of ancient Mayan cosmology. What is revealed is the prophetic vision concerning our present time and awakening on this planet. The ideas in this book are fascinating and beautifully inspiring.*

## The Global Brain
### Speculations on the Evolutionary Leap to Planetary Consciousness

By Peter Russell
1983/252 pages
**$9.95**
$12.35 postpaid from:
Jeremy P. Tarcher, Inc.
9110 Sunset Blvd.
Los Angeles, CA 90069

*Drawing on recent information from the physical, natural, and social sciences, as well as mysticism and philosophy, Peter Russell suggests that the human species is on the verge of achieving a quantum leap in evolution toward a core existence based on spirituality. This book leads us to understand how worldwide transformation, in individual consciousness and society as a whole, is not only possible, but very probable.*

# The Harmonic Convergence

The great return of Harmonic Convergence, then, is like an awakening from cultural trance. It is the opportunity for all to engage the Mayan Factor, and, in a word, to receive the galactic imprint. Though at first we do not appear to be Mayan, by the time we reach the moment for galactic synchronization our way of life shall be in every regard a modeling after the lifestyle of the Maya who preceded us in Central America. Only we shall find ourselves as planetary Maya, possessing a brilliantly simple and sophisticated technology based on the matching of solar and psychic frequencies which harmonize the "ratio of the sense-fields." Creating a nonpolluting technology, we shall allow ourselves to subsist comfortably in small bioregional groups, strung together as information nodes on a communications system that has finally dispensed with wires. And lastly, availing ourselves of the leisure time to which our genetic hardware had originally disposed us, we shall collectively come to know as one. In that knowing, our life shall pass into the greater life. The mystery of the unknown which has always beckoned us, by the light it contained in its question, will expand us into levels of being and knowing undreamed of by the strifeworn ego of the old mental house.

*- José Argüelles*
*From* The Mayan Factor

# Emergence

The concept of wei-chi allows us to appreciate the importance of both aspects of crisis. In recent years, our attention has generally been focused on the *wei*, on the many possibilities for global catastrophe and how to avoid them. This will continue to be necessary as we strive to deal with the very real problems that face us. At the same time, these crises may lead us to question some of our basic attitudes and values: Why are we here? What do we *really* want? Isn't there more to life? This questioning opens us up to the other aspects of crisis, *chi*: the opportunity to change direction, to benefit from the prodigious and breathtaking possibilities that could be before us.

*- Peter Russell*
*From* The Global Brain

## Megatrends
### Ten New Directions Transforming Our Lives

By John Naisbitt
1982/290 pages
**$4.95**
$5.95 postpaid from:
Warner Books, Inc.
P.O. Box 690
New York, NY 10019

*In this well-researched and insightful analysis, John Naisbitt has identified ten national trends for America, which may well set the pace for the world. Although Megatrends in no way associates itself with "the New Age" movement, its conclusions, not surprisingly, coincide directly with projections of New Age thinking.*

## Megatrends

1) Although we continue to think we live in an industrial society, we have in fact changed to an economy based on the creation and distribution of information. 2) We are moving in the dual directions of high tech/high touch, matching each new technology with a compensatory human response. 3) No longer do we have the luxury of operating within an isolated, self-sufficient, national economic system; we now must acknowledge that we are part of a global economy. We have begun to let go of the idea that the United States is and must remain the world's industrial leaders as we move on to other tasks. 4) We are restructuring from a society run by short-term considerations and rewards in favor of dealing with things in much longer-term time frames. 5) In cities and states, in small organizations and subdivisions, we have rediscovered the ability to act innovatively and to achieve results — from the bottom up. 6) We are shifting from institutional help to more self-reliance in all aspects of our lives. 7) We are discovering that the framework of representative democracy has become obsolete in an era of instantaneously shared information. 8) We are giving up our dependence on hierarchical structures in favor of informal networks. This will be especially important to the business community. 9) More Americans are living in the South and West, leaving behind the old industrial cities of the North. 10) From a narrow either/or society with a limited range of personal choices, we are exploding into a free-wheeling multiple-option society.

        *- John Naisbitt*
        *From* Megatrends

## Vision

By Ken Carey
1985/94 pages
**$6.95**
$7.95 postpaid from:
Uni Sun
P.O. Box 25421
Kansas City, MO 64119

*These words comprise a vision and message of hope as received by the author from the One Spirit at the source of all life. His single-hearted desire has been to record and share these words that they may serve as inspiration to all who read them and welcome the Holy Spirit into their lives.*

### The Awakening

Humankind has multiplied and filled the earth. The time approaches for me to awaken within the human family as a dreamer awakens within a single body. My awakening causes the fearful and the loving to separate as oil and water.

For millennia I have been guiding your species to greater intelligence that today I might bring this message to my people. I would that you join me in my awareness. Know my Presence behind your events. Beneath the fabric of a superficial world, see, as I do, the Kingdom Of Heaven appearing in all its brilliance.

During the earth's next few passages around the sun, your perception of the true world will increase. For this is my world, The Emerging Sacred Reality, and because of its appearance on Earth, all things shall be made new. The old world, the historical world, has been organized in fear. My world is organized in love. A New Earth begins to take form. An Emerging Reality, rooted in love, respect, and peaceful cooperation, begins to settle across the face of Terra. To you, my coming appears as a long process with a single event at its conclusion. To me, my incarnation is a single event, which humankind would only accept as a process.

Join me now, as many are doing throughout the Earth, making conscious in human time what is already the Reality in Heaven. Creator and Creation are joined in physical flesh; for it is One Life that pulses within every body. We have now only to be joined in consciousness, in awareness, and all will be fulfilled according to prophesy. For these days were destined to come and those who are alive in these times have elected to see them.

        *- From* Vision

# Vision

By Ken Carey, author of *The Starseed Transmissions*, with an introduction by Jean Houston.

# Global Concerns

## S.O.S.

Many of us worry about the situation of the world. We don't know when the bombs will explode. We feel that we are on the edge of time. As individuals, we feel helpless, despairing. The situation is so dangerous, injustice is so widespread, the danger is so close. In this kind of situation, if we panic, things will only become worse. We need to remain calm, to see clearly. Meditation is to be aware, and to try to help.

I like to use the example of a small boat crossing the Gulf of Siam. In Vietnam, there are many people, called boat people, who leave the country in small boats. Often the boats are caught in rough seas or storms, the people may panic, and boats can sink. But if even one person aboard can remain calm, lucid, knowing what to do and what not to do, he or she can help the boat survive. His or her expression

— face, voice — communicates clarity and calmness, and people have trust in that person. They will listen to what he or she says. One such person can save the lives of many.

Our world is something like a small boat. Compared with the cosmos, our planet is a very small boat. We are about to panic because our situation is no better than the situation of the small boat in the sea. You know that we have more than 50,000 nuclear weapons.

Humankind has become a very dangerous species. We need people who can sit still and be able to smile, who can walk peacefully. We need people like that in order to save us. Mahayana Buddhism says that you are that person, that each of you is that person.

*- Thich Nhat Hanh*
*From* Being Peace

---

## Being Peace

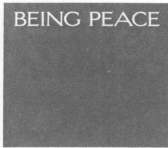

By Thich Nhat Hanh
1987/116 pages
**$8.50**
$10.00 postpaid from:
Parallax Press
P.O. Box 7355
Berkeley, CA 94707

*In this book of lectures to American peace activists and students of meditation, Thich Nhat Hanh — poet, Zen master and chairman of the Vietnamese Buddhist Peace delegation during the war — discusses the importance of being peace in order to make peace.*

## The Windstar Journal

P.O. Box 503
Snowmass, CO 81654

*A bimonthly publication of superior quality from the Windstar Foundation. The journal offers articles and poetry expressing ideas, methods and energy of a transformational planetary consciousness. Contributing authors include the leading thinkers and spokespeople from this emerging platform of planetary philosophy.*

## The Windstar Foundation
P.O. Box 286
Snowmass, CO 81654
203-927-4777
**$35.00**/Membership annually

*The Windstar Foundation is a non-profit education and demonstration center founded in 1976 by John Denver. Based on 1,000 acres in the Rocky Mountains, Windstar provides on-site educational programs in renewable energy and for production technologies, land stewardship and global resource management, conflict resolution, international citizens exchange and personal and community growth. Through conferences, publications, audio and video productions, and out-reach through a world-wide community-at-large, the Windstar Foundation connects people with one another and with vital information guiding the way to a peaceful, sustainable future.*

# Nuclear Free Zone:

Any well-defined geographical area, regardless of size, in which no nuclear weapons shall be produced, transported, stored, processed, disposed of, or detonated. Neither shall any facility, equipment, supply or substance for their production, transportation, storage, processing, disposal, or detonation be permitted within its borders.

## Tell the World

If you declare a Nuclear Free Zone, let people know. Besides the President and your representative and senators, you can tell members of your city and state governments. Nuclear Free America keeps a running total of NFZs, and would love to hear from you. In addition, the following nations possess nuclear weapons (or "peaceful nuclear devices"). Your action deserves their attention, and you can request to be taken off any target lists.

Office of the Ambassador
Embassy of the USSR
1125 16th St. NW
Washington, DC 20036

Office of the Ambassador
Embassy of the United Kingdom
3100 Massachusetts Ave. NW
Washington, DC 20008

Office of the Ambassador
Embassy of France
2535 Belmond Rd. NW
Washington, DC 20008

Office of the Ambassador
People's Republic of China
230 Connecticut Ave. NW
Washington, DC 20008

Office of the Ambassador
Republic of India
2107 Massachusetts Ave. NW
Washington, DC 20008

For more information, contact:
**Nuclear Free America**
2521 Guilford Ave.
Baltimore, MD 21218
301-235-3575

## Volunteers for Peace, Inc.
Tiffany Rd.
Belmont, VT 05730
802-259-2759

*Volunteers for Peace sponsors the International workcamps program. Sometimes described as a short-term "peace corps," these projects involve living and working in a foreign country for a specified period of time on a particular project to foster first-hand communication and cooperation among nations. A free sample newsletter is available. $10 annual membership fee includes annual directory of over 300 international workcamp opportunities.*

## Citizen Exchange Council
18 E. 41st St.
New York, NY 10017
212-889-7960

*An independent, nonpolitical, non-profit organization which sponsors exchanges between Americans and Russians, living both in the United States and the USSR. By serving Americans in the USSR, Russians in the United States and citizens of both countries wishing to learn and exchange from each other, the CEC provides a broad base of services from which to choose.*

## World Peace University
35 S.E. 60th Ave.
Portland, OR 97215

*The goal of the World Peace University is to contribute to the creation of a world free of war, where peace is the way of life, where hunger no longer exists, and where individuals achieve their highest degree of personal fulfillment.*

In March 1986 the University for Peace designated the World Peace University as a Center of the University for Peace, United Nations. The University for Peace is a United Nations affiliated organization in Costa Rica which was created by a United Nations Resolution in 1980. This designation grants the World Peace University the representation of interests of the University for Peace and the co-operative development of curriculum and projects.

# Understand Both Sides

Ths situation of the world is still like this. People completely identify with one side, one ideology. To understand the suffering and the fear of a citizen of the Soviet Union, we have to become one with him or her. To do so is dangerous — we will be suspected by both sides. But if we don't do it, if we align ourselves with one side or the other, we will lose our chance to work for peace. Reconciliation is to understand both sides, to go to one side and describe the suffering being endured by the other side, and then to go to the other side and describe the suffering being endured by the first side. Doing only that will be a great help for peace.

During a retreat at the Providence Zen Center, I asked someone to express himself as a swimmer in a river, and then after 15 minutes of breathing, to express himself as the river. He had to become the river to be able to express himself in the language and feelings of the river. After that a woman who had been in the Soviet Union was asked to express herself as an American, and after some breathing and meditation, as a Soviet citizen, with all her fears and her hope for peace. She did it wonderfully. These are exercises of meditation related to nonduality.

- *Thich Nhat Hanh*
*From* Being Peace

# Getting to Know the Other Side

## Summitry

In general, summitry simply means going to the top. We ordinarily think of the top as being occupied by officeholders rather than by citizens. Since war is conducted by nations, it's assumed that peace is likewise necessarily created "at the highest levels." All that citizens can do, according to this theory, is vote for the best available leaders and then acquiesce in what they do, unless their actions become flagrantly counterproductive.

A different perspective was offered, in striking terms, by Dwight D. Eisenhower, who had commanded a great army and who, when he spoke, was President of the U.S. "I like to believe," he said in 1959, "that people in the long run are going to do more to promote peace than are governments." He may have liked to believe this because he knew from direct experience how awful wars are — how awful they were even prior to the nuclear age — and also how awkward governments have generally been in preventing them.

"Indeed," he continued, "I think that people want peace so much that one of these days governments had better get out of their way and let them have it." Is this a bit of populist chatter from an old Kansan, or does Eisenhower have a deeper message than may at first appear? What would it mean for governments to "get out of (the people's) way"? And how could ordinary people possibly go about contributing to peace?

> *- Don Carlson and*
> *Craig Comstock*
> *From* Citizen Summitry

---

> *Most of the things worth doing in the world had been declared impossible before they were done.*
>
> —Louis Brandeis

## Citizen Summitry
### *Keeping the Peace When It Matters Too Much to be Left to Politicians*
Edited by Don Carlson and Craig Comstock
1986/396 pages
**$11.95**
$14.35 postpaid from:
Jeremy P. Tarcher, Inc.
9110 Sunset Blvd.
Los Angeles, CA 90069

*Aware of global dangers but not obsessed by them, citizen diplomats are taking thousands of initiatives to reach out to people on the other side and create networks of shared interests. This book is about their endeavors, their lives and philosophies in learning to envision a positive future and work together for it.*

## The Peace Packet
### *Institute of Noetic Sciences*

1982
**$12.95**
$14.45 postpaid from:
Institute of Noetic Sciences
P.O. Box 97
Sausalito, CA 94966

*Find your place in the peace movement! The packet is divided into three sections. The Readings section provides a historical and conceptual orientation to peace with emphasis on U.S./U.S.S.R. relations. The Inner work section offers suggestions on how to get in touch with your own attitudes about peace and how to use techniques such as relaxation, visualization, and affirmation to enhance your work with peace. The Outer Work section helps you discover your own opportunities and move easily into the roles that best fit you.*

## Paths to Peace
### *Exploring the Feasibility of Sustainable Peace*

By Richard Smoke with Willis Harman
1987/114 pages
**$10.95**
$13.45 postpaid from:
Institute of Noetic Sciences
P.O. Box 97
Sausalito, CA 94966

*Outlining nine basic approaches that have been used in the past to achieve peace, this books goal is to help the reader understand possible ways of eliminating the threat of nuclear war and feel impowered to take action. Including a scenario that may make a stable state of peace possible in the foreseeable future, this book is appropriate for all levels - from the upper echelons of government policymaking to the individual in action.*

## PEACEVISION

P.O. Box 271985
Houston, TX 77277
713-667-1413

*PEACEVISION is an organization committed to peace and planetary upliftment and is dedicated to producing and promoting ideas, individuals, and groups which are committed to peace and cooperation on a global scale.*

*PEACEVISION products focus exclusively on positive images and products of peace. Excellent for fundraisers.*

*Bumper stickers. 4″ x 12″, vivid sky* blue background with white lettering. 1-9 stickers at $1.00 each, 10-18 stickers at 50¢ each, 150 stickers at 30¢ each.

*Mini stickers 1-1½″ diameter. Also* available in a combination of languages. 15 for $1.00 or a roll of 500 for $15.00.

*T-Shirts.* Royal blue with white lettering. 50% cotton/50% polyester blend. S (34-36), M (38-40), L (42-44) and XL (46-48) $9.00.

Other products available include sweatshirt, Peace Trek poster and puzzle and HUGG-A-PLANET huggable 12″ globe.

# VISUALIZE WORLD PEACE

PEACEVISION  P.O.Box 271985  Houston, TX 77277

## National Campaign for Peace Tax Fund

2121 Decatur Pl., N.W.
Washington, DC 20008
202-483-3751

*A Peace Tax Fund is being proposed as an alternative fund in the U.S. Treasury. Every month, the IRS would be required to transfer tax receipts designated for the Peace Tax Fund into that special fund. Taxpayers who qualify to participate in the Peace Tax Fund may designate that their income, estate and gift taxes go to the Fund.*

### ◀How PTF Bill Would Work

*The Peace Tax Fund Bill would amend the Internal Revenue Code to provide that a taxpayer conscientiously opposed to participation of any kind in war could have his or her income, estate, and gift tax payments spent for nonmilitary purposes only.*

*That percentage of his or her taxes which equals the current military expenditures portion of the federal budget would go into a special trust fund administered by eleven trustees who have demonstrated a consistent commitment to world peace, international friendship, and the peaceful resolution of international conflict.*

*The PTF Bill will become law when our individual and united actions make clear to Congress how important its provisions are.*

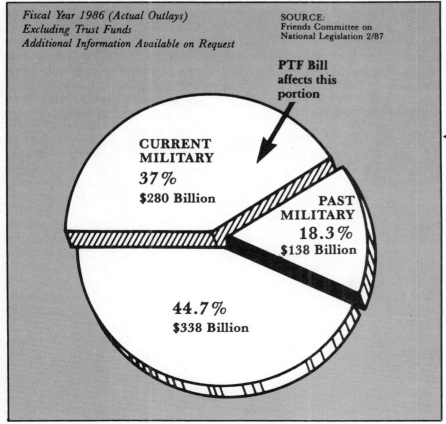

*Fiscal Year 1986 (Actual Outlays)*
*Excluding Trust Funds*
*Additional Information Available on Request*

SOURCE:
Friends Committee on
National Legislation 2/87

**PTF Bill affects this portion**

**CURRENT MILITARY**
**37%**
**$280 Billion**

**PAST MILITARY**
**18.3%**
**$138 Billion**

**44.7%**
**$338 Billion**

# Finding Effective Lower-Risk Means of Defense

George F. Kennan combines direct observation of the Soviet Union and of the American government, historical savvy, and the experience of diplomatic responsibility. Bold in argument yet circumspect in his treatment of evidence, deeply cultured, unblinking in his view of tyranny, imaginative in his sense of the future, Kennan is what the Japanese would call a "living national treasure."

From serving in Moscow during the time of Stalin, Kennan has long known in his bones that millions can suddenly be killed — as by a tyrant, so by the bomb. It can actually happen. Frustrated by prolonged arms control negotiations — which are not even about reducing the numbers of weapons, but simply about restraining further testing and deployment — he offers a simple proposal. If both sides would benefit from a deep cut in the number of weapons, let's not haggle over "asymmetries" in the "force posture" of the two sides. As a first step, let's agree to cut all categories of weapons by half, to be verified by the intelligence services of both sides. Then let's make another big cut.

Kennan knows that merely reducing the number of weapons will not save us. The current stockpiles are so grotesque that a tiny fraction of them could destroy our civilization. But making a deep cut would do what Don Carlson calls "breaking the trance." By reminding us that another way is possible, it would resuscitate our imaginations.

> - *Don Carlson and*
> *Craig Comstock*
> From Securing Our Planet

---

*It was a thought that built this whole portentous war establishment, and a thought shall melt it away.*

> - Ralph Waldo Emerson

---

## Securing Our Planet
### *How to Succeed When Threats Are Too Risky and There's Really No Defense*
Edited by Don Carlson and Craig Comstock
1986/396 pages
**$11.95**
$14.35 postpaid from:
Jeremy P. Tarcher, Inc.
9110 Sunset Blvd.
Los Angeles, CA 90069

*A companion volume to* Citizen Summitry, *this book draws together 36 chapters of powerful ideas on how to shift from threats to a network of positive relations.*

*Some of our country's most heralded spokespeople, past and present, offer their visions and plans for peace through economics, space exploration, and the collective efforts of all of humanity.*

## The Peace Catalog
### *A Guidebook to a Positive Future*
Edited by Duane Sweeney
1984/364 pages
**$14.95**
$16.95 postpaid from:
Press for Peace
c/o Penichet Publishing Co.
2514 South Grand Ave.
Los Angeles, CA 90007

*The Peace Catalog is an ideal resource for anyone interested in preventing nuclear war and attaining world peace. The catalog presents concrete, down-to-earth ideas for individual and collective action and a directory of over 1,000 peace organizations all across the U.S.*

In the declaration of Nuclear Free Zones, citizens and communities proclaim their unconditional opposition to the nuclear arms race by banning not only nuclear weapons from their midst but also any facility, equipment, or supply associated with them. This is the essence of being nuclear-free. Some communities may go further and also

renounce the right to be "defended" by the use or threatened use of nuclear weapons.

Nuclear Free Zones have proliferated in England, Europe, Australia, New Zealand, and Japan. All of Wales is Nuclear Free and there are broad-based popular campaigns toward the same end in Canada and the Pacific Islands. Nuclear Free Zones are thus an important global link. They bring diverse national peace movements closer together and, through "twinning" with cities in Eastern Europe and the Soviet Union, can link East and West.

> - *From* The Peace Catalog

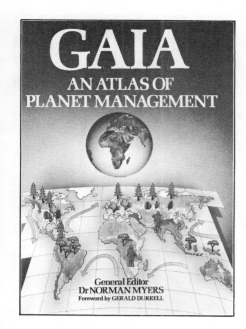

## Gaia
### An Atlas of Planet Management
Edited By Dr. Norman Myers
1984/272 pages
**$17.95**
$18.89 postpaid from:
Doubleday & Co.
501 Franklin Ave.
Garden City, NY 11530

*Described as an atlas, this is a colorful, oversize book packed with pictures and color drawings illustrating a concise, informative text. It examines the complex ecosphere, the earth we have inherited, and the earth we are creating.*

### Antarctic Convergence
The band of the Southern Ocean between 50° and 60°S is known as the Antarctic Convergence. Counter-rotating currents of cold and sub-Antarctic water travelling northwards (the East and West Wind Drifts) here pass under and interact with subtropical water moving south. The resulting turbulence drives nutrient-rich water to the surface, making the area highly productive, with great swarms of a crustacean known as krill forming the staple food for penguins, seals, squid, and whales.

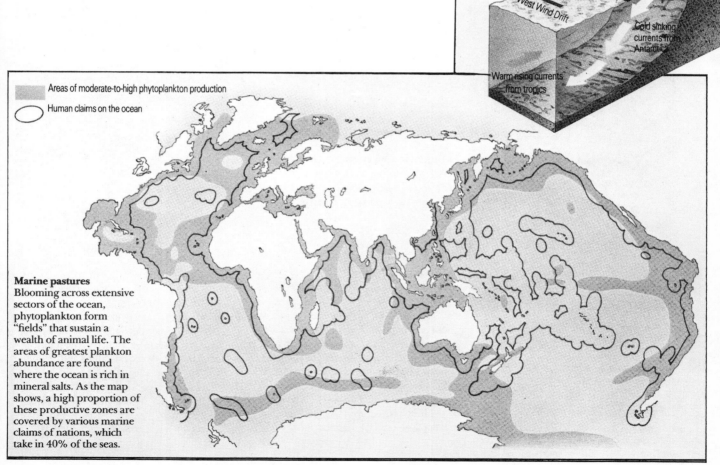

- Areas of moderate-to-high phytoplankton production
- Human claims on the ocean

### Marine pastures
Blooming across extensive sectors of the ocean, phytoplankton form "fields" that sustain a wealth of animal life. The areas of greatest plankton abundance are found where the ocean is rich in mineral salts. As the map shows, a high proportion of these productive zones are covered by various marine claims of nations, which take in 40% of the seas.

*- From Gaia*

# Earth Changes

One of the more consistent New Age themes is Earth Changes. From *The Book of Revelation* in the *Nostradamus Bible* to Edgar Cayce, there seems to be information saying that something is happening and will culminate sometime around the year 2,000. Ruth Montgomery's spirit guides say there will be a pole shift — the Earth will literally tip on its axis, spreading destruction and usher us into a Golden Age. Others say this is primarily a shift in human consciousness as evidenced by the great interest surrounding the Harmomic Convergence in August, 1987. The H.C. centered on the Mayan calendar which began its final 25 year cycle on that date.

What exactly will these Earth Changes be? It's up to you to decide ...

## Earth Changes Update

By Hugh Lynn Cayce
1980/130 pages
**$5.95**
$7.95 postpaid from:
A.R.E. Press
Box 595
Virginia Beach, VA 23451

*Edgar Cayce's readings in the 1920's and '30's frequently commented on Earth changes coming up at the end of the century. Here, Cayce's late son Hugh Lynn examines Cayce's predictions compared to news reports of geologic activity.*

# Cayce's Dream of Changes

This is a dream which Edgar Cayce had in 1936, on a train from Detroit to Virginia Beach. This followed court proceedings resulting from the family's arrest in Detroit for practicing medicine without a license. Edgar Cayce was troubled over the happening. How could the good he was trying to accomplish be so misunderstood? The dream:

"I had been born again in 2100 A.D. in Nebraska. The sea apparently covered all of the western part of the country, as the city where I lived was on the coast. The family name was a strange one. At an early age as a child I declared myself to be Edgar Cayce who had lived 200 years before.

"Scientists, men with long beards, little hair, and thick glasses, were called in to observe me. They decided to visit the places where I said I had been born, lived and worked, in Kentucky, Alabama, New York, Michigan, and Virginia. Taking me with them, the group of scientists visited these places in a long, cigar-shaped metal flying ship which moved at high speed.

"Water covered part of Alabama. Norfolk, Virginia, had become an immense seaport. New York had been destroyed either by war or an earthquake and was being rebuilt. Industries were scattered over the countryside. Most of the houses were of glass.

"Many records of my work as Edgar Cayce were discovered and collected. The group returned to Nebraska taking the records with them to study."

**These changes in the earth will come to pass, for the time and times and half times are at an end, and there begin those periods for the readjustments. For how hath He given? "The righteous shall inherit the earth."**

**Hast thou, my brethren, a heritage in the earth?**

- *part of the follow-up Edgar Cayce reading #294-185, June 30, 1936 From Earth Changes Update*

# The End Times & Armageddon
## *Dick Sutphen Asks the Experts*

*Is the Earth and its inhabitants changing? Dick Sutphen poses this question to Jess Stearn, Charles Cayce, Brad Steiger, Steven Halpern, Alan Vaughan, Edith Fiore, Freda Morris, and Bill Baldwin.*

*The second side of the tape discusses the Law of Grace. Can it alter destiny?*

# 1958-1998 A.D.

The earth will be broken up in the western portion of America. The greater portion of Japan must go into the sea. The upper portion of Europe will be changed as in the twinkling of an eye. Land will appear off the east coast of America. There will be the upheavals in the Arctic and in the Antarctic that will make for the eruption of volcanoes in the Torrid areas, and there will be the shifting then of the poles — so that where there have been those of a frigid or semi-tropical will become the more tropical, and moss and fern will grow. And these will begin in those periods in '58 to '98

- *Edgar Cayce reading #3976-15, January 19, 1934 From Earth Changes Update*

## 5/5/2000
### *Ice: The Ultimate Disaster*

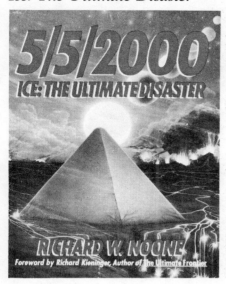

By Richard W. Noone
1982/358 pages
**$9.95**
$13.45 postpaid from:
Crown Publishers
34 Englehard Ave.
Avenel, NJ 07001

*5/5/2000 is the product of seven years of research and investigation. His thesis is simple: ice is building upon the South Pole. In the year 2,000 planets in our solar system will be aligned for the first time in 6,000 years. The combination of cosmic pull and the weight of the ice will create a pole shift with the earth literally shifting on its axis.*

## Pole Shift

By John White
1980/414 pages
**$5.95**
$7.95 postpaid from:
A.R.E. Press
Box 595
Virginia Beach, VA 23451

*Has the Earth shifted on its axis in the past? Will it happen again? John White gathers scientific evidence and intuitive insight to shed some light on this disturbing possibility.*

# Pole Shift

Hugh Auchincloss Brown collected material for his theory of pole-shift for more than fifty years, spending years and years on investigating such things as:

- What immense force quick-froze hundreds of animals in Siberia with grasses in their stomachs?
- By what process were entire tropical forests and volatile raindrops instantly arrested and fossilized?
- How could a soft jellyfish be quick-frozen along with oysters, clams, crabs, and starfish and turned to stone?
- How could a tree with fruit and leaves still on it be found in Siberia, quick-frozen?
- Why are there only but a few waterfalls on earth older than about 6,000 years?

These questions, one by one, Brown answers in his book. He eventually came to believe that a sudden and radical shift of the earth's axis is caused by a sudden and radical shift of one or both of the earth's icecaps. When the pole-shift takes place, continents and sea areas are rearranged, so tropical regions suddenly become lands of ice and snow, and lands of ice and snow suddenly become tropical. Brown ends Part One of his book by saying:

People of education and initiative must become awakened to full awareness of the lurking danger represented by this wanton titanic power which is ready, able, and destined to end our civilization — if left uncontrolled by man ... An awakening to the danger among the people at large is the first requisite ... It will indeed become a matter of great personal interest to many people ... once we know that our lives are at stake!

> *- Richard W. Noone*
> *From 5/5/2000*

---

The south becomes north and the Earth turns over.

> *- Egyptian Magical Papyrus*
> *Harris*
> *From 5/5/2000*

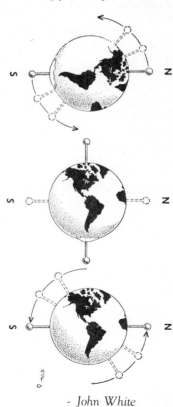

> *- John White*
> *From Pole Shift*

# Earth Spirit
## The Nature Spirits

Some people, possibly more than we realize, talk to the plants in their gardens and houses. Since nobody likes to be made to feel foolish, care is taken not to be caught in the act, and silent rather than voiced speech is used. Is it foolish to talk to plants? They do not move about like animals, and they are inarticulate; but they are alive and, in fact, have a kind of consciousness. People who are sensitive know this and are careful and considerate in the way they handle them.

It is essential to understand the true nature of the plants one cultivates in order to look after and handle them properly. (The word "plant" is used here to include all members of the vegetable kingdom: trees, bushes, flowers, fruits, vegetables and so on.) That plants are sensitive is now becoming a well-known fact. For some years a considerable amount of scientific research has been devoted to demonstrating the reality of this sensitivity. Probably one of the first to study the subject was the remarkable Indian physicist, Sir Jagadis Chandra Bose, who did his work in the early part of this century. For example, he believed that plants suffer severe shock in being transplanted, which delays their establishment in a new place and sets back growth. So before transplanting, he anaesthetized a plant by covering it with a glass bell jar into which he introduced chloroform vapor. Plants treated in this way took at once to their new environment, thus proving his point.

The work of Cleve Backster and Marcel Vogel in the U.S.A. has demonstrated that plants are sensitive even to human thoughts.

This does not mean that people with gardens ought, for example, to give trees a shot of anaesthetic before a branch is cut off or that flowers should be offered a whiff of nitrous oxide before being picked. It does mean that plants should be treated with care and consideration and, indeed, with appreciation for the service they give to man.

However, the true nature of plants cannot be described by scientific data only. My experience with the elemental kingdom has demonstrated that to me, opening up a deeper understanding of nature, and the nature spirits, the elementals.

Their realm is intangible and nonmaterial, and cannot be appreciated by means of the five physical senses, except in a condition of heightened awareness. The existence of the elemental kingdom

cannot be proved to the satisfaction of the scientist, nor can the reactions of its inhabitants be demonstrated in the laboratory. Yet to one perceiving with the higher senses, it is as real as any of the more material kingdoms.

When we see the leaves change color in autumn, we might wonder how this is brought about. The botanist has one explanation, based on observation and analysis. The elemental kingdom has another, attributing the work to the energy forms known as fairies and elves. Both are right. It all depends on the way you look at it.

*- R. Ogilvie Crombie*
*From* The Findhorn Garden

---

### The Findhorn Foundation
Findhorn, Movay IV36 0TZ
Scotland

*Findhorn offers many residential programs and workshops. Visitors are also welcome to share the Findhorn experiences located in northern Scotland.*

## The Findhorn Garden

By The Findhorn Community
1975/180 pages
**$11.95**
$13.45 postpaid from:
Harper & Row
2350 Virginia Ave.
Hagerstown, MD 21740

*This is the wonderfully magical story of the Findhorn Community. It was the world's first living proof of what mankind can do working in cooperation with the nature spirits and energies. Findhorn was founded by Eileen and Peter Caddy and Dorothy MacLean. Gardening experts from around the world visited there to see roses blooming in winter and flowers and vegetables growing double and triple their normal size. It became apparent, though that Findhorn was much more than a garden. It had become a learning center - a place that demonstrates the cooperation between man and nature and the organic nature of consciousness attuned to the oneness of all life.*

# The Findhorn Garden

Our work in the garden had deeply rooted the energies of love and light in the very soil of Findhorn. The forces of nature had been our teachers, providing us with physical and spiritual nourishment. Just as in the evolution of the planet, plants had provided the environment that made it possible for man to develop, each of the plants we had been guided to grow here

contributed its energies toward creating the proper environment for Findhorn's greater work: the transformation of the human soul.

Indeed, the growth of the garden is symbolic of the growth of the soul. The proper environment must be created, weeds that might choke out the finer, more delicate qualities of the soul must be removed, and all actions must be guided by the love that fulfills all laws. Just as you can create conditions for insuring the growth of plants, so the quality of life within the Findhorn community can be likened to a greenhouse environment where the growth and transformation of each individual is stepped up.

In the beginning, while we were in the midst of establishing the garden, we could not see what it was moving toward. Thus, we had to live in the moment with faith in God's guidance. Now, looking back, a clear pattern and plan can be discerned, each apparent challenge seen as teaching the perfect lesson. A man quite untutored in the techniques of gardening was placed in this unpromising terrain and challenged to create a garden. He was provided with all the necessary channels and situations necessary to revive in him the spirit of true cooperation with nature, under the guidance of the God within. And the garden grew.

Much has been demonstrated at Findhorn of what can be done in a

spirit of cooperation between man and nature. There is so much we have yet to do. In the new phase of experimentation we are moving into in the garden, we must begin to live more fully what we have been given. Some of the directives we have received present great challenges, but we know we must proceed as we have always done, step-by-step, in faith that we are revealing the oneness of all life.

*- Peter Caddy*
*From* The Findhorn Garden

## The Perelandra Garden Workbook
### A Complete Guide to Gardening with Nature Intelligences

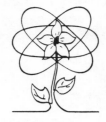

# THE PERELANDRA CATALOG

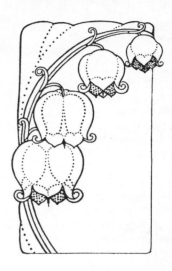

By Machaelle Small Wright
1987/250 pages
**$19.95**
$21.95 postpaid from:
Perelandra
Box 126
Jeffersonton, VA 22724

*A beautifully produced guide to conscious gardening by working with nature energies. This volume includes*

*how you can learn to communicate with the nature spirits (called devas), how to work with them in creating and maintaining your garden, selecting what to grow, improving the soil, fertilizing, harmonizing with seasonal and astrological cycles, harvesting, making and using flower essences, and much more. They also offer workshops, flower essences, and other helpful publications.*

---

# Deva of Soil

I wish to continue with the imagery of an orchestra — in particular, the concept of orchestration. As a plant germinates, grows and develops, it passes through a series of stages that when linked together as the full life cycle, creates a fine orchestration of movement, sound, pattern, light, intake, release. It crescendos and decrescendos. There are periods in the orchestration where the dynamic is that of a peaceful, still, summer lake. At other times, there is an explosion of life vitality of such magnitude one could liken it to fireworks in the sky. Just as one might sense the orchestration to be almost silent, there is suddenly a reverse and another swelling to a majestic crescendo.

The entire orchestration is created within the devic level of each plant

and is part of the blueprint. Once the Deva of the Garden has worked with you to position the various plants into the planting pattern, the blueprint energy of each plant, including its orchestration, begins to fuse into position within the garden itself. It is that fusion which enables me to get an accurate picture of what the soil will have to supply to each plant.

Usually, when humans consider fertilizing plants, they look at it as feeding for the purpose of facilitating growth. In one sense, this is accurate, but much too simplistic. We of the devic level see the soil activity as not just a support system but a comparable and fine orchestration in itself which, when played out, interweaves in harmony with the orchestration of the plant. The two orchestrations, one sounding from

above, the other from below, touch and intertwine in a way which creates one larger, fuller and more complex orchestration. When a garden is devically designed and positioned from above and devically prepared from below, the coming together of the two orchestrations occurs prior to seed and plant making contact with soil. This is one of the major benefits of such a garden. The orchestrations are already in place, interwoven, and playing out in perfect timing, and it is into this harmonious environment that seed and plant physically unite with soil.

*- The Deva of Soil
From* The Perelandra
Garden Workbook

# Landscape Angel to the Findhorn Gardeners

We would have you love the garden and all in it, putting your care and attention to it. But above all we would have you feel it all part of the One. It is not enough to grow plants merely for beauty, appearance or use. Grow them also because all are expressions of the whole.

You, too, are parts of the whole — part of that clod of earth, part of that tiny flower, part of the sunshine and the rain, the light in another's eye, the warmth of another's smile. And you are part of us, the angelic hosts who overlight and give life to the planet, who care for you all, though you know it not.

*- From* The Findhorn Garden

## The Secret Life of Plants
### *The Spiritual, Physical and Emotional Relations Between Plants and Man*

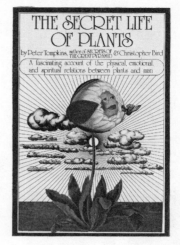

By Peter Tompkins and
Christopher Bird
1973/402 pages
**$9.95**
$11.45 postpaid from:
Harper & Row
2350 Virginia Ave.
Hagerstown, MD 21740

*Next time you cut down a tree, think about it. This is the classic book that explores the connections between plant and man. Yes, you can talk to your plants and, yes, they'll listen. The authors suggest that the most far-reaching revolution in the twentieth century might originate right in your garden.*

# Your Plant Knows What You're Doing

In another series of observations (measured by a polygraph), Backster noted that a special communion or bond of affinity appeared to be created between a plant and its keeper, unaffected by distance. With the use of synchronized stopwatches, Backster was able to note that his plants continued to react to his thought and attention from the next room, from down the hall, even from several buildings away. Back from a fifteen-mile trip to New Jersey, Backster was able to establish that his plants had perked up and shown definite and positive signs of response — whether it was relief or welcome he could not tell — at the very moment he had decided to return to New York.

When Backster was away on a lecture tour and talked about his initial 1966 observation, showing a slide of the original dracaena, the plant, back in his office, would show a reaction on the chart at the very time he projected the slide.

Once attuned to a particular person, plants appeared to be able to maintain a link with that person, no matter where he went, even among thousands of people. On New Year's Eve in New York City, Backster went out into the bedlam of Times Square armed with a notebook and stopwatch. Mingling with the crowd, he noted his various actions, such as walking, running, going underground by way of subway stairs, nearly getting run over, and having a mild fracas with a news vendor. Back at the lab, he found that each of three plants, monitored independently, showed similar reactions to his slight emotional adventures.

To see if he could get a reaction from plants at a much greater distance, Backster experimented with a female friend to establish whether her plants remained attuned to her on a seven-hundred-mile plane ride across the United States. From synchronized clocks they found a definite reaction from the plants to the friend's emotional stress each time the plane touched down for its landing.

*- Peter Tompkins and*
*Christopher Bird*
*From* The Secret Life
of Plants

## Behaving As If the God in All Life Mattered
### A *New Age* Ecology

By Machaelle Small Wright
1987/214 pages
**$9.95**
$11.45 postpaid from:
Perelandra
Box 136
Jeffersonton, VA 22724

*Machaelle Wright has created a Findhorn Garden in America where she cultivates the earth in cooperation with the earth energies, illustrating the oneness of all life.*

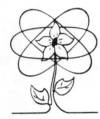

## To Care for the Earth

By Sean McDonagh
1986/224 pages
**$9.95**
$11.95 postpaid from:
Bear & Co.
P.O. Drawer 2860
Santa Fe, NM 87504

*If present trends continue, by the turn of the century we will face an environmental catastrophe as irreversible as any nuclear holocaust. Sean McDonagh's experience in the Philippines alerted him to the danger that threatens the Earth and the data he presents from other countries have reinforced this conclusion: In Mindanao, as in Brazil, forests are being destroyed; in Dublin Bay and in Central America pesticides poison air, water, and food; the lakes of Canada and Scandinavia and the German forests are polluted by acid rain.*

*Fortunately, awareness of the crisis is growing and ecology groups in many countries are calling for profound changes in the way human beings relate to the natural world. However, Christian churches have been slow to give a lead in this crucial area and McDonagh examines some of the reasons why this is so. He traces the cosmology and theology that underlie our modern thinking about the place of the human in relation to the rest of the Earth community and finds it wanting on a number of counts.*

# Connecting with the Devas

One evening in early January 1977, I walked into the woods and announced in a loud, clear voice, "I want to do at Perelandra what they did at Findhorn. I want to work with devas and I want to work with nature spirits. I invite all of you to make yourselves known to me. I am ready to learn from you."

Then I left the woods, returned to the house, put myself into meditation and waited.

At the time of "my declaration," I didn't know what I was doing. But years later, I realized that I had used a ceremony to ground a shift that was taking place in me. Ceremony is a physical vehicle used to ground energy from a higher level, thereby giving it form and greater accessibility to the people involved in the ceremony. It's a tool designed to give clarity and form to energy. To accomplish this, we use special settings, actions, words, music ... whatever is appropriate. On that night in January, I moved through a ceremony. I made a clear decision about what I wanted. I chose the woods as my setting. Then I moved through a series of physical actions via the use of words. I stated my intent. Clearly and simply. I invoked to myself what I felt I would need to carry out my intent. Then I sealed my declaration by physically acting on it — by going into meditation and opening myself to whatever was to happen next.

The response was immediate. In fact, I had the same experience that Dorothy Maclean had at Findhorn when she first connected with devas. I had a "crowd of voices" coming at me, all talking at the same time — all telling me that it was "about time." I connected in with them and found that they had been waiting for this for some time. I remembered that in the Findhorn book, when Dorothy described this experience, she said she simply asked the devas to speak to her once at a time. Having nothing to lose, I tried the same thing. Much to my amazement, they responded instanteously.

*Machaelle Small Wright*
*From* Behaving as if the God in All Life Mattered

# WILDERNESS SOJOURN

*Notes in the Desert Silence*
DAVID DOUGLAS

ILLUSTRATED BY JENNIFER DEWEY

## What Is a Deva?

Deva — the sanskrit word for "body of light." From the meditation standpoint, I found the devic level to be a level of consciousness very high in vibration. It's as if someone were to hit a bunch of tuning forks and we could distinguish the vibratory difference between them rather than the sound difference. I found the devic vibration to feel extremely high and light. It resembled nothing I had experienced in meditation previously. Its essence was clearly different.

The word "architect" has been used by others when describing what devas do — and I, also, find this to be the most appropriate word. It is the devic level that draws together the various energies that make up, for example, the carrot. The Carrot Deva "pulls together" the various

energies that determine the size, color, texture, growing season, nutritional needs, shape, flower and seed process of the carrot. In essence, the Carrot Deva is responsible for the carrot's entire physical package. It holds the vision of the carrot in perfection, calls together the energies required to formulate that perfection and holds that collection of energies together as it passes from one vibratory level to another on its route to becoming physical. Everything about the carrot on a practical level, as well as on the more expanded, universal level, is known by the Carrot Deva.

*- Machaelle Small Wright*
*From Behaving As If the God in All Life Mattered*

## Morning

I remain in my sleeping bag later than usual this morning. I slept poorly last night; it took some time to drift off, and I fell into a restless sleep only to awaken near midnight. The moon had climbed high and drenched the canyon in silver half-light. As I rose on one elbow, I saw the figure of an animal nosing the ground next to me. It was a ringtail cat, its huge curling tail diaphanous in the moonlight. I lay still at first, uncertain whether this was some relic from my unsettled rest, but when I muttered a few words aloud, it looked up at me. Separated by only a few feet, we stared unwaveringly into each other's eyes. Then, as the moon was enclosed by a tumult of black clouds, it slowly turned and padded away into the night.

I've seen few wild creatures so closely; most have been mere specters — the hindquarters of a bear, the shadow of a mountain lion — sightings so quick and tentative that I wondered whether I had seen anything at all. But as seldom as they are glimpsed, the wild animals sharpen the edge of our awe. Each creature — aside from existing as part of God's creation and the rich network of life — serves to rein in our sense of self-mastery. "We need to witness our own limits transgressed," as Thoreau once wrote, "and some life pasturing freely where we never wander."

*- David Douglas*
*From Wilderness Sojourn*

**Wilderness Sojourn**
*Notes in the Desert Silence*
By David Douglas
1987/102 pages
**$11.95**
$13.45 postpaid from:
Harper & Row
2350 Virginia Ave.
Hagerstown, MD 21740

*These are personal and poetic reflections on the spiritual values of the wilderness. Hauntingly touching.*

## The Art of Zen Gardens
### A Guide to Their Creation and Enjoyment

THE ART OF
*Zen Gardens*

A GUIDE TO THEIR
CREATION AND ENJOYMENT

A. K. DAVIDSON

By A. K. Davidson
1983/150 pages
**$9.95**
$12.35 postpaid from:
Jeremy P. Tarcher, Inc.
9110 Sunset Blvd.
Los Angeles, CA 90069

# Zen Gardens are Places Apart

More than 600 years ago, the Zen priest-gardeners of Japan developed simple techniques to create visually stimulating outdoor environments that are also oases of peace and serenity. *The Art of Zen Gardens* explains the history and philosophy behind this Japanese garden art and given step-by-step instructions for creating your own Zen garden, even in very limited space.

This practical volume provides more than 100 line illustrations showing you how to use gravel and stones to suggest the ripples and eddies of moving water, build earth mounds that represent mountains, create a small pond to serve as the "heart of the garden", select lanterns to use as focal points, enhance the sounds in a garden — the trickling of water, the clacking of bamboo, the crunch of a gravel path, construct small bridges and water-falls, develop the illusion of space using paths, rock formations, and shrubbery.

*From* The Art of Zen Gardens

. . . the Ryoan-ji garden is the product of a philosophical system—that of Zen Buddhism—as serious as that which inspired the ceiling of the Sistine chapel. . . . The Sistine chapel is magnificent, but it asks our admiration rather than our participation. The stones of Ryoan-ji, irregular in shape and position, by allowing us to participate in the creation of the garden may move us even more.

Donald Keene

*Karesansui*-style garden with grass.

*Karesansui*-style garden with gravel.

## Ancient Mysteries/UFO's/Etc.

# A Different View of Humankind's Past

*By Joseph R. Jochmans*

Walk into any modern history museum today, stroll past the various exhibits on humanity's earliest cultures, and what do you see?

Over the past two hundred years that the science of archaeology has been around almost all the artifacts unearthed have been neatly arranged to show how the development of humankind is *linear*. What this means is that we supposedly started as primitive cave people and very slowly worked our way up over thousands of years to achieve the first light of civilization in ancient Egypt, Sumer, India, Peru and Mexico. Now today we claim to be the most advanced beings to have ever lived on the planet. According to this view we have always been progressing upwards no matter what.

But there are serious problems with this view. Some are very obvious, especially when you look at such marvelous and stupendous ancient structures like the Great Pyramid in Egypt or Stonehenge in England or the gigantic stone heads of Easter Island. Here are construction projects from the distant past which had to have used some form of advanced technology to both plan and build.

Take the Great Pyramid as only one example. Here we're talking about two million three hundred thousand blocks weighing an average of two and a half tons each, or about eighty-five million cubic feet of material — that's enough stone to build thirty-five solid Empire State Buildings. The Pyramid's base covers a little over thirteen acres, yet from one corner to the opposite corner the whole thing is off only one-quarter inch from perfectly level. Almost six hundred thousand casing stones once covered the outside of the structure, each weighing sixteen tons and with less than one-fiftieth of an inch between their joints — or less than the thickness of your fingernail. Along one base edge of seven hundred and fifty-six feet the stones were laid out with an accuracy of just one-tenth of an inch deviation over that entire length — what can

only be measured with the best optical survey equipment today. Ask any modern engineer to duplicate such a structure with these kinds of specifications and you're likely to get a cold stare of disbelief added to the remark that it can't be done.

Yet the only answer archaeologists can offer us as to how the Pyramid was built — the only answer their linear theory allows them — is that it had to have been built by very primitive means only. If you get a few thousand tribesmen or farmers together with simple ropes and sticks and work them to death continually for twenty or thirty years without stop — presto, that's how you build a Pyramid and everything else.

The truth is, not all the artifacts found among ancient sites the world over can be neatly fit to conform to the linear view of history. There is a growing number of other artifacts which tell a very different story suggesting that history has not been linear but instead is *cyclic*. These other artifacts show that, contrary to the accepted view of history, there have been civilizations in the past as advanced as and in some cases even more advanced than ours today. The artifacts contain a level of sophistication not found in the ancient ruins out of which they came, but must have been the product of civilizations earlier still that for some reason were destroyed and forgotten. Global myths and esoteric writings, ancient scriptures and psychic visions are full of stories by long lost races and their cultures. Such names as Atlantis, Lemuria, Mu, Hyperborea, Polaria, Ys and Ultima Thule are but a few dim memories left to us. Were these real and can they be found again, like Schliemann's Troy or Bingham's Machu Picchu?

The answer the "out-of-place" artifacts give is a definite yes. Some of these include:

- Remains of electric batteries found in Babylonian ruins, along with gold electroplated objects dating back to 4500 B.C.
- A small wooden glider found in an Egyptian tomb at Saqqara that's

4,300 years old yet today can still glide a considerable distance.

- The Ashoka Pillar from Qutab Minar near New Delhi that shows no signs of rust on it after over 1,600 years' exposure to the Indian monsoons.
- The Mitchell-Hedges crystal skull found in Belize in Central America, possessing optical features inside it which modern crystallographers can't duplicate today.
- Maps such as those of Piri Reis and Oronteus Finaeus showing details of the geography of Antarctica as they once looked in 8000 B.C.
- Parts of a sophisticated spark plug embedded in a rock discovered near Olancha, California and dating back 500,000 years.
- A fossilized sandal imprint with two crushed trilobites in its center going back to early Cambrian times or 600 million years in age.
- Several dozen nickel-steel spheroids unearthed in South Africa, each engraved with three precision-made grooves, brought up from rock strata an incredible 2.8 billion years old.

The story these and many more artifacts like them tell us is a very different one we see in our museums today. Because these "out-of-place" artifacts don't fit into established views of our past, many experts would like to shove them under a rug of "unacceptability." But the rug is getting pretty lumpy and difficult to walk on these days. The artifacts and their implications of lost civilizations are getting harder and harder to ignore.

Humanity, it's now apparent, has gone through many forgotten cycles of growth and disappearances. They are but enticing remnants of these former worlds, coming through with the survivors who had to start their own new world all over again. There have been not one but many Noahs and many Arks saved from many Floods.

**Planetary Mysteries**
*Megaliths, Glaciers, the Face on Mars, and Aboriginal Dreamtime*

Edited by Richard Grossinger
1986/156 pages
**$12.95**
$13.95 postpaid from:
North Atlantic Books
2320 Blake St.
Berkeley, CA 940704

# The Face on Mars

### "A Human Face Where No Human Face Has Any Business Being!"

"It was a very striking countenance. It had all the interesting proportions — mouth, eyes, hair, nose, even features under the eye — that one would expect of a human face. It had a sort of beauty to it, an aesthetic quality. It's not, as one of our analysts years later wrote, 'just another face.' "

"It's obvious, if somebody did it, it was a *big project*, with purposes that were not trivial. I can look at it as a message. All the interlocking keys and codes reinforce the basic theme: This is intelligently designed, folks; come hither and find out something further ... It was an attention-getting device. It was not meant to be in the image of the guys who were there, it was meant to be in the image of the guys who were going to come there, namely *us*."

*- Richard Hoagland
From* Planetary Mysteries

**The Ghostly Register**
*Haunted Dwellings, Active Spirits*
By Arthur Myers
1986/378 pages
**$9.95**
$11.95 postpaid from:
Contemporary Books
180 North Michigan Ave.
Chicago, IL 60601

*Sign your name — if you dare — in* The Ghostly Register, *a spine-tingling guide to the most fascinating documented haunts in America. Read the eerie tales of spirits, bizarre occurrences, and unexplained phenomena. You will be spellbound by the account of ghostly manifestations of a tall Stetson-wearing figure aboard* The Wild Goose, *John Wayne's former yacht; the strange happenings and tragic history surrounding the Toys 'R' Us store in Sunnyvale, California; and the mysterious building in Idaho from which the trapped spirit of a mummified rat*

*makes its escape to the otherworld.*

*The ghosts whose exploits are described herein are good people, bad people, disappointed lovers, and the people who scorned them, murderers, murder victims, little old ladies, even prostitutes. Their personalities — and spooky activities — are as unforgettable as they are unsettling.*

**Mysteries of the Unexplained**
By the Editors of Readers Digest
1982/320 pages
**$19.95**
$21.89 postpaid from:
Reader's Digest
Pleasantville, NY 10570

*This is one of the best sources of information on unexplained happenings from strange stuff falling out of the sky to discoveries of live frogs in solid rock. UFOs are covered here as well as ancient mysteries, physical anomalies, unearthly fates, sea monsters, poltergeists and much more.*

One of the first written accounts of a UFO sighting — a fleet of flying saucers, perhaps — is the following excerpt from an Egyptian papyrus — part of the annals of Thutmose III, who reigned around 1504-1450 B.C.:

In the year 22, of the 3rd month of winter, sixth hour of the day ... the scribes of the House of Life found it was a circle of fire that was coming in the sky ... It had no head, the breath of its mouth had a foul odor. Its body one rod long and one rod wide. It had no voice. Their hearts became confused through it; then they laid themselves on their bellies ... They went to the Pharaoh ... to report it. His Majesty ordered ... (an examination of) all which is written in the papyrus rolls of the House of Life. His Majesty was meditating upon what happened. Now after some days had passed, these things became more numerous in the skies than ever. They shone more in the sky than the brightness of the sun, and extended to the limits of the four supports of the heavens ...

*This Egyptian papyrus, more than 3,400 years old, records the sighting of numerous brilliant round objects in the sky by Pharaoh Thutmose III, his army, and his scribes.*

*- From* Mysteries of the Unexplained

# The UFO

In the late 1940's a new phenomenon began to appear in the skies of Earth. These were silent flying craft unlike any men had seen before. They were called Unidentified Flying Objects or U.F.O.'s, though their disk-like or oval shape earned them the popular name of 'flying saucers'. To many, this phenomenon had no existence except in the imagination of science fiction writers and newsmen drawing for filler copy upon the sensational stories of various pranksters. Others, their minds conditioned by the memories of the recent war, wondered if these craft might not be some new kind of secret weapon, while still other individuals, noting the advanced technology that such craft seemed to represent, speculated that they might not be an earthly phenomenon at all but rather the appearance on our planet of visitors from outer space.

To whatever degree the public imagination was captivated for a time by these accounts of mysterious U.F.O.'s, the harsher realities of a world plunging deeper into a war of nerves and tension between the atomic powers soon relegated the phenomenon of these craft to a far back corner of human affairs. The Fifties and early Sixties were a time of one crisis following another in the arena of world politics and global confrontation. Armed with increasingly sophisticated weapons of nuclear power and mass destruction, the leading nations of East and West played games of brinkmanship as the populations of the world waited in seeming helplessness for war to erupt. Books and films of that period mirror well the fear and tension and the sense of resignation before the inevitable that seemed to grip people as they dug their fallout shelters and tried to face the realities of surviving a planetary holocaust.

During these years of crisis, many people upon Earth discovered that man had a strange new ally. Individuals in many lands found themselves being contacted by intelligence from the U.F.O's who claimed to be representatives from various extra-terrestrial races, 'space brothers' whose interest and desire were to help humanity into a new level of consciousness. These contacts spoke of the dangers of nuclear war and of the necessity for man to learn to see his world from a planetary and universal viewpoint, recognizing all men as brothers and all life as sacred.
- David Spangler
From Links with Space

# UFO Resources

### Guardian Action Publications
P.O. Box 27725
Salt Lake City, UT

*Channeled contact with aliens from other planets is a popular topic these days. This group claims to be in contact with the Space Commands circling planet Earth. They offer a free catalog of UFO material.*

### National Investigations Committee on UFO's
P.O. Box 5
Van Nuys, CA 91401

*Dr. Frank Stranges runs this UFO information center which claims ongoing contact with a Venusian named Val Thor. They publish books and a newsletter.*

### Aerial Phenomena Research Organization
3597 W. Grape Dr.
Tucson, AZ 85741

*This is one of the oldest UFO organizations in the United States. It sponsors field investigations of UFO reports.*

### Fortean Research Center
P.O. Box 94627
Lincoln, NE 68509

*This group investigates UFO's and other mysteries like miracles, Bigfoot and anomalous geologic formations.*

### J. Allen Hynek Center for UFO Studies
1955 John's Dr.
Glenview, IL 60025

*The late Dr. Hynek was America's most respected UFO researcher. The Center continues his work investigating UFO reports from all over the country.*

### Institute for UFO Contactee Studies
1425 Steele St.
Laramie, WY 82070

*This group helps people who say they've been in contact with UFO's and their crews. The group sponsors an annual contactee symposium.*

## Links with Space
By David Spangler
1971/42 pages
**$1.50**
$2.19 postpaid from:
DeVorss & Co.
Box 550
Marina Del Rey, CA 90294

*The question of life beyond our planet has always fascinated mankind. David Spangler (who wrote the introduction to this book) traces the history of UFO's and presents channeled material he says was received through his consciousness concerning extraterrestrial activity on and around our planet.*

## California UFO
1800 S. Robertson Blvd.
Los Angeles, CA 90035
**$15.00**/Bimonthly, six issues

*This is a relative newcomer to the UFO scence. It's editorial is a mix of UFO news and information, and other mysterious happenings.*

## Quest
## The Journal of UFO Investigation
106 Lady Ann Rd.
Soothill, Batley
England
**$25.00**/Bimonthly, 6 issues airmail

*This is Britain's leading UFO magazine, containing the latest of worldwide UFO research sightings and government reports.*

# We Must Keep Looking!

*By Mark DeMaranville*

"In man's analysis and understanding of himself, it is as well to know from whence he came as whither he is going." — Edgar Cayce

These words were spoken by the renowned medium Edgar Cayce during one of his thousands of trance "readings," and they underscore well the importance of seeking the truths about that shadowy part of our past termed prehistory.

Historically, the term *mysteries* referred to secret rites that were practiced in Egypt, Greece, Persia and other nearby lands. Today, the subject of *ancient mysteries* has taken on a broader context, encompassing such topics as the Egyptian pyramids and other massive structures of stone or earth; the quarrying and erection of megaliths, some weighing in excess of several hundred tons; the jeweler-like fit of cyclopean stones to tolerances of one one-thousandth of an inch; architectural designs that incorporated a precise understanding of advanced mathematics; site locations and building alignments that exhibited a knowledge of astronomy and subtle energies; and artistic styles suggestive of extraterrestrial origins. The weight of the evidence is becoming too great to allow the continued assertions that these great testaments of wisdom that dot our planet were simply the work of neolithic man.

There is a bounty of fertile situations awaiting further investigation. The discovery of extensive underwater stone constructions in the Bimini Islands in 1968 by Dr. J. Manson Valentine coincided precisely with predictions made decades earlier by Edgar Cayce that remains of the legendary continent of Atlantis would be found there in that very year. The

*Stonework of possible pre-Inca origin at Sacsayhuaman, Peru. The stones are cut and fitted together so accurately that a knife blade cannot be inserted between the stones ... even after thousands of years. How did ancient people's possess such skills and knowledge?*

collection of 14,000 ancient engraved stones in Dr. Javier Cabrera's private museum in Peru exhibit subjects such as detailed depictions of men with dinosaurs, flying apparatus, and heart and brain transplants. A room at the bottom of a well shaft in Egypt contains a huge sarcophagus of a different type of stone than the surrounding walls, and which is larger than the opening through which it would have had to pass. When queried as to how this was done, a dismayed Egyptologist who espoused simple answers for all enigmas blurted out, "Well, we don't understand *everything!*"

That's precisely why we must keep looking.

*- Mark DeMaranville is an esoteric researcher and President of the Light Ages Foundation, Inc.*

## Haunted England
### Royal Spirits, Castle Ghosts, Phantom Coaches & Wailing Ghouls

By Terence Whitaker
1987/212 pages
**$9.95**
$11.95 postpaid from:
Contemporary Books
180 N. Michigan Ave.
Chicago, IL 60601

*England has a rich and colorful ghostly heritage, with such famous spirits as Sir Walter Raleigh and Lady Jane Grey roaming the Tower of London, and the bulky ghost of Henry VIII shuffling along the battlements of Windsor Castle. Less well known but not less ghoulish are the panting ghost of London's Heathrow Airport, the Black Nun who still wanders through the Bank of England after 175 years, and the mysterious phantom horseman who forever rides the North Dorset countryside among the ancient burial grounds.*

# How to Order from This Catalogue

*You can order items from* The New Age
Catalogue *directly from the publisher, your local
book store or* The Body, Mind & Spirit Book Shop,
*the mail order division of* Body, Mind & Spirit *magazine.*

## Ordering from Publishers

If you are going to order directly from the suppliers listed in this catalogue, please be sure to follow the following recommendations to make mail order work better for you and the suppliers.

1. Include payment with your order. Always use a personal check or money order. Never send cash or stamps through the mail. You have no receipt of payment and chances are it may never make it to the recipient.

2. Include applicable sales tax if the company you're buying from is located in your state.

3. If you are ordering from outside the United States, be sure to use International Money Orders in U.S. dollars. However, it's best to inquire first since shipping costs will be higher. For inquiries, you can include an International Reply Coupon (available at your overseas post office) to ensure a reply.

## Order Anything Listed in this *Catalogue* from The Body, Mind & Spirit Book Shop ... Toll Free!

The Body, Mind & Spirit Book Shop carries every item listed in this edition of *The New Age Catalogue.* This is especially helpful if you are ordering multiple items. Call in your order toll free or send it to us using the following instructions:

1. Be sure to include your name, shipping address (don't forget Zip Code), and telephone number. We normally use the U.S. Postal Service, so box numbers are acceptable.

2. Print all information on your order. List the quantity, title, author, and any other information to help us identify the item you want. List its price (not the postpaid price, that's only if you're ordering directly from the publisher or company). If only a postpaid price is listed, that means that firm doesn't charge for postage and handling.

3. Total up the amount of your order. Rhode Island residents *only* add 6% sales tax.

4. Add $3.00 postage and handling for up to 5 books or tapes. For over 5 items, add 50¢ per item in addition to the $3.00 shipping charge. (For example, the shipping charge for 7 items is $4.00.)

5. For foreign orders, (including Canada), shipping is $4.00 for the first 2 items and $1.00 for each additional item. (For example, the shipping charge for 5 items is $7.00.) All foreign orders must be paid in U.S. dollars.

6. Payment in full by check or money order must be enclosed with your order. If you prefer, you may charge your order to VISA or Mastercard. Be sure to include your VISA/Mastercard number and expiration date. Your order cannot be processed without complete information.

7. Send your order to: Body, Mind & Spirit Book Shop, Catalogue Dept., Box 701, Providence, R.I. 02901.

8. Phone Orders: VISA/Mastercard orders *only* can be made by calling toll free 800-338-5216 from 9:00 am to 5:00 pm, Monday-Friday, Eastern time. For other business: 401-351-4320.

9. Gift Orders: *Catalogue* items make enlightening gifts. If you would like to give a gift order, give us the name and address of the recipient, your name, address and telephone number, and a brief message from you which we will put on the gift card that will accompany your gift order.

10. Subscriptions to *Body, Mind & Spirit* magazine can be purchased at a discount through the Book Shop. Subscriptions are: one year/6 issues for $11.95 (regularly $15.00) or two years/12 issues for $19.95 (regularly $24.00). A sample copy is $4.00. Simply indicate your subscription form and price on your Book Shop order.

11. Write us if you would like to be put on our mailing list for special offers, or for a current book list. The Book Shop also offers a special order/book finding service.

## Body, Mind & Spirit Book Shop
### Box 701
### Providence, RI 02901
### 401-351-4320
### *To Order Toll Free:*
### 800-338-5216

# Sources of Information

## Intuitive Development - Channeling
Charles H. Hapgood, *Talks with Christ and His Teachers*, Fine Line Books, 1984, ● Jon Klimo, *Channeling*, Jeremy P. Tarcher, 1987, ● Ruth Montgomery, *A World Beyond*, Random House, 1971, ● Ruth Montgomery, *Born to Heal*, Random House, 1976, ● Herbert B. Puryear, Ph.D., *The Edgar Cayce Primer*, A.R.E. Press, 1982, ● Raphael, *The Starseed Transmissions*, Uni-Sun, 1982, ● Jane Roberts, *The Nature of the Psyche*, Bantam Books, 1979, ● Jane Roberts, *Seth Speaks*, Bantam Books, 1972, ● Sanyana Roman and Duane Packer, *Opening to Channel*, Lumin Essence Productions, 1987, ● Pat Rodegast and Judith Stanton, *Emmanuel's Book*, Bantam Books, 1987, ● Helen Schucman, *A Course in Miracles*, Foundation for Inner Peace, 1975, ● Steven Lee Weinberg, Ph.D., ed., *Ramtha*, Sovereignty, 1986

## Intuitive Development - Psychic Functioning
Doris Agee, *Edgar Cayce on E.S.P.*, A.R.E. Press, ● June Bletzer, *Encyclopedic Psychic Dictionary*, Donning Company Publishers, 1986, ● Hal Zina Bennett, *Inner Guides, Visions, Dreams & Dr. Einstein*, Celestial Arts, ● Hugh Lynn Cayce, *Venture Inward*, Harper & Row, 1964, ● *Discover Your Rainbow Body*, The University of the Trees, 1985, ● Philip Goldberg, *60 Minutes to Unlocking Your Intuition*, St. Martin's Press, 1987, ● Enid Hoffman, *Develop Your Psychic Skills*, Para Research, 1981, ● Kreskin, *Expand Your Mind Power*, Listen USA, 1986, ● Djwal Kul and Kuthumi, *The Human Aura*, Summit University Press, 1972, 1977, 1986, ● Shale Paul, *The Warrior Within*, Delta Group Press, 1983, ● David and Lucy Pond, *The Metaphysical Handbook*, ● Dick Sutphen, *How to Rapidly Develop Your Psychic Ability*, Valley of the Sun, 1985

## Intuitive Development - Crystals
Gary Gold, *Crystal Energy*, Contemporary Books, 1987, ● John Milewski and Virginia Harford, *The Crystal Sourcebook*, Mystic Crystal Publications, 1987, ● Katrina Raphaell, *Crystal Enlightenment, Volume I*, Aurora Press, 1985, ● Katrina Raphaell, *Crystal Healing, Volume II*, Aurora Press, 1987

## Intuitive Development - Divination
American Society of Dowsers, Inc., Danville, VT., ● Ralph Blum, *Rune Play*, St. Martin's Press, 1985, ● Curtis W. Casewit, *The Graphology Handbook*, Para Research, 1980, ● Richard Geer, *Star + Gate*, Star + Gate Enterprises, 1986, ● Eden Gray, *The Tarot Revealed*, New American Library, 1960, ● Elisabeth Haich, *The Wisdom of the Tarot*, Aurora Press, 1975, ● Count Louis Hamon (Cheiro), *Cheiro's Language of the Hand: The Classic of Palmistry*, Prentice-Hall Press, 1987, ● Murry Hope, *The Way of Cartouche*, St. Martin's Press, 1985, ● Julia Lane, *The Numerology Workbook*, Thorson's Publishing Group, England, 1985, ● Cordelia Mansal, *The Astrology Workbook*, Thorson's Publishing Group, England, 1985, ● Henry Wei, Ph.D., *The Authentic I Ching*, Newcastle Publishing, 1987

## Create Your Reality - Transformational Journeys
Lynn Andrews, *Crystal Woman*, Warner Books, Inc., 1987, ● Lynn Andrews, *Star Woman*, Warner Books, Inc., 1986, ● Iris Belhayes, *Spirit Guides: We Are Not Alone*, ACS Publications, 1985, ● Claude Bristol, *The Magic of Believing*, Simon and Schuster, 1985, ● Laura Chester, *Lupus Novice: Toward Self-Healing*, Station Hill Press, 1987, ● Terry Cole-Whittaker, *The Inner Path From Where You Are To Where You Want To Be*, Rawson Associates, 1986, ● Shakti Gawain, *Creative Visualization*, The Good Living Catalog, 1979, ● John Harricharan, *When You Can Walk on Water, Take the Boat*, New World Publishing, 1986, ● Gerald G. Jampolsky, M.D., *Love Is Letting Go of Fear*, Celestial Arts, 1979, ● W. Brugh Joy, M.D., *Joy's Way: A Map for the Transformational Journey*, Jeremy P. Tarcher, 1979, ● Shirley MacLaine, *It's All in the Playing*, Bantam Books, 1987, ● Shirley MacLaine, *Dancing in the Light*, Bantam Books, 1985, ● Shirley MacLaine, *Out on a Limb*, Bantam Books, 1983, ● Ruth Montgomery with Joanne Garland, *Ruth Montgomery: Herald of the New Age*, Random House, 1986, ● Richard Moss, M.D., *The Black Butterfly*, Celestial Arts, 1986, ● Peter Rogers, *A Painter's Quest*, Bear & Company, 1987, ● Tom Rusk and Randy Read, M.D., *I Want to Change but I Don't Know How*, Price/Stern/Sloan Publishing, 1986

## Creating Your Reality - Self-Help
James Allen, *Become the Master of Your Own Destiny*, Whatever Publishing, 1987, ● Marcus Allen, *Tantra for the West*, Whatever Publishing, 1981, ● Henry Bolduc, *Self-Hypnosis*, A.R.E. Press, 1985, ● Charles Thomas Cayce, *Explore the Mysteries of Your Mind*, A.R.E. Press, 1986, ● Chris Griscom, *Ecstasy is a New Frequency*, Bear & Company, 1987, ● Stanley Mann, *Triggers: A New Approach to Self-Motivation*, Simon and Schuster, 1987, ● Dick Sutphen, *Master of Life Manual*, Valley of the Sun, 1987

## Creating Your Own Reality - Meditation
*Astral Sounds*, The American Research Team, 1973, ● Lawrence LeShan, *How to Meditate*, Bantam Books, 1974, ● Ram Dass, *Journey of Awakening*, Bantam Books, 1985

## Creating Your Own Reality - Dreamwork
Kenneth Kelzer, *The Sun and the Shadow*, A.R.E. Press, 1987, ● Julia Parker and Derek Parker, *The Compleat Book of Dreaming*, Crown Publishers, Inc., 1985, ● Mark A. Thurston, Ph.D., *How To Interpret Your Dreams*, A.R.E. Press, 1978, ● Montague Ullman, *Working with Dreams*, Jeremy P. Tarcher, 1979, ● Joan Windsor, *Dreams and Healing*, Dodd, Mead, and Co., 1987

## Creating Your Own Reality - Astral Projections/OBE's
Gavin and Yvonne Frost, *Astral Travel*, Samuel Weiser, Inc., 1982, ● Robert A. Monroe, *Journeys Out of the Body*, Doubleday and Company, 1977, ● Robert A. Monroe, *Far Journeys*, Doubleday and Company, 1985

## Creating Your Own Reality - The Search for Consciousness
Mark Davidson, *Uncommon Sense*, Jeremy P. Tarcher, Inc., 1983, ● Jean Houston, *The Possible Human*, Jeremy P. Tarcher, Inc., 1982, ● Charles M. Johnston, M.D., *The Creative Imperative*, Celestial Arts, 1986, ● George B. Leonard, *The Transformation*, Jeremy P. Tarcher, Inc., 1972, ● Michael Talbot, *Beyond the Quantum*, MacMillan, 1986, ● Charles Tart, *Waking Up*, Shambhala Publications, 1986, ● Fred Alan Wolf, *Star Wave*, Collier books, 1985, ● Roger N. Walsh and Frances Vaughan, eds., *Beyond Ego*, Jeremy P. Tarcher, Inc., 1980

## Creating Your Own Reality - Relationships
Marc Allen, *Friends and Lovers*, Good Living Catalog, 1985, ● Julie Henderson, *The Lover Within*, Station Hill Press, 1987, ● Bob Mandel, *Two Hearts Are Better Than One*, Celestial Arts, 1986, ● Sondra Ray, *Loving Relationships*, Celestial Arts, 1980, ● Sondra Ray and Bob Mandel, *Birth and Relationships*, Celestial Arts, 1987

## Creating Your Own Reality - Rebirthing
Jim Leonard, *Rebirthing*, Trinity Publications, 1983, ● Bob Mandel, *Open Heart Therapy*, Celestial Arts, 1984, ● Leonard Orr and Sondra Ray, *Rebirthing in the New Age*, Celestial Arts, 1983

## Creating Your Own Reality - Brain/Mind Technology
Tony Buzan, *Use Both Sides of Your Brain*, E.P. Dutton, Inc., 1983, ● Christopher Hills, *How to Recharge Your Brain*, University of the Trees Press, 1984

## Creating Your Own Reality - Inspiration
Eagle Walking Turtle, *Keepers of the Fire*, Bear and Company, Inc., 1987, ● Elisabeth Haich, *The Day with Yoga*, Aurora Press, 1983, ● Hannah Hurnard, *Hind's Feet on High Planes*, Living Books, 1986, ● Swami Amar Jyoti, *Retreat Into Eternity*, Truth Consciousness, 1981

## Creating Your Own Reality - Creativity
Betty Edwards, *Drawing on the Right Side of the Brain*, Jeremy P. Tarcher, Inc., 1979, ● Gabriele Lusser Rico, *Writing the Natural Way*, Audio Renaissance Tapes, 1987

## Transitions - Birth
Jeannine Parvati Baker, Frederick Baker, and Tamara Slayton, *Conscious Conception*, North Atlantic Books, 1986, ● Sondra Ray, *Ideal Birth*, Celestial Arts, 1985

## Transitions - Near Death Experiences
Raymond A. Moody, Jr., *Life After Life*, Bantam Books, 1975, ● Raymond A. Moody, Jr., *Reflections on Life After Life*, Bantam Books, 1977, ● Kenneth Ring, M.D., *Life At Death*, William Morrow and Company, 1980, ● Kenneth Ring, *Heading Toward Omega*, William Morrow and Company, 1984

## Transitions - Death and Dying
Derek Humphry and Ann Wickett, *The Right to Die*, Harper & Row, 1986, ● Elizabeth A. Johnson, *As Someone Dies*, Hay Horse, 1985, ● Elisabeth Kubler-Ross, *On Death and Dying*, MacMillan, 1969, ● Marie-Louise von Franz, *On Dreams and Death*, Shambhala Publications, Inc., 1984

## Transitions - Reincarnation
John Algeo, *Reincarnation Explored*, Quest Books, 1987, ● Joe Fisher, *The Case for Reincarnation*, Doubleday and Company, 1984, ● Joseph Head and S.L. Cranston, *Reincarnation: The Phoenix Fire Mystery*, Crown Publishers, 1977, ● Rudolph Steiner, *Reincarnation and Immortality*, Anthroposophic Press, 1970, ● Dick Sutphen, *You Were Born Again to be Together*, Simon and Schuster, 1976, ● Chuck Vadun, *In My Next Life I'm Going to be the Princess*, Valley of the Sun, 1984, ● Joel L. Whitton and Joe Fisher, *Life Between Life*, Doubleday and Company, 1986

## Transitions - Walk-Ins
Ruth Montgomery, *Threshold to Tomorrow*, Random House, 1972

## Spirituality - Mystics and Masters

Alice Bailey, *Education in the New Age*, Lucis Publishing Company, 1954, ● Alice Bailey, *Ponder on This*, Lucis Publishing Company, 1971, ● Philip S. Berg, *Kabbalah for the Layman*, Research Centre of Kabbalah, 1981, ● Dalai Lama, *Kindness, Clarity and Insight*, Snow Lion Publications, 1984, ● Deng Min-Dao, *The Wandering Taoist*, Harper and Row, 1983, ● Shems Friedlander, *When You Hear Footbeats, Think of a Zebra*, Harper and Row, 1987, ● Jeffrey Furst, ed., *Edgar Cayce's Story of Jesus*, A.R.E. Press, 1968, ● Benjamin Hoff, *The Tao of Pooh*, Penguin Books, 1982, ● Swami Amar Jyoti, *Spirit of Himalaya*, Truth Consciousness, 1985, ● V. Krishnamurti, *The Awakening of Intelligence*, Harper and Row, 1973, ● V. Krishnamurti, *You Are the World*, Harper and Row, 1972, ● Swami Nikhilananda, *Vivekananda: The Yogas and Other Works*, Ramakrishna - Vivekananda Center, 1953, ● Robert M. Pirsig, *Zen and the Art of Motorcycle Maintenance*, Bantam Books, 1974, ● Ram Dass and Paul Gorman, *How Can I Help?*, Random House, 1985, ● Paul Reps, *Zen Flesh, Zen Bones*, Doubleday and Company, ● Helen Schucman, *A Course in Miracles*, Foundation for Inner Peace, 1975, ● W.T. Stace, *Mysticism and Philosophy*, Jeremy P. Tarcher, Inc., 1960, ● Shunryu Suzuki, *Zen Mind, Beginner's Mind*, Charles E. Tuttle Co., 1985, ● D.T. Suzuki, *And Introduction to Zen Buddhism*, Grove Press, 1964, ● Swami Vivekananda, *Raja Yoga*, Ramakrishna - Vivekenanda Center, 1956, ● Alan Watts, *The Way of Zen*, Vintage Books, 1957

## Spirituality - Spiritualism

Ivy Northage, *Mediumship Made Simple*, Psychic News, 1986, ● Tony Ortzen, ed., *Silver Birch Companion*, Psychic News, 1986, ● Pam Riva, ed., *Light From Silver Birch*, Psychic News, 1984, ● M.H. Tester, *How to be Healthy, Wealthy and Wise*, Psychic News, 1972

## Spirituality - Native American

John G. Neihardt, *Black Elk Speaks*, Simon and Schuster, 1932, ● Omer C. Steward, *Peyote Religion*, University of Oklahoma Press, 1987, ● Mary Summer Rain, *Spirit Song*, The Donning Company, 1985, ● Wabun and Barry Weinstuck, *Sun Bear: The Path of Power*, Bear Tribe Publishing, 1983

## Spirituality - Earth Religions

Starhawk, *The Spiral Dance*, Harper and Row, 1979

## Spirituality - Women's Spirituality

Hallie Austen Inglehart, *Womanspirit*, Harper and Row, 1983

## Wholistic Healing and Health - Healing and Health

Jeanne Achterberg, *Imagery is Healing*, Shambhala Publications, Inc., 1985, ● Linda Cochran, *Beyond Dieting*, A.R.E. Press, 1983, ● Lew Connor and Linda McKim, *The New Holistic Health Handbook*, Viking Penguin, 1985, ● Harry C. Ehrmantraut, Ph.D., *Headaches*, Celestial Arts, 1987, ● Janet Goodrich, Ph.D., *Natural Vision Improvement*, Celestial Arts, 1986, ● Stanley Krippner and Albert Villoldo, *The Realms of Healing*, Celestial Arts, 1986, ● Michio Kushi with Alex Jack, *The Cancer Prevention Diet*, St. Martin's Press, 1983, ● Barbara Weber Ray, *The Reiki Factor*, Exposition Press, 1983, ● Dr. Harold Reilly, *The Edgar Cayce Handbook for Health Through Drugless Therapy*, A.R.E. Press, 1975, ● Meir Schnieder, *Self Healing*, Methuen, Inc., 1987, ● Bernie S. Siegel, M.D., *Love, Medicine and Miracles*, Harper and Row, 1986, ● Sam Ziff, *The Toxic Time Bomb*, Aurora Press, 1984, ● Jason Serinus, ed., *Psychoimmunity and the Healing Process*, Celestial Arts, 1986, ● Paul Reed, *Serenity*, Celestial Arts, 1987

## Spirituality - Oriental Medicine

Dr. Stephen Thomas Chang, *The Complete Book of Acupunture*, Celestial Arts, 1976, ● Mantak Chia, *Awaken Healing Energy Through Tao*, Aurora Press, 1983, ● Dr. Vasant Lad, *Ayurveda*, Lotus Press, 1984, ● Dr. Yeshi Donden, *Health Through Balance*, Snow Lion Publications, 1986

## Wholistic Healing and Health - Herbology

Jethro Kloss, *Back to Eden*, Back to Eden Books, 1983, ● Dr. Vasant Lad and David Frawley, *The Background of Ayurvedic Medicine*, Lotus Press, 1987, ● Humbart Santillo, *Natural Healing with Herbs*, 1985, ● Susun S. Weed, *Wise Woman Herbal for the Childbearing Years*, Ask Tree Publishing, 1986, ● Joan Wilen and Lydia Wilen, *Chicken Soup and Other Remedies*, Random House, 1984, ● Terry Willard, *Helping Yourself with Natural Remedies*, CRCS Publications, 1986

## Wholistic Healing and Health - Nutrition

Dirk Benedict, *Confessions of a Kamikaze Cowboy*, Newcastle Publishing Company, Inc., 1987, ● Coralie Castle, *The Complete Book of Steam Cookery*, Jeremy P. Tarcher, 1985, ● Leslie Cohen, *Nourishing a Happy Affair*, Larson Publications, 1982, ● Avelina Kushi with Alex Jack, *Complete Guide to Macrobiotic Cooking*, Warner Books, 1985, ● Michio Kushi with Alex Jack, *One Peaceful World*, St. Martins Press, 1987, ● Paul Saltman, Ph.D., Joel Gurin and Ira Mothner, *The California Nutrition Book*, Little, Brown and Company, 1987

## Bodywork - Movement

Ken Dychtwald, *Bodymind*, Jeremy P. Tarcher, Inc., 1986, ● Joseph Heller and William A. Henkin, *Bodywise*, Jeremy P. Tarcher, Inc., ● Deane Juhan, *Job's Body*, Station Hill Press, 1987, ● Milton Trager, M.D., *Trager Mentastics*, Station Hill Press, 1987

## Bodywork - Polarity Therapy

John F. Thie, *Touch for Health*, T & H Enterprises, 1973

## Bodywork - Massage

Bernard Gunther, *Sense Relaxation*, Newcastle Publishing, 1968, , ● Lucinda Hall, *The Book of Massage*, Simon and Schuster, 1984

## Bodywork - Acupressure

Michael Reed Gach, *The Bum Back Book*, Celestial Arts, 1983

## Bodywork - Yoga

Lorna Bell, R.N. and Eudora Seyfer, *Gentle Yoga*, Celestial Arts, 1987

## Bodywork - T'ai Chi

Cheng Man-Ching, *T'ai Chi Ch'uan*, North Atlantic Books, 1982, ● Richard Strozzi Heckler, *Aikido and the New Warrior*, North Atlantic Books, 1985, ● Chi Siew Pang and Goh Ewe Hock, *T'ai Chi, Ten Minutes to Health*, 1985

## Bodywork - Sports Self-Help

Dan Millman, *The Warrior Athlete*, Stillpoint International, 1979, ● Thomas Tutko and Umberto Tosi, *Sports Psyching*

## New Lifestyles - Communities

Corinne McLaughlin and Gordon Davidson, *Builders of the Dawn*, Sirius Publishing, 1985, ● M. Scott Peck, M.D., *The Different Drum*, Simon and Schuster, 1987

## New Lifestyles - Natural Products

Deborah Lynn Dodd, *Nontoxic and Natural*, Jeremy P. Tarcher, Inc., 1984

## New Lifestyles - Business and Investing

Christopher Hills, *The Golden Egg*, University of the Trees Press, 1979, ● E.F. Schumacher, *Small Is Beautiful*, Harper and Row, 1973

## New Lifestyles - Fiction

Ruth Mueller, *The Eye of the Child*, New Society Publishers, 1985

## New Lifestyles - Transformational Travel

Spa Finder, New York, NY

## Mew Lifestyles - Music

Steve Halpern, *Sound Health*, Harper and Row, 1985

## New Lifestyles - Visionary Art

Peny Prestini, *Illuminations: The Visionary Art of Gilbert Williams*, Visionary Publishing, Inc., 1986

## The Planet - Planet Visionaries

Jose Arguelles, *The Mayan Factor*, Bear and Company, 1987, ● Ken Carey, *Vision*, Uni Sun, 1985, ● Don Carlson and Craig Comstock, *Citizen Summitry*, Jeremy P. Tarcher, Inc., 1986, ● John Hogue, *Nostradamus and the Millenium*, Doubleday and Company, 1987, ● Barbara Max Hubbard, *The Evolutionary Journey*, Mindbody Communications, 1982, ● Dr. Norman Myers, ed., *Gaia: An Atlas of Planet Management*, Doubleday and Company, 1984, ● John Naisbitt, *Megatrends*, Warner Books, 1982, ● Peter Russell, *The Global Brain*, Jeremy P. Tarcher, Inc., 1983, ● George Trevelyan, *A Vision of the Aquarian Age*, Stillpoint Publishing, 1984

## The Planet - Earth Changes

Hugh Lynn Cayce, *Earth Changes Update*, A.R.E. Press, 1980, ● Richard W. Noone, *5/5/2000*, Crown Publishers, 1982

## The Planet - Earth Spirit

Al Davidson, *The Art of Zen Gardens*, Jeremy P. Tarcher, Inc., 1983, ● David Douglas, *Wilderness Sojourn*, Harper and Row, 1987, ● The Findhorn Community, *The Findhom Garden*, Harper and Row, 1975, ● Peter Tomkins and Christopher Brid, *The Secret Life of Plants*, Harper and Row, 1973, ● Machaelle Small Wright, *Behaving as if the God in All Life Mattered*, Perelandra, 1987, ● Michaelle Small Wright, *The Perelandra Garden Workbook*, Perelandra, 1987

## The Planet - Ancient Mysteries

Richard Hoagland, *Planetary Mysteries*, North Atlantic Books, 1986, ● Editors of *Reader's Digest*, *Mysteries of the Unexplained*, Reader's Digest, 1982

# Index